Try to Control Yourself

Dan Malleck

Try to Control Yourself
The Regulation of Public Drinking in Post-Prohibition Ontario, 1927-44

UBCPress · Vancouver · Toronto

21 20 19 18 17 16 15 14 13 12 5 4 3 2 1

Printed in Canada on FSC-certified ancient-forest-free paper (100% post-consumer recycled) that is processed chlorine- and acid-free.

Library and Archives Canada Cataloguing in Publication

Malleck, Dan,

Try to control yourself : the regulation of public drinking in post-prohibition Ontario, 1927-44 / Dan Malleck.

Includes bibliographical references and index.
Also issued in electronic format.
ISBN 978-0-7748-2220-6 (bound); ISBN 978-0-7748-2221-3 (pbk.)

1. Drinking of alcoholic beverages – Government policy – Ontario. 2. Liquor Control Board of Ontario – History. 3. Liquor laws – Ontario. 4. Drinking of alcoholic beverages – Ontario – History – 20th century. 5. Temperance – Ontario – History – 20th century. I. Title.

HV5087.C3M34 2012 363.4'10971309041 C2011-907432-X

Canada

UBC Press gratefully acknowledges the financial support for our publishing program of the Government of Canada (through the Canada Book Fund), the Canada Council for the Arts, and the British Columbia Arts Council.

This book has been published with the help of a grant from the Canadian Federation for the Humanities and Social Sciences, through the Aid to Scholarly Publications Program, using funds provided by the Social Sciences and Humanities Research Council of Canada.

UBC Press
The University of British Columbia
2029 West Mall
Vancouver, BC V6T 1Z2
www.ubcpress.ca

For K.E.L., who reads every word

Contents

Tables and Figures

Tables

Figures

Acknowledgments

I am sure that historians of alcohol and drugs quickly grow tired of people suggesting with a nudge and a wink that "the field research must be *fantastic*." Yes, it was fantastic, but not for the dissolute reasons suggested in the nudges and winks. Research for this project gave me the opportunity to work and consult with a variety of fantastic people, and although I will never remember all of their names, I will never forget their assistance.

The hard-working staff members of the Archives of Ontario have been especially helpful. Having to deal with a researcher whose requests for literally hundreds of boxes of files at each visit overwhelmed their storage capacity must have been one of the more onerous frustrations of their work. Ana Cassanova was most notably patient and competent in her assistance. The Access to Information staff helped me to negotiate the intricacies of the regulations, and I remain indebted especially to Ron Ward, who fielded too many questions from someone who, although critical of the process of government regulation, had internalized enough of the state-control discourse to want to do the right thing.

Beyond archival staff, a number of colleagues have provided valuable insight and support. Craig Heron's work and collegiality have been especially important. Having dug through the same sorts of materials for a project that far exceeds this one in quality, he has provided insight and ideas, discussions over pints, and a place to stay, all of which will remain some of the highlights of this field research. He read the entire manuscript at a late stage, and his thoughts, insights, and encouragement were invaluable. Members of the Alcohol and Drugs History Society (ADHS), that brilliant, sodden rabble whose field research is equally fantastic, have provided forums for discussion and insightful analyses that have opened up a variety of areas of new research and additional neuroses. James Nicholls, especially, suggested links between the Liquor Control Board of Ontario and the British Central Control Board (Liquor Traffic) that I have not yet fully explored. These links forced me to think more about the connection between different ideas of liquor regulation in the early part of the twentieth century. The ADHS has been an ongoing source of support and insight, and I have appreciated the collegial discussions over many, many pints at our various conferences. Bill Rorabaugh, Scott Haine, and Richard Hamm participated with me in an especially informative panel that helped to shape the later stages of this project. David Courtwright has been extremely encouraging of my mash-up of methods and theories. Colleagues at the Canadian Society for the History of Medicine have heard me thrash out a number of my ideas, helping me to legitimize my work as "medical history" even though medical use of alcohol was increasingly the deviation from the norm. Steve Hewett allowed me to invite myself to speak to his students and colleagues at the University of Birmingham, where I was able to work out some of the main ideas in the last chapter; Alex Mold and Virginia Berridge hosted a talk at the London School of Hygiene and Tropical Medicine that made me feel like a big kid who had been allowed to play with ideas in an intellectual sandbox. Other good hosts and colleagues have included Jonathan Reinarz, Catherine Carstairs, Tricia Barton, Jim Mills, and Val Curtis, whose different perspectives, collegiality, humour, and hospitality have been invaluable.

I am especially grateful to the staff at UBC Press. I have had the privilege of working with a tremendously talented editor, Melissa Pitts, who has become a good friend, sharing pints and conversations as well as good editorial advice. The anonymous reviewers gave valuable insights and encouragement. As the manuscript wound its way through the production process, I was continually impressed with the good nature and professionalism of the staff with whom I had the privilege of working.

Many of these connections, and all of this research, have been made possible by the support of an Associated Medical Services – Canadian Institutes of Health Research Development Grant and also by funds from various pots of gold hidden at Brock University. This funding permitted me to hire several research assistants in the first few years of the project. Alanna Jenkins, Julia Ladner, and Trevor Campbell did much of the hard slogging through newspaper microfilm and digital files. Alanna deserves special acknowledgment for her diligent and detailed work over several years of this project, and the binders she put together have helped me out of many a difficult referencing problem.

Parts of Chapters 6 and 8 appeared in different versions in earlier publications. I thank the editors of the *Annals of Leisure Research* as well as the University of Toronto Press, publisher of *The Real Dope* (2011), respectively, for permission to reproduce that material here.

Although most of the time we slog it out in solitude, we cannot survive without a support network of friends, family, and co-workers. My colleagues in the Department of Community Health Sciences at Brock University –

often, I am sure, baffled about why they have a historian in their midst – have, by their very diverse approaches to scholarship, opened my eyes to a variety methodologies and perspectives. The staff at my own local public drinking space, the Merchant Ale House, unknowingly attended the birth of most of the chapters in this book. Thanks to them for the company and the many pints. My family continues to be supportive, resigning themselves to my absences and occasional silences. More than anyone else, Kim Landon had to put up with my semi-presence, need for isolation, various research and conference trips, ridiculously extensive collection of microbrews, and poor sleeping habits. She accepted it all with heroic fortitude. Although she has now moved on to other adventures, she still deserves credit for her presence and support throughout the life of this project. It is for this reason that this book remains dedicated to her.

These people inspired, supported, and sustained me while I tried to figure out what all of this material meant, how to frame it, and how to make the results of this labour seem useful. Of course, any failure in this work remains mine alone, although I wish I could blame Zeeba.

Preface: The Word on the Street

Of the dozen streets in the south-western Ontario village of Thorndale (pop. 400), where I spent the second decade of my life, one of the shortest is Temperance Street. It is literally a road to nowhere: roughly 150 metres long, it boasts a whopping three houses, and terminates in a farmer's field. When, in 1984, the township of West Nissouri – of which Thorndale was the municipal capital – voted to end local option, making it legal to have a licensed premises, or even, God help us, a liquor store in the town, I, a cynical, slouching teenager, was baffled at the idea that there had been any kind of prohibition up to this point. I was raised in a family of moderate social drinkers, and still pride myself on what I call my healthy relationship with alcohol. Although one grandfather might be considered to have had a drinking problem (stories abound of my parents fetching him from the Hespeler Hotel's beer parlour), my parents were social drinkers who enjoyed cracking a cold one when friends and family dropped by. Needless to say, we had many friends and family dropping by.

Soon after local option was overturned in West Nissouri, a licensed restaurant opened up. It was located on the corner of Temperance Street. When, decades later, the Liquor Control Board of Ontario began to open "Agency Stores," contracting private convenience-store owners in remote parts of the province to sell booze under licence, the store in Thorndale that got the licence was, you guessed it, on the other corner of Temperance Street. Fearing that the street would soon be renamed, since this positioning seemed to me too brilliant an irony to last, I asked my mother to keep an eye out for a name change. If they changed the name, I told her, I wanted that sign. My mother is clever, and our town is small; she went to the municipal office (a short stumble from Temperance Street) and paid to have a new "Temperance St." sign hung. I have the original in my kitchen. The street's name remains the same.

I tell you this not because I find my experience particularly fascinating but because the story of the moistening of Thorndale's Temperance Street offers a useful metaphor for the story in this book. The end of prohibition did not see the end of temperance in Ontario. That movement was strong, vocal, and persistent. Just as Temperance Street's name became increasingly irrelevant as liquor gradually moved in at the end of West Nissouri's own prohibition era, the creation of the Liquor Control Board of Ontario necessitated a gradualist approach to changing the system, requiring regulations that struck a balance between temperance sentiments and "wetter" inclinations. It was a bureaucratic solution to what was considered a widespread social problem. More important, it was a bureaucratic solution to a deeply divisive *political* problem. As a result, we still have many seemingly archaic and remarkably frustrating liquor regulations and laws in the province. We are not alone. Most Canadian provinces, and I would suspect American states, are riddled with bizarre and seemingly regressive regulations that limit the free flow of booze or impose certain expectations on the proprietors of public drinking spaces and on the people who want to consume alcohol. Visitors from abroad may be baffled by our laws. A friend from Edinburgh, Scotland, once told me of the odd looks he got when he and his wife, fresh off a long bike ride in Banff, Alberta, strolled the path around Lake Louise while sipping from cans of beer. They were unwittingly breaking the law, and some people were aghast.

It is this sort of reaction that inspired the research that has led to this book. The end of prohibition was a tense and difficult time for government regulators. On the one hand, they had the evidence of what appeared to be the utter failure of prohibition, at least when viewed from the perspective of social order. On the other hand, they had many constituents who still believed that liquor was the devil's drink and that the legalization of booze would lead to the downfall of society. I am not belittling these people. Many of them were progressive, socially minded individuals who believed that their ideas would elevate society, help to end poverty and social decline, and pave the way to a better world. Politicians also took them seriously. They were not mindless reactionaries, antiquated old biddies, or crazed radicals. They were voting citizens who were organized, passionate, and respectable.

As a result of this tension, the liquor control regime that emerged was full of contradictions. From a contemporary perspective, it can appear to have been a frightening, hypercontrolling surveillance regime. But such an interpretation would be based both on a limited understanding of the goals of the regulatory system and on the tensions between the ideal and the actual. The functioning of the law and regulations, the system that emerged, was shaped by people – politicians, bureaucrats, and everyday citizens – who had to negotiate the implementation of the regulations. This book is a story of the social, political, economic, and cultural forces that moulded the system with which they all interacted.

Try to Control Yourself

Figure 1 The LCBO required hotel beverage room operators to send photos of their public spaces. This one, including a rare glimpse of a patron, is additionally remarkable for the signs of a recent, cursory mopping. The neat and clean beverage room was an indication, however superficial, that the management was trying to keep things in order. *Source:* Undated photo, Rex Hotel, Port Arthur, AO, RG 36-1-0-1149.

Introduction: The Emergence of Liquor Control Bureaucracy in Ontario

With its own attempt at the "noble experiment" of prohibition a dismal failure, the Province of Ontario took the moderate route. In 1927 the Liquor Control Act (LCA 1927) overturned provincial prohibition, legislated by the Ontario Temperance Act, in favour of government-run liquor distribution, replacing the prohibition-era Board of License Commissioners with the Liquor Control Board of Ontario (LCBO) and ushering in the provincially managed distribution of alcoholic beverages.

Liquor control was supposed to solve the problems of prohibition, the "noble experiment" gone awry. In spite of much fear mongering from the temperance forces, rhetorical hyperbole from the media, celebration from the drinkers, and – undoubtedly – hand rubbing from the brewers and distillers, the end of provincial prohibition did not usher in utter social chaos.[1] Although the "Drys" (often pluralized like that) feared that the Liquor Control Act would renew society's slide toward iniquity, the advocates of liquor control chose a temperate modification to the status quo. The Liquor Control Act legalized alcoholic beverages in a manner that aimed to encourage a moderate approach to drinking. The LCBO began to reconstruct residents' relationship with drink, how and where they could consume it, and in effect their perception of a mind-, body-, and (for some) soul-altering substance.

Since the LCBO's early work involved both controlling the sale of liquor to the public and the regulation of the places in which people could drink their booze, a study of the entire scope of the board's work would be far too complex for one book, at least if there is any hope of giving it a fair analysis. This book, therefore, considers public drinking, leaving to others the issue of government sale for private consumption. What I am interested in here is the way that the *public* consumption of alcoholic beverages was regulated in post-prohibition Ontario, how government control placed constraints and expectations on the population, and how the regulatory process created a dynamic interaction between the government agency and the general public. Residents who wanted to drink and those who wanted to sell it to them blatantly or surreptitiously challenged and in some cases modified the system that was envisioned by the regulators.

It is tempting to create a sharp dichotomy between the two sides of the equation – the government and the people – but it would be a distortion. Neither side was homogeneous. "The government" was, and is, a complex system comprising politicians, self-interested career civil servants, idealistic administrators, and partisan appointees. They had diverse agendas and were often working at cross-purposes. The same can be said of "the people." Owing to the distinct communities in which people lived, to the background, gender, ethnicity, or social class of the individuals, and to the values that drove them, the members of the general public were equally diverse. So studying the regulation of public drinking involves dissecting a complex relationship between the regulator and the regulated. To understand state regulation of the individual, we need to look at a variety of interests from a variety of perspectives, all under the disarmingly simple term of "liquor control."

Among Canadian provinces, Ontario was no leader; by the time the LCBO opened its offices, ordered its stock, hired its staff, renovated its first liquor stores, and deputized its inspectors, provincial liquor boards were becoming somewhat commonplace in Canada.[2] For most provinces, prohibition had been a wartime innovation (ostensibly to address wartime resource scarcity), which the Dominion government enacted through a series of prohibitionist orders-in-council. Consequently, immediately after the war, several provinces dismantled their prohibitory regimes. Quebec rescinded prohibition as soon as possible, allowing sales in stores in 1919 and reintroducing public drinking in 1921. British Columbia and Yukon Territory followed soon after, introducing their own liquor control regime in 1921; by 1925 both had opted to permit the public consumption of beer (passing "beer by the glass" legislation).[3] Other provinces soon followed suit, with Manitoba (1923), Alberta (1924), and Saskatchewan (1925) beating Ontario onto the liquor control bandwagon, although not necessarily permitting beer by the glass so quickly. Whereas Albertans could drink in bars the same year that they could buy alcohol at stores, Manitobans had to wait until 1928, and Saskatchewan's residents had to wait until 1935, fully a year after Ontarians had reopened the beverage rooms.[4]

From a twenty-first-century perspective, the metaphor of "jumping on the bandwagon" seems apt; given the limited nature of its early liquor control system, the province might appear to have remained almost completely "on the wagon." Indeed, regulation was deliberate and slow, and in its operations the LCBO presented a sober face in a process that encouraged moderation.

The LCA (1927) erected a complex system of oversight, what some have hyperbolically described as Nazi-like surveillance.[5] People could buy liquor at government-run stores, but public drinking remained illegal. The consumption of beverage alcohol had to take place in an individual's private residence. Notwithstanding that the act defined "private dwelling place" remarkably loosely as "any building or part of a building or tent where a person resides," which included private guest rooms in hotels, it would be another seven years before people could drink regular-strength beer in public with their friends and neighbours.[6]

Yet a closer look calls into question the often-stated opinion that Canada's seemingly restrictive, abstemious provincial liquor control regimes were an extension of temperance ideology. Liquor control was, in my view, almost a revolutionary innovation for two reasons. First, looking forward from 1916, the creation of the LCBO was a reversal of the direction in which the province had been heading. Temperance rhetoric and the temperance movement had been strong in Ontario. In the 1898 plebiscite, Ontarians had voted overwhelmingly in favour of prohibition. Similarly, a 1902 provincial plebiscite geared to eliminating public drinking in favour of centralized liquor licensing – the License Act (1902) – was supported by a majority of electors, although it failed to receive adequate support to become law.[7] Nonetheless, many Ontario municipalities had passed "local option" plebiscites, which banned the sale of liquor, beer, and wine within their boundaries. Wartime prohibition was continued after a resounding majority of voters agreed in a 1919 plebiscite on the issue. In 1921 another prohibition plebiscite reiterated this decision. Thus, far from embracing temperance ideology, liquor control was pushing against a process of drying out the province that had peaked in 1916 with prohibition.

The second reason that the LCA (1927) might be considered revolutionary is the nature of the regime that it enacted. A centrally organized Liquor Control Board, based on modern principles of governance, was what Gerald Halliwell called a "socialist system" of government oversight.[8] The social problem of alcohol consumption was to be managed by tight control over the distribution of the troubling beverage. The board would be Janus-faced, charged with discouraging indulgence while profiting from sales.[9]

It was, however, a moderate revolution. There were many consistencies with the past. The LCBO replaced the provincial Board of License Commissioners (BLC), which had been in existence for the decade of prohibition. The BLC was itself a centralized board, but its mandate was to oversee the distribution of liquor for medical and industrial purposes and to make sure that the Ontario Temperance Act was enforced.[10] It was also responsible for inspecting and licensing "Standard Hotels," a component of its work that was a holdover from the decade before prohibition when the public consumption of liquor in Ontario was normally confined to hotels. Finally, the administrative apparatus was already in place: the LCBO hired back most of the staff of the BLC.

For the first seven years of its existence, the LCBO was occupied mainly with controlling the distribution of alcohol for personal consumption. It closely monitored activities within the liquor stores, posted inspectors at each distribution point for alcohol (i.e., breweries, distilleries, and wineries), and simultaneously investigated the conduct of premises licensed to sell light beer. This beer, approximately 2.2 percent alcohol by volume, was known colloquially as "4.4 beer" in reference to its proof level.[11] The board also collected data on the drinking habits of Ontarians, collaborated with social service agencies to keep an eye on the trouble drinkers, worked in close contact with various police authorities to root out illegal sellers (i.e., bootleggers) or illegal drinking places (often called "blind pigs"), and made sure that all beverage alcohol was distributed under its watchful administrative eyes.

In 1934 the board's work expanded considerably. As a result of pressure from consumers, combined with the end of prohibition in the United States, the Conservatives under Howard Ferguson's successor as provincial premier, George Henry, introduced to the Ontario Legislature "An Act to Amend the Liquor Control Act, 1927," more commonly known as the Liquor Control Act (1934). Its major, and most controversial, change was to permit the sale and consumption of regular-strength beer and wine in public places, commonly called "beer by the glass" legislation. The law was passed by the Conservatives in an attempt to curry voter favour in the 1934 election. This political strategy did not work. The Conservatives' main opponents, the Liberals, were led by the young and charismatic Mitchell Hepburn, who vowed to uphold the LCA in his stated attempt to depoliticize prohibition as an election issue. The Liberals won, and Hepburn was left to figure out how his party, which drew considerable support from the quite vocal and active temperance movement, would make this new legislation work.[12]

Hepburn's task was made easier by the ambiguity of the 1934 legislation. The LCA (1934) did not clearly state where public drinking could take place. The Conservatives had apparently planned to extend the permission to several types of public establishments, including restaurants and hotels. Doubtless, many who voted for the Liberals thought that they would be able to buy a beer at their local restaurant or "snack bars," both of which had been permitted to sell light beer, and certainly many restaurant owners presumed this would be the case. They were mistaken. Hepburn and his newly selected chief commissioner, former federal Liberal member of Parliament Edmond Odette, decided that the best way to operate the LCA (1934) was to limit the sites of public drinking. The LCBO, therefore, focused its efforts on hotel beverage rooms and dining rooms, private clubs, steamships, and trains.

By far, the most prominent drinking space quickly became the hotel beverage room, a place rooted in several decades of public-drinking tradition. Within the span of a few weeks in the summer of 1934, the LCBO received well over one thousand applications from hotel proprietors seeking the privilege of selling beer in their beverage rooms or beer and wine with meals in their dining rooms. Hotels that received such permission were issued a beer authority or a beer and wine authority (and although it was the proprietors who applied, the authority was attached to the premises). In late July, Ontarians returned to the revivified hotel beverage rooms.

What they found would have surprised and disappointed many of them. The beverage room of 1934 was considerably different from the archetypes of the past. The LCA (1934) was heavily restrictive, and the LCBO expanded on the legislated rules with its own set of regulations. According to the LCA (1934), no gambling, drunkenness, or "riotous, quarrelsome, violent or disorderly conduct" could take place in the beverage rooms. No slot machines or gambling devices were allowed. The stand-up bar, a mainstay of the pre-prohibition saloon, was prohibited, replaced by a screened-in "taproom." Beer could not be served for off-premises consumption. Hotels were not allowed to have any financial association with breweries, and breweries could neither own nor provide free services or products to hotels. The LCBO's regulations were more specific. Only beer could be sold in beverage rooms. Beer and wine were allowed in hotel dining rooms as long as a reasonably sized meal was also purchased. In the beverage room, customers had to sit at a table and be served their beer by waiters – whose tidy appearance was also mandated by the regulations. To the clause on disorderly conduct in the LCA (1934), the board added "music, singing, dancing, disorder, quarrelling, profane or obscene language or misbehaviour." Radios and music boxes being played in other parts of the hotel should not be loud enough to be heard in the beverage room. Food was not allowed in beverage rooms, although in the early rules "the Board will make no objection to the placing of a small bowl of either pretzels or potato chips on each table ... providing no charge is made for the same."[13] As we will see, the board created many more regulations, governing all aspects of a hotel's operations.

Disinterested Management

In placing the control over drinking in the hands of a central board, the Ontario government was following the lead of governments around the world. The centralization of both distribution and control over liquor consumption was based on the principle of "disinterested management" pioneered in Scandinavia in the last part of the nineteenth century. Under this arrangement, also called the Gothenburg system, government controlled both the manufacture and the sale of alcoholic beverages. Such management was "disinterested" because managers did not have a financial stake in selling more alcohol; their focus was supposed to be control. Ontario's approach was a modified Gothenburg system: the manufacture of alcohol remained the purview of private industry, but the LCBO ran the stores. Breweries and wineries were allowed to sell their own products from their own stores, but an LCBO inspector was on site. The 1934 act continued this mix of private and public management: the drinking establishments were privately owned but were authorized by the board and closely watched by the local inspector. Management of all aspects of liquor consumption remained, ultimately, the purview of the state.

The centralization of liquor control in Ontario created a system in which individual behaviour intersected with state regulation. This of course is nothing new, but the process of liquor control was a major expansion of the state oversight into individual lives. It is an example of "governmentality," an idea Michel Foucault introduced to characterize governance in the modern era, or as he explained it, "the conduct of conduct" *("conduire des conduits")*.[14] As Mitchell Dean notes, "government entails any attempt to shape with some degree of deliberation aspects of our behaviour according to particular sets of norms and for a variety of ends."[15] As an agent of governmentality that attempted to "conduct the conduct" of citizens, the LCBO attempted to construct a social vision based on a specific set of values and ideas about social order. It created a system of control that defined moral and immoral activities, compelling individuals to conform to idealized behaviours in order to get direct benefits – a drink in public with their friends.

To further Foucaultize the discussion, I would argue that the LCBO's activity was the expression of *biopower*. Biopower is the active principle of biopolitics, the process by which government's role expands from the simple management of trade and other *external* facets of life to the subtle but pervasive management of the *internal* life of the individual, the way we conduct our physical selves.[16] Biopolitics is not just social control with a newer name. Whereas social control is the imposition or implementation of a specific value system on others, the "power" in biopower is a neutral force that both oppresses and empowers: certain activities and beliefs are permitted and even encouraged, whereas others are suppressed and discouraged. Biopolitics is therefore a process of negotiation and modification. The LCBO's biopower was subtle but extensive. It sought to reshape the individual's relationship with his or her body by internalizing self-control over the consumption of liquor and to restructure an individual's ideas about the physical and neurochemical effects of that substance. Whereas prohibition simply prohibited the consumption of alcohol, liquor control *permitted* consumption, although under certain conditions that were controlled by the state but negotiated with the citizen.

The mechanisms of the LCBO's biopower were complex and pervasive. The very consumption of something that brought pleasure and psychic transformation was framed by various notions of propriety and validity, discourses like those found in temperance, medical, and social-reform rhetoric, each of which contained specific ideas of what was dangerous to the physical body and the body politic. These mechanisms forced people who wanted a drink to run a series of bureaucratic gauntlets before they could indulge and relax. In the liquor stores, the customer had to buy a permit book, fill in a form listing a substance he or she wanted to buy, and be evaluated by the liquor store employee.[17] (The employee's actions, of course, were also controlled.) As I noted above, after 1934 the customer who wanted to have a legal drink with friends was also subjected to a series of state-prescribed constraints on behaviour. There was slightly more leeway in the licensed hotel dining rooms, but here again the individual's desire for the physical pleasure of drinking was severely constrained. Moreover, the system contained several layers of control: the hotel management was overseen by the state; staff was overseen by management; the customer was both served and regulated by the staff; and members of the public could report back to the state about activities in the hotels. (As we will see, the apparatus of the state was also scrutinized by the public.) The authority of the central administration was diffused throughout the system by various paid and unpaid agents.

Those familiar with the work of Max Weber will recognize this structure since the LCBO's biopolitical project was facilitated by the bureaucratization of government. Weber's dissection of bureaucratization helps us to see the structural implementation of central values. He and his intellectual descendants provide an appreciation of how government works in a structural way and of how bureaucrats who are invested in the system place considerable value in the bureaucracy as a way of injecting rationale into chaos.[18] Weber's "ideal-typical" bureaucracy, which strives toward an objectivity that is devoid of subjective value judgments and personal interest, is a valuable tool for understanding the LCBO's regulatory project. A bureaucracy derives its power from "well-defined spheres of competence, continuous performance of official duties, an orderly hierarchy of control ... decision-making based on written records ... and a style of decision-making which consists of applying general rules to particular cases."[19] These structures permit a form of governance that would otherwise be impossible. Hence the structure was functional: "The whole point about bureaucratic administration as a means of domination is that it carries out tasks which cannot technically be performed by the employing agent itself."[20] A well-structured bureaucracy allows management of people from a distance.

What makes Weber's ideas of bureaucratization useful to a study of the LCBO is that this idealization of an objective, rule-based bureaucracy stands in stark contrast to emotionally charged temperance discourse of moral regulation and social disaster. By the 1930s the manufacture, sale, and consumption of beverage alcohol had been the focus of reform organizations in North America for at least a century. Even though many considered prohibition – the outcome of the anti-alcohol movement – to be a failure by the 1930s,[21] the temperance movement remained a strong and very active force in local and provincial politics. So the activity of the LCBO was viewed from both sides, the Drys and the Wets, in emotional and passionate ways. The Wets saw the board as restrictive; the Drys saw it as facilitating a social danger. Indeed, that the LCBO's first few years brought enough money into the coffers of the provincial government to virtually erase its debt further added to the Drys' concerns about the dubious connection between liquor and the management of the state. To them, these connections created the danger of the pre-prohibition regime, in which alcohol licensing was an intensely political activity. In contrast, the Wets were not really a cohesive movement. Yet, although not as organized or vocal as the Drys, they certainly expressed their interests through their actions. The many arrests, licence suspensions, and investigations into illegal activities in both hotel beverage rooms and the pervasive unlicensed "blind pigs" made it very clear that the people wanted to drink in public and could not easily shake off the forms of sociability that had been normative in the past. Such behaviour is fundamental to understanding the operation of and the limits to the bureaucracy of the LCBO. No matter how well-organized this bureaucracy was (and the LCBO was by no means a perfect system), it was run by, and organized to control, the actions of humans, all of whom had their own values, ideals, expectations, and demands.

The Governmentality of the Bureaucracy

Although it may seem odd, the ideas of bureaucratization and governmentality intertwine quite nicely. Bureaucratization is the development of a complex organization in which rules and ultimate power are centralized but decision-making authority is diffused throughout the system. Governmentality is the discursive construction of this regulatory system. Mitchell Dean has described a variety of components of governmentality that are useful for this current analysis. Most notable are the means by which government functions and the point at which it ceases to function: the "regimes of control" of government. These regimes sit within the bureaucracy's "field of visibility" and are shaped by a variety of technologies, what Dean calls the *"techne"* of the system. "Fields of visibility" are the areas in which a government functions and on which a governing activity focuses. I like to think of a spotlight in the dark: it brightly illuminates certain things while obscuring everything outside of the spot. So the government's vision is limited to that which it chooses to see; governmental discourses ignore certain behaviours, ideas, and values. Similarly, the *techne* restricts the form of governance: the technologies, documentation, mechanisms, and apparatuses of the governing body enable a certain delimited form of observation and data collection, but they also limit the mode of governance to the parameters of the physical functionality of these technologies.[22]

The complex bureaucracy of the LCBO relied on diverse technologies of communication and surveillance – including paperwork, statistics, observations, and photographs – that facilitated a certain degree of standardized data collection presented in a form that was understandable to the central administration. Moreover, communications tools, such as the telephone, the telegraph, letters, and personal meetings, further shaped the nature of the LCBO's governance, that is, the way conduct was conducted. Here, we see the limits of the *techne*. Certain aspects of public behaviour were hidden from the eyes of the bureaucracy, whereas others faced increased scrutiny. Still others may have been ignored, to extend the analogy, through a sort of selective blindness. Moreover, the bureaucracy's view was additionally obscured because it relied on a degree of subjective evaluation by inspectors who were from the regions under scrutiny and who thus had their own biases about the communities. For example, local hotel inspectors could (and some did) exploit their official positions to advance their own interests, but this activity was often invisible to the central administration (and sadly, to historians), owing to the nature of the techniques of regulation. We learn of this behaviour only when a proprietor or community member chose to complain, and even then the veracity of the complaint is questionable. As well, the structure of the bureaucracy, which required a degree of trust in the system's distant agent, made it difficult both for the central administration to accept such criticisms and for the complainants to make their case.

Here, we get back to my assertion that liquor control was revolutionary: its expansion drove the centralized control of behaviour deeper into the lives of individuals, as a solution to a "problem" that had plagued the state for decades, and in the process constructed a new discourse of governance. Government became an agent of moderation; the late-nineteenth- and early-twentieth-century temperance movement's insistence on absolute prohibition was replaced by an earlier form of moderation (or "true temperance"), regulated by the state but made real by the self-governing individual – you had to control yourself if you wanted to drink. This revolution was possible because the alternative was social chaos. On the one hand was prohibition, which had been reframed as a state of lawlessness under an extremely restrictive legal regime, not to mention an egregious violation of individual liberties. On the other hand was the unregulated drink traffic, which had been framed by the prohibition and temperance movements as a steep and slippery slope to social disaster. Liquor control was the compromise between the two extremes. Just as, with public health inspection of factories, schools, and other public or semi-public institutions, the government infiltrated the bodies of individual citizens, so with liquor control the government entered another aspect of the lives of citizens: their bodies at rest. It deployed the ideal of what I call the "citizen-drinker": one who indulges, but responsibly, within the constraints imposed by the state and in a way that does not upset the existing social order.

Possibly the key to understanding the specific biopolitical perspective of the LCBO's bureaucracy is the notion of a politics of moderation. Just as excessive drinking wreaked havoc on an individual's body, excess was the enemy of the body politic. Overly permissive liquor distribution in the pre-prohibition period resulted in prohibition, which was excessive restriction. Neither worked. In his 1929 report to the provincial Legislature, the board's second chief commissioner asserted that the board was interested in moderation in all aspect of its work: "After the test of prohibitory laws, it may be affirmed that moral advance and their personal acceptance of voluntary limitation, if not voluntary abstinence, is the real solution to evils arising from the abuse of intoxicating liquors."[23] In other words, prohibition failed because it was legislative excess rather than moderation. To be too restrictive would be to drive erstwhile legal drinkers into the arms of the still-prevalent bootleggers or operators of "blind pigs." As a result, the board had to be responsive to the demands at the local level. It recognized that the only way to create a successful regime of control was to create a system that was both sufficiently lenient to discourage people from seeking illegal means of satisfying their craving and sufficiently restrictive to prevent social disorder.

To understand this process of regulation, the interplay of often contradictory interests, and the negotiation of respectability, this book examines the LCBO's operations at the community level, excavating its relationship to the individual drinker and vendor while considering how its system of control was a mechanism enforcing a biopolitical agenda. It looks at the operation of the Liquor Control Board in six Ontario communities: (1) Essex County; (2) Waterloo County; (3) the "Niagara region" of Lincoln, Niagara, and Welland Counties; (4) the Thunder Bay district; (5) the city of Ottawa; and (6) the city of Toronto. These communities were chosen in an attempt to embrace geographic and demographic diversity, and the specific social and demographic characteristics of these communities are provided in the Appendix. The study ends in 1944 because in that year new legislation was passed that bifurcated the work of the LCBO, creating the Liquor Authority

Control Board to oversee the regulation of booze consumption in public places.[24] Most of the current study concentrates on the period 1934-44, the first decade of "beer by the glass" legislation.

By reading all of the available LCBO Establishment Files for these communities, I was able to construct an impression of the type of forces at work in each area: the local politics, the community opposition to or support of public drinking, and the various social and cultural factors that affected the board's ability to enforce its rules. This multicentred approach is far preferable to any other form of sampling, such as a random sample of all of the establishments across the province, because it permits us to see the communities as places with their own character and cultures. The context of these activities was established by an examination of at least one newspaper from each region. Municipal and other government records, such as letters to the premier of Ontario, round out main sources for the work. Since much of the material and many of the investigations into the drinking spaces were filtered through official eyes, it is important to remember that what we have here is a biased view of public drinking. Some things are missing. For example, there is no indication, even in reports on the beverage rooms of a city as diverse as Toronto, that some of these spaces were used for homosexual socialization, even though it is likely that they were.[25] This is not a cultural history of drinking in post-prohibition Ontario; it is a social, cultural, and administrative history of the development of the control of public drinking in the province.

Drinking and Regulation in History

As a study of liquor regulation, and of government bureaucracy, this work fits into several historical traditions. Since the LCBO was mandated to restrict access to alcohol, its creation and most especially its early history inform aspects of the broad history of the prohibition and temperance movements. Conversely, in attempting to shape the way people viewed alcoholic beverages, the LCBO is part of an emerging history of drinking culture. Moreover, as a government agency that emerged in the interwar period, the LCBO also adds to the literature on the functioning of government bureaucracy. It is valuable to look at these historical traditions in turn.

For several decades, the social history of alcohol was for the most part a social history of anti-alcohol movements. Research on "temperance" is broad and deep.The temperance movement was a remarkably important and influential social force in North America, and by the end of the nineteenth century, it was international in scope.[26] The Woman's Christian Temperance Union (WCTU), which began in the United States and quickly spread to Canada and around the world, established what Ian Tyrrell has called a "Woman's Empire."[27] The WCTU was not alone in its efforts, and male-dominated organizations like the Anti-Saloon League in the United States and the Dominion Alliance for the Total Suppression of the Liquor Traffic in Canada joined the WCTU to push the prohibition agenda in the political realm.[28] By the beginning of the First World War, many states and several provinces had already passed some form of prohibitory legislation. These histories are important because they help us to understand that, far from some group of sour, boring old crackpots who wanted to stop decent people from having a nice drink with friends, members of the temperance and prohibition movements viewed themselves as progressives, hoping to elevate society from the potential downward spiral of an industrial age. They just wanted to do it without what they saw to be the fundamentally demoralizing and socially disruptive influence of beverage alcohol. This is why, in Canada, they allied themselves politically with the Liberals.

Although the history of the temperance and prohibition movements is extensive, an increasing number of historians are looking at those on the other side of the barroom door: the drinkers. Several historians of early modern drinking have demonstrated that the tavern was an important social space in a variety of urban and rural settings.[29] For Upper Canada, historian Julia Roberts has shown that the rural tavern was an essential community centre.[30] As industrialization expanded, the urban tavern in North America appears to have become more firmly a place of working-class socialization. Historians of working-class culture have found the tavern to be an important, if not the most important, cultural institution for the industrial working class.[31] Craig Heron's recent research into the place of the working-class tavern in Canada and his tremendously important larger study of booze in Canada have gone a long way toward rectifying this gap, but more examples from more places across Canada will expand our understanding of this important social space.[32]

Since most of the studies of historical North American drinking cultures and their opposition reasonably set the onset of prohibition as their end point, the history of alcohol (both temperance and consumption) exhibits an uneven appreciation of the prohibition and post-prohibition drinking environments. Prohibition itself has not been understudied, but there has been a decided lack of rigour in much of the popular prohibition-era histories. With gangsters, rumrunners, and speakeasies, the prohibition era has seen tremendous attention in popular history and popular culture. Much of this attention has been highly sensationalized, placing "myth above reality."[33] In contrast, academic historians have attempted to understand prohibition as government policy and social formation.[34] Some studies of prohibition-era policy creation have taken the examination of government regulation forward into the post-prohibition era. In the Unites States, where liquor policy is developed at the state level, several historians have begun to dissect the field of post-prohibition liquor policy.[35] Some valuable studies have considered the relationship between Canada and the United States during American prohibition, including Greg Marquis's examination of how Canadian post-prohibition policies affected US attitudes toward liquor control and other studies of the situation along the Canada-US border.[36] In Canada, given the provincial jurisdiction of liquor policies, the situation has also been studied mostly at the provincial level.[37]

This book engages with these various historical traditions. For historians of the temperance and prohibition movements, the LCBO's work to limit access to and curtail the consumption of alcohol offers important insights into how the messages of these large social movements impacted public policy after their big success – complete prohibition – was seen to have failed. For historians of drinking cultures, the LCBO's mandate to facilitate but control drinking provides important insight into how uses of alcohol within a social setting were viewed by the predominantly white, middle-class bureaucrats who were interested in normalizing a specific type of drinking within a narrowly focused notion of respectability. Finally, for historians of government policy and government bureaucracy, the LCBO's work provides key insights into the functioning of an administration that, although constructed to deal with the significant political challenges presented by public drinking, did not seem to be able to please anyone, except maybe the politicians who hid behind its apparatus.

The book is divided into two sections. After a brief examination of the unique political and social situation regarding public drinking from 1927 to 1934, the book turns to the various aspects of regulation of space and behaviour. The first section examines the ways the LCBO attempted to restructure, physically and discursively, the public drinking space. Here, we are concerned with the bureaucratic methods of the LCBO, Dean's *techne* of governmentality (Chapter 2), the geospatial arrangement of the drinking space (Chapter 3), the social and political forces that influenced the LCBO's work (Chapters 4 and 5), and the ways that the hotel proprietors resisted or attempted to modify the board's approach to entertainment and recreation (Chapter 6). The second section is concerned with the way the LCBO sought to regulate specific types of people within the drinking space. The board sought to address the sticky problems of women in bars (Chapter 7) and of ethnic groups whose relationship with beverage alcohol was different and therefore a challenge to the LCBO (Chapter 8). The last chapter is an examination of how the board's work, forged in the Depression of the 1930s, changed during the Second World War. The brief Conclusion considers the board's legacy in 1944, when new legislation divided its operations, transferring the oversight of public drinking to a new government agency.

Post-prohibition liquor control is a story of how the temperance movement, various drinking cultures, politicians, and the emerging bureaucracy interacted in the reformation of public alcohol consumption and in the construction of a new subject, the citizen-drinker. He or she consumed legally purchased alcohol in legal spaces and tried to behave but acted in a way that accepted the need for social order. By looking at the activities in the communities, the book attempts to go beyond the "high-policy" approach to studying governance. It considers the implementation and modification of policy at the community level and how these local contexts affected the achievement of some homogenized version of the citizen-drinker. The attempted objective implementation of centralized rules intersected with the subjective interest of a diverse population. Temperance Street would never be the same.

1
Liquor Control Bureaucracy and the Mechanisms of Governance

As a complex regulatory bureaucracy, the Liquor Control Board of Ontario (LCBO) developed or adapted a series of systems and technologies to do its work. Some of the board's approaches have been addressed by other writers, notably Scott Thompson and Gary Genosko in *Punched Drunk* and Mariana Valverde in *Diseases of the Will*.[1] Both of these studies conceptualize the board as an essentially oppressive agency that kept Ontarians under tight surveillance. Although it is true that, like most developing government bureaucracies, the board was increasingly technological and complex in its functioning, such extreme characterizations miss the limits of the bureaucratic apparatus. As discussed in the Introduction, both the presuppositions and the technology of control affect the view of the observer. What one looks for, and where and how one looks for it, restricts the range of possibilities of what one finds. It is useful, then, to examine both the context in which the LCBO was created and the procedures the board developed to undertake its work.

When it was formed in 1927, the LCBO adopted some of the apparatus of its predecessor, the Board of License Commissioners, but with a much larger and growing bureaucratic organization. Initially, the LCBO's central administration consisted of three men: chief commissioner D.B. Hanna and commissioners R.J. Manion and Stewart McClenaghan.[2] By 1934, before the new Liquor Control Act (LCA) of that year came into place, this body had been reduced to now chief commissioner McClenaghan, supported by deputy chief commissioner J.M. McNamara.[3] Premier Mitchell Hepburn reduced the number of commissioners to one: chief commissioner Edmond Odette.[4] Through its first seven years, the LCBO reported to the attorney general. Under Hepburn's Liberals, the board began to report to Hepburn himself, likely because he was not only the premier but also provincial treasurer.

Although the precise internal organizational structure of the LCBO remains unclear, extant records offer us a basic quantitative impression of the board's operations. In 1927 the head office included a commissioner's staff of five, a general manager's staff of two, a comptroller's office of eight, and a general office of several hundred. Including the inspectors and store and warehouse staff, the LCBO in 1927 had 785 employees.[5] By 1934, prior to the new LCA, although the total number of commissioners had declined, the office staff had increased to seven in the chief commissioner's office, four in the general manager's office, and eleven in the comptroller's office. Although the total number of office staff appears to have been reduced, likely as a result of Depression-era reductions, increased inspection, store, and warehouse employees meant that, before the new law came into place, the LCBO's staff numbered 1,066, a 36 percent increase in employees.[6] After the beginning of the operation of the LCA (1934), and despite significantly adding to the hotel-inspectorate branch, the LCBO's staff declined to 904.[7]

The LCBO rapidly became an extensive, complex regulatory bureaucracy. Its activities reached to the edges of the province, into the homes of any resident who chose to purchase and consume alcohol, and into the public spaces in which they were permitted to do so. Through its operations, it sought to reshape not only the behaviour and very self-perception of drinkers but also the attitudes of the managers and owners of drinking establishments. The board employed inspectors and staff across the province and deployed various forms of regulatory technology and bureaucratic language to fulfill its mandate. To reconstruct the citizen-drinker, a concept based on intermingling discourses of social order and respectability, it deployed an authoritative language of control that radiated from the central administration to its operatives at the periphery, where it was modified to suit local conditions.

Hotels throughout the province were the main focus of the LCBO's public-drinking regulatory activities. In the early part of the twentieth century, most hotels remained small, independent businesses that were often run by a married couple or less frequently by a widowed woman or (less ideal to the board) a male bachelor. Far from the large, multistorey hotels owned by multinational corporations, with which readers may be more familiar, a typical Ontario hotel at this time was relatively small, with no more than a handful of rooms, several of which could be occupied by the proprietor and his or her family. The building might be either owned by the proprietor or leased, leading to a variety of individuals who were interested in the successful operation of the business. Building owners might repeatedly dismiss problematic proprietors until one who could properly do the job was found. Or owner-proprietors would struggle along, hoping to make enough money to improve their business, and either prosper or sell out and move on. So when an inspector reported back to the central administration about the activities within a hotel, he often framed his assessment in a personalized manner, making subjective assessments of the situation that added nuance to what could, at a distance, seem a clear case of rule violation or poor management.

Hotels were an important part of life in Ontario. Julia Roberts has shown how the colonial tavern functioned as a way station in the pre-mechanized travelling life of the province.[8] This aspect persisted, transformed by the development of railways and automobiles.[9] Business travellers needed hotels, and most older hotels had some kind of "sample room" where travelling salesmen could store or display their wares. Peter Delottinville's description of Joe Beef's Tavern in Montreal as a place that included facilities for workers to sleep further illustrates how hotels could cater to a variety of classes.[10] Many hotels, especially in times of affluence or in areas of increased industrial or economic activity, housed workers either temporarily or on a semi-permanent basis. In north-western Ontario during various economic booms, the hotels could be full of "bushmen" or temporary labourers. Across the province during the Second World War, hotels were pressed into service to house transient or newly arrived labourers in wartime industries. Also, most hotels, especially those in smaller towns, usually had large rooms that could be made available to the public for banquets or other functions. Whereas large, corporate, and respectable hotels like Ottawa's Chateau Laurier, Toronto's Royal York, and Windsor's Norton-Palmer were frequented by elite travellers, many more modest establishments, family-owned and -operated, squeaked by in a competitive market. These businesses received the most intense scrutiny from the LCBO.

With so many small hotels, the board could be selective in its licensing decisions. The "Standard Hotel" licence was considered by many to be a mark of quality, and not all hotels received it. In 1927 the LCBO licensed 1,258 standard hotels, and by the time the legislation changed in 1934 the number had risen to 1,463 (most, but not all, of these were licensed to sell light beer).[11] It also denied many applications, deeming the premises to be unsuitable for any number of reasons, ranging from physical layout to potential problems in the surrounding community.[12] The accommodation business was competitive. As Karen Dubinsky has shown in her work on Niagara Falls, there was considerable tension between owners of standard hotels and those individuals who operated "tourist homes," which were licensed, if at all, by municipal authorities.[13] To further complicate things, the board distinguished between rural and urban hotels. Initially, a rural hotel could have only four bedrooms, and an urban hotel needed a mere six. Likely as a result of applications from people who hoped to create a country drinking space by sparsely furnishing four "bedrooms" and calling their place a hotel, the LCBO quickly modified its regulations. Within the first year of the operations of the LCA (1934), a rural hotel needed six rooms, and an urban one needed twelve.

When an individual applied for a standard hotel licence and, after 1934, usually accompanied this application with one for a beer authority or a beer and wine authority, they subjected themselves, their family, and their premises, as well as the area in which their property was located and its residents, to the regulatory gaze of the LCBO. This gaze was authoritative and appeared ubiquitous, but it was also limited and biased, shaped not only by the values of the members of the central administration but also by the very apparatus of the LCBO's bureaucratic structure. The technology used to enforce regulations both shapes and limits the activities of the governing agency.[14] Having examined the surveillance techniques of the LCBO over a broad span of time, Gary Genosko and Scott Thompson argue that the various means of recording and tracking liquor purchases of individuals "could transform the most private interests into public matters, in the process re-categorizing individuals and redefining their material possessions and property."[15] In this view, the private individual fell under the oppressive gaze of the public agency.

Although this interpretation is useful, it tends to understate the functional limits of the surveillance techniques and the restrictions that extant communication methods placed on the ability of the central administration to enforce its authority. To use Dean's terminology, the *techne* restricted the field of visibility available to the board's scrutiny. What follows is a dissection of the various forms of communication between hotel proprietors and the board. It demonstrates the limits of the technology of control, suggesting that silences were created by documentation that asked for specific information, and it exposes the expanding impersonalization of the process. This all began with the application for a standard hotel licence and for a beer and wine authority.

The Application

The initial contact between the hotel proprietor and the LCBO was often through the application for a standard hotel licence. Prior to 1934 the licence application form was a single standard-sized page, which included a few lines indicating the proprietor's desire for a light-beer authority. On the rare occasion when a hotel did not wish to apply for a light-beer authority along with the standard hotel licence, the light-beer section might be crossed out or not completed. After 1934 the hotel proprietor had to complete an application for a standard hotel licence and a separate application for a beer authority or a beer and wine authority. These applications were much more comprehensive than the pre-1934 form, being four pages long and asking for a range of information from physical layout of the building to the management structure of the business. The applicant also had to forward three letters of reference from respectable community members – a politician, a police official, and another respectable community member, usually a business owner. All had to attest to the proprietor's good character and suitability for running a hotel. Finally, possibly further attesting to the proprietor's financial stability and credibility, the application had to be accompanied by the appropriate fees: $1 for a standard hotel licence and $300 for an authority. The latter fee was not as high as it might appear since the board then credited back to the hotel $300 off the "gallonage fees" the management paid on beer purchases.

Although ideally an application would be followed by a visit from a local inspector or less frequently a police officer, in the first few months of the operation of the LCA (1934), this process was often impractical. In the summer of 1934, the board received well over one thousand applications but had yet to add the staff required to enforce the new rules. Not surprisingly, the local inspectors could not undertake inspections of the premises prior to granting an authority, and many were granted "site unseen." This situation caused some concern when, in November 1934, after the initial phase of the LCA (1934)'s operation, and at the end of the fiscal year, many of these authorities were revoked.[16]

Less frequently, prior to an application being filed, the board would receive a letter asking whether an application would have any chance of success. Many of these letters came after the initial flurry of applications and the granting of authorities in the summer of 1934 and permitted the board to undertake a much more comprehensive evaluation of the establishment than it had in the first few months. Having an inspection prior to submitting an application provided the proprietor the opportunity to make changes that the board required in order for the hotel to conform to a more idealized vision of a standard hotel. It also provided the inspector with an opportunity to comment on the character of the proprietor (and owner if they were not the same person) and to provide other subjective information, such as the suitability of the location for a hotel and the "desirability" of the hotel in the location. In the first few months of the 1934 act's operation, the board promised to grant authorities to a few proprietors based on assessments of pending renovations.[17] By the end of 1934, the board had changed its policy: no more promises would be made before renovations were completed.

Once the licence and authorities were granted, the normal procedure was for the inspectors to file an annual report and monthly "Authority Holder's Conduct Reports" (AHCRs). The annual reports were standardized four-page forms, with roughly three pages of checkboxes and fields that the inspectors needed to complete and with space at the end for additional comments. The AHCR was a shorter document, one single-sided page, that had a series of fields with yes or no questions or brief items that needed to be filled in, such as listing the temperature of the glass-cleaning water or the state of the beer kegs. An open field at the bottom of this report, about ten centimetres of space, was left for comments, and the opposite side of the page had lines for additional information. Some inspectors routinely used all of this space. Inspector D.W. Downey from Toronto's east side had large, scrawling handwriting and filled a page and a half with comments; other inspectors might have five lines of tightly typed information or nothing more than a word or two.

Depending on the location and the time of year, these monthly AHCRs were often filed irregularly. Probably owing to the number of hotels he had to inspect, and the problems he found in a number of them, inspector John Kidd from Toronto's west side (whose district included the city's rambunctious Jarvis Street) often filed AHCRs with several dates in the "date inspected" field, suggesting that, whereas he inspected frequently, he filed reports only occasionally. In contrast, inspector George Skuce of the Thunder Bay district found that some of the more remote locations were difficult to reach, especially in the winter, and therefore would apologize to the central administration when he could not visit every hotel on a regular basis. These forms, both the annual report and the AHCR, permitted a degree of subjective information to accompany the specific fields to be included. So the inspector's perspective was essential to the technology of control; he could choose which aspects of the establishment's operation to include or ignore.

By the 1940s the board had modified the format of both the long report and the AHCR to assert more specific control over the type and format of information being requested and over the activities of inspectors. Indeed, the AHCR was changed to the "Authority Holder's Monthly Conduct Report" (AHMCR), suggesting a standardization of the use of time. In both report forms, the requisite objective data expanded, and the space for additional subjective information declined. The long report now had a note at the bottom of the fourth page indicating that additional information should be submitted on a separate page, something that most inspectors rarely did. The AHMCR had about three centimetres of space; often inspectors entered brief, generic information, such as "A well run hotel," or more often simply left it blank. The subjective input from inspectors was reduced by these forms, although the priorities of each local inspector (e.g., whether he always checked the temperature of the dishwater or was preoccupied with the cleanliness of basements) could reappear in letters sent to the board or in additional pages. As a result, the inspector became more of a calculator for the central administration. Although it is impossible to determine the impact of such expanded objective formatting on the inspectors, it is telling that, after the AHMCR replaced the AHCR, the reports became increasingly bereft of additional comments. One can imagine an inspector becoming a form-filler; from Max Weber's perspective, this outcome is the fundamental dehumanizing aspect of bureaucratization, but it is also what makes the ideal-typical bureaucracy so valuable to the central authority since it affords increased control of the type and format of information gathered. At the same time, by removing the opportunity for the inspector to make quick and insightful observations, the board reduced the effectiveness of its main source of information about the context in which the hotel operated.

Oversight of the Hotel Proprietor

Although reports were the main face-to-face contact between the LCBO and the establishment, the board's central administrators also communicated directly to hotel proprietors using a variety of methods. Most communication involved letters to deal with specific occasional problems and generic circulars to deal with broader, system-wide issues. Members of the central administration would, at times, travel to the area in question and visit a variety of establishments. Telegraphs also flowed both ways, as did telephone calls, although much less frequently. Finally, in extreme cases the board would invite an establishment's proprietor to visit the board's offices on University Avenue in Toronto. Sometimes these invitations were, quite clearly, commands.

Circulars were fundamental to the communication strategy of the board.[18] Indeed, on the liquor store side of board operations, circulars were sent out with remarkable frequency. Between 1927 and 1934, over 1,600 circulars were sent to the store employees (nearly 230 circulars per year), and in the next ten years the number doubled. This tremendous amount of contact indicates how important tight control over the operation of the retail liquor stores was to the board. It may have been a result of the fact that spirits, traditionally considered more problematic than wine or beer, were being sold there. Circulars were also sent to licensed beverage rooms, the "establishment side" of the board's operations, although not nearly to the extent that they were sent to the liquor store employees. By 1944 hotel proprietors and club managers had received only 198 circulars, averaging fewer than two dozen annually.

Circulars were valuable components of the board's control efforts, most especially in the first few months after the LCA 1934 came into effect, when the board often changed or added new rules in the course of a few weeks. Many of these circulars simply reiterated for proprietors the laws or regulations in the LCA or in the annual *Digest of Rules, Orders, Regulations and Legislation* that the board sent to all hotels. Usually, hotel managers were expected to send back a brief acknowledgment of the circular. For example, the board required a reply confirming that the management had "read and understand[s] the contents" of the circular that was sent out in March 1938 reminding proprietors that the law forbade them from seeking "assistance [from brewers or distillers], either by way of donations of Beer, money or equipment, nor must an Authority Holder seek funds from the advertising of personal greetings on behalf of Brewers or their employees in proposed programmes or pamphlets."[19] These were static forms of control, issued from the centre to the periphery, that enabled the board to speak *at* the managers but did not facilitate any sort of dialogue or allow the local context to be taken into consideration.

A somewhat more dynamic form of interaction was possible through sometimes frequent back-and-forth correspondence between the central administration and either the proprietor or the local inspector. These letters could relate to routine aspects of the hotel operations, such as the number of fire escape ropes in rooms, or to more troubling issues, such as stories of drunkenness, prostitution, or violence in the hotel. The letters were quite often spurred by the content of an inspector's report or letter, which Arnold Smith, the deputy chief commissioner after 1934, or William Mair, the assistant director of hotels, read carefully, highlighting items of concern with a ubiquitous red pencil and occasionally making notes in the margins. A letter would then be issued to the proprietor informing him or her of the rule violation and often including a reminder that such behaviour was unbecoming of a hotel licensed by the board. Often the response would be a simple reply apologizing for the transgression, but at times the board and hotel proprietor could engage in protracted discussions about facets of the hotel's operation and about the unique characteristics of the location or the establishment that the hotel proprietor felt the board should consider.

At times, letters were not enough. In many cases, hotel proprietors would decide, or be ordered, to visit the board's offices in Toronto to discuss a specific situation. Often such visits were made when a hotel's authority was suspended or when the board repeatedly refused to grant an authority in the first place. At other times, members of the board's central administration might embark on a tour of different parts of the province. For example, Arnold Smith visited the Thunder Bay district at least once, in 1935, and Essex County that same year; he also spent some time in Ottawa (he was from Cornwall) and in the Niagara region. Edmond Odette, the chief commissioner, spent a good amount of time at his home in Tilbury and was a frequent visitor to nearby Essex County, although whether he was enforcing, inspecting, or glad-handing is never clear. In Toronto, staff members of the central office might take it on themselves to drop in on nearby establishments; proprietors in that city would also phone or visit the board's offices much more frequently than those who lived outside the provincial capital.

The demand for a proprietor to meet with the chief commissioner or deputy chief commissioner was among the most serious requests in the operations of the board.[20] When made of hotel proprietors in more distant areas, such a demand was often a measure of last resort, designed to reiterate the importance of the board's rules and to remind proprietors that they faced severe consequences if they continued to cause or allow trouble. Although no transcripts exist of the discussions in these meetings, a memo was occasionally included in the establishment's files giving some details. Usually, these memos ended with some generic statement of proprietor compliance, such as in April 1941 when Mr. McMillan of Toronto's Variety Hotel "promised future cooperation."[21] If the board's authority was not heeded in these situations, the proprietors were usually out of luck: a change of hotel ownership or management would usually follow.

Inspectors

To function with any hope of effectiveness, the LCBO's regulatory regime relied on the activity and integrity of its regional inspectors. As a bureaucracy, the LCBO required a degree of consistency in the enforcement of its rules, but within a system that recognized the unique characteristics of each community. The LCBO relied on its inspectors to provide insight into the specific contexts of individual cases. Given the importance of a beer authority or a beer and wine authority to the economics of a hotel, inspectors could wield considerable power among local hoteliers. The LCBO, therefore, had to keep an eye not only on the hotels but also on the inspectors.

Government inspectors were not a new sight in 1927. From at least the early part of the twentieth century, government inspection of a variety of private industries and public agencies had represented an increased infiltration of the government into the lives of everyday people. Most inspectors were focused on ensuring that revenues, generated by various forms of licences, were collected, whereas others, notably the factory inspectors, scrutinized the activities of industry (and faced more rigid opposition). Liquor inspectors in the early years of the province's post-Confederation life were locally appointed individuals who were normally focused on collecting fees and, since these were local patronage appointments, not usually concerned with regulating behaviour.[22] With the centralization of liquor-licensing bureaucracy in 1915 – a change that was followed almost immediately by (and may have intentionally predated) provincial prohibition – liquor inspection began to shift into a more hands-on concern with the behaviour of licence holders and the operations of their premises. Also in the early part of the twentieth century, increasingly complex regulatory bureaucracies, such as those necessitated by Children's Aid and Mother's Allowance, required a specialized, nearly professional inspectorate that was preoccupied not with revenue collection but specifically with evaluating behaviour.[23] LCBO inspectors straddled these two traditions. They were expected to have some (however limited) expertise in the hotel business, they definitely paid attention to behaviour, and they were the conduit through which the board ensured that fees were collected. Judging by the reports that inspectors regularly submitted, the work of the LCBO's inspectors after 1934 was focused predominantly on evaluation of proprietors and their premises and on intervening when things went wrong.

Yet who were the inspectors? Unfortunately, personnel files for the inspectors, if they ever existed, have not survived. Thus much of the information about them has been gathered from assorted records in various hotel files, asides on letters, and the premier's correspondence files. Normally, outside of Toronto, each region had one inspector. Toronto appears to have begun with one inspector, but with the advent of "beer by the glass" legislation, new inspectors were added to that city's roster. Among all of the communities studied, only one, Ottawa, had the same inspector from 1934 through 1944. The backgrounds and training of the inspectors are difficult to determine. Some appear to have worked in the hotel business. General inspector John Pitt, who had been an inspector at least since the operation of the Board of License Commissioners, was described in 1930 as "a thorough hotel man."[24] Inspector U.G. Reaume of Essex County may have worked in the real estate business: in one case, he mentioned that, prior to his appointment with the board, his office had handled the sale of a particular hotel property.[25] Others were clearly partisan appointments. Several letters in Premier Hepburn's correspondence files were from individuals thanking him for helping them to get their positions with the board, usually as clerks in stores but occasionally as hotel inspectors. At the same time, at least one inspector, Toronto's A.A. Montgomery, appears to have lost his position in 1934 owing to complaints that he was favouring Conservative hotel proprietors. Montgomery had been appointed under the previous administration, and although this was not an automatic reason for dismissal (Pitt had also been an inspector prior to 1934), his partisan activities were viewed poorly by influential Liberals.[26] As I discuss in Chapter 5, the partisan nature of some appointments does not necessarily suggest that the individuals were not suited for their jobs since there were far more requests for patronage than the government could honour.

Inspectors were busy. As noted earlier, inspector Kidd consolidated several months' worth of inspections on one form, suggesting he had limited time to fill in the form or maybe even to inspect. More explicit information about the inspector's workload can be seen in a March 1936 letter to Odette written by Windsor barrister A.J. Gordon. The writer, whose office was in the same building as inspector Reaume's, had agreed to take messages for the inspector one Saturday afternoon and was struck by the number of calls and by the diversity of the issues they covered. Claiming he had not informed inspector Reaume that he was sending the letter, Gordon observed that "he never complains; but I just want you to know how onerous his duties are and ask that your Board bear with him." To add weight to his argument, the correspondent reproduced the list of twelve calls, detailing the issues that Reaume's work encompassed. Odette replied that "it is quite apparent that poor Inspector Reaume is greatly over-worked" and explained that he was sending the letter to Hepburn so that "he may lay [the issue] before the house [provincial Legislature]."[27]

Given the importance of the beer authority to the hotel industry, it is not surprising that inspectors often became the targets of complaints and allegations of misuse of power. Regularly, the central office received letters complaining of the activities of the inspectors. These letters might be from disgruntled hotel proprietors who felt that the inspector was being unjustly severe in enforcing the rules, or more often they might comprise anonymous complaints about a hotel that suggested the inspector was not doing his job properly. Although these sorts of complaints were generally either not heeded or found to be fictitious, the board did recognize that some of its inspectors needed to be watched closely for various reasons. Whereas some inspectors appear to have had tremendous integrity in the eyes of the central administration, a number of them made decisions and evaluations that quickly brought their ideas and actions under closer scrutiny by the board. The complaints about Waterloo's Norman Ratz were so persistent that the board appears to have done remedial work with him, sending the chief inspector (initially John Pitt and later Harry Simington) or inspectors from other regions to accompany him or to check up on his work. Eventually, Ratz was dismissed under allegations that he was participating in corrupt and illegal activities (something against which he protested vigorously to the premier).[28]

The board also became concerned about the inspection and opinions of Ottawa's Alfred Larocque. Rather than suggesting that Larocque was conspiring with criminals, the board began to question his ability to provide objective evaluations of hotels identified with a range of social classes. Larocque was somewhat sycophantic, favouring clubs and hotels frequented or owned by people in power while being dismissive or overly critical of hotels of a lower status. Most glaring was the case of the Bridge Club of Ottawa, which inspector Larocque continued to insist was respectably run. Deputy chief commissioner Arnold Smith visited the club and found it was being operated without any regard for the specific regulations for private clubs. He informed Larocque that he had received information about the club's substandard operation but did not tell the inspector that he had visited it personally. When Larocque attempted to contradict this report, claiming that Smith's informant was mistaken, Smith reprimanded the inspector for being biased and sloppy.[29] The board rejected such overt favouritism, and throughout the 1930s Larocque's decisions became increasingly both questionable and questioned. However, that Larocque was never dismissed indicates that his behaviour was not so egregious as to undermine the operations of the LCBO.[30]

Formal training of inspectors, if there was any, is also absent from the records. Apart from occasionally being accompanied on their rounds by senior inspectors John Pitt or Harry Simington, local inspectors appear to have been left on their own. The records indicate only one time when all inspectors were brought together for something akin to a conference. At that time, in late 1936, they visited a variety of Toronto hotels in groups and wrote reports on all of them. Although this exercise may have been an attempt to enforce some sort of standardization among the inspectors, its effectiveness is difficult to gauge. It does make for interesting reading of the various ways that inspectors interpreted behaviour.

The relative autonomy of the inspectors forces us to consider the limits of their reports. Given that the inspectors were familiar with the local situation – often appearing to have been friendly with many hotel proprietors and certainly to have been sympathetic to the plight of many of these small business people – they were as much advocates for hotel proprietors as they were conduits between the central administration and the individual hotel management. So evaluations of the inspectors' communications with the board, as detailed and rich a source as they are, must be qualified with the understanding that it is likely the inspectors did not report everything. Although the administrators in Toronto were likely to demonstrate some leniency of their own, they tended to be intolerant of the inspectors' tendencies to arbitrarily enforce (or not) specific rules. These sentiments could be reiterated when the board might send an inspector from one region to do a surreptitious evaluation of the premises in a different region. Several times, the reports back to the central administration presented pictures very different from those painted by the inspectors. Such episodes, combined with the stories mentioned above about inspectors Ratz and Larocque, demonstrate that although the board's managers, especially Arnold Smith, were interested in the functioning of the hotels as viable businesses, they felt that control – and therefore power – should remain in the offices on University Avenue. In the language of governmentality, the subjectivity of the inspectors' view limited the central board's field of visibility.

The Language of Control

The LCBO's inspectors visited the hotels and reported on their operations, but apart from the inspectors' immediate observations, most of the rule enforcement was done through correspondence from the central authority. It is valuable, then, to examine the language of control in order to see the mechanisms through which the LCBO exerted its authority. This analysis also enables us to examine the language of bureaucracy, how the board, a relatively localized government administration that oversaw a geographically broad network of employees, attempted to create the perception of objectivity through its words. Communication was coded in an administrative jargon that reiterated certain discourses of power and authority.

As in any bureaucracy, the esoteric jargon of the LCBO held both blatant and subtle discursive associations. The LCA did not create a system of liquor licences; it created a network of beer and wine "Authorities." The term "Authority" was usually capitalized, which suggests increased weightiness in the word. Hotels with standard hotel licences were "Authorized premises," and the proprietor was an "Authority holder" (whether capitalized or not). The language of "authority" is powerful, but beyond the power of the term is its discursive meaning. Having the "Authority" of the LCBO was a greater burden than simply being licensed by the board; it imbued the beverage room and hotel with state sanction, and in the eyes of the board it also added important responsibility to the hotel proprietor. The hotel was, in effect, an extension of the state apparatus; indeed, it was legally defined as a public place. The board expressed the importance of keeping the hotel doors open at all hours for the "travelling public," noting that the hotel lobby was a public space and also that the hotel proprietor, who often lived in the hotel, was significantly restrained in what he or she could do as a private citizen-drinker. Demonstrating the increased responsibility of the authority holder, hotel proprietors had to apply for a special permit to keep liquor and beer for personal consumption in their private rooms in the hotel. According to the LCA, liquor could be consumed in the privacy of your own home, but the nature of the hotel business meant that the authority holder had to be extra careful. Not only was it too easy for private liquor to end up in the public spaces of the hotel, but the proprietor was an ostensible agent of the government and needed to act appropriately.

This additional responsibility of the authority holder was not restricted just to alcohol possession. The place of the authority holder between private citizen and public agent meant the board could scrutinize any range of negative actions. So when a senior administrator at the board received letters from creditors complaining that a hotel proprietor had not paid a bill, he would explain to the creditors that the board would not act as a collection agency. At the same time, he would usually write the proprietor a stern letter saying that nonpayment of bills was not the sort of behaviour the board expected from an authority holder. This was the significance of the term "authority" – an extension of biopower that was permissive (i.e., granted permission to sell and profit from beer and wine) but simultaneously restrictive (i.e., imposed increased scrutiny on what would normally be private behaviour).

Other language was similarly encoded with weighty meaning beyond seemingly innocent terminology. Authorized premises were "Standard Hotels," which might have an authorized "beverage room" but not a "tavern" or "saloon" or "pub." Was this term used to enforce a knowing vagueness about what took place in these spaces or, conversely, to reinforce the discursive distance from the pre-prohibition saloon? It is difficult to determine, but newspaper evidence suggests that, official labelling notwithstanding, people employed a variety of terms, such as "beer parlour," "tavern," and "bar," when describing the hotel beverage room. The elimination of the saloon – a stand-alone drinking place – from pre-prohibition legislation, which began in 1897, suggests that the goals of legislating away the problem of the saloon predated the LCBO. Of course, "beverages" are any kind of consumable liquid, but the term also functioned commonly as a euphemism for alcoholic drinks, just as does the term "drink" itself. So a beverage room was a place where people went to consume alcoholic beverages. As I discuss further in the next chapter, outside of its beverage and dining rooms, the hotel could sell "soft" beverages. The standard hotel licence gave rights for hotels to sell a range of products, for which other businesses required separate municipal licences. With the term "beverage" attached to alcohol, the flexibility in advertising and signage was constrained. Newspaper or poster ads were not allowed to have any reference to alcohol. So to announce that a hotel's dinner dance included "a meal and beverages" or even "a meal and refreshments" was to attract the ire of the board.

Moreover, the term "beverage room" seems to have been a compromise that enabled the space to be described for the purpose of the administration of the law, but the term was not always used within the hotel. The board was not consistent on this practice, but at times it required hotels to post "Men's Entrance" and "Ladies and Escorts' Entrance" over the doors to the respective beverage rooms. This practice stripped this public space of any indication of what actually took place within, although it is unlikely that anyone would be fooled. Here, we see the discursive restructuring of reality: hotels, which had beverage rooms – and which were the only public spaces where people could buy and consume alcoholic beverages – were simultaneously public but hidden. We will see this feature repeated when considering the physical reconfiguring of the beverage rooms.

In the daily operation of the LCBO too, its administrators deployed a series of terms that both reinforced the sense that its actions were objective and created an idea of broader surveillance. The LCBO was constructed as an impersonal, remote organization. Consider, for example, Arnold Smith's reply to the request by Fort William's Elks Club to hold a New Year's Eve dance in 1939. "The Board have decide[d] that if any Club wishes to hold such a dance, the Board will not object, but wish to point out that they certainly feel that it is very poor policy for any club to hold such a dance, as they will certainly not meet with public favour."[31] Here, the "Board" is a regulatory construction, and the use of plural verbs suggests that the "Board," or central administration, consisted of many members. After 1934 the central administration of the LCBO was essentially a one-man body, consisting of Edmond Odette, although at times in the Ontario Legislature Smith was stated to be a second member. This construction was bolstered by the passive voice, such as when William Mair noted to the managers of the city of Kitchener's American Hotel (who wanted to open a hotel in the nearby town of Preston), "I am requested to advise you that the Board will consider no further authorized premises in the Town of Preston."[32] Indeed, such linguistic obfuscation makes the actual membership of this "Board" impossible to determine. Smith suggested in the Elks Club quotation that he was responding to the directives of some group, but Odette alone was the only person superior to Smith in the LCBO's reporting structure (apart from the elected politicians). At times, the facade of a remote, all-powerful "Board" was dropped. Smith often slipped between the generalized, impersonal use of the term "Board" and the personal pronoun. So when the Nipigon Hotel wanted to use one room as an all-purpose space, Smith wrote to inspector George Skuce, "the Board cannot give him permission to use this room as a sample room once a week, a beverage room during the daytime and a bedroom at night. I do not mind giving him permission to use it as an overflow beverage room when it is needed but certainly not as an all round purpose room."[33] More telling was Smith's reply to an inquiry about the status of Toronto's Avonmore Hotel: "The hotel was one of the early ones to receive an Authority and was one of the first whose Authorities I cancelled."[34]

As a number of these quotations indicate, one common bureaucratic discursive form, employed often in corrective messages to the hotel proprietor, was the passive or indirect voice. In this context, the language of the bureaucracy connects with ideas of discipline as expressed by Michel Foucault, and here we can merge it with Max Weber's notion of rationalization through bureaucratization.[35] The passive voice implies objectivity of processes by removing an actor from the process. It is used in scientific writing to suggest that the people doing the experiment do not matter and to thereby lend the language a sort of universality.[36] Just as the use of the plural term "Board" suggested a larger decision-making body, the use of a passive voice, or indirect language, strengthened the sense that the work of the LCBO was guided by bureaucratic objectivity. It most definitely permitted the source of information or decisions to be obscured. Often when an inspector or the police reported on a particularly unsavoury activity in a hotel's beverage room, the letter to the proprietor would contain the words "As the result of reports received" or "Complaints have been received."[37] These passive or indirect constructions do not indicate who made the reports, suggesting that the proprietor could not escape the ubiquitous gaze of the LCBO (nor could the inspector – it was this kind of language that tripped up inspector Larocque). Some proprietors attempted to talk their way out of a situation by implying that the reports were not true, even when they had come from a viable source, such as an inspector or other official. For example, when the board refused his request for permission to have dancing in the dining room of his British American Hotel in Windsor, citing problems in the management of the hotel, Elias Doumani replied, "not only [do] we consider your reports you received are untrue, but realy [sic] believe that there are some great mix up in this affairs." Unfortunately for Doumani, the reports came from William Mair, director of hotels, who had personally, surreptitiously, visited the hotel.[38]

Like the passive or indirect voice, another obfuscating term that reinforced the mystery of the bureaucratic process was often deployed on reinstatement of a suspended beer authority. When a beer authority or a standard hotel licence was suspended, the board gave specific reasons for doing so but rarely indicated the length of the suspension. Usually, an authority was suspended "indefinitely," a term that suggests the premises would be dry for a long time while the proprietor straightened up. When the authority was reinstated, the board usually explained the decision as resulting from "representations" made to the board. When the city of Windsor's St. Clair Hotel requested permission to have dancing in the dining room, the board gave permission "as a result of representations made and after careful consideration."[39] In 1942 the Embassy Hotel in St. Agatha (Waterloo County) had its authority suspended "indefinitely" on 25 June, and it was reinstated on 26 July "as a result of representations made."[40] For the historian, such obfuscation can be frustrating since it does not permit us to trace the reasoning behind these decisions. Did the "representations" come from influential politicians or simply from an inspector's or administrator's review of the situation? Or, conversely, was there no "representation" at all? Could the board have made a predetermined decision about how long the authority would be suspended but have told the proprietor that it was an "indefinite" suspension to frighten him into behaving? Of course, this was the very point of such language: its obscurity imbued the board with a seemingly impenetrable opacity. The bureaucracy moved in mysterious ways, and therein lay its power.

A final form of obfuscation that the board used when denying an authority application was the explanation that there were "sufficient authorities" in the area. At first glance, this term may seem entirely reasonable, as I discuss in Chapter 3, given the need to keep the number of beverage rooms in a specific area to an acceptable number. A closer look reveals that the suggestion of an objective calculation helped to obfuscate a more subjective evaluation. For example, in September 1934 inspector M.G. Dean reported that the proprietor of the City Hotel in Humberstone, near Fort Erie, had a "very chequered career and there is certainly a very strong feeling that this authority should not be granted." Another local resident explained to the board that "the people of Humberstone are not opposed to the City Hotel having a [beer] permit but are very much opposed" to this particular family's application. When a barrister wrote on behalf of the family in question to ask for an authority, Smith replied that "the Board could not see their way clear to the granting of such License and Authority, they being of the opinion that there were sufficient Licenses and Authorities to meet the needs of the locality."[41] In a similar case, where the board's reply was even more clearly intended to be obfuscatory, the proprietors of the Belmont Hotel in St. Catharines applied for an authority and included in their application the required recommendation from a city official – in this case, the mayor of St. Catharines, Frederick Avery. The board was prepared to issue the authority, but then Avery called to withdraw his recommendation, explaining that he had been "wrongly advised regarding the character of the applicants."[42] Mair removed the authority from the mail and wrote to the applicants' barrister explaining that "the Board have decided that in view of the present commitments they are of the opinion that the City of St. Catharines will be adequately served in the matter of Hotel and Beverage Room accommodation."[43] The seemingly objective calculation obscured a subjective evaluation and a potentially embarrassing political situation. It is probably not insignificant that Avery was a Liberal who would run for provincial office two years later.

Limited by the Technology

As the above example suggests, the technology of the bureaucracy of governance had limits and flaws. The inspections, reports, memos, letters, and circulars permitted a persistent but restricted form of control over the actions of the beverage room management. Although the board's rules could be ignored or at least tempered by proprietors who had a good rapport with the inspectors or who could appear to be doing their best, the central administration also had to read between the lines of each report, letter, and memo. So some features of the hotel management that may have been legitimate or valid in a given community could appear, when translated through the static media of letters and inspectors' reports, to be problematic and in need of correction.

The board occasionally used form letters to apprise proprietors of broad, province-wide issues or, in specific regions, to deal with issues germane to an area. Although efficient for communicating general directives, the form letter could undermine the impression that the LCBO had a panoptic view of the hotel operations. For example, in Waterloo County in 1935 the board began to issue letters to several hotels about the sale of beer in the dining room after beverage rooms had closed at 11 p.m. The standard text of the letter included the following observation:

> Owing to reports having been received that your Hotel, which does a very small dining room trade in the day time, is doing a tremendous eleven to twelve pm beer trade in your dining room which clearly proves that this is just a means of serving Beer from eleven to twelve, you are hereby notified

> that all service of Beer must cease at eleven (11) P.M. or in other words, when the beverage room closes at 11 o'clock, no Beer may be served in your Dining Room.[44]

This letter usually produced an apologetic response from proprietors. Sometimes, however, such generalizations could undermine the board's attempt to imply its omniscience. In the case of the Central Hotel in Preston, which received a copy of this form letter, the proprietor wrote back in surprise, "I have never opened my dining room for that trade, thus you have been misinformed of this hotel."[45] Given that generally good reports on the hotel were filed on other occasions, his protests seem valid.

Bureaucratic oversight could also be limited due to its reliance on the impressions of individuals familiar with the local situation. In this business, there appear to have been no innocents. Although most of the inspectors seem to have had the interest of the board's regulatory integrity at heart, the stories of inspectors Ratz and Larocque indicate the limits of any assumption that there was perfect integrity among the inspectors. Thunder Bay inspector George Skuce, moreover, was characterized by the local member of the provincial Legislative Assembly (MLA), Charles Cox, as "rather incompetent."[46] Yet Cox's evaluation drips with irony since Cox himself was exceedingly biased in his assessment of local hotel premises: not only was he the MLA, but he was also the mayor of Port Arthur. He could exercise undue influence over the fate of a hotel's authority application, as I discuss in Chapter 5. So, although the LCBO's procedures relied on well-established individuals to give a trustworthy opinion about the situation "on the ground," the reports to the central administrators were also shaped by any range of political or personal biases. The central administrators were not unaware of these flaws in the system and appear to have tried to work around them (rather than simply being an extension of the partisan political machine) but were not always successful. Thus, although the ideal-typical bureaucracy would have credible operatives at the periphery, the LCBO was limited by the character of the people and by the often obscure intricacies of local personal politics and partisan intrigue.

A final limit of the processes of the LCBO was its reliance on other agencies for evaluation. In undertaking its work, the board liaised constantly with local and provincial police departments. Often a decision to suspend an authority was made after the police informed the board of a raid on a hotel or of a proprietor's conviction for personal violations of the LCA. These reports were formal and employed their own dry, bureaucratic formats. Moreover, they tended to be valid. Yet in other ways, police officers could be less reliable. Numerous reports came to the board about police officers being given free drinks by hotel proprietors (which was against the law). Yet none of these reports came from police officers themselves. If the allegations were true, and at least some of them appear to have been so, then the limits to the police's law enforcement practices would have constrained the board's ability to enforce its own rules. If police officers were favouring a particular hotel, it was unlikely that they would raid it.

In still other ways, the evaluations of the police could be suspect. In 1931 the LCBO sought input from the Fort William Police Department on the application for a standard hotel licence for the Queen's Hotel. The local police chief, W.J. Dodds, said the applicant "had been a resident ... for a number of years and bears a good reputation." When William Dingman, the director of permits, refused the application, he explained to Dodds that it was based on "an adverse report from the Provincial Police." He concluded his letter with the observation, "I regret to find that two much esteemed [police] authorities differ in their reports."[47] The fundamental flaw of any bureaucracy appears to be that it has to be operated by humans.

Understanding the processes of regulation is essential to understanding the operations of the LCBO. The regulatory project was shaped by the technologies, forms, reports, and individuals that were involved in developing and enforcing the board's rules. Each of these elements affected the regulatory authority of the central administration. The paperwork forced often subjective evaluations to follow a standardized format; the richness and diversity of the local context were squeezed into a uniform configuration. Doubtless, some elements remain invisible to contemporary historical investigation. Nevertheless, the very volume of material that the board generated, the personalities and preoccupations of the individual inspectors, and the competing interests of the community meant that the board's regulatory project was a diverse and complex, if flawed and limited, endeavour.

2
The Public Life of Liquor, 1927-34

Although the Liquor Control Act (LCA) of 1927 fundamentally changed the social landscape of Ontario for people who wanted to buy alcoholic beverages and drink them in their homes, the act did not change in any noticeable way the prohibition on the public consumption of alcohol. The 1925 decision to allow light beer to be consumed in licensed public places continued, but public sale and consumption of regular-strength beer (what some called "the good stuff") was still illegal. Just as the Board of License Commissioners had done, the Liquor Control Board of Ontario (LCBO) assumed the role of inspecting and licensing "Standard Hotels" and granting light-beer permits. There was some administrative logic in the connection between liquor control and hotel licensure. In the years prior to 1916, hotels had been the main site for liquor consumption in the province. And in some ways, little changed in 1927: even the applications for the standard hotel licence were essentially the same form. Taken from this perspective, the regulation of public beer drinking was merely old wine in new bottles.

Yet the bottles made that old wine taste different. Whereas under prohibition all forms of liquor were illegal, under the LCA (1927) liquor was no longer prohibited, but its public consumption was. Moreover, the decade of prohibition had left a bitter aftertaste on the palates of regulatory authorities, and the astringency of criminality flavoured the reputations of many hotel premises and proprietors. Hoteliers who had been convicted under the Ontario Temperance Act were followed by the unpleasant aroma of their criminal records, which, after 1927, seemed increasingly irrelevant. Moreover, since the 1927 law permitted people to buy booze and drink it in their hotel bedroom, subtle nuances of the hotel operations had changed. For example, hotel proprietors were often asked to put a patron's beer "on ice," a service that created some trouble when the police showed up looking for illegal drinking and found iced beer in the kitchen. Meanwhile, police often discovered beer-drinking parties going on in hotel bedrooms, with the actual role of the hotelier in the festivities remaining in question. So from 1927 to

1934 the LCBO continued the work of the Board of License Commissioners but with the added responsibility to negotiate the new relationship between the public and alcoholic beverages. How did the character and substance of the LCBO's regulation of public spaces develop?

Before investigating this question, it is useful to make two important qualifications. First, the regulation of hotels appears to have been a very minor part of the LCBO's early activities. Much of its work involved the management of stores and distribution of beer, wine, and liquor. Even the people involved in overseeing hotel operations seem to have been seconded to the distribution side. The main correspondent with hotel managers was often William Dingman or his successor A.K. Coulthard. Their title was director of permits, a position that ostensibly entailed overseeing issues related to private liquor permits. Many hotels received little more than a cursory examination by one of the six general inspectors on the board's staff. Second, it is important to resist imposing a presentist bias on this examination. Although we know that the board's mandate broadened in 1934 to include the sale of regular-strength beer and wine in hotels, this change was not apparent until well into 1933. So it is historically inaccurate to look at the LCBO's work from 1927 to 1934 as a sort of ramping-up of public drinking. Even though many people may have been pretty certain that beer by the glass was coming, in 1927 this prospect was a distant hope for some, a fear for many, and an administrative nonissue for the LCBO. Nevertheless, it is important to look at the patterns of the period preceding the LCA (1934) to understand or at least contextualize what happened after the act was passed. Although many of the senior managers of the board and the politicians to whom they reported changed in 1934, there was a consistency in the application of the rules and in the approach to hotel licensure.

This chapter examines the approaches, assumptions, and priorities of the LCBO management as it sought to license hotels under the new liquor control regime. It explores the relationship between the bureaucracy and the hotels – the regulators and regulated – and the way that the legislation limited the board's operations. It further demonstrates that, rather than being an agency of policing, the early LCBO was an agency of standardization that built cultural authority by enforcing a specific value system in a way that shaped people's activities to a certain vision of proper citizenship. The bitter tang of pre-prohibition drinking cultures, and the prohibition-era patterns of consumption and illegal sales of liquor in hotels, flavoured the work of the LCBO. The board's work implementing the LCA was split between addressing preconceived ideas of these public spaces and shaping new attitudes of respectability and responsibility. Many proprietors were motivated, it seems, by pre-prohibition assumptions about what would be permitted in the public drinking space and by the desire to profit within the new system. In the last part of the chapter, I consider the agitation for "beer by the glass" legislation that began around 1931 and picked up steam over the next two years. Although this "wet" agitation was centralized, with the proponents of more liberal drinking policies badgering the premier and his cabinet, it also had a localized element, building a grassroots agitation against what many considered a deeply flawed liquor control regime.

The Pre-prohibition Hotel as Drinking Space

The government's decision in 1934 to confine public drinking to hotels was based on an association between public drinking spaces and accommodation that had been a legal reality for at least a quarter-century. In 1906 the government passed the "Act to Amend the Liquor License Laws," which added significant detail to the earlier iterations of this act. This and other amendments to the liquor licence laws tended to add restrictions to the number of places in which drinking was permitted. This tendency can also be seen in the annual "Report on the Operation of the Liquor License Acts, Ontario," printed in the provincial Sessional Papers. These reports often emphasized the reduction of the number of licences, and the laws mandated a gradual increase in licence fees. The 1906 legislation, similarly, restricted the definition of a "tavern" to "an hotel, inn or other public house of entertainment kept for the purpose of providing refreshment and accommodation, which shall include board and lodging, for the public."[1] The latter phrase suggests that all such places must include board and lodgings, but it was not until three years later that this relationship was confirmed. The 1909 act of the same name added a qualification to the definition of the type of tavern that could receive a liquor licence: "No tavern license shall be issued to any saloon, tavern or other premises not having all the tavern accommodation required by law ... and such license may hereafter in the discretion of the Commissioners be issued without there being the hotel accommodation required by law."[2] The apparent conflation of the terms "tavern accommodation" and "hotel accommodation" demonstrates the connection between the two, suggesting that in the enforcement of these rules, a tavern without bedrooms for rent might not receive a liquor licence.

Prior to prohibition, when the provincial government was contemplating prohibitory legislation, both dry and wet forces lobbied for or against such a law. One of the key arguments the Wets employed was that prohibition would ruin hotels because much of the business of a hotel was dependent on the drink trade. As noted in the previous chapter, most hotels were small, independent operations that were family-run and dependent on a variety of revenue sources. The *Toronto Globe,* an advocate for prohibition, scoffed at such characterization in the months leading up to prohibition in 1916. Along with editorials and regular articles deriding wet sentiments, the *Globe* published a series by Norman Lambert entitled "Hotel Accommodation in

Ontario Minus the Bar."[3] In this series, Lambert provided a variety of examples of Ontario communities that had been under local option, vividly contrasting the degraded hotel accommodation of those communities that had continued to be wet with the high-quality hotels of dry communities. Steeped in temperance rhetoric, Lambert's articles demonstrate that Ontarians had been debating the relationship between drink sales and hotel accommodation for some time. Moreover, his argument about the degradation of communities with licensed hotels suggests that more than just drinking would be eliminated through prohibition. Prohibition would run incompetent and bad hoteliers out of business, and the community and the "travelling public" would be better for it.

This association between drinking and hotel operations, and the need to address both, was reiterated in the Ontario Temperance Act of 1916. The prohibitory law retained the provincial Board of License Commissioners (BLC) which had been created only a year earlier in an attempt to centralize liquor law administration. The BLC was charged with overseeing all aspects of the manufacture and sale of liquor and all aspects of the inspection and licensure of hotels, creating a new category of accommodation: the "Standard Hotel."[4] These hotels adhered to a set of guidelines regarding the number of rooms, type of services and amenities the establishments provided, and quality of the physical structure. In return, hoteliers whose establishments were granted standard hotel licences were permitted to provide a series of money-making services, such as selling tobacco and nonintoxicating drinks as well as operating restaurants or ice cream parlours without further fees.[5] As Karen Dubinsky shows for Niagara Falls, hoteliers presented the standard hotel designation as a mark of quality.[6] By 1927, then, the connection between drinking and hotel accommodation had been established, at least legislatively, for decades.

Pushing the Boundaries under the Shadow of Prohibition

During prohibition, numerous hotels had been modified with various architectural innovations to skirt the law, and between 1927 and 1934 these physical attributes continued to cause problems with law enforcement. In the Royal Hotel in Elmira, police found a "chute" down which bottles would be thrown in the event of a surprise raid and a "hide" in the bathroom containing "one part quart of Walker's Rye whiskey and one pop bottle of whiskey." The "hide was concealed and by taking of[f] the moulding a side of a wall moved out."[7] In New Hamburg's King Edward Hotel, police also found a hide; the local police inspector described the hotel as "a bootleg Hotel and nothing else." Granting a light beer permit would simply cause further enforcement problems since it would be used only "to cover up on illegal sale of strong beer."[8] In 1928 a raid of the Bodega Hotel by the Ontario

Provincial Police (OPP) revealed "a sort of wicket arrangement ... in the door of the proprietor's room."[9] The proprietor could keep booze in his room and hand it out through this wicket. Many of these hotels were in smaller and rural communities, the remoteness of which would have also assisted in the proprietor's ability to avoid the eyes of the law. In 1933 inspector John Pitt refused to recommend that Niagara Falls' Hillcrest Inn receive a licence "owing to the locality in which it is situated[,] it being about 500 yards off the Street[,] and of late years has been used for nothing else but Bootlegging purposes."[10] The ghosts of prohibition-era bootlegging would haunt the LCBO for at least the next decade.

One of the main temptations for hotel proprietors was the lure of easy money from the illegal sale of alcohol to Americans. Most notably in the Niagara region and Essex County, the tourist trade presented many temptations. Heavy tourist areas were especially hard hit by the fact that strong beer could be purchased in stores but not in hotels. The manager of the Long Beach Hotel in Wainfleet, west of Fort Erie, wrote in 1927 asking for a permit to sell "the new strong beer" in his hotel. "I was granted a liscense [sic] to sell 4.4 [beer] on May 28 of this year but since the government stores have opened in this locality there is no sale of 4.4 whatever."[11] The manager of the Pickwick Arms Hotel in Fort Erie, across the river from Buffalo, claimed to be applying for a light-beer permit with some hesitation, explaining to the board that, although the hotel had not intended to apply for a permit, "we find quite a demand for light beer and feel that it is necessary to have the permit."[12] This was granted, but a year later William Dingman wrote to the company that owned the hotel complaining that "our reports about this hotel ... are latterly unfavourable, in that the manager's idea of a hotel seems to be largely to cater to drinking parties from the US and in consequence the place has been allowed to deteriorate."[13] The manager was replaced a week later.

Fear of the potential for this temptation could also shape the board's attitude toward applications for light-beer permits. In Crystal Beach, near the border with Buffalo, xenophobia coloured the assessment by the local member of the Legislative Assembly (MLA) of a newcomer's application for a light-beer permit: "I am inclined to think that this man being a new arrival and of the foreign race [Italian] he might use it as a guise to screen the good stuff, as the police inform me he comes from Toronto and is unknown as to character at the Beach."[14] A Niagara Falls OPP constable informed the manager of the venerated Clifton Hotel that his sign reading "Tap Room 4-4 beer and ale" was "illegal and must be changed." The management protested to the board, but even the Clifton Hotel's reputation could not save it from such a blatant attempt to lure in thirsty American tourists.[15] When Toronto's Waverly Hotel received a circular reminding proprietors of the restrictions on advertising 4.4 beer, the proprietor assured him that they would not be advertising the beer at all. "The whole thing, Mr. Dingman, is a first class joke. No one can sell this stuff ... you can be sure we are not going to kill the dignity of our hotel by posting any signs on it to sell beer, even if it was good beer."[16]

The temptation to cater to visitors was not incidental; the LCA had always been presented as at least partially intended to accommodate the thirsts of American tourists. Visitors, of course, could purchase liquor for their own consumption in their "homes," the LCA's definition of which included hotel rooms (along with tents). A visitor had to purchase a visitor's liquor permit, and before the Twenty-First Amendment was passed to end US prohibition, the implication was that American visitors would have to drink their purchases while still in Canada. So it might not be surprising that many hotel proprietors, especially in border communities, sought to manipulate the rules for their own gain. For example, in early May 1927, prior to the LCA coming into effect, the board received an application for a standard hotel licence from the Point Pelee Beach Club on Ouellette Street, in downtown Windsor (quite a distance from Point Pelee). The application provoked some consternation. The plan was to create about two dozen small rooms on the third floor of an otherwise retail building, accompanied by a kitchen, lockers, and possibly a dining area. Writing to the club's representative, Dingman noted that "the real question" was whether it would be a genuine club or whether the establishment, located next to the ferry docks, was "to be of service mainly to persons of the sporty, thirsty type."[17] No licence was granted. A year later, another individual attempted to secure a standard hotel licence for the premises, which were now described as the location of the "defunct Point Pelee Club."[18] Inspector Pitt reported that the building was entirely unsuitable as a hotel since "it is nothing more than a joy house and he only wants a license for to [sic] cover up some of his illicit doings."[19] The Ouellette Street premises demonstrated an attempt to cater to "the sporty, thirsty type" by creating small rooms that could pass as individuals' hotel rooms, where they could stay and, in theory at least, drink their legally purchased liquor. Despite being a notable attempt to innovate within the parameters of the law, it failed because it was clearly a space intended for drinking, not for accommodations.

Possibly the most audacious yet successful attempt to manipulate the parameters of the LCA was made by R.A. Bailey, the proprietor of the Ravine Hotel, near Harrow, in the rural south end of Essex County. In May 1930 Bailey inquired about how best to accommodate about three hundred (mostly American) representatives of the steel industry at his hotel. He especially wanted, first, to ensure that they could drink booze using their own temporary visitor's permit and, second, to determine whether it would be permissible for him to have beer delivered directly to the hotel patrons by the local Walkerville Brewery. Individual beer delivery was a normal service and entirely legal. Dingman replied that there was nothing improper about these requests, just as long as "whatever liquor these various persons procures [sic] is got upon temporary or individual permits ... and provided the law is respected, the liquor being kept and used only in the private rooms of respective individuals." Reminding the proprietor of his responsibility to keep an eye on things, Dingman added, "I trust you will do what you can to assist moderation and judgement in the use of liquor so that there will be no over-indulgence or unseemly behaviour."[20] As long as the law was respected and order maintained, the visitors could have their booze and drink it too.

This trust was misplaced. Soon after the convention, Dingman received reports of significant drunkenness and illegality by the conference attendees. Reportedly, people were driving drunk throughout the countryside; at least two serious car accidents occurred, and a farmer's horse was let out onto the road and struck by a "United States car."[21] But most egregious, in the board's eyes, was the situation in the hotel itself. Dingman's letter is worth quoting at some length:

> I am advised that a cottage was erected with a bar in the main room, behind which were two one-half barrels and one one-quarter keg of beer on tap, also a large metal tub for the bottle beer, on the bar being some fifty glasses, and nine tourist liquor permits also behind the bar. There is said to have been no furniture in the cottage, a second room being [a] bar and the third room fixed up with four homemade bunks with blankets on them, as if intended to accommodate four men. You were asked about this room and are reported to have stated you built it on my advice in order to comply with our regulations, which if you so stated, was untrue. You are also said to have been asked if this cottage had been built for the occasion and you replied that it was your intention to have several other United States organizations hold conventions at your place and that you would be using this cottage for them, stating that in a conversation with me I said whenever you wanted permission for another of such conventions to let me know, as we are anxious to get all the American dollars over here that we can. I know very well I never used such exuberant language of that kind.[22]

Through his solicitor, the proprietor explained that he had assumed that by putting up a cottage, and leasing it to the patrons, he was creating the conditions for a house party, where beer and liquor from outside the area could be obtained on permits. He contradicted a number of the reports the board had received, explaining that the horse had been hit, but not hurt, by one of the partiers, that only one person from the party had been in a car accident, and that this man had not been drinking. Interestingly, the board appears to have accepted the response.[23]

In 1931 Bailey applied again with a request to be allowed to accommodate the same convention. It seems that he saw the profitability in conventions, as he began to hold several of them. With the first repeat request, Dingman wrote to OPP district inspector F.E. Elliott to discuss the proposal. He explained that Bailey was penitent and that the proprietor wanted to make sure that his activities were legal but that he could still accommodate the conventioneers. Elliott was not impressed; he reminded Dingman that the police had faced considerable trouble from the group, that the hotel did not have the space to accommodate such a group, and that "this is nothing, more or less, than a drunken brawl and I do not think that we should encourage or be a party to Americans coming over there for nothing more or less than a drinking bout."[24] Dingman, however, was inclined to permit the activities, explaining in a memo to Elliott that, since the law had now been explained to him, "Mr. Bailey cannot ... claim to be under any misunderstanding as to what is expected of him."[25] Apparently, this party also got out of hand, and the subsequent year the OPP visited the hotel to find that another similar party was going on but without permission from the LCBO. When making his report to the chief commissioner of the OPP, district inspector S. Oliver complained that it seemed unfair to his officers that these parties should be allowed to continue: "I add too that it is the Ontario Provincial Police that are criticized through the press when an occasion of this kind comes to light, not the person who is responsible for supplying beer and liquor to permit holders for booze parties of this nature."[26] This was a not-so-subtle complaint about the functions of the LCBO. The writer intended to make his case to every level of administration he could. Since the LCBO relied heavily on the work of the local police, he reasoned that it did not seem fair to ignore their advice and allow their officers to be the targets of complaints.

The Ravine Hotel example provides an extreme case of an attempt to skirt the law while claiming innocence. The appeal of thirsty American conventioneers, combined with the rural location of the hotel, proved to be an irresistible temptation. At the same time, given the proprietor's appeals for leniency and his claims of ignorance and innocence, the board's reaction is most significant: it relied on the hotel proprietor to keep an eye on the activities of the patrons and to make sure that everything was conducted within the parameters of the law. This is a fundamental aspect of bureaucracy: the distribution of power to the periphery. Unlike a standard model of a bureaucracy, however, given the board's limited inspectorate, power was conferred upon the proprietor, a holder of a licence granted by the board, who was expected to act accordingly. Here the character of the proprietor was paramount. The board had to trust him to operate appropriately and had to trust the local police to keep an eye on him. So the power of the regulatory bureaucracy was, in some ways, extended beyond its own control. Likewise, with the OPP and the complaint of the local inspector, we see that the police's power to manage such social disorder was restricted by the board's apparent willingness to permit disorder. At the hyperextension of their reach, the bureaucracies collided.

The police and the board worked together, and sometimes at cross-purposes, because the job of the police was to deal with illegality and to prevent lawbreaking, and the board's job was to nurture good behaviour. Both were focused on illegality, but one was punitive whereas the other could be supportive. The proprietor's character was a fundamental aspect of the board's operations, and his or her apparent good intentions could be shaped and coaxed along the right path by a kindly, paternalistic central administration. This appears vividly in the case of the Kimberly Hotel in Port Arthur. When Godfried Burstrom, the hotel's owner, applied for a personal liquor permit in June 1928, he did so as the proprietor of a hotel with a bad reputation in the eyes of the police. In a working-class district of the port town, the hotel was what a later observer would call "a cheap class of workingmen's hotel."[27] Moreover, Burstrom, who was blind, had trouble managing the hotel since, it was alleged, at times some of his staff would repeatedly take advantage of his condition and slack off or break the rules. Although Burstrom did receive a light-beer permit, Dingman wrote to him to reiterate the responsibilities of a hotel manager with respect to the personal purchase and consumption of liquor:

> I would advise you to make sparing use of the permit privilege in view of the vulnerability of hotel men in the matter of liquor and especially in your own case, from your location etc. Hotel men keeping any considerable quantity of liquor in their private quarters are apt to be importuned for drinks and it is a short step from yielding, even without charge, to trafficking and trouble. Thus it would be irregular for you to serve liquor even without charge to other persons. I offer this suggestion for your protection.

The "protection" that the director of permits offered was double-sided. In one respect, he was offering Burstrom protection from potentially exploitative staff or customers, but at the same time he was offering the man protection from the circumstances. This advice came with a healthy dose of moral obligation and guilt: "You will remember that your record formerly had been unsatisfactory, but finally I arranged for renewal of standard license to you on the expectation that all irregularity was at an end. I am glad to say that the reputation of your place is greatly improved and I would like to see it keep its good reputation."[28]

The sentiments in Dingman's letter underscore a fundamental thread running through the work of the LCBO from 1927 to 1934. The LCBO sought to reinforce a vision of order through paternalistic and none-too-subtle appeals to personal and moral responsibility on the part of hotel management.

So Dingman may have also made this appeal based on the little he knew about Burstrom's personality. According to many accounts, he was a meticulous and tough manager, something that the board would have appreciated. In the Kimberly Hotel case, which was unique given Burstrom's blindness, the letter probably served an additional purpose of instructing staff. Since someone would have had to read the letter to the manager, at least one other member of the hotel staff would have understood the gravity implied in the situation. It should be noted that Dingman did tend toward the sanctimonious in his advice to hotel proprietors. Having observed that several hotel proprietors in Lincoln County (Niagara region) had made large purchases of liquor on their permits, Dingman informed the head of the local hotel association that "any considerable quantity of liquor in [hotel proprietors'] private quarters is apt to invite importunities for liquor, and if the least latitude is allowed it is a short step to trafficking and serious trouble. I have therefore counselled them to be sparing in liquor orders owing to the vulnerability of a hotel men on these points."[29]

The letter to Burstrom also draws attention to a second, and I think more crucial, theme in the early operation of the LCBO: the opportunity for second chances, which was tied to the functional value of the hotels themselves. As I discuss in the next chapter, the board's work in evaluating and licensing a hotel space was tied to an idea of the need for a hotel in the particular location. Despite being a rundown workingmen's hotel, the Kimberly may have served a need for accommodations and other facilities among a specific demographic in the area. This circumstance, along with Burstrom's management skill, may have given the board confidence in the hotel's prospects, justifying its decision both to continue licensing the place and to grant the manager a personal liquor permit.

A proprietor's reputation could hold considerable weight in convincing the board to license a dubious hotel proposition. The National Hotel in Allan Water, which was a remote trading community approximately 200 kilometres north of Port Arthur, had received a standard hotel licence in 1927. The town was difficult for the inspector to access, and when the manager renewed his application in 1930 under the name of the Allan Water Hotel, the board asked the local Ontario Provincial Police detachment to report on the place. The OPP constable noted that the place did not seem appropriate as a hotel, and its licence and beer permit were denied. The hotel's manager, Dallas Gastmeier, argued against this position, explaining to Dingman that he did not feel his hotel, which had always been run properly, should be denied this privilege. Dingman was moved by the argument and wrote to the OPP for a more precise report, noting that "Mr. Gastmeier writes so reasonably that I cannot help feeling his case may be entitled to more favourable consideration."[30] The OPP explained that the layout of the hotel was such that beer would be served in an area frequented by "Indians" who came in to town to sell their furs. As I discuss further in Chapter 6, Aboriginal people were prohibited by the Indian Act from consuming alcohol.[31] Nevertheless, the board granted the licence, and when the OPP reported two years later that the number of "Indians" in the hotel could result in them drinking light beer in the beverage room, the new director of permits, A.K. Coulthard, decided it was probably best just to let the licence run its course and simply not renew it when time for renewal came.[32] This decision was moot, for the next licence-renewal period was November 1934, after the LCA (1934) came into operation, and the hotel did not meet most of the requirements for a standard hotel under the revised regulations.[33]

The significance of this second chance should not be underestimated. Many hotels received a second chance on the strength of the hotel's value to a locality or the good reputation of a proprietor; but many hotel managers who had received standard hotel licences and light-beer permits succumbed to the temptations against which Dingman so sternly cautioned Burstrom. Many of them lost their licences and their livelihoods.

To explore the intersecting and often competing priorities of establishing a viable hotel system and addressing a proprietor's criminal past, we can consider the case of the Thompson Hotel in Fort William. In 1930 Mrs. Rossi (not her real name) applied for a light-beer permit for her hotel. Unfortunately for her, the OPP reported that she and her three sons had a string of past convictions, or what the police and the board often referred to as "irregularities." As the owner of the building, Mrs. Rossi decided to find another person to manage the business, but this new applicant was also deemed unsuitable; the police felt that he was simply a "front." Dingman told Rossi that she needed to remove herself entirely from the operations of the hotel: "We will entertain no proposition for a Standard License for this hotel for any party who is not entirely independent of yourself and family so that he will be in full and genuine control of the hotel, unencumbered by the presence therein either living there or directing things, of yourself or any member of your family."[34] A subsequent applicant was charged for having kegs of strong beer on the tap in the beverage room.[35] At this point, in the spring of 1930, Dingman confided to the chief of the Fort William Police Department, "It seems that the Thompson Hotel and the [Rossi]s are fated to be a perennial subject with both of us, but I live in hopes that we will get things squared up sometime and in satisfactory condition, though I doubt if that will happen before this place entirely changes hands."[36] An unrelated individual applied in April, and although he had one conviction, dating to 1927, the board determined that he was suitable. The licence was granted with the proviso that "your said license and permit is liable to immediate cancellation if we find that any member of the said family is employed in or resides in the Thompson Hotel, or is found to be doing any business about his hotel, other than for the purpose only of occasionally inspecting the property and collecting the rent."[37] This new manager impressed the police with the improvements he was making to the hotel, but a month later he was gone.[38]

The Rossi family continued to try to have the hotel licensed, and after a few more failed applications, OPP district inspector W.G. Ingram suggested to Dingman in 1931 that perhaps the patriarch, who was the only person in the family without some kind of conviction under the Ontario Temperance Act (OTA) or LCA, could be granted a licence.[39] This solution, made with strict conditions that the three troublesome Rossi sons not come near the hotel, came with a caution from Dingman, not unlike the message he had sent to Burstrom a few years earlier:

> You must be aware that there has been trouble from various members of your family, and this consent is given mainly on the basis that you yourself have no police court record and have never been in difficulty with the police. I hope you recognize the importance of not merely maintaining this good record of your own, but exercising such scrutiny and control over every person in the hotel as to ensure their good behaviour and the generally creditable management of the hotel. I hope that you will succeed, and am willing that your family should have a chance through you of rehabilitating themselves on the terms above mentioned.[40]

The faith was misplaced: in September 1932, fifteen months after Rossi received the licence, the police raided the hotel and found his son Nick in charge, a keg of strong beer on the tap, and no indication that he had purchased the keg on his permit. Nick Rossi had no personal liquor permit. He was found guilty and fined $100 and costs, a standard fine in such cases.[41] The police raided a few weeks later and found that Nick still lived in the hotel and that another brother was there often; the third brother was being held on charges of arson. Nevertheless, the board granted the father a licence once again, with the proviso that the sons get out and stay out. This time, it seems, they heeded the warnings. One year later, a new manager with no dubious past took over the hotel, and after that point the place was run well.

The case of the Thompson Hotel raises the question of why the board bothered to continue with this hotel. Owned by a family of dubious reputation, the Thompson Hotel should, one expects, simply never have received a standard hotel licence, let alone a light-beer permit. Yet this hotel's situation clearly illustrates the underlying motivation behind the LCBO's early hotel-licensing activities. Central to the board's mandate was to license hotels for the service of the "travelling public," a term often repeated in the board's letters. The Thompson Hotel was a suitable structure and in an important location, but it was owned by a family whose members had repeated trouble with the law. The first explanation might be that partisan politics underlay the approval of these applications. This might have been the case, but there is no indication from other government records, most notably from the records of Premiers Howard Ferguson and George Henry, that this case gained any special attention. Moreover, in the extensive records of this hotel, there is no indication that there was any political influence.

If we rule out politics, we can speculate on the intersection of a viable hotel and the need to oversee its actions. Since hotels had been the site of public drinking in Ontario for at least a generation, they were the ideal site for illegal beer consumption. Moreover, the repeated appearance of kegs of strong beer on the hotel's taps indicates that the facilities for drinking were being abused. If the board had denied a standard hotel licence and light-beer permit, it would simply have been turning its back on the operation of a potential illegal drinking premises, or "blind pig." To continue to license the hotel was to continue to add a layer of oversight to the hotel's operations. Moreover, as the patronizing letter from Dingman indicates, the board's communications were attempts to correct behaviour or to impart proper habits to the proprietors. Rossi Sr. was an Italian immigrant, and although it is not stated in the records, the board may have seen its role as instilling foreigners with correct British discipline. Moreover, there was a sense of obligation to the Rossi family. Mrs. Rossi argued to Dingman that she had spent over $22,000 to improve the hotel so that it would conform to the standards of the board. It would have been unfair to deny a hotel licence after such an excessive sum had been spent to create a suitable hotel space.[42] This sense of fairness was, in fact, a motivator in many of the interactions of the board, both before and after the LCA (1934) came into effect. Finally, related to the renovations, and from an entirely functionalist perspective, the needs of the community may have been served by a hotel of the size and layout of the Thompson Hotel. To deny a standard hotel licence was to deny the community this necessary resource.

Hotels were important parts of communities, and as we will see, the role of a hotel as a community meeting place often influenced the board's regulatory decisions. But the "Standard Hotel" designation carried additional importance: it indicated a mark of regulated quality. To this end, and notwithstanding its liquor control name and mandate, the LCBO was interested in constructing a viable and respectable hotel system in the province. When, in May 1927, the proprietor of the New Royal Hotel in Galt applied for a standard hotel licence, Dingman informed him that the board was holding the application "in abeyance" and explained, "We must have Standard Hotels conducted not only in strict compliance with the law, but in a creditable manner generally, especially since this Province has begun to attract tourists. We feel that undesirable hotels are apt only merely to give dissatisfaction to our own citizens but may repel visitors whom we want to attract."[43] This was the reason the Windsor hotel Chez Mario lost its short-lived licence in 1929. Soon after the licence was granted, inspector John Pitt observed that it was completely inappropriate: "I was not very much impressed with the condition of the place or with the class of people who frequent it[;] *too many painted women* about the place[,] and from the environment[,] place looks as if it might be used for other purposes."[44] Two weeks later, it was closed.

The board, then, wanted to discourage unappealing hotels and to encourage good ones. In 1929 the Windsor House Hotel in Kitchener, which was called by a local MLA "one of the best small town hotels I have ever visited" but which did not have a standard hotel licence, was fined for selling items that the LCA (1927) allowed only a standard hotel to sell.[45] Dingman wrote to the manager claiming that "there is an easy alternative to any hotel which desires to obey the law and run a good hotel, and that is for the proprietor to make up his mind to that intent and apply for and receive a Standard Hotel License."[46] Similarly, when Joseph Zuber, the proprietor of the venerable Walper Hotel, also in Kitchener, faced conviction under the LCA, Dingman wrote to him in a somewhat fawning manner, noting that "we would be glad to consider your application for a Standard Hotel License, on the basis of course of your absolute observance of the law."[47] In writing this letter, Dingman appealed to the man's wealth and supposed respectability in order to suggest that following the law should not be a problem. Moreover, his tone suggested that having such a well-respected hotel listed as a standard hotel would be a credit to the LCBO:

> You are not a man who is struggling to make his way in the world and who may think he needs to take liberties with the law to procure a livelihood. None of these considerations need to trouble you, and we wonder now if you are not enough of a sport to change your reputed policy and take rank as you can among our very best Standard Hotels and show an all round example, not merely of running a good hotel, but of respecting the law in every way ... We are preparing a booklet of Standard Hotels for early issue.

He closed the letter with an odd suggestion that Zuber's high self-perception might interfere with his own business decisions: "We are wondering if this letter will amuse you or whether it will evoke a response. We suppose you will write us at any rate."[48] Zuber did take out a standard hotel licence, and his status permitted a rare degree of leniency in the eyes of the police. In a report about two of the more prominent hoteliers in Waterloo County, OPP district inspector Ingram noted, "I have had some information that this place is dabbling a little in illegal handling of liquor, but ... this Hotel is no doubt the best in the City for public accommodation and might deserve a little consideration."[49]

Since the standard hotel designation itself was improved when a good hotel sought licensure, a standard hotel that was found to be poorly managed devalued the standard hotel designation. The board had an interest in rooting out even the suggestion of illegality. Although the board may have been lenient with respect to one or two convictions under the OTA, it viewed with considerable disdain constant indicators of ongoing problems. In 1927 the proprietors of Niagara Falls' Alexandra Hotel lost their standard hotel licence after a police raid found

> 8 Cartons 96 qt bottles Taylor and Bates ale in pantry off main dining room of hotel
> 36 qt bottles Taylor and Bates in ice box in bar room
> 3 cartons 36 quarts Taylor and Bates ale in buffette [sic] in bar-room
> 1 case of Canadian club whisky in basement of hotel

Moreover, the owners' liquor permit included the purchase of "15½ dozen [bottles] of ale [and] 1 case of whisky."[50] When the case came to trial, the charge was reduced from "keeping for sale" to having liquor in a place other than a residence; the proprietors pled guilty, were fined $300, and lost their personal liquor permits, and the standard hotel licence and light-beer permit were suspended. Immediately, their lawyers wrote to the LCBO to dispute the suspension of the permits. They argued that since the charge of "keeping for sale" had been dropped, the proprietors were not "convicted publicans" and should not have lost their standard hotel licence.[51] Dingman's reply suggests the assumption of an authority that superseded the law: "I find that the search showed in all fourteen dozens of beer in three places ... and one case of whiskey ... all indicative of intent to violate the law."[52] After the lawyers challenged this conclusion, Dingman reiterated his position: "It may be that the officers failed in securing conviction for selling or having for sale, from lack of evidence of sale, but the presence of all this liquor is hardly to be misunderstood, and the magistrate evidently felt that something was wrong when he imposed a fine of $300 and costs."[53] A month later, when the proprietors again asked to have their standard hotel licence reinstated, Dingman wrote the local OPP to ask its opinion. OPP district inspector C. Airey argued that the licence should be refused "in fairness to other hotel keepers whom we have every reason to believe have strictly and conscientiously observed this law."[54] A few months later, the licence and light-beer permit were renewed on the advice of an unidentifiable LCBO staff member who, on visiting the hotel, had noted that the proprietor "was an old English war veteran who had tied up his money in this hotel and was liable to lose all unless he was given further opportunity of making good."[55]

Leniency, combined with a healthy dose of paternalism, permitted an amount of abuse by proprietors. In 1929 a woman, Mrs. Labelle, sent a request to the board that clearly moved Dingman. She asked that, for New Year's Eve, she be permitted to close her hotel to the general public in order to have a private party for her family:

> That's the only day that I could received my childrens [sic] and can enjoy it ourself with little beer without the law come in ... I know it is against the law but I always respect the law good and I just received my license I can['t] afford to lose it ... but if I had a permit from the Board well everything is allright [sic] with the law just for that day I will show this permit everything be fine. Please do that for me I don't want my children nor my relation to be in trouble I have been 26 years and I ha[ve] always had my children with me for that day and never had no trouble.[56]

Observing that "this is the only request of the kind which I recall in nearly fifteen years of hotel administration, and in the belief that it is honorably asked," Dingman granted the request.[57] His generosity was misplaced: he soon learned that she held a party that was open to the public and that she had previously been involved in some "blind pig" activities in her hotel. Moreover, making the situation more unusual, he learned that she was using an assumed name and was known by three different names (her maiden name and two others). When the matter was eventually cleared up and Mrs. Labelle wrote once again asking for a standard hotel licence and promising to obey the law, Dingman's paternalistic tendencies returned: "The way you can best please me, however, is by being a real good girl and absolutely observing the law, and keeping clear of doubtful acts of any kind whatever."[58]

These cases suggest an aspect of the board's operations that was prevalent in the pre-1934 period: the importance of leniency, supplication, and clemency. Except for extreme cases of persistently problematic proprietors with long histories of bootlegging, the board was willing to give many hotel proprietors second and even third chances. This evidence challenges the notion of an overly restrictive post-prohibition control board, replacing it with an impression of one that was attempting to break from the past in order to construct a hotel system based on self-control and redemption. Not surprisingly, but probably not intentionally, these two values were fundamental to the rhetoric of the traditional temperance movement. Through self-control and intervention (by God), the drunkard would be redeemed. The prohibition era undermined this classic sin-penitence-redemption cycle with the intervention of the state, which did not require self-control because the government supplanted individual will with an external control mechanism. Theoretically, without access to booze, respectful citizens no longer had to control themselves since there was no temptation. When prohibition ended, the need for self-moderation and self-control returned. In a secular state, the Liquor Control Board took the place of the forgiving God.

In many of these cases, leniency was practised despite advice from the police that a proprietor should not have a beer authority. The reasons for this discrepancy are difficult to determine. There may have been some elements of political influence in certain cases. When the proprietor of Kitchener's American Hotel was busted for bootlegging in 1931, the police forwarded to the LCBO the man's standard hotel licence and light-beer permit, noting that the hotel has been taken over by Karl Schmidt, "a notorious bootlegger. We will be on guard in the matter of any application from [Schmidt]."[59] In keeping with the trend of ignoring police advice, the board granted the licence when Schmidt applied. A few years later, Schmidt was convicted of illegal selling and went to jail for four months, but the board does not appear to have taken any action. There may have been some outside influence – on the back of the letter informing the board of Schmidt's conviction, someone scrawled a cryptic but suggestive note: "No Action. P.A."[60] Did this mean that the board had decided to take no action, or did it mean that the board had been informed to do so by someone initialled "P.A."?

Certainly, there were several examples of the board's decisions being directed by politics and outside influence. As I discuss in much more detail in Chapter 5, after 1934 such influence was not uncommon but not as prevalent as one might expect. Only occasionally do the records indicate political influence, and although many undocumented discussions may have led to decisions being changed, there are also documented cases when the board ignored or disagreed with attempts to influence its decisions. Although the Ferguson and Henry regimes may have been politically and culturally different from Premier Mitchell Hepburn's, with the leadership of the board changing significantly, there was a decided consistency in attempts by the board to dissociate itself from politics. This effort was aided by Premiers Ferguson and Henry, both of whom – when responding to letters that asked them to use their influence to gain licences or patronage, such as jobs at liquor stores – insisted that they would not interfere with the board's operations. This was a standard response that Hepburn also used after 1934.

The Intersection of the Legal and the Illegal

The board's leniency when dealing with specific hotels probably also related to one of the primary mandates of the LCBO: to create a viable alternative to the bootlegger. Although the LCA was designed to address the concerns about illegal drinking, it also created a situation in which hotel proprietors who felt they were acting legally found that their efforts to follow the law were undermined by the existence of illegal drinking spaces. In 1927 Thomas Innes, proprietor of the King George Hotel in Comber (Essex County), wrote to the board to complain that it was not worth his time to continue to sell light beer when "the Blind Pigs which are allowed to run in this district sell real beer for 25 cts to 35 cts per bottle so my sale[s] of light beer are practically nil." His complaint had two layers. First, he was concerned about the restrictions and conditions he faced by following the law. Second, by describing the "blind pigs" as being "allowed to run" he made a subtle complaint about the lax enforcement of the law, which made honest hotel proprietors unable to run a decent hotel:

> I run a decent respectable house – and there are only about four Hotels in Essex County that are run so, if I am to continue in the Hotel business I must have some support and it seems to me that I am paying out good money for license etc and running a decent house and getting no favors. Nothing in exchange for the fee and the Blind Pigs are allowed to flourish and pay no license fee directly to the board.[61]

In response to this complaint, Dingman forwarded the letter to the OPP, promising Innes that the local detachment would "give attention to the law violation of which you speak in your district" and asking Innes to provide the information to the officers.[62]

Confronting illegality while dealing with the exigencies of a community's position was a difficult task that involved a variety of influences and often unsatisfying outcomes. Consider, for example, the notorious Edgewater Hotel in Riverside, which attracted considerable attention from the police and the local newspapers and may very well have been one of the hotels that caused Innes such concern. The hotel was managed by Mrs. Bertha Thomas, whose antics, and those of her son, were followed by the *Border Cities Star* as well as by newspapers from farther afield. Also known as the Thomas Inn, the establishment was a popular roadhouse with a large dance floor and a heavy tourist trade. In 1927 the board consulted with the local OPP, deliberating about whether to grant to both the Edgewater and the nearby Island View Hotel only a restaurant light-beer permit, which would have required the proprietor to apply and pay for individual licences to sell tobacco and to run a restaurant.[63] In consulting with the OPP, Dingman asked district inspector J. Gardner to recommend what the board should do. Dingman noted that the establishments were basically restaurants with a few hotel rooms attached and concluded that "whatever rooms they have being rather incidental and small in number ... a hotel business in the real sense is hardly done."[64]

Inspector Gardner agreed with Dingman's assessment, and his suggestions on how to proceed demonstrate the intricate link between hotel management, illegality, and the respectability attached to the standard hotel licence. While noting that there had been no conviction against either the Thomas Inn or the Island View Hotel since the LCA came into effect, Gardner observed that the Island View Hotel "is certainly much the superior and is the most up-to-date roadhouse in the Border Cities and I believe is entitled to a light beer permit but not a Standard Hotel License as they do not have sufficient sleeping accommodation." The Thomas Inn, by contrast, "is certainly not deserving of a Standard Hotel License." He noted that the expense and trouble that would be caused by an application for a restaurant permit were not necessarily a bad thing since the hotel "is certainly not deserving of any consideration." Moreover, he concluded, although neither had been convicted under the LCA, the Thomases had "caused us a great deal of trouble." He claimed that he suspected they had broken the law frequently but that the police had not been able to gather enough evidence for a conviction.[65]

The Move to Beer by the Glass

Secret beer stashes, regular-strength beer attached to light-beer taps, illegal selling through a hole in the wall: such aspects of the hotel beverage trade after the passing of the LCA (1927) represented a hangover from prohibition. As the 1930s opened up and the Depression deepened, the United States debated the repeal of prohibition. Arguments for liberalizing the liquor laws multiplied. By the early 1930s, increasing numbers of voices rose in favour of "beer by the glass" legislation, which would permit regular-strength beer to be sold in licensed establishments. Before examining the outcome of this legislative change, the LCA (1934), we need to understand the context in which it was created.

By 1932 the Depression had created tremendous pressure on the government to enact a variety of reforms that would boost revenues and get people back to work. It had also generated increased concern among socially active reformers to protect the poor and the vulnerable from unnecessary expenses and indulgences. In the issue of public consumption of alcohol, both the Drys and the Wets viewed their solution as the most economically and socially responsible. The temperance movement continued to be active through church groups and influential, locally active societies such as the Woman's Christian Temperance Union (WCTU). The Wets were not as united. Various workers' organizations, trade unions, and trades and labour councils often expressed workers' demands for a decent glass of beer. They were joined in their wet activities by business people, notably various Hotelmen's Associations. Often the loudest wet voice came from the Moderation League, a national organization headed by business leaders and other prominent individuals who had been lobbying for the end of prohibition since 1919.

No history of the Moderation League has been written, and some of its work remains unclear, but by the 1930s it had been in existence across the provinces for well over a decade. In keeping with the provincial nature of Canadian liquor legislation, the league was organized provincially but appears to have had various local-action committees. Like the anti-prohibition leagues in the United States, the league also mobilized bourgeois women to present a respectable wet counterpart to the respectable women's temperance groups across the country, such as the WCTU, church-based Women's Missionary Societies, and Women's Institutes.[66] In its campaigns, the Moderation League did not push for a return to the saloon, preferring instead the values of moderation and "true temperance" and the government control that would facilitate them. For example, in British Columbia in 1919 the Moderation League pushed for government sale of "sealed bottles of liquor and the sale of beer and wine with meals in restaurants."[67] It was not interested in the return to the saloon. As Craig Heron has noted, its elite leadership "wanted a return of deference, respect and restraint among the mass of the population."[68] As we will see, some tensions between workers and the Moderation League persisted.

In 1931 the Moderation League began to ramp up its pressure on the government to reintroduce "beer by the glass" legislation in the province. Premier Ferguson had been adamantly and steadfastly opposed to this in 1927, and his hand-picked successor, George Henry, a former United Church Sunday school teacher, retained the opposition to any loosening of the laws.[69] The Moderation League, however, was persistent. It presented several important arguments to counter dry assertions about the degradation that expanded laws would cause the province. First, it argued that "beer by the glass" legislation would improve business in hotels and restaurants, attracting even more American tourists and keeping visitors from travelling to Quebec, where the liquor laws were much more liberal. In a series of letters and a monthly periodical tellingly named *New Business,* the Moderation League presented statistics and anecdotes reiterating the value that "beer by the glass" legislation would have for Ontario's economy. The *New Business* also included assertions that Ontario was unnecessarily burdening its population with an outmoded form of control, comparing Ontario with more liberal regimes in British Columbia, Alberta, Manitoba, and of course Quebec (see Figure 2).

The economic argument about the increase of business was joined by socio-economic arguments about the damaging financial and social effects that such restrictive laws had on the province. Since they could not have a bottle of "the good stuff" in their local beverage room, Ontarians continued to patronize illegal sellers, either buying bottles from bootleggers or patronizing underground drinking places ("blind pigs"). Such businesses were doubly problematic: not only were they holdovers from the troublesome prohibition era, and entirely outside of the eye of the government's regulators, but they also received revenues that could have gone directly into government coffers (see Figure 3). Although much of its rhetoric appealed

Figure 2 Provincial comparison, from the *New Business,* 1 September 1932. *Source:* Archives of Ontario, RG 3-8-0-227 (MS 1749), Premier George Henry's Public Correspondence Files, "Liquor Control – Operation of #2."

to the need of the common man for a respectable glass of beer, the Moderation League did not have wholehearted support from labour. In September 1932 R.H. Russell, a delegate to the District Trades and Labor Council in Toronto, expressed his disappointment that Moderation League banners were included in the recent Labour Day Parade. "The man who is running the Moderation League," he argued, "is absolutely opposed to organized labor in any way shape or form."[70]

This opposition notwithstanding, the Moderation League was aware that its argument could be heard best through the voices of the masses. In the agitation against prohibition at the end of the First World War, the league mobilized returned soldiers, who gathered names on petitions and in many provinces successfully saw prohibition end. In the early 1930s it used workers for similar ends. Rather than petitioning door to door, the league embarked on an extensive "straw poll" project in factories and workplaces across the province. It had sympathetic supervisors and foremen conduct polls based on the question "Are you in favour of an amendment to the Ontario Liquor Control Act to obtain the sale of beer and light wines to both Ontario citizens and tourists through standard hotels, clubs and certain approved restaurants?" In an additional strategic move, the league had these foremen

HE LIKES THE DEPRESSION

Bootlegger—"You're driving the tourist away Boss, but you've saved the home market for me"

Figure 3 "He Likes the Depression," from the *New Business,* 1 July 1932. *Source:* Archives of Ontario, RG 3-8-0-227 (MS 1749), Premier George Henry's Public Correspondence Files, "Liquor Control – Operation of #2."

send the results to both Premier Henry and the league's offices. As a result, the premier was flooded with dozens of letters informing him of the outcome of the straw poll. In the vast majority of cases, workers voted overwhelmingly in favour of this proposal. According to the league's own count, submitted to the premier, out of 502 factories approached, 340 (68 percent) allowed the vote. At these factories, 35,239 people voted, with 29,242 (83 percent) in favour of the proposal and 5,997 opposed. When the league's poll was challenged by the *Toronto Telegram,* which argued that it was not representative of Ontarians and especially not of women, the league retorted that, in the 25 factories in which over 75 percent of the workers were women, 3,638 people (84 percent) favoured the proposal, evidence that women supported beer by the glass.[71] In Henry's letters, there are only two indications of employers who refused to allow this poll to be taken. One of them was Henry himself, who, on a request by the league to have civil servants polled, replied tersely, "as I have already intimated to some members of your League, I am not favouring your campaign at the present time and I do not see why I have been asked to consent to a straw vote being taken among the civil servants of the province."[72] Yet he could see the pressure building.

Despite being a vocal and seemingly well-funded organization, the Moderation League was not the only wet voice being heard in the premier's office. As noted above, various labour organizations and Hotelmen's Associations also expressed their interest in a loosening of the liquor laws. For example, in June 1932 the Hamilton District Trades and Labor Council forwarded to the premier a resolution passed in conjunction with the Labor Educational Association of Ontario that urged granting "local autonomy to municipalities" in the issue of beer and wine sales and that deemed the increase in beer and wine prices, along with the existing control regime, to be "class legislation" that did not "meet with the needs and desires of the workers" and was furthermore not "in the interest of true temperance."[73] Similarly, hotel proprietors presented economic arguments in favour of "beer by the glass" legislation while adding their own unique economic perspective. On 9 September 1932 a large delegation of the Hotel Association of the Province of Ontario met with Henry to press its case. The premier insisted that no "beer by the glass" legislation would be forthcoming. Following this meeting, the association forwarded a resolution to the premier arguing that "the granting of the request to sell beer and wine would result in the employment of a large number of people," and it provided statistics from other provinces that "show[ed] conclusively that License Law is more desirable than Prohibitory Legislation." Furthermore, the association argued that the increasing "unfair and unjust" competition from unregulated tourist homes, camps, and other lodgings was exacerbating "the seriousness of the financial condition of the overwhelming majority of the standard hotels."[74] The resolution concluded by expressing the association's extreme disappointment with the premier's perspective.

The hotelmen were the second front of the wet attack, and accordingly the Moderation League saw them as allies. One of the most prominent members of the Moderation League, R. Home Smith (its treasurer), was a well-known real estate developer and entrepreneur whose activities included playing a key role in the redevelopment of the Toronto waterfront, which included the Sunnyside Amusement Park. Smith was also a restaurateur, having opened the Old Mill Tea House in Toronto in 1914.[75] Accordingly, the league appears to have directly contacted hotel proprietors, encouraging them to sign a resolution and send it to the premier. Proprietors like Francis G. Venables, the owner of several hotels in Toronto, explained in a letter accompanying the resolution that whereas he would normally "consign to the waste-paper basket chain letters," the Moderation League's letter "appears to me to be such an admirable document and co-incides so completely with my own views ... that I feel I must sign." The document, entitled "Request," was over three pages long and presented the arguments for beer by the glass from a comprehensive but decidedly business-friendly perspective. It argued that tourist money was being lost and that hotels and restaurants were threatened by the current economic situation, that these and other businesses would benefit from the increased trade created by permitting "beer by the glass" sales, that rich and poor alike were forced to drink only in their homes, where many might not want to drink, and that such legislation would make regulation and government control easier since liquor drinking in semi-public areas would not be confined to bedrooms and other private places such as cabins and camps. It concluded with the assertion that the premier must "investigate freely to establish the truth or falsity of these statements."[76]

Such lobbying efforts appear to have had some impact on George Henry, whom Sharon Jaeger characterizes as indecisive and lacking the political wits of his predecessor, Howard Ferguson, or of Mitchell Hepburn, the new and dynamic leader of the provincial Liberals.[77] At the September 1932 meeting with the hoteliers, Henry reportedly observed that perhaps it would be possible to work out some "scheme" to allow people who already had liquor permits to "have beer and wine with their meals in hotels."[78] This statement spurred a backlash from the Drys, who had already been urging Henry to stay the temperate course. Not only did they argue that he should resist the overtures of the Wets; some also argued that further restrictions on liquor sales would be the most prudent fiscal and social policy. In reaction to the meeting with the hotel proprietors, Ben Spence, one of the most influential leaders of the temperance forces in Ontario, wrote to congratulate Henry for resisting the temptations of the Wets. In a dense, eight-page letter, Spence provided Henry with various statistics that either challenged assertions of the Wets or reiterated dry perspectives on the social impact of drinking. He concluded with the observation that the current liquor system "has proved itself ... to be a tremendous success from the standpoint of the people who make and seek to derive a profit from the sale of liquor and also of people who drink." He then made his plea, turning the language of the Moderation League on its head by arguing that the premier should "give 'serious consideration' not to the negative question of how might the sale or use of liquor be least harmfully extended, but rather to the positive constructive and imperatively urgent question of how best may that sale and use be immediately curtailed and how soon can it be entirely abolished."[79] To Spence, and his dry colleagues, liquor control was merely a brief deviation from the onward march toward legislated national sobriety.

In contrast to the often terse replies that Henry would send to the Moderation League, he drafted a warmly worded letter to Spence of slightly over three pages, responding to specific points. He thanked Spence for the temperance leader's detailed extrapolation of sales and permit statistics, which he admitted that he had not had time to explore in depth. Then, congenial but not agreeable, Henry pointed out several flaws in reasoning. Observing that "you have been such an enthusiast in the cause of temperance and prohibition that your views are apt to be extreme and ... your reading of figures and statistics may be somewhat biased," he dismissed a number of misinterpretations, including Spence's argument that the consumption of alcohol was going up (Spence compared annual expenditures, but Henry divided them by the increasing number of permits, demonstrating that, per person, expenditures had dropped by about 20 percent). In conclusion, Henry argued that a closer inspection of Spence's statistics would demonstrate that liquor control was achieving the goals of moderation and temperance and that "as long as we have a people who desire liquor the safest law is one in which the Province has control of the distribution." Henry, who may have been indecisive, certainly understood the complexity of the situation and the inconsistencies of biased interpretations of policy.[80]

As 1932 ended, a further complication, long dreaded, became manifest: prohibition was ending in the United States. Although the Twenty-First Amendment did not become law until December 1933, some predicted the country would repeal prohibition by the spring of 1933. In December 1932 the Moderation League sent a letter to Henry, accompanied by a collection of clippings from various newspapers, about the impact that the end of prohibition would have on the economy of Ontario. First, it observed that, under US prohibition, many American visitors who came to Ontario continued on to Quebec, bypassing Ontario's hotel industry. This situation was bad enough to the Moderation League, but with the changes in the United States, even fewer tourists would be coming to Ontario, whether or not they wanted to visit Quebec. Second, it noted that many Ontario residents visited the United States. In 1931 Ontarians spent $26 million south of the border; with "the added attraction of a sane beer law in the United States," this number would not decline and likely would increase.[81]

Under the weight of such arguments, a year later Henry was beginning to change his perspective. When in November 1933 a correspondent criticized Henry for espousing the Moderation League's cause, the premier replied that it was not the league that had convinced him to consider "beer by the glass" legislation but rather "the changed attitude of the people in the United States." He writes, "we cannot close our eyes to the fact that in many ways the social life of our country is interlocked with that of the United States, not I will admit in entirety because I quite feel that the way the problem is being handled in the United States would not be acceptable to our people in this Province."[82] Although the social life of Ontarians may have been intertwined with the United States, Henry's political future remained firmly entwined with what happened in Ontario. So although he may have argued that the Twenty-First Amendment was the instigator for his changed opinion on the LCA, he also knew that within a few months he would have to go to the polls. The political situation was uncertain, but the tide had shifted in favour of beer by the glass. Liberal leader Mitchell Hepburn declared that he wanted to "peel" the "dry label" from his party and espoused much wetter views than his predecessors; and although the Progressive Party continued to urge tight liquor control (if not prohibition), during an economic depression that was now nearly five years old, this party had a narrow band of supporters. Moreover, a significant contingent within the Conservative Party was pushing for a loosening of the law. Henry probably knew that to continue to favour the status quo was to court political disaster.

Change happened quickly. In March 1934 Premier Henry presented a bill to significantly amend the Liquor Control Act; it passed with little fanfare and with only a handful of votes in opposition. On 19 June 1934 the people of Ontario went to the polls; on 20 June 1934 Mitchell Hepburn was the premier-elect. When the new law came into effect, it was under a significantly different political administration. The act named the places in which beer or beer and wine might be sold as "standard hotels and ... such other premises as the regulations may provide and define."[83] Newspapers expressed surprise when, after the Liberals took office and implemented the act, only standard hotels received the privilege. The decision not to allow beer in restaurants was political, made by the Liberal cabinet soon after the party took office. In July 1934 the *Toronto Star* observed that "only very gradually will restaurants be licensed, if at all."[84] One year later, Premier Hepburn assured temperance workers that he had no intention of permitting beer in restaurants.[85]

When the LCA (1934) became law, the LCBO's mandate expanded. Although it was still charged with overseeing the sale of liquor across the province, and with licensing hotels, the decision to set hotels as the main sites of legal public consumption of liquor meant that the hotel side of the

LCBO's business expanded tremendously. Yet, in spite of the change in leadership, which did cause a shake-up in the personnel of the LCBO, its priority remained to construct and support a hotel system across the province that was guided by the principles of respectability and social order and driven by bureaucratic efficiency. The rest of this book draws mostly on the much more detailed and rich records of the post-1934 period, yet it does not ignore the 1927-34 phase of the LCBO's operations. In many ways that will become clear, the regulation of hotels involved a fundamental reorganization of the relationship between residents of the province and the water(s) of life.

3

Idealistic Form and Realistic Function: Restructuring Public Drinking Space

In 1937 inspector Harry Edgecombe of the Liquor Control Board of Ontario (LCBO) inspected the American Hotel in Sandwich, Ontario, and was not sure what to do. This was not his district, but he was visiting Essex County on a somewhat routine assignment to provide a second opinion on some of the establishments in the area. He could not decide whether he liked what he saw or not:

> Tap room is very well equipped, ladies and men's beverage rooms are fair but I do not like the low partition between these rooms, no privacy whatsoever, open passageway between ladies beverage room and so called dining room ... The above lay-out is like one room with low wood partitions designating each room, kitchen and mens' [sic] lavatory fair. Bedrooms and bath are in opposite end of building and are of course private, furniture is fair and rooms are clean, decoration just fair. Summing up general appearances, it is nothing for us to be proud of as a licensed hotel but apparently all the owner can afford and serves the community and volumn [sic] of business is small ... [The proprietor] recently lost his wife, leaving seven children and the poor devil is trying to make a living. I have made several trips out there, not being able to reconcile myself to the place at all, but I found it well conducted.[1]

Edgecombe's evaluation of the physical space of the American Hotel illustrates the interplay between the moralistic and pragmatic in the regulation of hotels. He paid attention to the potential mingling of single men and women in the hotel, a factor that could have a significant impact on the morality of the hotel, but gave equal time to the furniture, the condition of the kitchen, and the decorations, more pragmatic aspects of the hotel's operations. At the same time, his sympathetic reflection on the proprietor's personal troubles and his note that the current situation was "all the owner can afford" demonstrate that there were a variety of considerations when evaluating a hotel's layout; each situation had to be assessed on a variety of points comprising an interplay of fiscal reality and bureaucratic idealism.

A major component of post-prohibition liquor control was a literal as well as a metaphorical restructuring of drinking in Ontario. The LCBO's regulatory activities involved reshaping both the way people constructed legitimate and illegitimate public drinking practices and the way people constructed public drinking spaces. Few hotels represented a model post-prohibition public drinking space, and the LCBO demanded that premises undergo a range of physical alterations in order to conform to its idea of a well-managed and manageable beverage room. Yet, although they may have been motivated by some idealized vision, the LCBO's central administrators and inspectors recognized that this ideal would not be achieved. What they hoped to accomplish was more modest: a balance between a suitable premises and reasonable management of that space. Moreover, since the LCBO was charged with inspecting and licensing the entire hotel premises, not just the drinking spaces, its evaluation of the viability of hotel space extended far beyond simply an assessment of the hotel as a beverage room. The shape, functionality, and management of nondrinking spaces – bedrooms, kitchens, basements, and other areas necessary to a well-functioning hotel – were equally, and often more, important to the board's evaluation of a hotel's suitability for licensure.

With a few notable exceptions, the organization and reorganization of public drinking space is a relatively understudied topic; we must look beyond drink studies per se to find the conceptual tools with which to understand the governmental project of revisioning and rearranging the beverage rooms. However, the exceptions are significant. David Gutzke argues that British brewery owners undertook a restructuring of their public houses in order to conform to progressive ideals of social order and propriety.[2] Robert Campbell's examination of Vancouver's beer parlours includes discussions of the gradual transformation of beverage room space within a moral framework that was imposed by the British Columbia Liquor Control Board but also negotiated and shaped by the interests of the patrons, staff, and proprietors themselves.[3] Mariana Valverde has argued that the regulation of drinking spaces was one part of a broader reconfiguration of the relationship between the individual and the state.[4] Evaluating the moral discourse behind the spatial arrangements of public drinking spaces, Valverde considers the relationship between post-prohibition public drinking spaces and the physical characteristics of the imaginary, demonized pre-prohibition saloon. She argues that government liquor control agencies attempted, in vain, to construct regulations and parameters for the arrangement of the drinking space that promoted morality and self-regulation.[5]

Valverde's work leads us into other examinations of the spatial arrangements of government regulation: into the biopolitics of space. Possibly the best-known example of such a spatial arrangement, as examined by Michel Foucault, is the Panopticon, Jeremy Bentham's utilitarian prison design in which all inmates are visible to a seemingly unblinking gaze of authority.[6] Recently, geographers have discussed with great interest Foucault's ideas of governmentality and space. A key aspect of governmentality is the production of a specific type of truth; governments deploy this truth in a variety of organizational and physical structures, using different spatial rationalities depending on the context and function of the specific branch or activity of the government. The LCBO's work fits into what Margo Huxley has called "dispositional spatial rationality," which "aims at drawing boundaries and producing order that will foster correct comportments." Such rationality is intended to "bring arrangement and visibility to bear on individuals and populations problematized as chaotic and uncontrolled."[7] The problem is "dispositional" because of the threat of chaos, disorder, and inverted social systems caused by "spaces of debauchery, drunkenness, idleness that produced poverty, disease and death." Clearly, the LCBO's work, in making certain behaviours visible and manageable, reflects this aspect of governance, but as we will see, its work in shaping hotel spaces also paid attention to the healthful spaces that hotels should become. This aspect of governance was a form of *generative* rationality, in which "the qualities of environments are held to be catalysts in generating disease or health, immorality or virtue."[8] As one board official explained, "the layout of the ground floor of a Hotel where beverage rooms are conducted has much to do with the conduct of the patrons and a poorly laid out Hotel generally results in disturbances which are not conducive to good conduct or good sanitary conditions."[9] This statement captures precisely what Huxley discusses: both health and morality can be affected by the arrangement of a hotel space. According to the LCBO's spatial rationalities, the arrangement of space was an important factor in making certain problematic behaviours visible and manageable and, as a result, in generating new, morally or physically healthful behaviours. It is this simultaneous constraint *and* facilitation of behaviour that typifies the idea of biopower.

For our purposes, of interest in these examinations is that, whereas most studies of space and governmentality are related to official spaces (e.g., hospitals and prisons) or to public spaces (e.g., idealistic visions of model cities), the LCBO was concerned with the spatial arrangement of a publicly used but privately owned space. The publicly regulated hotel was a private business, being owned by private citizens or legal corporations. Oversight and control of these spaces were negotiated between government agencies (e.g., the LCBO, fire marshal, and city building inspectors) and private interests. The regulatory discourses of generative and dispositional rationalities confronted the exigencies of context. Foucault himself recognized such limits when he wrote about the Panopticon that "if I had wanted to describe 'real life' in the prisons, I wouldn't indeed have got to Bentham ... The actual functioning of the prisons ... was a witches' brew compared to the beautiful [Panopticon]."[10] As Huxley explains, "schemes and 'diagrams' such as the Panopticon serve as models, tests and ongoing aims against which programmes of government are evaluated and adjusted."[11] The ideal may never be achieved, but the effort and effect of these governmental activities provide insight into practices of regulation.[12] So, although the administration of the LCBO may have employed an idealized sense of what a hotel should be and how it should function, this ideal was challenged and modified based on the context and individual situations the board confronted. In each case, the LCBO's central administration and local inspectors needed to determine whether modifications to the ideal were possible or whether such changes would deviate too radically from the dominant ideal of social order encapsulated by the board's generative and dispositional rationalities.

The Calculus of "Need"

Whereas the larger issues such as what type of establishments to license were political, the finer details of what constituted an appropriate or inappropriate establishment for licensure were left to the post-1934 LCBO to determine (in consultation with its political masters). Initially, the board reasoned that only hotels that had been in operation prior to prohibition would receive the beer and wine privileges. Yet these guidelines, expressed as policies, were much more flexible than the board admitted publicly. Within a few weeks of the LCA (1934)'s operation, the board received applications from property owners and other entrepreneurs inquiring about the potential to renovate storefronts and apartments in order to make them suit the definition of a "Standard Hotel." The board needed to reconsider its initial policy in response to its evaluation of the "need" of the area.

The reference to "need" represents a form of obfuscating bureaucratic language, discussed in Chapter 1, that permitted the board to give a reason for its decisions that seemed rational and objective but may have been neither. The term "need" was dualistic: its more precise meaning was related to a set of considerations associated with the LCBO's broader mandate to create legal, orderly drinking spaces. Some areas, such as the main tourist quarter in Niagara Falls and King Street in downtown Toronto, required more hotel accommodation for tourists and travelling business people than did areas that were visited by fewer travellers. The importance of licensing hotels in these areas was often not debatable since many of these hotels were full-service establishments that saw the beverage room in the way the board expected: as a service to the "travelling public." Other areas might simply have no other hotel nearby. This was the case for St. Catharines' Belmont

Hotel, which an observer noted "is located in [a] business Section on Geneva Street [with] no Hotels for five blocks and is Well located for a Hotel."[13] Still other areas might need accommodation for longer-term residents, such as itinerant workers in industrial areas or in north-western Ontario boom towns. Port Arthur's Star Hotel was described favourably in the context of the specific requirements of the town: "There are 27 bedrooms in all, in cubicle style, fairly clean, 24 upstairs and three down. These meet a need and ... cater to Polish, French and English customers."[14] Such hotels, if their rooms, layout, and amenities could meet the standards the board required, or at least be adequate enough for the specific location, would receive a standard hotel licence and be eligible for a beer and wine authority. In Ottawa, for example, hotels in the Byward Market area were patronized by farmers attending the market. Inspector Alfred Larocque explained, for example, that the City Hotel "serves an urgent need in accommodating farmers comming [sic] to By-Ward market."[15] Part of this hotel's appeal was that it had adequate stabling facilities for the horses.

The "class" of the patrons was important: it could result in the denial of an authority, but it could also be the cause for special accommodation, related to a further meaning of "need." The American Hotel in Sandwich was directly across from a foundry, and the inspector noted that it "does seem to answer a need in the locality with regard to serving beverages to the labouring class of this particular part of the city."[16] A year later, inspector U.G. Reaume added an additional perspective on the value of this hotel in its area:

> It is very difficult to keep this place clean because of the smoke, dust and soot from the foundry ... Men go into the beverage rooms and their clothes are greasy and it necessitates washing the furniture every day, sometimes more often during the day." Yet as other local hotel owners explained to Reaume, this place "renders quite a service because the workmen would not feel like going into the others [hotels] in their working clothes.[17]

Similarly, Waterloo inspector Norman Ratz argued that the rural Breslau Hotel should be allowed to continue to serve meals in its beverage room because "there certainly would be a nice odor in a well set up dining room if a farmer came in to a hotel from a manure yard, and asked to be served a sandwich and a glass of beer, or if a greasy trucker sat down to a white table cloth to eat a 10c sandwich."[18] Since hotels served a variety of purposes for a variety of peoples, the board recognized the importance of evaluating each establishment's place in and suitability to its community.

Based on these inspectors' recommendations, establishments in areas that had little call for travellers' accommodations also received standard hotel licences and beer authorities based on "need." Here, the need was simply for licensed, controlled sales of beer and wine for the local residents. This sort of need involved providing an alternative to bootlegging, and often the factor determining the need was related to the demographics of the area. The foundry workers in Sandwich were an example of a group whose desire for beer would likely be served by bootleggers if not accommodated by the board's rules. Inspector Larocque reported on Ottawa's Preston Hotel in October 1934, making a similar observation about the area's need, although his criterion was ethnicity, not class. He argued that such a hotel could be desirable because "it is in a locality where an authority might not be amiss, being located in a foreign district." However, since the hotel did not have enough rooms (it had four) and since "the general housekeeping is bad and [the] place is lacking in quality," Larocque concluded that it should not receive an authority.[19] Toronto's Venezia Hotel was the target of a number of unfounded complaints charging that many immoral activities took place within.[20] Inspector John Kidd attributed the letters to local bootleggers, who, he reasoned, felt that the hotel was cutting into their business. Their attempts to sabotage the reputation of the hotel, he reasoned, were evidence that the hotel was addressing a need to damage the bootlegging business.[21]

The type of people living in a specific location might provide a reason for laxity in enforcing rules, but the demographics of an area could also require extra attention to the rules by the proprietor and more surveillance by the board's inspector. When reporting on the Avonmore Hotel's application for an authority, Toronto inspector D.W. Downey argued that "there is no need of a hotel *of this type* in this section. However, I do believe that a respectable looking hotel should be located in or around this particular section."[22] The Avonmore was located on Jarvis Street in Toronto. The board faced considerable pressure from local residents and temperance advocates in the city, all of whom demanded a reduction in the number of hotels in the area. Downey suggested that the owners "be called in for a conference and see if they are prepared to put the place in shape. As it stands at the present time it is an eyesore and provides a target for the critics to shoot at."[23] A bad hotel in an overcrowded section, Downey claimed, would cause nothing but disorder in the community and bring disgrace on the board.

The evaluation of the need for a licensed hotel in a particular area was one way that the board defined the field of visibility of its control activities. More is said about the considerations of an area's suitability for an authorized premises in the next chapter, which examines the response of the community to hotel beverage rooms. Of importance here is that the factors the board used to evaluate the space in which a hotel operated were not simply moral. The pragmatism in the inspectors' reports, how the features of specific hotels suited the specific requirements of an area, often superseded the simple issue of morality. Order was important, but, as the example of the American Hotel in Sandwich suggests, sometimes a hotel could be valuable by containing and circumscribing a problem that could otherwise spread to other hotels. Other times, however, such as with the Avonmore on Jarvis Street, the proprietors had to do extensive alterations before their premises would suit the board's requirements. I now turn to considering the extent of these alterations and the interplay of pragmatism and idealism that underlay the restructuring of the drinking space.

Constructing a Better Beverage Room

The restructuring of the drinking space by the liquor control authorities has been described as an exercise in "moral architecture," on the one hand, and as a progressive reconfiguration, on the other. Valverde argues that the regulatory efforts of the LCBO were designed specifically to create a moral environment that represented certain bourgeois discourses of social order and morality. She sees things like an inspector's concern with the condition of the basement or the washrooms as an assessment of the moral capacity of the proprietors. Yet, since Valverde bases her interpretation on a single study of the most atypical community in the province (the city of Toronto), the multifaceted nature of such inspections might have been understated in her source material.[24] Nevertheless, as research on the reconstruction of English public houses demonstrates, an aesthetically appealing drinking space did have both moral and functional value. Gutzke argues that the restructuring of pubs was a progressive approach that merged form with function and that the function was both practical and broadly moral. "Improved pubs" were places in which alcohol could be consumed in pleasant, home-like surroundings rather than in the derelict environments of a pre-war "local."[25] This "progressive" viewpoint, of course, was also bourgeois. James Nicholls contends that the British pub-improvement movement "opened a new frontline in the battle for control over the working-class drinking place."[26] The British experience provides a useful insight into the reform activities of the LCBO. Replace "gin palace" with "saloon" or "bar-room" and you have one of the primary motivations of the LCBO: it wanted drinkers to choose the hotel beverage room (and try to behave) rather than the illegal bootlegger (and thereby misbehave), and it wanted to construct a new kind of drinking space that would be above the reproach of mostly middle-class temperance forces.

One aspect of the inspection was to evaluate the hotel's capacity to function as a *supervisable* space. The ideal hotel layout was one that provided the opportunity for observation and control of the patrons. Normally, a hotel patron would enter the foyer and register for a room at the front desk. These characteristics – the foyer, the front desk with an attendant, and the registration book or registration card file – were standard features of a hotel. A registration system was a legal necessity that allowed surveillance of patrons and, when the register was scrutinized by police or LCBO inspectors, surveillance of the management and staff of the hotel. Standard hotels were also required to have dining rooms and usually at least one beverage room. In the ideal hotel space, these rooms would be accessible from the foyer, thereby permitting observation (and intervention) of potential customers. As Arnold Smith told the proprietor of the Grandview Hotel in Shuniah, Ontario, "The proper plan of an Hotel calls for the following requirements: One must be able to enter the office and lobby and from that point reach the Dining room, Ladies' or Men's Beverage Room or show guests their rooms without in any way passing through any other room."[27] Although Smith explained this "proper plan" – a sort of idealized hotel layout – in the language of customer convenience, such a layout also permitted a manager to keep an eye on what was going on in his or her hotel. In one case, a hotel proprietor was praised in the inspector's report because he spent every evening sitting in his foyer keeping an eye on everyone who went into the two beverage rooms.[28] Ideally, a hotel customer, whether headed for a bedroom, dining room, or beverage room, would be easily observable from the moment he or she entered the hotel.

Yet, just as Bentham's perfect Panopticon was elusive, so too was the ideal structural arrangement for a hotel not always achieved, and many concessions to financial and physical constraints were common. In the flurry of applications that followed the LCA (1934), the board licensed many places that simply did not have the basic elements of a hotel. Restaurateurs evicted tenants in apartments above their business and subdivided the space into makeshift bedrooms, store owners took over adjacent storefronts to create the necessary hotel "departments," and the owners of large houses hung out a sign and began to serve beer in their front room. In the months after the first authorities were issued, the board's inspectors visited and evaluated each space, recommending continuation, cancellation, or at times significant modification. On 1 November 1934, after three months of the LCA (1934), many hotels that inspectors deemed to be inadequate lost their authority and usually their standard hotel licence.

Whether a hotel was in a purpose-built structure or the proprietor was planning extensive renovations, the board made specific requirements based on the hotel's role as accommodation for the "travelling public" and also as a means of regulating social behaviour. Here, we find examples of both moral architecture and hotel functionality. Every hotel application was supposed to be accompanied by at least one photo of the hotel; ideally, the proprietor would submit photos of the main components of the establishment, including beverage rooms, dining rooms, and foyer or lobby. If a hotel needed renovation, the board required the proprietors to submit drawings of the building's layout. Some sent complete architect's blueprints, whereas others submitted simple pencil sketches. An inspector might also forward a small sketch of his own to illustrate some aspect of the hotel's layout that needed attention. Usually, these plans were evaluated by inspector William Hart, who travelled throughout the province examining existing structures of hotels and making recommendations for renovations based on his consideration of the ease of surveillance and, often more important, fire safety and toilet facilities. Except for a few instances in 1934, a hotel would normally not receive even the promise of an authority until the renovations were completed.

The Victoria Inn in Niagara Falls was not built to be a hotel. Previously McHenry's Inn, the place was a restaurant that "merely sold beer." Finding that this was a losing enterprise, the proprietor sold the business to Bruce Biggar, who took over some rooms in an adjacent apartment building in a vain attempt to meet the requirements of a standard hotel. After two proprietors failed to run a successful business, the building's owner, Louis Sacco, took it over himself in order to try to make the place turn a profit. Sacco "put a few cheap beds and mattresses in a few of the rooms upstairs, but the premises do not conform to hotel requirements in any way."[29] When in 1937 the board informed Sacco that it would not renew his licence, he approached the local member of the Legislative Assembly (MLA), William Houck, in an attempt to influence the decision. Inspector Wilson Wylie was told to inspect the space again, and he balked, noting that when he had inspected it the year before,

> the place did not in any degree set forth either in the kind of building or the quality of service which the Board desired hotels should provide for the public, and I felt that to further transfer to another person however efficient he might be would necessarly [sic] fail unless on a proposal for the expendature [sic] for a very large sum of money to have the place conform to the regulations.

Another inspection, he argued, would be futile: "The whole lavatory system is seriously at fault [and] bedrooms are of a kind in ... which should not be longer tolerated."[30] According to deputy chief commissioner Arnold Smith, Sacco would have been much better off returning the sections of his business to their original uses: a restaurant on the ground floor, three apartments above the restaurant, and a dance hall at the top floor. In any case, Smith reasoned, there were more suitable hotel accommodations nearby.[31] Despite sending letters to Premier Mitchell Hepburn – entreaties that referenced Sacco's twenty-five-year loyalty to the Liberal Party – the authority was never granted, and the Victoria Hotel ceased to exist. Sacco's story was not exclusive: the same situation played itself out in communities across the province.

Yet modifying nonhotel space did not always result in failure; more capable proprietors with the resources to make modifications could find success in converting storefronts and apartments to a hotel. When Victor Hagerman applied to have a set of stores on Toronto's Bloor Street turned into a hotel, inspector Hart visited the place and agreed that these rooms could be renovated to become a good hotel. Much to the chagrin of the local Businessmen's Association, the board promised Hagerman that it would grant an authority on the condition that he would make the necessary renovations.[32] (This promise was made only weeks before the board ceased to grant such assurances.) When inspectors John Kidd and Joseph Cheeseman visited the hotel in March 1937, they called it "nothing but a series of Beverage rooms, basement, ground floor and upper floor" and suggested that the drinking spaces be reduced and removed from the bedroom space. The hotel remained in operation.[33] Unlike Sacco's hotel, which was near to other, more suitable premises, the Bloor Hotel served a need in the community, being the only hotel within a few blocks of a busy business district. Yet, although the hotel did offer rooms that suited the board's guidelines much more so than those in Sacco's unsuccessful venture, this was primarily a drinking space.

More indicative of the importance of the spatial rearrangement of hotel beverage rooms is the attention that the board gave to hotels that were traditional hotel buildings but troublesome operations. In 1937 Arnold Smith wrote to James Deadey, proprietor of the Royal Cecil Hotel in Toronto, requesting Deadey follow through on a promise to submit a plan to change the layout of his hotel. Situated on Jarvis Street, the Royal Cecil was patronized by "a class of people that are not very welcome at any hotel."[34] It was notorious for drunkenness, fighting, and sexual impropriety; the full range of the "constellation" of vices was projected onto the Royal Cecil and not without some justification.[35] Smith reminded Deadey that "the type of people that you have to deal with in connection with your beverage room can easily cause you considerable trouble, and your present layout does not lend itself to the proper handling of these people."[36] The changes were substantial. Deadey had to move his kitchen and dining room to the main floor, rearrange the beverage rooms, install adequate washrooms on the main floor so that customers did not have a reason to go to the second floor (close to the bedrooms) to use the facilities, and move the entrance of the ladies' beverage room to the outside. The latter requirement was considered necessary because, as the hotel was currently arranged, the doors between the two beverage rooms were directly across from each other, allowing "the ease of communications by patrons" between the two beverage rooms.[37] As inspector Downey noted, "if a complete separation of the rooms are made ... we can control the situation."[38] (Also interesting in Downey's words is the "we," suggesting that here the board could have direct control over the patrons.) These alterations were completed, although they did little to improve conditions at this hotel. The Royal Cecil Hotel continued to be a euphemism in the popular press for the worst hotel in the city.[39] As general inspector John Pitt noted in 1939, "There is more criticism regarding the conduct of this hotel than all the other hotels in the Province put together."[40] Physical renovation notwithstanding, the hotel remained a persistent trouble spot that "we" could not control.

As the Royal Cecil example demonstrates, two aspects of the architectural ideal of hotels that governed the morality of the hotel's patrons were surveillance and segregation. The board wanted to ensure that responsible staff could oversee the activities of the hotel's patrons (outside of the private bedrooms) but at the same time wanted to reduce the direct connection between troublesome situations, such as the ease of accessing those bedrooms and the closeness of the men's and ladies' beverage rooms. Physical arrangements gave the board an opportunity to try to "control the situation." Such oversight required both the architectural reorganization of space and the training of staff to make sure patrons acted appropriately. Whereas hotel management would train the staff, the board had the final word on a hotel's arrangement.

A rational physical layout also allowed the board to manage not only the separation of the various operations of the hotel but also the problematic (to some eyes) intermingling of certain hotel patrons. By the end of 1934, the board had begun to insist on the separation of the sexes. "The problem of mixed[-sex] drinking," chief commissioner Edmond Odette explained, "is one of the most vexing we have." As a result, the board "ordered separate beverage rooms for men and women in some hotels. It depends on the district and the class of the clientele."[41] This policy was soon extended to all hotels, and only a few exceptions permitted the creation of only a men's beverage room. Indeed, as I discuss in looking at recreation and entertainment in Chapter 6, for many hotels, the most popular drinking space could be the ladies and escorts' room because men could go there with female friends and meet other women. This situation became significant enough that, in March 1937, the board sent out a circular reminding proprietors that unescorted men could not be served in the ladies and escorts' beverage room and that all hotels had to provide a men's beverage room. Even this rule was flexible, depending on the "class" of the hotel. Benjamin Neale, the manager of the Royal York Hotel, which was arguably the most elite hotel in the province, informed the board that he was not going to create a beverage room for men only: "I fully believe that the possibility of ladies accompanying their male escorts in our beverage room tends to increase the tone of business and I feel that it would not be a good feature if we were compelled to maintain a room specially for the use of male customers."[42] The board's solicitor replied that "there is considerable merit in your suggestion," and it appears that the board did not enforce the rule in this instance.[43]

The Royal York was a special case since, along with catering to a wealthy clientele, it was a large hotel with plenty of room separating beverage room customers; other hotels were not so well apportioned. As a result, the divisions incorporated other aspects of surveillance into the operation of the beverage room. Notably, the tap man, who appears to have been considered the most responsible member of a beverage room's service team, would do double-duty as an observer of patron behaviour. Like the Royal Cecil, the Kimberly Hotel, which inspector George Hanrahan called "the lowest class hotel in Port Arthur," had a corridor dividing the two beverage rooms, with doors across from each other.[44] When the proprietor renovated late in 1937, he proposed an arrangement that "will give better supervision and will have a service room between the Beverage rooms."[45] In January 1938 inspector Kidd noted that the taproom in Toronto's Alexandra Hotel was arranged so that waiters had to leave the beverage rooms and cross a hall to get their orders. This layout limited oversight since "the tap man is unable to see what goes on [in] the men's or Ladies room." He recommended a change that "would entirely separate the men from women" or, alternatively, "to serve beer only in the Men's room."[46] After making a special visit to the establishment, Hamilton's inspector Cheeseman suggested an alternative: that the "Service bar be placed between the ladies and Escorts and Gents Beverage Room regardless of what space it takes from existing rooms."[47] Such restructuring allowed better supervision of the patrons of the hotel, constructing a hierarchy of observation in which the tap man was the stationary individual responsible for observing and presumably correcting misbehaviour.

Although many physical requirements were designed to separate drinking patrons from each other, other physical components sought to isolate drinking from the broader public view. On his tour through north-western Ontario, inspector Hanrahan stopped at Port Arthur's Rex Hotel, where he found that the outside door to the beverage room was open, "giving a full view of interior to passersby, who would naturally turn to look in because of the excessive noise."[48] This was not acceptable. Visiting Windsor's British American Hotel in 1939, inspector Reaume "told the proprietor to tilt [shut] the Venetian blinds around the beverage rooms."[49] The proprietor continued to ignore this rule, and in 1943 inspector Harry Simington observed that the hotel needed to keep its blinds shut, "as this beverage room is close to the main street and when these blinds are open there is a view from the sidewalk of some 15 feet."[50] So whereas the staff inside the hotel could keep an eye on drinkers, the same activity was to be hidden from public view.

Similar to keeping drinking away from the curious eyes of the public, the board required advertising and hotel signage to provide minimal indication of drinking. Although a hotel sign could include the words "purveyor of beer and wine by authority of the LCBO," it could say nothing else about beverage alcohol nor draw undue attention to its sale. Ottawa's Gilmour Inn had such a sign, but the words "beer and wine" were illuminated in neon. When Arnold Smith told the proprietor to remove it, the proprietor complained to Smith that "you, on your various calls to Ottawa, saw the signs and did not object to them."[51] In a confusing back-pedal, Smith wrote that "we are not at the moment objecting to existing signs, but point out that no further signs of that kind may be used. By next year we expect that the illumination of the words 'beer and wine' on existing signs will be eliminated."[52] This, it should be noted, was not what Smith had initially said. After a few months, the board reiterated that "beer and wine" must not be illuminated.

Although the process of making the signage rule is obscured in the board's records, this is likely a case of the board creating ad hoc regulations as the need arose. Neon provided a particular challenge. In 1937, when the Embassy Hotel in Toronto contracted the E.L. Ruddy Sign Company to make a hotel sign that included the word "Dancing" in neon, the sign company contacted the board to make sure this was permitted. Ruddy's manager, V.T. Pegg, noted that the St. Regis Hotel had purchased a similar sign, with the words "Supper Dance" illuminated. The board informed Pegg that the St. Regis had been told to disconnect the specific troublesome words and that it would be best if the Embassy's sign did not have "Dancing" on it at all.[53] This case is especially noteworthy because it was the tradesperson who was functioning as a rule enforcer. The board's control over signage resulted in tradespeople internalizing rules that did not directly affect them.

Yet the board's rules on signage were not absolute. In several cases, and for no clear reason, the board was more lenient than usual. All of the cases of such leniency that I found were in the Niagara region. In 1935 the owner of the Pickwick Arms Hotel in Fort Erie asked the board whether he could put the word "Tavern" on the outside of his hotel "owing to the type of our hotel being English in construction." Both the local inspector and deputy chief commissioner Arnold Smith agreed to this request.[54] Also in 1935 the managers of the prominent Leonard Hotel in St. Catharines asked whether they could have a sign in "Old English lettering with merely the wording ... of 'Leonard Tavern'" on the entrance to the beverage room from inside the lobby. Again, Smith permitted this sign to remain, although a similar sign had to be removed from the hotel exterior.[55] But two years later, the board found such signage caused criticism. The Pickwick Arms sign "is a regular subject of complaint to other Hotels in the district on the grounds that the Board in this matter shows discrimination." The hotel's owner was ordered to take the sign down.[56] A year later, Smith wrote a sort of *mea culpa* to the Leonard Hotel:

> In view of the fact that many others have started to erect signs like them I have had to make them remove them and I must ask you to do likewise as you can understand I cannot make fish of one and flesh of another and your signs are the cause of a great deal of embarrassment to me. However, since these signs have been put up you have had the benefit if any benefit has

> accrued. It is contrary to have signs of this kind and I trust you will remove same immediately.[57]

Such language was rare and reflects the value Smith placed in a respectable hotel, which the Leonard Hotel had been. When it opened in 1929, the Leonard was lauded by the industry journal the *Canadian Hotel Review and Restaurant* as a modern, reputable, and innovative hotel.[58] Although by the 1940s the hotel had begun to decline in local prestige (and by the 1990s had become an image of urban decline), the Leonard Hotel was the city's Royal York or Chateau Laurier. Smith's letter of apology demonstrates the emphasis the board placed on fairness, especially to respectable institutions.

The case of signage, notably the reaction of the Gilmour Inn proprietor to the board's letter, raises the question of how proprietors responded to these rules and demands for physical alterations. Certainly, they did not appreciate all of the modifications, however minor, that the board demanded. Hotel proprietors who had been in the business for decades and were used to doing things a certain way, along with proprietors whose business was small, such as in country hotels, might resent or resist changes. Indeed, many of the conflicts that hotel proprietors had with the LCBO were about the speed at which the proprietors made the changes or about the extent to which the demands were met. Often, when the central office required changes to be made immediately, proprietors would ask for more time and might even receive the support of their local inspector. In November 1935 inspector Norman Ratz reported of the Bridge Hotel in Bridgeport that "all reccomended [sic] improvements are being attended to as finances permit. This is going to be a little hard sledding for this man for a while, to make all the necessary improvements, such as decorating and attending to the floors. Business is none too good, so I would suggest a little patience for this winter."[59] Teresa Schneider of St. Clements Hotel in Waterloo County explained that she also didn't have the means to do the renovations and complained that the board's rules were impeding her ability to survive: "Now that beer is back again and a person could get back on their feet again we have to repair and decorate and put in convenience that are not within our means."[60] She was out of business a few months later.

Few proprietors reacted as bluntly as did Mr. Haverluck, the proprietor of the Savant Hotel in Savant Lake (Thunder Bay district), who wrote in response to demands for significant alterations made by a board hundreds of miles to the south:

> As I feel that these plans are rather too elaborate for the place I'm forced to ask you if you would not consider changing your plans for the following reasons. The place hardly warrants a "Ladies Beverage Room" as this is a mining town and there are few ladies here, and if one was put in as per your

> plans it would do away with the staff's bedrooms. Regarding the lobby, we feel that the dining room is much larger than required and a part of this could be partitioned off.[61]

He writes in a subsequent letter:

> It is impossible to have inside toilets as there is no sewerage system and is impossible to install any as the hotel is set on bed rock.[62]

These communications demonstrate a few factors about the relationship between the board and the proprietors. First, the board often enforced a vision of hotel structure that was out of pace with the realities of the situation. The place did not need a ladies' beverage room, and the dining room requirements were smaller than necessary. Second, and more significant, strongly worded letters such as these were still deferential and respected the board's view. After more discussion with the local inspector, Haverluck worked out an arrangement for a much smaller ladies' beverage room, and the renovations proceeded.[63] The motivation in these cases was not public safety or morality as much as it was the image and legitimacy of the LCBO. This issue reappears in many of the chapters in this book since, in different conflicts between the beverage room in practice and in theory, what often mattered most was the public perception of the board's work.

As a government bureaucracy that was working to restructure public behaviour and simultaneously reinforce its own legitimacy, the LCBO sought to restructure the hotel social space in a way that ensured the hotel layout would facilitate orderly behaviour and surveillance. Its inspectors and architect insisted on manageable and functional social spaces that provided a public service while making sure that public behaviour was either orderly or could be kept under a close watch. This work was a fundamental aspect of the "conduct of conduct." The board, through its inspectors, sought control over the hotel drinking space so that hotel management and staff could, in turn, exercise their control over the drinker. Yet at the same time, the board did not disregard either the functional or financial challenges that its requirements might force on hotel proprietors. I now turn to considering the more pragmatic aspects of the operations of the hotel and the role of regulating the pragmatic, functional, and non-liquor-related aspects of the hotel business.

The Pragmatic Aspect of Hotel Management

The ideal hotel was a "full-service" operation, with drinking considered "incidental" to the hotel's financial viability, so the hotel inspector spent considerable time investigating the other aspects of the hotel operations. The annual "Hotel Inspector's Report" was four pages long, with the first three pages dedicated to describing and quantifying various non-alcohol-related features of the hotel. The inspector evaluated the fire protection, the physical state of the building, and various aspects of the different "departments" of the hotel. In each section, the inspector was asked to evaluate the quality of these elements. This form also provided a small space to evaluate the "character or reputation" of the licensee and "his conduct." Only the last section was an assessment of the beverage room, in which the inspector was required to describe the number of tables and chairs, condition of furniture, cleanliness of the beverage room, number of toilets, windows, doors, cleanliness of glasses, condition of the beer-drawing equipment, and number of cuspidors. Of all the sections of the report, the beverage room inspection was proportionally the largest, suggesting that, although the other elements were important, the inspector would spend most of his time evaluating the beverage room facilities. This proportional domination of the beverage room inspection was also reflected in the single-page monthly "Authority Holder's Conduct Report." This report's priorities inverted those on the annual report: beverage rooms were evaluated first, followed by dining room, lavatory, and fire protection. In the routine inspection, the board placed a high priority on the operations of the hotel beverage room.

Yet, although the structure of the forms might suggest the board was preoccupied with the beverage room operations, the information that inspectors chose to provide shows that they were looking at everything. As noted in Chapter 1, several inspectors were considered "hotel men." Moreover, often the standard hotel licence or beer authority would be withheld, suspended, or threatened to be suspended due to an ongoing issue with something that had nothing to do with beverage room operations. Inspectors spent much of their time paying attention to ensuring that the hotel was safe, clean, and fully functioning.

Safe

The safety of a hotel was an essential component for a government agency that was charged with licensing hotel accommodations. Fire alarms, extinguishers, ropes to escape from rooms, the steepness of stairs, the sturdiness of handrails, and other components occupied considerable space in the reports. Most of these elements were not directly related to moral regulation or drinking, although an aspect such as the steepness of stairs might be mentioned as a problem because people who had consumed too much alcohol might have difficulty scaling or descending them. Yet there is a persistent connection in the discourses of safety to a broader biopolitical project; an unsafe hotel that was licensed by the government could both endanger citizens and discredit the licensing agency.

Fire was a persistent threat to hotel operations and often appeared in a bitterly ironic fashion. Several hotels burned down in the 1930s, and many of these were wooden buildings that were completely gutted by fire. Hoteliers in Niagara Falls probably remembered the spectacular fire of the elite Clifton Hotel in the winter of 1932; no one was injured in this fire because, as a summer hotel, it was occupied only by the caretaker and his family.[64] Ironically, six months prior to this fire, the board had criticized the hotel for not having adequate fire escapes.[65] In 1940 inspector M.C. MacDonald in the Thunder Bay district observed the fire hazards of two Jellicoe hotels, Allen's Hotel and the Algoma, noting that "the fire hazard is serious, and the two hotels are far too close together for safety, or to allow the placing of adequate fire escapes ... When I stay in this hotel myself, I usually feel (after putting out the coal oil lamp) like sleeping with my flash light in one hand, and one ear and eye open for emergencies."[66] Six months later, they too were destroyed by fire. The proprietor of the Tudor Hotel in Toronto was chastised for dragging her heels on required improvements to fire safety, especially regarding dodgy wiring. In the winter of 1943, when she asked to be allowed to delay the renovations until spring, the board said that this was not possible. One week later, the hotel burned to the ground.[67]

Not surprisingly, given these experiences, the board spent a good deal of time addressing fire code violations. When considering applications from establishments that were built predominantly of wood, with wood or coal stoves or boilers, and often converted from previous functions, the LCBO took tremendous care to ensure that patrons would be safe. In 1931 William Dingman, then director of permits, wrote to the proprietor of the Commercial Hotel in Ottawa noting that the board was hesitant to renew its standard hotel licence

> because of fear of trouble ... yours being a wooden building of three storeys, old and inferior and crowded by another building erected along side which has closed up the windows of three bed rooms, though they are reported to have small windows high up which admit a little light, but which afford no chance for exit by means of a rope in case of fire.[68]

Six months later, an internal memo that reported on fire prevention discussions between the board, Toronto's fire marshal, and a fire prevention engineer noted that "the services of a practical man to assist the hotel inspectors is necessary, in order ... to give our hotel inspectors some training along the lines of a technical nature."[69] This may have been the impetus for hiring inspector William Hart, whose position originally straddled the LCBO and the provincial fire marshal's office.[70] Indeed, in 1936, when responding to a criticism about the inspectors not keeping a good enough watch on the activities of the St. Charles Hotel in Ottawa, Arnold Smith explained that "Inspectors of this Board are largely for the purpose of seeing that the hotels are safe from fire hazards, etc."[71] Although this statement might have been an exaggeration since the inspectors certainly spent considerable effort overseeing other aspects of the operation, it does provide a sense of how important fire inspection was to the activities of the board's inspectors.

The board's experience with fire code violators ranged from proprietors who immediately complied to those who presented persistent resistance to change. Often this resistance appeared to be due to a lack of money, but unlike in cases noted above where the issue was renovations for more aesthetic reasons, the board was generally unsympathetic to such excuses. Elias Doumani, the proprietor of the British American Hotel in Windsor, faced repeated criticism from the board over his poor management with respect to fire code provisions. When inspector Reaume reported that the various passageways in the hotel were poorly lit, suggesting that the proprietor simply needed to buy more light bulbs, William Mair, the assistant director of hotels, wrote to Doumani informing him that "under the Provisions of the Fire Accidents Act ... you, as proprietor of the above hotel, will be liable for damages should any inmate or patron of your premises suffer any accident."[72] Over the next several years, Reaume had to constantly remind the proprietor to make improvements. In 1939 the *Windsor Star* reported that, after a major fire at the Queen's Hotel in Halifax, Windsor's fire chief had insisted that his department would strictly enforce regulations. Reaume informed Smith that "the Windsor Fire Department and I have co-operated right along with reference to fire hazards in this district but there are still a few hotels who do not co-operate with us. One in particular [is] the British American Hotel."[73] Then in 1943 the fire marshal reported that he was concerned about the number of small fires that had been reported in the hotel. Since 1938, he explained, at least nine fires had occurred, possibly more, and "I have every reason to believe that two or three deliberate attempts have been made to either burn the building or create a condition of panic which would no doubt be followed by serious results." He was concerned that the hotel was similar to others across the country in which many people had died in fires.[74] An inspection by a fire prevention engineer a few days later resulted in a detailed report, with eleven recommendations for upgrades. Doumani began to make changes almost immediately.[75] Although the suspicion of arson at the British American Hotel was not typical of other hotels under the board's purview, fire prevention and safety features were a major concern and a persistent fixation of the board's inspectors.

Since concerns over fire hazards in older hotels were persistent, it is not surprising that the board's inspectors approved of "modern, fire proof" constructions. When inspector Downey reported on the new Maple Leaf Hotel in the east end of Toronto, he wrote that it was "an absolutely fire proof Hotel and was constructed in accordance with the new city by-law," and he recommended that it receive an authority.[76] In 1940 inspector Kidd noted that the Edgewater Hotel on Toronto's Roncesvalles Avenue was a "modern, fully equipped fire proof hotel ... This building is a credit to the hotel industry in the City of Toronto, being second to none in everyway other than its size."[77] When Philip Kamin proposed to build the Queensway Hotel in St. Catharines, the board was initially unwilling to grant it an authority. Kamin promised it would be a "very modern, wholly fire-proof hotel," and when it was built, inspector Vern Buchanan agreed, saying that "there is nothing as beautiful or as modern in the whole Niagara district."[78] Licensing such hotels would be a credit to the board.

The idea of modernity as a palliative for social ills is nothing new, and it was a fundamental feature of progressive thought in this period. In England the restructuring of pubs, mostly undertaken by brewers themselves, was intended to advertise the modernity and respectability of the brewery while emphasizing bourgeois refinement.[79] In Canada the urban-planning movement emphasized the modern ideas of "efficiency and scientific innovation" to alleviate class tensions.[80] These perspectives enable us to reframe the LCBO's efforts to upgrade standard hotels and its enthusiastic embrace of the "modern." Modern, updated hotel premises would be safe for the patron, respectable for the drinker, and an indication of the progressive approach of the LCBO itself.

Yet modern and fireproof hotels were not immediately granted authorities either; the calculus of need was omnipotent. Kamin's Queensway Hotel was initially denied a standard hotel licence and beer authority. Similarly, when proposals were submitted to the board for a hotel at the corner of Dundas and Roncesvalles in Toronto, the promise was that the proprietor would construct a "fire proof building" that would be "a credit to the locality." However, since the board faced considerable opposition to the creation of any authorized premises in that section of the city, the hotel was not built.[81] In 1937 the Beardmore Chamber of Commerce enthusiastically endorsed a plan by Mr. N. Rotshstein to invest heavily in the town by building what the chamber described as a "modern fireproof theatre" and a "fully modern hotel of about thirty six rooms ... You will have an idea what a building such as he plans means to this community."[82] A modern hotel (which, if the theatre was any indication, would also be fireproof) built by a wealthy landlord would secure the future of the town. The board rejected this proposal because the town already had two hotels and because, with Beardmore's economy in decline, there was no immediate need for additional hotel accommodation.

The matter of fire code and general-safety violations tested the board's insistence that its *primary* concern was the safety of the "travelling public." These violations were serious issues for the board, but were they serious enough to merit suspension of licences? While Reaume was apparently banging his head against Doumani's apathy, how did the board act to correct Doumani's behaviour? In this case, Doumani was repeatedly warned that his hotel was in violation of the rules, and the language of the letters of warning suggested that the board would penalize him, but there does not appear to have been any action. Perhaps the dark hallways were not as dire a concern as other fire code violations in other cities. In contrast, the Empress Hotel in Toronto had its authority suspended after repeatedly being told to upgrade fire escapes, fire exit signs, and extinguishers.[83] In other instances, the board did not need to exercise its punitive authority. Toronto's Victory Hotel, which was a generally well-run establishment on Bay Street, was repeatedly told to improve its fire escapes. Eventually, the city fined the proprietors for not complying with a fire marshal's order.[84]

Yet failure to suspend authorities or licences when fire regulations were not observed should not lead us to conclude that the board was simply paying lip service to the need for fire protection. What we need to remember is the purpose of a regulatory bureaucracy and the effect that suspension would have on public safety. Without a standard hotel license, an establishment fell outside of the purview of the board's work. By remaining within the board's "field of visibility," the hotel continued to be observed and its management's actions documented. Fire regulations, then, were a part of a broader regulatory system designed to reconstruct the management of a hotel premises; they were linked to the relationship between pragmatism and idealism and between centralized regulatory bureaucracy and the activities on the periphery.

Clean

The relationship between cleanliness and moral capacity has been discussed by many scholars in relation to both governmental regulatory projects and moral reform in general.[85] For the LCBO, cleanliness was an ideal but was also relative, being a matter of the context in which the hotel was situated and a variety of unique circumstances. The forms filled in by the inspectors asked many questions about cleanliness, employing both binary (yes or no) and more qualitative evaluations. Waterloo's inspector Ratz was positively ecstatic when praising the Central Hotel in Preston as "spotlessly clean, floors are exceptionly [sic] clean, to find dirt would almost be impossible, floor coverings are of the best, Bedrooms, and Beds are in perfect condition."[86] The subjective assessment of a hotel's cleanliness could be connected to the evaluation of the proprietor's ability to run the more troublesome aspects of a hotel. In 1940 Arnold Smith wrote to the proprietor of the New Port Hotel in Port Dalhousie chiding him for his lax attention to the hotel's operations. Smith's letter is worth quoting at length given the discursive connection between cleanliness and orderly behaviour:

> For some time past the board have been receiving complaints regarding the operation of the dining-room of your Hotel, and after a personal

> investigation, I am quite convinced that the complaints are warranted and the management of your dining-room is most unsatisfactory. The place is not kept clean, and we have every reason to believe that when you are not personally present in the Hotel, that liquor is being sold in your dining-room, and the general appearance of the help in your dining-room cannot be tolerated. Dirty uniforms are worn by your help, there is entirely too much familiarity among your help, wandering all through your dining-room, etc., and I must insist on you making a complete change in regard to the operation of this dining-room. The kitchen and dining-room must be thoroughly cleaned and a new and efficient staff engaged for the dining-room service.[87]

Without placing too much emphasis on the proximity of the ideas in this passage, it is worth noting what Valverde calls "slippages" between discourses.[88] One sentence mentions the dirty hotel and illegal liquor sales; the next connects dirty uniforms on staff with "familiarity," meaning overly friendly and unprofessional behaviour. The last sentence insists on a thorough cleaning of the space and on the hiring of new staff – in effect, a physical and moral cleansing of the hotel.

A hotel's cleanliness could provide a good reason for granting a licence or authority. Evaluating the Windsor Hotel in Geraldton, inspector George Skuce noted simply, and tellingly, "everything is clean and tidy but of course [it] is not a first class Hotel but I believe if he had the money he would fix it up satisfactory."[89] Inspector W.T. Nugent of the Ontario Provincial Police visited the Lakeland Hotel in Port Arthur after bad reports had been made of its operation. He contradicted these reports, calling the hotel "one of the cleanest small hotels I have ever been in ... I cannot ascertain any reason why authority should not be granted."[90] In both instances, the cleanliness was placed at the forefront as an indicator of a proprietor's competence to properly manage a licensed standard hotel.

Yet we would be wrong to see cleanliness as the sole or main determinant of the proprietor's capacity to run a good hotel and, conversely, wrong to see filthy conditions as necessarily causing a loss of authority or licence. Both effort and context were important. As noted earlier, the American Hotel in Sandwich was understandably dirty. It was located near a foundry, and the very dirtiness might be considered functional given that the workers, the hotel's main patrons, might feel less comfortable messing up a clean hotel. Also, inspector Ratz's evaluation of the Breslau Hotel's need to allow dirty truckers and farmers to eat sandwiches in the beverage room because they would mess up the clean dining room suggests that the context and the function of the hotel could affect perceptions of ideal cleanliness.[91] Essex County inspector Reaume recommended that the Dixie Hotel receive an authority "because of the amount of money that the proprietor has expended to operate it as a hotel ... However, if the license is granted I would recommend that the proprietor be asked to paint and decorate the hotel throughout as it does not present a clean appearance."[92] At this hotel, the proprietor's effort and financial outlay needed to be taken into consideration. Granting a licence would then permit him to tidy up his hotel. Clearly, cleanliness was an ideal, but the hotel's location, patronage, and other contextual factors could militate against the importance of conforming to this ideal.

Fully Functioning

A standard hotel, according to Edmond Odette in 1934, required at least "one lobby, one dining room, one kitchen, one store-room, a laundry, a sample room," bedrooms, and suitable bathroom accommodations.[93] The LCBO's own rules were much more detailed, and various local Hotelmen's Associations might add their own criteria in order to elevate the hotel to a more respectable status. But Odette's description provides a useful outline since these components presented both the necessary amenities for the benefit of the "travelling public" and an indication of the functions expected in a hotel. The mention of the sample room indicates the role of the hotel as a part of the province's commercial infrastructure since this was a place where "commercial travellers" could store and display their products.[94]

Failure to meet the basic requirements of a hotel, no matter how clean the place was kept, usually resulted either in a failure to receive a licence or in the licence's cancellation. Prior to the advent of the service of full-strength beer, when examining an applicant's hotel in Niagara Falls in 1932, the local inspector described it as "clean well furnished and apparently well conducted but lacks the necessary qualities to give it the status of a standard hotel."[95] With the creation of the LCA (1934), an examination of the hotel facilities that were not related to the beverage room provided an additional means of classifying, evaluating, and possibly rejecting a potential hotel premises. The assessment of such facilities was a way of ensuring that proprietors were running more than just a "drinking joint." Considering the attempts by the proprietor of the St. Clements Hotel in Waterloo County to bring his establishment up to the board's standards, inspector Ratz noted the importance of such amenities: "I do appreciate ... your effort to make a real hotel of the place, but it is not the desire of the board to encourage the saloon type of hotels, or to make beverage rooms all over the premises."[96] Although the board was quite aware that many hotels were being licensed mostly so that the proprietors could sell beer, the requirements of full hotel service provided a bureaucratic solution to a moral problem. By erecting a framework of rules, all of which the proprietor had to follow, the board was able to reinforce the self-governance of the individual proprietors and simultaneously, at least in theory, filter out unsuitable management. After all, to successfully manage a kitchen, dining room, and bedroom accommodations along with the beverage rooms, managers would need to demonstrate responsibility and skills well beyond those needed to sling booze. Moreover, a fully functioning hotel should not need the revenue from beer sales to remain financially viable.

For a hotel to receive a standard hotel licence, the board usually demanded a properly functioning bedroom service. Counting bedrooms was a regular component of hotel inspectors' work, especially in the first few months of the LCA (1934)'s operation. Since some aspiring beverage room operators erected flimsy walls to create bedrooms that conformed to the board's quantitative requirements, inspectors had to evaluate the quality of these rooms. Niagara inspector Wilson Wylie described the utter unsuitability of Teal's Hotel in Crystal Beach, explaining that the proprietor, a well-connected citizen of the town, was trying to circumvent the board's basic rules: "Lay out is but a cheap attempt to provide an office and Hotel rotunda. Bedrooms built of beaver board one section of which has not yet doors. There are five bedrooms in all ready and no lavatories as yet for patrons of these rooms."[97] General inspector John Pitt's description of the St. George Hotel in Ottawa illuminates a variety of aspects of hotel operations and spatial organization that the board found important:

> Poor affair ... it is poorly conducted and gives no service other than the selling of Beer, has only six rooms for guests and two of these are inside rooms [i.e., with no windows]. Do not operate the Dining room and kitchen is never used. What was the Dining room on second floor they have turned it into what they call a Grill room, but it is nothing more than a Beverage room with an Orchestra playing and Dancing goes on from nine o'clock until midnight. The only food served in this so called Grill room is a couple of soda biscuits on a plate, and the noise about the places, while dancing is going on is deafening ... in my opinion it gives no service and is not needed and these kind of places should not be encouraged as it reflects up on the Board, to a certain extent.[98]

The insubstantial number of rooms, their use exclusively for guests to drink in private, no notable dining room service, an unused kitchen, a dinner dance that had no food, and "deafening" noise: all of these features indicated that the hotel was roundly unsuitable for a hotel.

The term "poor affair" and "cheap" were often used to describe substandard hotels or potential hotels. Such language generally described working-class hotels or those that were established to accommodate itinerant labourers, especially in north-western Ontario. Yet we should not rush to conclude that shabby, working-class hotels were immediately determined to be inadequate. Although the board asserted a notion of bourgeois respectability, it was not absolute in enforcing such a class-centred ideal. Of importance, as noted earlier, were the proprietor's attempt to make the place respectable and the hotel's value in its geographic context given the characteristics of its intended patronage. Skuce's assertion that the proprietor of Geraldton's Windsor Hotel would be able to "fix it up satisfactory" if he had the money was directly related to the intended clientele in that north-western Ontario town.[99] So, although the evaluation of the ideal hotel emphasized financial capacity and implied a bourgeois notion of physical layout, we must remember that it went beyond simple categories based on financial means or the character of the patrons. The specific purposes that the hotel would serve and the proprietor's willingness to follow the board's rules were of paramount importance. When Essex County inspector Reaume reported on the persistent problems he had with the proprietor of the Highway Hotel in Windsor, he drew broad conclusions about the proprietor's unsuitability to run a standard hotel: "I believe it is impossible to have this proprietor conduct the hotel properly. He has made many promises to me but they all prove to be the same."[100] Within the year, the place changed hands.

When evaluating the suitability of a hotel for licensure, the LCBO demonstrated flexibility in deploying idealized notions of the public hotel and drinking space. It considered physical layout, geographic location, and other spatial components that contributed to the generative and dispositional rationalities of biopower. These spatial rationalities drew on idealized notions of a hotel's layout, safety, and cleanliness but were in no way wedded to them. An establishment that was safe and clean and that offered appropriate hotel facilities reflected an ideal vision of public accommodations and reinforced the board's authority as a regulatory agency. But the board was pragmatic and recognized the esoteric factors that could impede the achievement of the ideal. Its expectations were mediated by the geographic location, anticipated or actual clientele, and functional purposes of the hotel (e.g., near a market or providing accommodation for labourers), as well as by the character of the management, often demonstrated in a proprietor's efforts to follow the rules. Evaluations of the hotel from people on site, architectural drawings or pencil sketches, maps of the location and proximity to other civic institutions (e.g., churches, schools, and other hotels), and similar evidence informed the board's decisions on how best to proceed. Such evidence contextualized the assessment of the *need* for a hotel in a community. "Need" was a tremendously flexible and utilitarian concept, and its essential meaninglessness allowed it to be deployed in any way necessary. As we will see in subsequent chapters, the needs represented by spatial layout or geographic location often interacted with broader social, cultural, and political characteristics that extended well beyond the beverage room doors.

4
Hearing the Voices: Community Input and the Reshaping of Public Drinking Behaviour

Liquor licensing in Ontario had been a municipal issue for decades before prohibition. Even after the new liquor laws in the early part of the twentieth century centralized licensing administration at the provincial level, legislation recognized the rights of (enfranchised) residents of each municipality to determine whether they would permit alcoholic beverages to be sold in their area. Dominion and provincial local-option legislation provided a mechanism for determining the wetness of a community. The Liquor Control Act (LCA) preserved this system; a significant proportion of both the LCA (1927) and the LCA (1934) dealt with the mechanisms of local-option votes regarding the placement of liquor stores in the community. Moreover, after some debate and public uproar in the 1930s, the courts determined that the act would not supersede pre-prohibition local-option votes, mandated by the federal Canada Temperance Act of 1878. In 1934, prior to the election that ended his brief career as premier, George Henry promised not only that local option would be respected but also that "the new ['beer by the glass'] legislation won't affect portions of a municipality which doesn't want it, even if they are not under local option."[1] The effect of alcohol on the individual community, then, was a central concern in provincial liquor regulation.

The Liquor Control Board of Ontario (LCBO) was well aware of the importance of the community's reaction to beverage rooms. The many variables involved in the calculus of need, although often subjective, were not nearly as subjective as the most crucial factor in this calculus: the voices of the people. These voices were disparate in their perspectives: some were radically opposed to public drinking; some were wholeheartedly in favour; some thought a well-run beverage room could be a boon; and some argued that, although they were not opposed to drinking, the specific place in question or the management was not adequate to carry out the job. In the calculus of need, the input from the public was the most variable variable of all.

This chapter looks at the many ways that community voices affected the work of the LCBO. Here, the term "community" indicates both the people who lived near the proposed authorized premises and those who might represent them. The term "voices" refers to the various forms of communication that reached the LCBO – including letters, petitions, and in-person meetings, which were the three main ways of expressing concern – as well as the way the community's issues were represented in the press. Looking at how they "affected" the board's work includes considering direct influences on LCBO decisions and how they may have effected a change in the LCBO's broader regulatory behaviour, including written or unwritten policies. Since almost every beverage room application was accompanied by some form of community feedback, several examples from the broader application process reveal the intricacies of the relationship between the central administration and local interests. Ultimately, however, although local perspectives provided essential information, final decisions were shaped by the dominant bureaucratic vision of a respectable and orderly system of public drinking in the province.

Community Reaction to Beverage Room Applications

It was difficult to disguise a hotel proprietor's attempts to have their establishment authorized. Along with the application (which was a notarized public document), the three letters of reference sent to the board would make the application process public or at least semi-public knowledge. In most municipalities, significant physical alterations to the building required application to the local government, a process that would make any changes a matter of public record. Moreover, renovations would be obvious to the neighbours. Finally, the inspector was often a familiar figure in the community. Even in a place like Toronto, the inspector's visit would be noted by vigilant observers. And the Drys were nothing if not vigilant. Many of the opponents of beverage rooms were well organized and familiar with the board's system, and they kept an eye out and an ear to the ground for new beverage room applications. At the same time, proprietors who faced opposition to their application from the neighbourhood could also muster their own support.

Although it would be easiest to characterize the debates around the creation of beverage rooms as pitting the Wets against the Drys, such a sharp dichotomy would not accurately portray the cast of players involved in the beverage room drama. It is more appropriate to see reactions to a new beverage room on a spectrum from bone-dry temperance forces who felt that alcohol was the great social destroyer to libertarians who felt that the Liquor Control Board was too restrictive in its enforcement and that liquor sales should be wide open. Many people sat between these extremes, moderately concerned about the types of businesses being established in their neighbourhoods but not diehard prohibitionists. Insisting that they were not "temperance cranks," many correspondents to the board claimed that they enjoyed a beer as much as most people and that they had problems only with the activities in a certain establishment or were troubled by the impact of a new hotel on the character of their neighbourhood.

The variety of community voices could result in a complex and conflicted situation in the local context, and several examples help to illustrate some of the major themes. Consider what happened to Olga Sandell, manager of St. Catharines' Rosdol Inn. In 1936 she wrote the LCBO an eloquent letter in precise script on expensive blue paper explaining her reasoning for applying for a beer and wine authority:

> At the time of taking possession of this Inn, it was not my intention to even think of the Beverage end of it, but, I have found through folks coming in – perfectly satisfied with the delightful surroundings, and the excellent cuisine offered – they would have to be referred to a Hotel where they could be served with beer and wine – thus losing their patronage.

She described her hotel as "a beautifully located and a perfectly operated Inn for accommodation of twenty-four guests, in our most luxuriously furnished rooms catering to the most fastidious of clientele, and I wish to apply for a license to sell Beer and Wine, in bottles, to accomodate [sic] such a class of trade."[2] She presented her hotel as respectable and her interest in having beer and wine as simply incidental to the operation of a well-run hotel. It was near the downtown, in the former mansion of city founder William Hamilton Merritt, and adjacent to Highway 8, one of the main routes through the region. It was also at the edge of one of the most affluent residential sections of the city.

Immediately on hearing of the application, dozens of community groups wrote in protest. The Local Council of Women forwarded to the LCBO a package of letters from various social and church groups (see Table 1). These correspondents generally expressed traditional temperance sentiments when faced with the prospect of a drinking establishment, drawing on the metaphors of the saloon. Isabel Irvines of the Graduate Nurses Association wrote that she and her colleagues were opposed, "first, because it is a place where young people go for their parties and because of its nearness to two of our parks and intoxicated men or women loitering in these parks would be very objectionable to rate payers of this city of ours."[3] The secretary of a local Young Women's Mission Society wrote that "the privileges of dispensing liquor ... would be a temptation and would doubtless be taken advantage of by thoughtless young people."[4] The Local Council of Women took these

Table 1

Organizations that wrote to oppose the Rosdol Inn application	
Carry-on Bible Class of St. Paul Street United Church	Undated
Women's Association of St. Paul Street United Church	Undated
City Mission	16 June 1937
Women's Missionary Society of the First United Church	16 June 1937
St. Catharines Ministerial Alliance	17 June 1937
Women's Missionary Society of St. Paul Street United Church	17 June 1937
Woman's Christian Temperance Union	17 June 1937
St. Paul Street United Church Men's and Women's Bible Class	17 June 1937
Protestant Women's Federation	18 June 1937
Ladies Aid Society of Queen Street Baptist Church	18 June 1937
Women's Missionary Society of the Welland Avenue United Church	18 June 1937
Woman's Association of Welland Avenue United Church	18 June 1937
Women's Association of First United Church	18 June 1937
Women's Missionary Society of Westminster United Church	18 June 1937
Memorial Woman's Association	18 June 1937
Graduate Nurses Association	19 June 1937
Young Women's Mission Circle of the Queen Street Baptist Church	19 June 1937
The Honorary Chair Club	19 June 1937
Official Board of the Welland Avenue United Church	20 June 1937
Welland Avenue United Church	20 June 1937
Welland Avenue Men's Club	20 June 1937
Memorial Women's Missionary Auxiliary	21 June 1937
Golden Rule Class of Queen Street Baptist Church	21 June 1937

Source: Archives of Ontario, Liquor License Board of Ontario, Standard Hotel Case Files, AO, RG 36-1-0-622.

letters to the city council, claiming to represent twenty-three organizations, all opposed to an authority for the Rosdol and opposed to any further authorities in the city.

In spite of this opposition, the Rosdol received an authority. The board did not outline its reasons for granting authorities, but we can see two main factors driving this decision. First, the Rosdol application had support from powerful community members, including the chief of police; a manager of a local bank; Archie Haines, the local Liberal Association president and a future member of the provincial Legislative Assembly (MLA); Frederick Avery, the local MLA and a former mayor; and A.S. Goxing, an alderman, who said that Sandell, "by her clean high class and corteous [sic] services to the public in general has received great favourable comment ... I therefore not only on the half of myself but the public in general, reccommend [sic] her to the board and all consideration you extend to her you can feel assured will be mutually appreciated."[5] Moreover, the city council voted to support the application. Second, we can speculate that the LCBO saw Sandell's hotel as representing the sort of establishment that it wanted to see in Ontario. Sandell was respectable, her hotel was first-rate, and she clearly put the bedroom accommodation and dining business ahead of any need to sell more beer. The Rosdol had the potential to be a signature standard hotel. In the end, however, the temperance forces won the day. Although the application was approved, within a year the hotel closed due to a severe decline in patronage. It appears that the respectable, middle-class locals, the Rosdol's customers, abandoned the business.

As the Rosdol Inn case demonstrates, opposition from the highly mobilized evangelical Christian groups could be devastating. Often these evangelical organizations worked together to protest a proposed new beverage room. And they terrified local politicians. When Niagara Falls' Elliott Hotel applied for an authority in May 1935, it resulted in a telegraph to the board registering protest because the hotel would be "within one hundred and twenty five yards of our church and Sunday school."[6] The local MLA, William Houck, explained that "it would be suicide to issue this man a permit."[7] The Ormond Hotel in Thorold saw similar protests from a church that MLA E.J. Anderson explained was approximately five hundred feet from the hotel, a distance, Anderson contended, that did not justify the church's claims that the hotel was too close.[8] The Finnish Pentecostal Church in Port Arthur protested the application of the Royal Canadian Legion Hall, which was situated right across the street, saying "a hall opposite a church is bad enough influence as it is."[9] The calculus of need factored proximity into the equation.

Other protests included a good dose of xenophobia, reflecting concerns more generally about the impact of an authorized hotel on a small town. For example, when the hotel in the town of Bloomingdale, near Kitchener, applied for an authority in 1935, a local minister, on the suggestion of the inspector, petitioned the area and found that only two people supported the authority, six were neutral, and thirty-four opposed it. He argued that "we fear the consequences of such a place where lawlessness can prevail as a subidsay [sic] to the Kitchener debauchees. There are greater temptations to lawlessness in a rural place."[10] The fear of the transplantation of big city "debauchees" was combined with the classic temperance metaphor of the tavern as a centre of immorality. A letter thanking the board for cancelling the authority of the Dorking Hotel, at the northwest corner of Waterloo County, noted that "it was just a place for the young girls and boys to come here from nearby towns that wouldn't accommodate them at home."[11] The board's decision may have been influenced by the fact that Dorking was a small town far enough from larger centres to be difficult for police or inspectors to visit regularly.

Although the board received complaints about authority applications from churches in communities across the province, nothing compared to the level of vigour of the evangelical groups in the provincial capital. In Toronto, church protests were practically a routine feature of a hotel application. Here, the evangelical opposition was well organized and appears to have been well financed. For example, when petitions arrived at the LCBO offices in opposition to the application by the proprietor of the Royal Arms Hotel on Jones Avenue in east Toronto, they were on dozens of pages of professionally printed forms (with the declaration against the proposal printed at the top), rather than on handwritten petition forms, which were more frequently received.[12] The petition was about two centimetres thick, which amounted to hundreds, if not thousands, of names. Likewise, the signatures on the petition against the Royal Hotel on Danforth Avenue, according to the letter that accompanied it, totalled 2,197 names. The Danforth Avenue area of Toronto had several hotel applications that faced serious opposition. This residential district was home to several churches that banded together to voice their opposition. Other parts of Toronto where a strong evangelical temperance opposition arose against new hotel propositions included Bloor Street just west of Yonge Street, the Parkdale area, and Roncesvalles Avenue.

The rhetoric in the protests across the province was typical of evangelical temperance arguments against beverage alcohol. A letter form the Clerk of Ottawa's Parkdale United Church protesting the authority of the Carleton Hotel noted its proximity to churches, schools, and a hospital, claiming "you will therefore see the environment in which this moral menace is proposed to operate."[13] The secretary and president of the Church of the Nazarene in Toronto pulled no punches in manifesting the sensational temperance imagery of the drinking place:

> With young men and women fast becoming drunkards (since the existence of the Beverage rooms) mothers coming to our workers, with breaking hearts as they tell of the breaking of happy homes through the cursed drink and little children living in poverty in homes once comfortable, but now robbed of that comfort by parents who are pawning the very furnishings of their homes to buy BEER, these and other evils compel us in the name of Him who has said "In as much as ye have done it until one of the least of my little ones, ye have done it unto me" seek this favour from your hands.[14]

Similarly, C.D. Farquharson of Windsor's Westminster United Church claimed that the Driving Park Inn was near four churches, two public schools, and a Catholic school. Instead of launching "a vigorous campaign" against the hotel, he decided first "to write you and ask if you will not rid us of this outrageous and evil thing at once."[15] A correspondent from Dunnville, at the southwest corner of the Niagara region, informed the board that "every evening small children are seen waiting in the Queen's Hotel ... for parents who are drinking."[16] The safety of children, the integrity of the family, and the uplift of society were central tropes in temperance rhetoric, and they were constantly reiterated in letters to the LCBO.

The passion of evangelical churches was supported by the work of the Ontario Temperance Federation, notably its general secretary, A.J. Irwin. Irwin, the author of *Alcohol: A Brief Manual for Teachers and Young People* (1930), was a professional temperance advocate. He corresponded with a variety of politicians and leaders throughout the country, and his opinions were often sought by dry newspapers. Irwin wrote many letters to the LCBO, discussing in clear and respectful prose any number of issues ranging from violations of the Liquor Control Act, which were stated as matters of law, to specific issues relating to the placement of a beverage room in a specific neighbourhood. His correspondence to the LCBO was often in response to complaints and rumours he had received about the activities in hotels throughout the province. For example, in a letter of June 1935 to the attorney general (who forwarded the letter to the LCBO), Irwin claimed that the LCA was being violated by the New Statler Hotel in St. Catharines: "Recently ... the information came to me from a credible source that in connection with the equipping of the [New] Statler Hotel in St. Catharines the bill for supplies ... was o.k.'d by an official or prominent employee of Taylor and Bates Brewery." Citing the relevant sections of the LCA prohibiting beverage room proprietors from taking donations from breweries, he reiterated his concern: "You will of course be aware that the matter of interest on the part of brewers and distillers in liquor-selling establishments, exercises a very vicious influence on the conduct of the trade."[17] Such law-breaking would lead to moral decline. In a letter of December 1934, Irwin claimed that the proprietor of Waterloo County's Hespeler Hotel was attempting to evade the board's rules requiring meals to be purchased by people who were dancing in the dining room.[18]

Although motivated by evangelical Christian principles, Irwin often couched his arguments in a number of competing discourses of social order. Consider his letter to the board in September 1934 regarding a proposed hotel on Bloor Street in Toronto:

> It is in close proximity to two very large schools and to several churches. It is in such relationship to valuable property that it is bound to damage the

> values very materially. It is on a line of very heavy road traffic and the parking which would likely attend it will add seriously to the congestion of the situation. It cannot be held that there is any need of additional accommodation for travelers in the vicinity; there are other hotels and other means of accommodation within easy reach if such were necessary so that the institution would resolve itself primarily into a beer saloon which would be a menace to the youth and a serious deterioration to the whole neighbourhood.[19]

Although concerned mostly with morality and legality, Irwin touched on issues of the impact of drinking on property values, traffic, and general public safety. Elsewhere, he drew on his impression of the will of Ontarians when he lectured the LCBO on how it should be approaching the touchy issue of beverage room licensure:

> I think it is fair to say that what was in the minds of the people in the Province of Ontario in the last election was that the ordinary standard hotel would get authorities, and while the Act included restaurants and other places, the public did not anticipate the widespread extension of the privilege beyond the existing standard hotels. The granting of authorities to a large number of additional premises where hotels have never been, or have not been for nearly a generation; where the accommodation is questionable, where there is no need for entertainment of travelers, and where the obvious reason for the esistence [sic] of an authority is primarily for the sale of beer is contrary to the intention of the people of the province and will involve repercussions that will not be to the advantage of the Government.[20]

The logical structure and reasoned arguments of Irwin's letters presented a contrast to the often impassioned and reactionary letters received from other opponents of beverage rooms.

Although the most vocal, the evangelical temperance organizations were not alone in protesting the creation of beverage rooms. Each community under examination had its own unique character, something that is clear in the opposition to beverage rooms. In Ottawa a number of hotels faced opposition not from evangelical Christians but from members of the Catholic Church. The Ambassador Hotel was close to the Rideau Street Convent, and the Baxter Hotel was one block from the Convent of St. François d'Assise, both of which opposed an authorized hotel near their premises. The Baxter Hotel's application was protested by parents whose children attended the school attached to St. François. We have already seen how, in Waterloo County's rural communities of Dorking and Bloomingdale, the concern was representative of a rural-urban tension. In the Thunder Bay district, concern about the combination of alcohol and unmarried labouring men in the mining and lumber industry or among those working on the construction of the Trans-Canada Highway often resulted in questions of who would run licensed hotels. The comptroller of the Brompton Pulp and Paper Mill opposed the application by the proprietor of a local hotel in Red Rock, arguing that "it would be detrimental to the best interests of our employees if he is granted this license as we should have no control over the hours during which beer would be sold on these premises." He said that the company would prefer to operate its own hotel since one that is owned by someone independent of the company "might well not be good for the community which we are endeavouring to build up."[21]

Many correspondents expressed their concern about what the hotel would do to the character of the neighbourhood. The town council of Riverside, near Windsor, sent a letter to oppose the licensing of the St. Clair Hotel. The letter explained that, although the town had several prominent dance pavilions and licensed hotels that catered to tourists, the street on which the St. Clair Hotel was located had been zoned residential. In Toronto the Bloor District Businessmen's Association opposed the creation of a hotel in the Dovercourt area, explaining that "the small merchants feel that if another Hotel is allowed in this section it will mean the drying-up of purchasing power for necessaries."[22] A nearby resident explained that such a hotel would be a "menace and depreciate the value of my property."[23] The application to create the Rosedale Hotel in Ottawa East triggered three petitions from residents, amounting to over fifty pages of signatures. The argument of the petition was simple: "We the undersigned, believing that it would be detrimental to this residential community to have such a beverage room, respectfully request that no such authority be granted."[24] In most of this correspondence, whether it was from evangelical temperance organizations, business people, or private individuals, the dominant discourse was characterized by intertwining concerns about social order and respectability and motivated by a clear understanding of the community's rights to oppose such an imposition.

Compared to the well-organized temperance voices, the Wets were less homogeneous yet similarly spoke a language of social order and respectability. For many, a neighbourhood beverage room would be a boon to the community because it would discourage the patronizing of illegal drinking places, or "blind pigs." Others argued from a point of view of fairness to the hotel proprietor or to the local residents. When the proprietor of the Royal Arms Hotel was denied an authority, a local resident wrote to argue against this decision: "I find myself in the position now like a good many more of having to pay transportation to give myself the priviledge [sic] of having a glass of beer."[25] The proprietor polled the neighbourhood and found a majority in favour of the authority.[26] But these appeals were unsuccessful, and the hotel did not receive an authority. The nearby Stafford Hotel was more fortunate. One resident wrote in October 1934 that as long as the hotel was run properly, there should be no reason not to grant the authority, adding, "we in this section of Danforth should have the privilege of refreshments in our own neighbourhood."[27] A week later, another correspondent made the same point, arguing that he and his neighbours felt it was not fair that they had to travel so far to have a beer or that "I have to get off ... the streetcar to get a glass of beer and then pay another car far[e] to get to my home." This correspondent also criticized Irwin's tactics: "He will not take [a petition] from door to door, but just to those he knows are always against [liquor]."[28] The Stafford Hotel's authority was granted.

Outside of Toronto, voices supporting beverage rooms presented similar arguments combining the rights of the residents and the respectability of the hotel proprietor. When the Log Cabin Hotel in Belle River, Essex County, lost its authority in 1936, the town council wrote in protest, calling the hotel "the best building in the village, as well as a very respectable place for the citizens to frequent."[29] This authority was not renewed, the board explained, due to poor hotel management and the existence of enough authorized establishments in the area.[30] When the Dorking Hotel was denied an authority, the proprietor forwarded a petition in support of his application, alluding to the potential problems that not having an authority would create in the neighbourhood:

> Instead of having to go to a bootlegger to buy their beer these people would come to me. These people are practically all law abiding citizens but they will not drive for 8 or 12 or 15 miles to get a drink of beer when they can get it from a bootlegger by just driving one mile or in some cases to the next neighbor for a drink of beer at the same price as a hotel keeper sells it. Not only that this country is infested with bootleggers and as far as I know their [sic] is only one or two in this locality against us having a hotel here.[31]

As with many of the other examples here, this petition's entreaties fell on deaf ears. The Dorking Hotel did not receive its authority. In 1929 Peter Schummer, a clerk of Wellesley Township, described the St. Clements Hotel as a place where

> people are waited upon with good meals and we are told by the travelers that they appreciate it very much to come here now ... I might say that I haven't seen a drunk person around the hotel since the last five years and if people should be seen in that case they get it from the bootleggers and probably the hotel-keeper is blamed for it when he is entirely innocent. Stop the bootleggers and you'll see no drunkards.[32]

After the new LCA came into effect, and the hotel lost its authority, Schummer's son wrote to explain that "it is our right in this village to demand a beer priveledge [sic] ... 90 percent of the people here want to see [the authority] reinstated."[33] The hotel's authority was reissued a few days later.

Although petitions in support of a hotel were the exception rather than the rule in the southern part of the province, in the Thunder Bay district, many communities petitioned for hotels to receive authorities. As with the Dorking Hotel's application, many correspondents argued that to deny authorities to decent hotels was to encourage bootlegging and other social problems. Merchants in Savant Lake urged the LCBO to grant an authority to the Savant Hotel, explaining that they could get a petition if necessary: "Everyone wants a beverage room in preference to all these bootleggers."[34] Two petitions came from Dorion, signed by 176 people, with the observation that "if our Community is to be deprived of a legitimate system of sale, 'bootlegging' will again make its appearance."[35] A letter accompanying a petition in support of the Loon Lake Hotel in Loon Lake noted that there were over three thousand people with cottages on the lake and that without an authorized premises they would have to drive to Port Arthur; it predicted that this drinking "might not be to the same excess if there was available within a reasonable distance some place where moderate drinking could take place."[36] Petitions also arrived from Beardmore, Nipigon, and Nakina, all supporting hotel authorities. The common thread in these petitions was that to deny such authorities was to encourage bootlegging, whereas to authorize hotels run by respectable individuals was to encourage moderation and social order.

Dry voices expressed concern about the moral impact of a beverage room on their communities, whereas the supporters of beverage rooms were often focused on the positive impact of the hotel on the community. The petitions from communities in the Thunder Bay district are indicative of this rhetoric, arguing that an authorized hotel was much more desirable than a "blind pig" or purchasing from a bootlegger. Government officials were often also concerned with the financial impact of a hotel on the community. When protesting the suspension of the Log Cabin Hotel's licence, the town council of Belle River (Essex County) claimed that the proprietor "pays very heavy taxes and we feel he should have some sort of revenue."[37] Farther down the Detroit River, the council of Sandwich West protested the LCBO's decision not to renew the authority at the lively Elmwood Hotel, noting that the Elmwood was a source of considerable revenue for the town.[38] The MLA for Ottawa wrote to protest the board's decision not to allow dancing on the LaSalle Hotel's new rooftop patio. He based his argument on fairness, claiming that the local inspector had promised that once the patio was built dancing would be permitted, but also on financial considerations. Denied a place to dance in Ottawa, patrons would "cross over to Hull where the money they spend is lost to Ontario citizens and [to] the Ontario government in the form of greater revenue."[39]

When considering such requests, local inspectors often prioritized the function of a hotel in the community over its revenue-generating potential. Premises that might have seemed, on the surface, to be unlikely to receive special treatment were viewed favourably when found to serve a special need in the social fabric of the neighbourhood. Port Arthur's Kimberly Hotel was not the best place around, but inspector George Skuce reported in February 1936 that "the Salvation Army captain told me today he didn't know what they would do without [the hotel's proprietor] for during the cold winter he has a big pot of soup on [the] stove every night for those who want it."[40] Inspector Norman Ratz observed that the proprietor of the Embassy Hotel in St. Agatha should be allowed to have banquets with card playing since "the country villages ought to have a place for recreation to improve rural conditions."[41] The combination of respectability of the proprietor and social order was the central theme in H.B. Arkell's letter to Premier Mitchell Hepburn that supported the application of the Ambassador Hotel in Ottawa. Arkell claimed to be an opponent of the LCA, but he nevertheless supported the proprietors' application:

> Most of use who are opponents of the existing legislation cannot but wish it administered to a manner that will best suit the highest interests of the people. It is on this basis that I desire to present the matter for your further consideration ... [The proprietors are] two men whose integrity and character will ensure that, if the License is granted, this hotel will be managed under the law as a reputable and respectable institution.[42]

Arkell's argument, presented in the language of respectability and social order, appealed to the board's need to encourage reputable and well-managed hotel operations. All of these hotels remained in operation.

Although the supporters of beverage rooms were not organized like the temperance forces, there was one wet voice that caught the board's attention: the Moderation League. As noted in Chapter 2, the league had been active in Canada since 1919, first lobbying to end prohibition and then attempting to convince the government to bring back "beer by the glass" legislation. Unlike Irwin of the Temperance Federation, after the passage of the LCA (1934), the Moderation League in Ontario seems to have confined its actions mostly to Toronto, at least among the six communities studied here. The league's work in Toronto was extensive; it spoke the language of respectability and was dedicated to ensuring orderly beverage rooms as a way of alleviating the criticisms of temperance organizations. In August 1935 H.S. Pritchard, executive secretary of the league, wrote a letter to chief commissioner

Edmond Odette in which Pritchard stated the league's allied interest in the work of the Liquor Control Board. He explained that the league's work dated back to 1921 and that it was concerned that a petition had been circulating in Toronto demanding a plebiscite on the issue of continuing the sale of beer and wine in authorized hotels.[43] Pritchard explained that in the Moderation League's view, its work now lay in making sure that authorities are "not granted to improper or incompetent persons or organizations," and authorized hotels and clubs are not "conducted in improper or inadequate premises or improperly conducted."[44] He explained that the work would be carried out in Toronto and in those places "so immediately adjacent thereto as to affect the vote in the City of Toronto."[45]

Subsequently, the league's members acted as a sort of shadow inspectorate, reporting to the board on the types of unsavoury activities taking place in specific hotels throughout the city. These reports were far more detailed than most inspectors' reports and covered a range of issues relating to the overall operation of a hotel. They were often organized into three sections: "Conduct of Hotel"; "Condition of Premises"; and "Our Comments," which gave an overall impression of the place. For example, commenting on the Commerce Hotel on Danforth Avenue, the league's inspector wrote,

> [Food] of indifferent boarding house quality ... No liquor is served ... those who inquire for it are referred to "Frankie Bull" ... Handbooking is in effect on the premises, through the head barman, through the waiters ... Furnishings are cheap ... Hustlers patronize the place, apparently working on their own ... The general sense of the investigation is that the house is a poor specimen of what one expects of a city hotel and is obviously run as a tavern ... Investigator who stayed at the hotel says it was noisy all night ... Premises are reasonably well kept ... [Proprietress] seems very industrious and is on the job to the best of her ability but has little or no idea of what is demanded in operating a hotel ... General: It is our observation that these are make-shift premises which do not cast any credit upon the operation of the industry in the City; in the hands of improper personnel, which reflects itself in the operation of the premises to the discredit of the industry.[46]

In another report in January 1937, the league complained that the Alexandra Hotel, a notoriously bad establishment on Queen Street West, was being operated "more or less in the manner of a common brothal [sic]."[47]

Despite writing collegial and respectful reports to the board, the league was clearly not an ally of the LCBO. The subtext of these letters was that the board was not doing enough to make sure that acceptable premises were being operated in the city. In a three-page report on the Nealon Hotel, on King Street in the city core, Pritchard concluded,

> We are firmly determined that the existence of such places shall not contribute to the [anti-alcohol] plebiscite ... or affect the result of one, if held. Therefore, we are not marking this communication confidential. We ... reserve the right to make its contents known to the press of the City in the event his place is not made a standard hotel and conducted as such in the hands of proper personnel competent to do it.[48]

The Moderation League's interest was fundamentally bourgeois, presenting a discourse of respectability that required constant vigilance over the more troublesome elements of society. As I noted in Chapter 2, and as Craig Heron has also discussed, the expectations of the more elite Moderation League members often clashed with the conditions and interests of working-class drinkers.[49]

The league got the board's attention. Immediately on receiving the report on the Nealon Hotel, Arnold Smith made a personal inspection. He found several "irregularities," notably the limited menu of the hotel's dining room and the restricted number of bedrooms in operation. He suspended the authority on 1 October 1935, pending attention to a list of problems. Two days later, in an internal memo to William Mair, the assistant director of hotels, Smith explained that the changes had been made, and he reinstated the authority. When he wrote to the Moderation League, he explained that his inspection contradicted the league's report on almost every point, from the conduct of patrons to the number of storeys in the building. Nevertheless, after these problems were addressed, he explained, "I feel quite confident that there will be no more trouble in connection with this Authority." His confidence was possibly naive, as the hotel continued to be a trouble spot. Notable here is that it was the Moderation League's letter that made the board jump.[50]

The reaction to the Moderation League's reports is intriguing and can be interpreted several ways. Since the hotel inspector was usually known to the hotel manager, having someone like an anonymous Moderation League member visit a hotel during the busy period could give the board valuable insight into the operations of troublesome hotels. The board itself routinely ordered inspectors from one district to visit and comment on the hotels in another district, often with very fruitful results. Yet at the same time, Smith's reaction to the report on the Nealon Hotel suggests that, although the Moderation League's reports were insightful, Smith was not willing to consider the idea that an independent body could do a better job at inspecting the hotels than the board's own members. Such a possibility would contradict fundamental values of bureaucracy, which needs to imbue in operatives on the periphery the authority to function semi-independently while simultaneously following the directives of the central administration. To begin to react to the impetus of an external body, regardless of its professed allegiance with the board's own mandate, would be to undermine the board's authority.

Thus the reaction to the Moderation League's reports was consistent with the board's operations and converged with its political bureaucratic priorities. A key aspect of a bureaucracy's operations is the need to preserve the integrity of the organization itself. This could be achieved in a number of ways. In the LCBO's case, there were two key political considerations that had to be addressed. The first was the need to avoid offending its political masters. The second, which I will consider briefly here and which is a central theme in this book, was the need to appear to be effective, objective arbiters of social order. In other words, the board was persistently preoccupied with making sure that its operations both had the approval of the public and appeared to be effective.

A poorly run hotel could reflect badly on the board's image as an effective control agency. When inspector John Pitt investigated the German Inn in East Windsor, which had been granted an authority in July 1934 but likely without an inspection, he urged the board to cancel both the Standard Hotel licence and the beer authority because "everyone [is] laughing at it."[51] When the Ambassador Hotel in Ottawa applied for an authority, inspector Alfred Larocque warned the board that it was a touchy local issue: "We have stepted [sic] into a hornet's nest ... some of the objectors expressed to me in no uncertain way their determination to cretesize [sic] the Board openly in the Press, if that Authority was granted."[52] When inspector George Hanrahan visited the notoriously rough Royal Cecil in Toronto, he concluded his damning report with the observation, "I cannot too pointedly emphasize this; A well meaning public would be quite justified in a severe criticism of it."[53] Similarly, correspondents from outside the board suggested that a hotel's bad image damaged the board's reputation. One writer attacked the authorities granted to several establishments in Windsor, saying that they "simply make the Liquor Control Board look ridiculous ... If authorities are restricted to bona fide hotel premises owned and operated by reputable Canadians the public will respect the administration. If not – blooey!"[54] Niagara Falls MLA William Houck wrote to the board to ask that it consider cancelling the authority of that city's Arlington Hotel, explaining the political interest of him and the board: "Such places as this man is running are certainly a detriment, not only to myself, but to the Liquor Control Board."[55] In these views, if the board let such establishments continue, it risked being seen as an ineffective regulatory agency.

Letters of Complaint and Community Surveillance

Much of the tension around the granting of beverage room authorities demonstrates how contentious liquor was in the post-prohibition period. Drinking and especially the availability of public drinking spaces were political hot-button issues and continued to be sources of major social tension. The creation and licensing of a hotel engendered tremendous pressure on the Liquor Control Board to act according to the will of the people. In these cases, the board had to weigh a variety of issues, from the suitability of the proprietor and premises to the broader social conditions of the neighbourhood, the amenability of the surrounding community, and broader political factors, including the impact on and input of municipal politicians and the impact on the profile of the board itself and on the government of the day. Once the hotel was licensed and the furor eased, the board had to address daily complaints and observations from the general public regarding the operations of authorized premises.

Indeed, complaints from the public were essential to the LCBO's work; anonymous public eyes saw much more than the official gaze of the government. Actively seeking or simply receiving input from neighbours was not an unusual aspect of regulatory administration. As both Margaret Little and Xiaobei Chen have demonstrated, provincial government agencies relied on such surreptitious and often anonymous surveillance.[56] Much information, like that presented by the Moderation League, was framed as detailed and respectable advice and operated as a sort of second level of surveillance for the board. In most communities, the board's inspectors had many hotels under their purview and certainly could not visit every hotel every night to make an inspection (nor could the police). Although the inspector was expected to submit his "Authority Holder's Conduct Report" (AHCR) on a monthly basis, the details were often sketchy, and some inspectors were unable to provide the level of complexity the reports required; the inspectors in Toronto appear to have been overwhelmed and at times submitted one AHCR that supposedly represented several visits over the span of a number of weeks or even months. Other inspectors, especially George Skuce in the Thunder Bay district, had trouble reaching all of the communities in his jurisdiction. With this workload, the input of the public could be a welcome support to the board's own oversight.

Yet there were significant bureaucratic and administrative challenges to the information provided by the public. As with the work of the Moderation League, before the information provided by correspondents could be acted on, it needed to be verified by board staff. Even when the board asked local police detachments to investigate a hotel, inspectors often had to follow up on the reports with a visit to the hotel premises or even to the residences of correspondents. Part of the problem was that many of these complaints were simply false. When the board received a letter of complaint at the main office, most of the time a letter was dispatched immediately to the local inspector, with a copy of the complaint, asking him to investigate. If the complaint was signed, the inspector would attempt to contact the correspondent and discuss the details of the letter. If the letter was unsigned or signed anonymously, the inspector would usually do his own inspection of the premises, meet with the hotel proprietor, and try to figure out whether the complaint was valid. In many, if not most, cases, the letter was determined to be false or at least seriously exaggerated. Responding to such a letter, Essex County inspector U.G. Reaume argued to Smith that "any one writing a letter of complaint who is not manly enough to sign his own name is not worthy of consideration,"[57] yet he still investigated its contents. In every case, the inspector had to write back to the central office to explain the situation and recommend the sort of action that needed to be taken. So the additional eyes, while supplementing the board's capacity for surveillance, also increased the workload of the inspector.

The importance of social norms and social order is threaded through those letters in which the correspondents recognized that the LCBO had to be aware of the scrutiny of the public, or more particularly, the public press. Numerous letter writers, with valid or invalid complaints, threatened to take their grievances to the press if they did not see some sort of action. Some were quite vehement; an anonymous correspondent who claimed to be "A member of the Methodist Church" complained that the manager of the Venetian Hotel in Niagara Falls was a bootlegger and was serving to minors and that if "I do not see any change I shall publish it in the Mail and Empire" – interestingly, a wet newspaper but politically Conservative.[58] A correspondent named "Fed Up" complained that Windsor's Schramek Hotel was "a dirty hell hole," accused the board of being in the pocket of James Clark, the local MLA, who was a notorious defender of the wet interest, and threatened to write letters to the Detroit, Windsor, and London newspapers.[59] A letter listing a series of inflammatory charges about the Austin Hotel in Port Dalhousie threatened that "if the board can not do something about this place, maybe we can all get together and get the newspapers to help us."[60] Inspector Joseph Cheeseman found that the hotel was run admirably and that this letter was most likely written by a rival hotel owner.[61] Nevertheless, in each case, regardless of how inflammatory the letter's contents, the board sent out inspectors to investigate.

These complaints, charging the LCBO with being biased, partisan, or simply incompetent, resulted in actions that reinforce the impression that the LCBO worked to minimize criticism as a way of bolstering its own authority. Avoiding criticism, or at least reducing it, was central to the LCBO's regulatory activities: only a board with inscrutable authority could enforce standards of respectable behaviour. So when in 1936 the board faced condemnation in St. Catharines over its decision to grant an authority based on the recommendation of the local MLA, its need to protect its own authority trumped partisan politics. The MLA, Frederick Avery, had initially approved of Marck's Hotel on Queenston Street, but when the community in the area launched a protest against that hotel, Avery flip-flopped. Exasperated, Smith wrote to Avery explaining the dilemma the board faced:

> As pointed out to you in the very beginning, it makes it very awkward, as I have to acknowledge these various protests, and when at heart, I feel that they are expressing my own view, it makes it doubly hard, and I imagine before this thing is through, there is going to be plenty of trouble, and many deputations registering protests, and as it is not the policy to mention anything about your desire in the matter, perhaps you can offset things by notifying these people who are likely to protest that you are anxious for the Hotel, and in that way, it might prevent some of the protests coming to this office, as I certainly feel there are going to be plenty of them.[62]

Although the board was not allowed to mention publicly when it was acting on the wishes of a politician, Smith felt that the board faced too much pressure as a result of what he determined to be this member's capriciousness. He cleverly (yet unsuccessfully) asked Avery to show his own hand in order to place the blame on the politician's head and thus save the LCBO from an excessive degree of criticism.

Here, then, we see connections between the functional mechanics of a government agency and its bureaucratic political reality. The LCBO needed to establish, as best it could, an orderly or at least not overly disorderly public-drinking system that subjected the citizen-drinker to the oversight of government administration and necessarily struck a balance between being overly restrictive and overly permissive. It required the input from the community to help it to determine the parameters of acceptable enforcement. So to achieve its basic goals, the board needed to consider what the community wanted and what it could tolerate. Thus community voices provided the board with information about how it could continue to legitimize itself. Avoiding criticism was important, but in a complex society, especially in urban areas, with a collection of competing interests and conflicting perspectives on order and disorder, morality and immorality, right and wrong, the board's administrators could not please everyone. At times, they could work only to minimize the extent of criticism. The following case study, in which the demands of the community and the mandate of the board were in direct contradiction, vividly illustrates the hills, valleys, forests, and fields of the political landscape that the LCBO had to navigate.

Mass Community Protest in Toronto

As noted earlier, in Toronto, agitation against hotel beverage rooms could be excessive, as impassioned and, dare we say, intemperate as one could

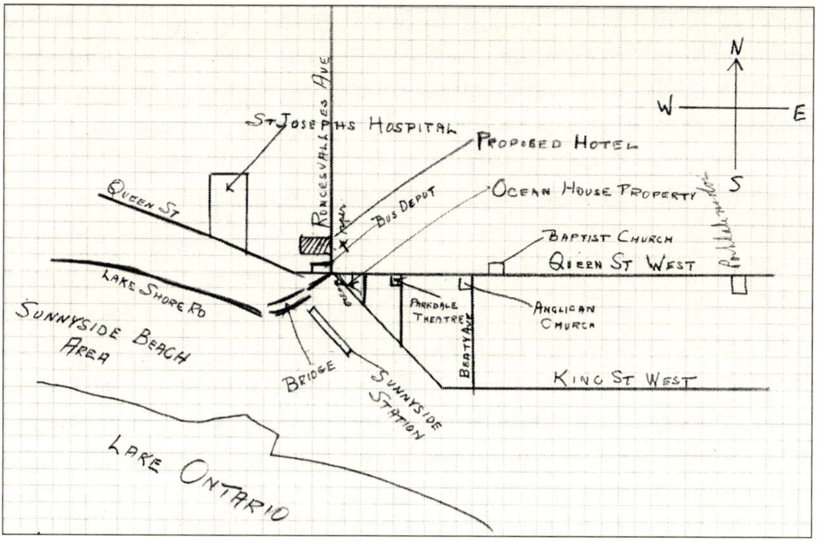

Figure 4 The intersection of Queen, King, and Roncesvalles in Toronto. *Source:* Archives of Ontario, Liquor License Board of Ontario, Standard Hotel Case Files, RG 36-1-0-1335.

imagine. Within a few weeks of the LCA (1934) coming into force, along with hundreds of applications for beverage room authorities, the LCBO and the premier's office began to receive protests against those applications. As noted above, the major opposition came from the Danforth Avenue area, the district near High Park, and neighbourhoods along Bloor Street, both in the core and at the west end. The latter area was particularly notable because the former town of West Toronto was dry. Each of these sections had a vocal cohort of temperance advocates who actively resisted any proposed beverage rooms.

A good example of how community pressure could impact the board's decisions can be seen in the area that adjoined the Sunnyside Amusement Park and that sat along the beach just south of the three-way intersection of Queen Street, King Street, and Roncesvalles Avenue (see Figure 4). This area contained no standard hotels with beverage rooms. From the beginning of the LCA (1934), applicants had applied for authorities for establishments that were not proper hotels. In July the operators of the Sunnyside Park pavilion applied for an authority and were denied because the pavilion was "situated in the Sunnyside amusement park area, which is not considered a desirable location."[63] A few months later, another potential manager wrote to Edmond Odette asking what the chances were that he could obtain an authority. He explained that the pavilion could be renovated to include ten bedrooms and that in the 1933-34 season it had catered to over fifteen thousand patrons.[64] The board denied the application.

Although these were individual letters to the board and sparked no public reaction, once stories emerged about the potential for authorized hotels to open nearby, voices of opposition arose quickly. In October 1934 a rumour spread that the Ocean House Hotel, which had closed in 1916 and been subdivided into retail space, was going to be renovated and reopened as a hotel. Immediately, local residents began to petition the board against such an application. In a memo, William Mair observes: "A delegation consisting of incumbent of every pulpit in the locality waited upon the Chief Commissioner ... protesting against any issue in the area."[65] The existing occupant, a store owner, stated that he had never been told to leave the building but rather that the landlord had told him that if someone were interested in reopening the hotel, and if the LCBO granted an authority, he would have to vacate. Nevertheless, the board continued to receive several strongly worded letters of protest. In response, the building's owner wrote to the board explaining that he was not sending an application but wanted only to make sure that any decision the board made would not be prejudiced by "untrue reports."[66] Likely, the owner was looking for a buyer and did not want to damage the property's prospects by having the board make a decision against an authority in the area before he sold the building. Arnold Smith was not encouraging. He replied that "owing to the very strenuous opposition which has developed in Parkdale [the district in which the hotel was located], the board has decided not to grant any Authorities in that part of the City." He explained that "the Ocean House Property would not receive an Authority if an Application were to be filed."[67]

In 1937 two hotel proprietors purchased a piece of land in the same area, with plans to build a new hotel. Smith wrote to Odette (who was on vacation) noting that this location "is a very congested centre and you have always considered this out of the question for an Authorized premises."[68] Odette agreed, instructing Smith to tell the applicants "or any other interested parties" that no authorities would be considered in the area. "Be sure and make your letter as emphatic as possible."[69] Reporting on the situation, William Mair wrote that the board had received a petition in opposition with over one thousand names, organized by ministers from the "Parkdale Presbyterian, Dunn Avenue United, St. Mark's (Anglican), Erskine United, Parkdale Baptist, North Parkdale United, Parkdale Tabernacle and Church of the Epiphany (Anglican)."[70] To reinforce his point, he drew a small diagram of the area, noting the presence of several churches and the hospital (see Figure 4). In view of the considerable pressure the board was facing in this section of the city, it reiterated its resolve that no applications for authorities would be considered.

Two years later, this resolve disappeared. Fred Hammer applied in June 1939 for an authority at the northwest corner of Roncesvalles Avenue and Queen Street, the same place that, in 1937, Mair had found to be problematic. Hammer was a popular and successful hotel proprietor who owned racehorses and yachts.[71] Contrary to its general practice, the board granted an authority before the hotel had been built. The local uproar was considerable: local clergy threatened to hold a sit-down strike near the construction site; politicians claimed they had been betrayed by the board. One city alderman reminded the municipal council that, a year earlier, the city had asked the LCBO to cease granting authorities in Toronto and that the board had agreed. The local churches, with the support of the city council, held a rally in opposition. To demonstrate that this assembly represented the will of the neighbourhood, the organizers claimed that they had received no assistance from other organizations, suggesting that this uproar was entirely indigenous to the area. Premier Hepburn, however, refused to interfere with the board's decision. The new chief commissioner, Arthur St. Clair Gordon, argued that he had received many letters of support and that the decision was final. The Woman's Christian Temperance Union (WCTU) argued that this decision was "the first step towards the downfall of democracy."[72] The city council noted that it could not legally block construction. Hammer's Edgewater Hotel opened in January 1940, described by inspector John Kidd as a "modern, fully equipped fire proof hotel ... a credit to the hotel industry in the City of Toronto, being second to none in every way other than its size. It will service a district badly in need of a first-class hotel, and also being located close to the Sunnyside Railroad Station, the [Toronto Transit Commission] bus terminal and St. Josephs Hospital."[73]

What had changed? What variables in the calculus of need influenced the outcome most strongly? Although no clear reason can be found in the records of the board and although the LCBO, typically, did not explain itself publicly, we can piece together a clearer picture of the factors that affected this decision. First, the area was, as inspector Kidd noted, desperately in need of a hotel. With both a bus depot and train station, the three-way intersection of Queen, King, and Roncesvalles must have seen its share of travellers in need of accommodations; a hotel would be an asset to the area. The agitation by opponents to a licensed hotel meant that no decent lodging space had been built in several years because, without a beverage room, a hotel might not have been considered viable. This issue of viability is further suggested by Hammer's need to have the guarantee of an authority before building. Second, and related, 1939 saw an increase in industrial output and economic activity. Although war was not declared until a few months after Hammer applied for his authority, the months immediately before the war did see a shift in economic capacity. Third, and possibly most significant, was the issue of leadership. Edmond Odette, the chief commissioner since 1934, died of a heart attack on 31 March 1939, and his successor, Arthur St. Clair Gordon, had approved of Hammer's application. Unlike Odette, who was a former politician but not an elected MLA while heading the LCBO, Gordon was a sitting politician and in his second term as provincial Liberal member for Kent West. The relationship between politics and clientelism, which is addressed in much more detail in the next chapter, although not a driving force behind the LCBO's operations, could influence its decisions in profound and often bizarre ways.

The fourth factor in this case was a limited usefulness of community protest in general. Faced with the persistent and clear need for a hotel in the location, and one which was likely to be operated in a manner in keeping with the board's central values of social order and responsible management, the board chose to ignore the voices of what may have appeared to be an unrealistic opposition. This was the case both with the Edgewater hotel, where city council's opposition occurred prior to the economic changes of early 1939, and the Rosdol Inn, where influential politicians stood in opposition to the temperance forces. To create a functional accommodation environment, the board sometimes had to ignore the loudest voices.

Giving Meaning to the Voices

The process of investigating and establishing hotel beverage rooms required the LCBO to consider the multiple views of competing community voices. In Toronto the voices of the dry forces often held sway over the board's decisions, although notable deviations suggest that other interests and considerations could influence the decision-making process. Although not the exclusive factor driving the board's decisions, community input was fundamental to the board's work. It was by hearing the voices of the community that the board would determine what course of action would (usually) face the least amount of criticism and cost the least amount of political capital. Once hotels were established, the board relied on the eyes of the community to provide ongoing surveillance of these spaces. The reasons for this surveillance were complex, and forms of denunciation could range from the opportunistic to the altruistic. Beyond motivations, the LCBO's management and inspectors had to determine which voices were most convincing and which evidence was most conclusive. In the process, the board undertook a persistent dialogue with the community, probing and perhaps moulding dominant value systems, both constructing and working within established discourses of deviance, and erecting a pervasive and nearly ubiquitous control regime.

Paying attention to the many voices of the community was a major component of the LCBO's regulatory activities; listening to its political masters was another. The board sought to strengthen its bureaucratic authority by minimizing opposition. At times, this effort required it to determine the more prudent choice of action: to license or not to license. At other times, its work was much more overtly political, intended to placate politically powerful individuals. Likely, the latter strategy would strengthen its authority, although we cannot dismiss that, since many of the senior bureaucrats were Liberals, they likely were also inclined to support the decisions of their political masters. We see this in many cases, both in the macropolitics of provincial partisan activities and in the micropolitics of the communities. The next chapter digs further into the complexity of the political forces at play in the LCBO's work. It is not adequate to argue simply that the LCBO was just a puppet of the provincial government. Although this perspective is appealing to the twenty-first-century political cynic, it does not do justice to the historical record. Just as the board's approach to community voices was multifaceted, so too were its activities within the political system.

5

"As a Result of Representations Made": The (Dys)function of Patronage in the LCBO's Regulatory Activities

In February 1935 alderman N.J. Lacasse of Ottawa wrote to Arnold Smith of the Liquor Control Board of Ontario (LCBO) to complain about the board's decision not to grant a beer authority to that city's Baxter Hotel. The board had ruled that the hotel was too close to schools and churches. It would simply face too much criticism from members of the community. "I sincerely believe," Lacasse griped, that "if we were ready to give a large bonus to some politician, that it would not be long that the license would be granted. I know for a fact that other hotel keepers had to pay in the same case." He threatened to bring this information about influence peddling to Premier Mitchell Hepburn.[1] Smith, himself a former politician, was nonplussed; he had heard this all before. "I can assure you," he wrote back, "that no politician could get the Board to change their attitude in this regard. You mention that Hotel Keepers have had to pay a bonus to get their Authority and all I can say ... is if they pay anyone to look after their case it will receive no more consideration than if it had been presented by themselves, as all Applications are treated on their merits only by the Board."[2] For Smith, there was no place for politics in the operation of the Liquor Control Board.

Although accusations like Lacasse's charge of influence peddling were relatively rare, political pressure was rampant in the operations of the LCBO. This is not really surprising. The liquor licence was lucrative, a golden fleece of the hospitality industry. For politicians, whose careers were usually built on the support of grassroots social networks, the ability to influence the granting of liquor licences must have been a major spoil of office. Before liquor licensing was centralized by the province in 1906, the liquor licence was a major partisan tool and a reward for loyalty.[3] This was a clientelistic system, with positions filled based on personal relationships rather than individual skills or merit. Moreover, hotels had traditionally been community meeting places, locations for both free expression and partisan activity; political action and the local tavern went hand in hand.[4]

So politicians may have wanted to reward supportive hotelkeepers with the significantly competitive advantage of the authority to serve beer and wine.

Yet to do so, these politicians needed a compliant Liquor Control Board, something that was more difficult to attain than they might have expected. During the 1934 election campaign, when Mitchell Hepburn decided to support the new "beer by the glass" legislation, he stated that he wanted to depoliticize liquor control. He may have been responding to a general impression that liquor licensing was a highly partisan political activity, or he may have been making a more specific reference to the political scandal that tainted the LCBO just prior to the dropping of the 1934 election writ. In late 1933 and early 1934, when the Conservatives were still in power, the board had been the centre of a highly publicized and damning political "toll gate" scandal. British distillers, it was claimed, had paid bonuses to Conservative politicians and workers to stock their products. During the election, these allegations resurfaced.[5] So for Hepburn to make liquor control non-political was to suggest the integrity of his party's intentions relating to the administration of liquor regulations, in contrast to the partisan scandal attached to the previous administration.

In 1930s Ontario it was easier to talk about removing politics from liquor control than actually to achieve this goal. Hepburn's first act relating to the LCBO was to appoint Edmond Odette, a former Liberal member of the federal Parliament and a personal friend, to the position of chief commissioner. Arnold Smith, Odette's former Liberal colleague in the federal Parliament, became the director of hotels and personnel, with the position soon elevated to deputy chief commissioner. Several inspectors hired under the new administration also had Liberal connections. Moreover, when the Liberals took office, they replaced 481 of the board's more than one thousand employees with 265 of their own supporters.[6] Hepburn also was concerned with maintaining control over the hiring practices of the board; in November 1934 he berated Odette for not being available when the premier wanted to discuss personnel issues. He immediately restructured the board, handing personnel to Arnold Smith, who seemed never to leave the office.[7]

Yet one cannot conclude, on the basis of some high-level political appointments, that patronage was *fundamental* to the LCBO's regulatory decisions. First, not all staff members were political appointments. Several members of the senior administration had worked for the board prior to 1934, under the Conservatives, including William Mair, the deputy director of hotels; William Common, the board's solicitor; William Hart, the architectural inspector; and several others not named William, notably the highly respected general inspector John Pitt.[8] Second, something that may seem blatantly partisan might actually be practical; filling a politically sensitive regulatory bureaucracy with members from your own political party is a convenient way of ensuring that decisions reflecting directly on your government's operations are made by people whose judgment you trust.[9]

The story of victorious politicians rewarding their loyal members is not new. Several historians have shown that patronage was essential to the early politics of Canada, with parties and specific individuals using patronage as a way of establishing strong networks of elites who helped to build national unity or provincial power bases.[10] It could also work in a local environment. Alan Gordon has shown how patronage at the constituency level could create a complex and reciprocal set of relations among local individuals, which helped to forge connections between erstwhile disparate groups.[11] He outlines an intricate system of checks and balances in which government appointments, notably jobs in various sectors of the civil service, were doled out in a systematic way through consultation with local party hierarchies. This system diffused authority, reducing the potential power of any one person. Gordon observes that, in the years before the First World War, people had begun to criticize the "loose bureaucratic methods" of the federal civil service. Prime Minister Robert Borden had planned an overhaul of the civil service, along the lines of "the principles of scientific management," but his plans were interrupted by the Great War.[12] These institutions were presented as able to transcend the problems of patronage by replacing party loyalty with experience and education as criteria for hiring and advancement. Career advancement based on impersonal evaluations of skill and experience were a central feature in Max Weber's ideal-typical bureaucracy.[13]

Studies of patronage and clientelism, a system that doled out favours based on personal relationships rather than merit, have centred on the way that government jobs were distributed; less clear are the ways that certain privileges were obtained. This is important in the LCBO's case because, although it was generally easy to fire and hire individuals to fill certain jobs, granting hotel licences and beer authorities required the party loyalist to have a hotel that could at least appear suitable for the task. Here, patronage, generally something carried out surreptitiously, had the potential to become intensely public since, as we saw in the previous chapter, a hotel space that was inadequate or poorly run could reflect badly on the LCBO and the government.

So what was the role of partisan politics and clientelism in the board's work? It is a difficult question to answer, but a quick response might be that partisanism was present and could be functional, whereas clientelism was considered to be dysfunctional but not absent. Since the board's reputation was so closely connected to the reputation of the Liberal government, it drew on the perspectives of individuals who claimed allegiance to the Liberals both to help evaluate applications for authorities and to keep an eye on the situation on the ground. So here, partisanism was useful. But clientelism was anathema to an administration that attempted to distribute standard hotel licenses and beer authorities based on the merit of establishments and their proprietors. It contradicted the ideal of objective regulatory practices superseding subjectivity.

The importance of patronage in the LCBO's operations is difficult to determine. Sharon Jaeger insists that the board was rife with patronage, citing Premier Hepburn's own admission that he was not above influencing the board's decisions.[14] Doubtless, the political culture in the province held out the *expectation* of partisan favours. John A. Smith, the proprietor of the Walker House, a "coloured" hotel in Windsor, wrote to the LCBO in 1939 explaining that "for my service with the Liberal party, I would have had an appointment in Niagara Falls if I hadn't of [sic] been coloured. All the rest of the boys that I worked with all got their appointments and something to do."[15] He was concerned that the board was being overly critical of his hotel's operations because of the colour of his skin and that of his customers. William Houck, member of the provincial Legislative Assembly (MLA) for Niagara Falls, wrote in 1938 to complain that he had not been consulted on the appointment of the new inspector. "Naturally, as the Member for this riding," he wrote to Smith, "I believe that co-operation should be displayed and when new appointments are being considered I should either be consulted or notified." Smith did not comment, although inspector M.G. Dean seems to have been moved out of Niagara soon afterward.[16]

Giving board jobs to party members is one thing; doling out authorities and licences to dedicated Liberals is quite another. The board received hundreds of letters that contained references to party loyalty or partisan perspectives. When Louis Sacco was refused an authority for his Victoria Inn in Niagara Falls, he wrote a last-ditch letter to Hepburn complaining that "after working for forty-seven years I am being put out of my property by the Liberal Party for which I have worked and supported all my life."[17] The proprietor of the Dorking Hotel in Waterloo County submitted a petition from the community demanding that he receive an authority, explaining that "the signers on that petition are almost one hundred perscent [sic] Liberal[;] why cannot these people have a little convenience?"[18] Joseph Eassy of Kitchener was more forthright in asserting his political entitlement in 1939: "My affiliation with the Liberal Party of Waterloo County has been well known ever since I located in Kitchener more than forty years ago. At all times I have worked for the advancement of Liberal policies and for the support of Liberal candidates."[19] In spite of a number of letters of support from local Liberals and attempts to restructure his building to conform to the board's requirements, Eassy did not even receive the application forms.

Along with appeals from proprietors, the board received many letters from party insiders advocating for special consideration of local supporters. Houck was a persistent correspondent to the board. Along with advocating for "good" Liberal residents like Louis Sacco, he attempted to use his influence with the board to gain favours for powerful local politicians. For example, in August 1934 Jane Teal, the sister of the reeve of Crystal Beach, applied for an authority for her establishment. When the board refused to grant the authority, arguing that the building was a firetrap and simply not suitable as a hotel, Houck wrote increasingly desperate letters to Smith explaining that Teal was a respectable woman, had recently lost her husband and deserved a break, and was politically connected.[20] When Houck told Smith that the community was up in arms that Teal was being denied an authority whereas another hotel, run by an outsider named Sheehan, had received one, Smith explained that the Sheehan Hotel "is a real hotel in every sense of the word, while the Hotel that was operated by Mrs. Teal is just one section of a large fire trapped building, and was not a hotel, and I felt very nervous all last summer at it holding an authority from this board."[21] Finally, Houck laid his cards on the table:

> I must admit that I am going through more or less of a hellish stage at this time in regard to this application. The only reason that I am taking it on the chin and trying to be of material assistance to her is the fact that the Teal family command the greater majority of the electorate of Crystal Beach.[22]

Eventually, Smith convinced Teal to buy better premises and, in order to assuage Houck's fears about political recrimination (which Smith suggested to Houck were overblown), informed Teal that Houck had done everything in his power to help her obtain an authority.[23]

Houck was not alone in using his position to attempt to win favours from the board for constituents, although among the communities studied here he may have been the most persistent. In Ottawa the Queen's Hotel was owned by the son of a Liberal senator, and one correspondent wrote to Smith in October 1934 that "if there is anyone in Canada who deserves consideration from the Liberal Party it is [he]."[24] Edward J. Anderson, the MLA for Welland, wrote to Odette in support of an application by Rafael Serravelli, explaining that Serravelli

> is the first Liberal worker to make an application for a license in my riding. He organized two groups of Italians and has been to a great extent responsible for changing the town of Thorold from a 700 Tory majority to a Liberal majority of nearly 400. If this license is not granted we will lose our grip on the whole foreign born population in Thorold.[25]

In Essex County a correspondent wrote to support an application for the Ducharmes Hotel, noting that "these people have always been staunch supporters of the Liberal party ... [and] have always played an active part in the elections."[26] In all of these cases, we see the expectation of partisan favours, often through the accepted networks of high-level Liberals in the community.

Although there is little doubt, then, that the liquor licence was a prized political spoil, the question remains as to the impact of such political machinations on the LCBO's activities. The previous examples provide a good illustration of the trickiness of interpreting this situation. Serravelli did receive his authority, whereas the Queen's and Ducharmes Hotels did not. Did Anderson's partisan entreaties impact Serravelli's chances, or did the board rely on the evidence of the physical layout and on its calculus of need? Certainly, inspectors considered the physical attributes of the Queen's and Ducharmes Hotels to be unsuitable spaces for a beer authority, whereas Serravelli's Ormond Hotel had been a hotel before the end of prohibition. Did Houck's persistent partisan letters convince the board to grant Teal the several extensions of an authority on her unsuitable premises, or was it Teal's respectable place in the community that allowed the board to justify granting extensions on the grounds that she would eventually take over a more suitable building, which she could run according to the board's rules?

Although these tantalizing questions are unanswerable, there are clear cases where political connections were worthless, demonstrating that party loyalty was not everything, and others where politics drove the board's actions, often in spite of the better judgment of the central administration itself. When the National Capitol branch of the Native Sons of Canada applied for an authority, it had the support of both the Ottawa West Liberal Association and the South Ottawa Liberal Association but did not receive the authority.[27] Likewise, Albert Brady had loaned space during an election campaign to the Ward Four Liberal Association in Toronto, but in spite of its letter in support of his application, he did not receive an authority.[28] J.M. Dalrymple wrote to support the application for an authority by the Lakeshore Pavilion in Toronto, explaining that the operators of the pavilion had been "of great assistance to me in forming my 'Twentieth Century Liberal club' and I am very much in favor of them having a permit."[29] The authority was not granted because the pavilion was, as mentioned in the previous chapter, in an "amusement park area, which is not considered a desirable location."[30]

In these examples, party loyalty was not enough to supersede the physical deficiencies of the building or the simple fact that there was no perceived "need" in the area. So it is fair to conclude that partisan politics were not a singular driving force behind the board's regulatory decisions. When the proprietor of the Atlanta Hotel in Toronto complained to the board about its refusal of his authority application, he stated that he had been turned down because he was a Conservative. Smith replied that such a statement "is ridiculous ... as a great number of Liberals have applied, and received exactly the same answer."[31] It is notable that these letters came from Arnold Smith, who, as the deputy chief commissioner, had the often difficult task of overseeing all aspects of the board's operations.

So although Hepburn may have replaced over four hundred LCBO workers with his own supporters, hotel management was not so similarly affected by clientelism. Supporters of McMullin's Hotel in Fort William argued that too many "Tories" had been granted hotel licences and that this privilege should not go only to members of the Opposition. The local Liberals became involved, writing a letter evaluating the situation in Fort William and urging the board to grant the authority. Most notable in this letter is how the correspondent, C.W. Wilson, a local merchant, invoked both the justice of granting an authority to a party member and the value of the hotel based on local conditions and the hotel's potential ability to assuage problems:

> I would like to point out ... facts in connection with this application
> 1st Ninety per cent of the Hotel men of Fort William are Tories, in fact all of them, with possibly one exception. They are, therefore, anxious to keep a Liberal from securing a license.
> 2nd The Section in which Mr. McMullen will build his hotel has a distinct and separate population of more than five thousand people. There is no hotel of any sort and everybody living in this section is compelled to come up town to have a beer or to secure hotel accommodation.
> 3rd Not having an hotel in that section encourages co-called "Joints" which are difficult for inspectors, or even police, to check.
> 4th Mr. Joseph E. Crawford, [MLA], for Fort William, is not against an authority being granted to Mr. McMullin.
> 5th Fort William has four or five thousand more people than has Port Arthur but one less Hotel Authority. In view of all this I feel it would be in our interest to grant Mr. McMullin an Authority – in fact I know it would.[32]

When the application from McMullin's Hotel was rejected, the proprietor wrote to insist that the LCBO make a partisan stand, but Smith countered, "you can hardly expect that this Board ... should issue authorities to any man because he is a good fellow or belongs to any particular society, nationality or politics."[33]

The non-partisan assertions of the board may, in fact, have been a personal preference of Smith himself. For Smith, making decisions based on partisan politics or personal assessments interfered with the effective operation of the board. Several times he explained – to insiders as well as to the general public – his views on how politics and personal appeals would undermine the work that the board was doing. When Waterloo County inspector

Norman Ratz explained that he had recommended an authority for a hotel that turned out to be troublesome simply because he felt pressured by the community and because the proprietor "seemed good for it," Smith reprimanded him:

> I am not in any way interested in playing politics in the granting of Hotel Authorities regardless of the party. The hotel is either needed or it is not needed and the premises are either correct or not correct, and I do not want the Board to be placed in a position at any time of granting an Authority just because someone is a good fellow, and have the premises reported OK and then later have it turn out that the man is undesirable, and then take the stand that there is something the matter with his premises.[34]

Here, the problem was fairness to the proprietor since basing initial decisions on subjective personal issues would not stand up to scrutiny if the premises themselves were inappropriate. Inspector Ratz was an especially problematic partisan inspector, and he would eventually be dismissed for some shady dealings in association with a local MLA. Smith made a similar appeal to fairness when responding to William Houck's attempts to obtain an authority for Jane Teal in Crystal Beach. Smith explained why he was troubled by persistent clientelism: "I do not believe it is right for a person to spon[s]or something that is not just and right, and there is no justice in granting Mrs. Teal an Authority to operate a restaurant as a Hotel, even though she does stir up an agitation amongst a few people."[35] For Smith, politics and personal appeals interfered with the operation of the board. Although this may seem an odd perspective for a former politician, he had also been involved in the hotel business and may have been more interested in the respectability of the hotel business than were many of the people who attempted to place partisan pressure on the LCBO. Then again, Smith's dislike of partisanism and clientelism might explain why he had been only a one-term member of the federal Parliament.

Although Smith defended the integrity of the board's operations against partisanism, he may have been a lone (if influential) voice in the partisan wilderness. Several of the board's inspectors made clear partisan overtures, although it is true that some others did tend to view political machinations with the same sort of disdain as Smith. We have already seen inspector Ratz's decision to overlook some shortcomings in one hotel's layout due to his poor evaluation of the proprietor's character. When reporting on the City Hotel in Waterloo in September 1935, Ratz noted a number of physical problems with the hotel, problems that normally would exclude a hotel from receiving an authority. Ratz explained that he had not mentioned these problems before for reasons of a personal and political nature: "In the first place I wanted to give [the proprietor] a chance to get some of the money back that he had spent on improvements, in the second place, Mr. Devitt, the owner and his entire family are very prominent Liberals, so you will understand where a little pressure would be brought to bear."[36] Also troublesome was Alfred Larocque, the inspector for the Ottawa district and, as noted above, a former Liberal organizer. Larocque was both openly partisan and also somewhat sycophantic, giving good reviews to sometimes undeserving elite clubs and hotels while denigrating simpler establishments that, nevertheless, were well run. Some cases are considered below, but it is important, first of all, to understand the context in which Larocque was working. Ottawa was overwhelmingly a political town. As noted with the application of the city's Queen's Hotel (owned by the son of a Liberal senator), the LCBO had to deal with powerful federal and provincial politicians on a regular basis. Indeed, many politicians from outside of the city stayed in hotels, making themselves even more closely interested in the operations of the Liquor Control Act (LCA). This sort of influence must have been difficult to resist, especially to a relatively low-level employee like Larocque, who might have aspired to greater things. Moreover, the city was politically divided. In the 1934 provincial election, the Ottawa East riding was taken by a Liberal, M.C.D. Paul Leduc, who became the minister of mines. The Ottawa South riding was held by Conservative Arthur Ellis. The Carleton riding, surrounding the city, was held by Conservative Adam H. Acres, and the riding had been Conservative for decades. So partisan politics were more significant in Ottawa than in communities like Essex County or Niagara, where all of the members were Liberal.

Whereas Smith had some control over the actions of the inspectors, he had little control over the powerful provincial politicians who signed his paycheque. Although evidence of partisan favouritism was not as blatant as the words of people like Larocque or the entreaties from frustrated hotel owners, in many instances we find minor suggestions of political influence, often in the form of marginal notes on records, cryptic messages about "representations made on your behalf" sent to proprietors, or even the simple reissuing of authorities after proprietors had been told under no uncertain terms that they would not receive a renewal. Determining whether such episodes are cases of patronage or partisan favouritism is difficult, especially since often no paper trail remains. Paper records of partisan decisions would be unnecessary when Odette merely had to walk into Smith's office to make his decision known.

However, as illustrated by Hepburn's frustrated 1934 letter complaining that Odette was never available, Odette was often out of the office, so at times the communications between Smith and Odette were necessarily part of the public record. For example, when Odette travelled to California in December 1936, Smith wrote several letters outlining some issues for which "I would appreciate your instructions."[37] The issues with which they dealt involved generally mundane aspects of hotel regulation: proprietors planning to build a hotel and wanting assurance they would receive an authority (which Odette would not give); a hotel that had a bad report from police (Odette told Smith to use his own judgment); and the plan of the Taylor and Bates Brewery to sponsor a radio show in Hamilton (Odette said there was no problem as long as they observed the rules).[38] This letter suggests that Odette was consulted on the routine activities of the board; it also suggests that Odette trusted Smith to make many decisions relating to the regulation of hotels.

In the communities examined for this study, three stand out as having the most obvious examples of partisan or personal favouritism for hotel proprietors: Ottawa, Essex County, and Toronto. This is not surprising. We have already considered the partisan life in Ottawa. Similarly, Toronto, the seat of provincial government and the location of the LCBO's offices, presented ample opportunity for hotel proprietors or interested individuals to attempt directly to influence board decisions. But most notably, Essex seems to have been lousy with politics. This condition was the result of several key factors. First, Odette's home of Tilbury was on the eastern edge of Essex, although part of Kent County. Moreover, Essex was the home of several active and influential politicians who were vocal advocates for the hotel and beverage industry and worked the partisan machine quite often.

Partisanism in Essex County

In September 1934 inspector John Pitt evaluated the situation in Essex and reported back to the board that "there are too many places having Standard Licenses and Authorities that are not worthy of the Status of a Standard Hotel." This was explained by the culture of influence peddling within the area: "There has been too much interferences [sic] from outside parties in regard to obtaining Standard Licenses and Authorities. For people who are anxious to get into the hotel business and who will meet with their demands and no small sum is demanded."[39] Although the "outside parties" were not identified, given that Pitt had been an inspector since at least 1927 and tended to have little time for partisan activities, it is likely the "outside parties" were individuals outside of the board's administration but not outside of politics.

Three of the four Liberal members of the provincial Legislative Assembly for Essex County were active advocates for hotel proprietors in the area: James Clark, David Croll, and A.C. Trottier, members for Windsor-Sandwich, Windsor-Walkerville, and Essex North, respectively. The fourth member, L.P. Wigle of Essex South, occasionally wrote to the board regarding hotels in his district but does not appear to have actively campaigned for hotels. Clark and Croll were barristers, Trottier a physician, and Wigle a farmer. This was a powerful collection of influential politicians. Clark became the speaker of the House in 1939 and had previously been a dynamic ward boss. Croll was something of a wunderkind; born in Moscow, Russia, in 1900, he was elected to the Legislative Assembly in 1934, becoming minister of public welfare and minister of municipal affairs in the summer of 1934 (he was the first Jewish cabinet minister in Ontario) and minister of labour in May 1935. He held all three ministerial posts until he resigned in 1937.[40] Given that Premier Hepburn's own riding of Elgin was also adjacent to Essex County and that Odette was from Tilbury, we can see the potential for considerable patronage and favouritism based on both partisan and personal connections.

As in other communities, these politicians attempted to use their influence to gain concessions for favoured constituents. When writing about the decision of Raymond Lappan, the proprietor of the Walker Road Hotel in Windsor (a different hotel from John A. Smith's Walker House), to conduct dances in his dining room contrary to the directions of the board, inspector George Hanrahan wrote Smith a confidential letter outlining the role of politicians in this action:

> On receipt of your letter Mr. Lappan in company with one Mr. F.X. Chauvin called at the office of Major Jas. H. Clark, and told him he had been denied the privilege of conducting dancing in the dining room of his hotel. Major Clark's answer to him was to go ahead and conduct dancing, that the Prime Minister the Honorable Mr. M.F. Hepburn had told him it would be all right for dancing to be conducted in any place where it was desired. He further told Mr. Lappan he would be responsible in the matter. Mr. Lappan's hotel is located in the riding of Dr. Trottier. If you have any comment you want to pass on to me I shall be glad to hear from you.[41]

Smith told the hotel to stop holding dances immediately. Later that month, Trottier wrote to Odette supporting Lappan's application for dancing. He called Lappan a "Gentleman of good reputation" and explained that in granting a licence "your Board will confer a favour to me personally."[42] Odette forwarded the letter to Smith, and both Mair and Smith replied. They reiterated that, although the hotel may be a well-established place and suitable for a Standard Hotel licence, it was not suitable for dancing. They remained steadfast in spite of the political machinations. In August 1934 the secretary of the Worker's Ex-servicemen's League wrote to Hepburn complaining that the proprietor of the Plaza Arms Hotel was operating a sham hotel next door to the league's meeting rooms. The proprietor, the correspondent claimed, was attempting to take over the league's rooms and turn them into cheap bedrooms in order to give the appearance of a hotel. When members of the league approached the proprietor about these plans, he explained that "he had sent an Attorney to Toronto with $150 in his pocket to secure a license for him but he returned without it, but the same night he got in touch with Major Clarke [sic] ... A couple of telegrams were sent to Toronto, and next day he had a license."[43] Odette cancelled the authority on 7 September, but the proprietor still took over the rooms and received an authority when he had made the upgrades. The Plaza Arms continued to cause trouble for the board, and in spite of complaints about its operations, it continued to receive authorities. The hotel was represented by the law firm of Croll, Brody and Meretsky.[44]

James Clark's influence is worth closer examination. Possibly the most vocal Liberal critic of the LCBO, Clark was a barrister who often defended hotel proprietors who were being charged under the LCA. He was a persistent thorn in the side of the board since he often argued publicly that its rules pandered too much to the temperance forces. Although apparently sincere, Clark's argument was also ironic given that Odette and Hepburn were often characterized, as Sharon Jaeger puts it, as having a "fondness for the bottle."[45] When writing to the board in his capacity as solicitor, Clark was simply doing his job for his client; but given that he was a member of the Liberal caucus before becoming speaker, he was in a position to exert notable influence on the board. This sort of conflict of interest was not unusual, especially in Essex County. As indicated above, both Croll and Clark represented hotel proprietors in their dealings with the board. The example of the Walker Road Hotel illustrates Clark's belief that he had considerable sway over the board. This may have been the case, but it is not fair to the board's administration or to Clark to conclude that Clark always had the power to manipulate the board. Clark's influence did not go unnoticed. As noted earlier, in August 1935 an anonymous letter signed "Fed Up" was sent to inspector Hanrahan complaining about the conditions at the American Hotel in Windsor and concluding with, "who is running your office you or Jim Clark?"[46] Given that the board was concerned about its image as an objective bureaucracy, and about its social authority, it may have chosen to tread lightly with Clark; as a persistent critic of the board and of the LCA, he may have been the sort of person whom it was better to placate than to antagonize.

Clark, Croll, and Trottier were clearly attempting to affect the board's decisions in ways that were politically and personally beneficial, but the silent partner in all of this activity was Odette himself. His hand is not as clear in the decisions, but some conditions in Essex County were so blatantly contrary to the law and the philosophy of social order upheld by Smith that one cannot help suspecting that Odette insisted on leniency toward hotels in the area for personal or political reasons. Occasionally, we see the politics bubble up from under the surface. For example, in 1937 Smith received a call from Croll (acting in the capacity as solicitor) about the Dixie Hotel in

Windsor. He wrote to Odette asking for guidance because of the promises that were being made:

> Upon my advising him [Croll] that [an authority] had not been issued, he told me that he had been talking to you and that you had told him that you had given me instructions to issue same. I informed him that I had received no such instructions, and if you had issued them, they must have gone astray in the mail and I would communicate with you at once. Hence this letter.[47]

The terse frustration in this letter was probably the result of the persistent politics of Essex County. A few cases should provide an impression of the complexity of the politics of familiarity that ran through many of these accounts. The story of Belle River's Taylor Hotel illustrates the intricate connections between community context, politics, and the challenges of liquor regulation.

The Taylor Hotel was located in the resort area of Belle River, about halfway between Windsor and Odette's own Tilbury. It sat where Belle River met Lake St. Clair and was (and remains) a popular tourist resort. Like the town of Riverside closer to Windsor, Belle River was appealing to American boaters, and this appeal led to some concerns over the behaviour of hotel managers.[48] The Taylor Hotel was one of at least three licensed hotels in Belle River, the others being Emery's Corners and the Log Cabin Hotel. All posed problems for the board and police because they were attractive places for out-of-town people to go for alcohol and dancing since they were considered far enough away from Windsor to be outside of the eyes of the Ontario Provincial Police. They were not. Each was raided a number of times, and the Taylor Hotel was found to be quite troublesome.

The hotel had existed long before the passing of the LCA (1934). In 1931 the owners reportedly spent $3,000 to improve the property. When writing to Odette to ask the board to expedite the hotel's licence-renewal application, Herbert Taylor, son of the owner, Sarah Taylor, explained that the hotel was "four years arrears in taxes and two years arrears in payments." He made his case based on the suitability of the hotel for a licence and on the financial need of the proprietors, for whom the hotel was their livelihood: "It will be very evident to you that further delay in granting a license ... means that some other agency of the government must take care of [my parents]." He concluded with the observation that the hotel

> happens to be about the oldest in Essex County ... There can be no question as to its reconition [sic] as a hotel, but still I'm informed that such license and authority as necessary under the new act has not been granted. In other

> words, this is a hotel, it has been a hotel, and there seems to be no reason not to grant an Authority.[49]

Leo Sylvestre, a local barrister, wrote in support of the application, claiming that he had investigated the location and concluding with an argument about the legitimacy of the hotel as a fully functioning and desirable establishment:

> This hotel would serve the east end of the Village which is clamoring for it. The people living there do not patronize very much with the other hotels. As a result, the opening of this hotel at that point would help the local population and would not hurt the other hotel-keepers. I have found out also that the proprietor of the Taylor Hotel caters to outsiders ... Many people from Detroit and many people attending dances at the Lake View Pavillion would patronize this hotel.[50]

Taylor also had the support of the municipal council of Belle River, which petitioned the commission to grant the licence, arguing similarly that "the said Hotel, has by virtue of its ancient establishment and its proper accomodation [sic] merited the issue of your commission's authority for the said privelege [sic] and ... has retained its status as a bonified [sic] and standard hotel."[51] Soon after, the authority was granted.

Nearly six months later, the hotel began to run into trouble. In January 1935 the proprietor to whom the Taylors had rented the space had some kind of violent breakdown in the hotel owing to family trouble, and as a result the hotel was transferred to the management of Theo Fontaine, who was also the mayor of East Windsor.[52] Although Fontaine received a good character review from inspector Hanrahan, problems arose. Hanrahan visited the hotel at 12:40 a.m., Sunday, 24 March, and found dancing and drinking going on inside. Dancing, as I discuss in Chapter 6, was a significant issue for the board, and in July 1935 it issued new regulations on dining and dancing in hotels. Around the same time, it sent a special letter to hotel proprietors in Belle River, where the board determined that "there is no need for this form of entertainment in the hotels in the vicinity" since there was "a commodious dance pavilion, erected especially for that purpose," nearby.[53] Likely, this is a reference to Lake View Pavillion, mentioned by Sylvestre, which, ironically, he had suggested was a good reason for the hotel to receive a licence and authority in the first place.

Trouble continued. In early August, Hanrahan again found the hotel holding dances and wrote to ask "if permission has been granted there will you kindly advise me so as I may be guided in the matter."[54] The hotel had not received permission, although a few days later Fontaine wrote directly to

Odette asking for the privilege.[55] In the summer, the hotel was raided and police found people holding drinking parties in private bedrooms and two twenty-one-year-old men entertaining two underage women. The hotel management was found to have been encouraging and accommodating this behaviour; Denis Fontaine, Theo's brother and the hotel's manager, admitted that he had served this group, but another man was found guilty and fined $100 and costs. In a telling and too typical turn, Denis Fontaine paid the fine.

Smith seems to have become frustrated with this hotel and appears to have been troubled by the political machinations behind the scenes. After the case had concluded, he sent a letter to Odette, who was in Tilbury, outlining the details of the case and complaining that Odette was seriously contemplating permitting the hotel to have dancing. His letter was steeped in frustration and sarcasm: "Under ordinary circumstances I would be inclined to think, in view of the clarity of the original police report and the subsequent apparent fixing of the charge, the Authority covering this Hotel should be suspended indefinitely, instead of an extension of dance privileges; however, I am leaving the matter to your discretion."[56]

The hotel did not receive permission for dances, but it did not stop holding them and was not reprimanded. At the heart of the matter was partisan politics. In September 1935, when writing to general inspector John Pitt to request that he look in on the Taylor Hotel, Mair wrote a letter that was subtly telling about the politics behind the situation:

> The manager of the above hotel has been endeavouring to obtain the Board's permission for the conducting of dancing in his premises. So far he has not been successful in obtaining written permission, but it is understood that he has been conducting dancing nevertheless ... The Board have obtained certain information from various individuals on which they base their opinion that the place is not properly constituted for that form of entertainment, nevertheless they do not wish to antagonise Mr. Fontaine at the moment ... Would you be good enough to visit the hotel and if dancing is in progress advise us but do not interrupt him. Steps will be taken to see that dancing is not permitted positively, after the coming Election.[57]

The "election" to which Mair referred was likely the federal election, held on 14 October 1935, in which William Lyon Mackenzie King would win a massive Liberal majority over R.B. Bennett's Conservatives, taking 45 percent of the popular vote and 71 percent of the seats in the House of Commons. The Liberals swept Essex County.

The conclusion of the election did not immediately change the Taylor Hotel's prospects. In November inspector Hanrahan reported that he had once again found drinking after midnight on a Sunday morning and that "within the past 4 or 5 months the police found sales conducted here in one of the bedrooms on a Sunday. It would seem time to take some action on this kind of practice and I would recommend some type of the same."[58] But he did not seem to be at all confident in the possibility that the board would deal any serious blow to the hotel. When the hotel's licence was suspended later in December, it was due to nonpayment of beverage taxes. In a routine practice, Hanrahan confiscated the beer order-books and authority document. Whereas he normally would have sent the books to Smith, in this case he wrote cryptically, "perhaps I should hold the books pending your action," knowing that the board would restore the authority soon, which it did do. Authorities were to be renewed each March, and in February 1936 the inspector again recommended against renewal. "The business is run primarily for dancing and sale of beverages," he noted. The rules required dancing to be permitted only as an adjunct to meals, and in spite of its having three dining rooms with eighteen tables and sixty-eight chairs, "there was not enough food in the refrigerator to feed a half dozen people."[59] The political situation may have finally turned against this hotel. Trottier wrote in mid-March recommending "that you do not renew the license of Taylor Hotel, that hotel not being as efficient as the others."[60] Two days later, Mair wrote a letter informing Fontaine that his authority-holding days were numbered:

> The Board have reluctantly decided to consider the renewal of Standard Hotel License and Authority ... You will also accept this communication as a final warning that if the Regulations of the Board are not properly observed in every detail during the course of the coming license year, that immediate cancellation of the License and Authority privileges will follow on receipt of the first adverse report.[61]

It is possible that Fontaine realized he had used up his political capital. Instead of applying for a full-year licence, a week after Mair's letter he applied for and received a "summer hotel" authority, which permitted him to sell beer from 31 May to 31 October. In April 1937 Fontaine applied to take over the authority of the Log Cabin Hotel, which had been shut down by the board in March 1936. The new inspector, U.G. Reaume, noted that Belle River did not need any more hotels but recommended the authority be granted. Likely unfamiliar with Fontaine's history, Reaume reported that Fontaine "would be a good hotel man."[62] The authority was granted, although Fontaine sold out six months later and troubles continued at the Log Cabin.[63]

The Taylor Hotel file offers some evidence of the functioning of local politics with respect to the LCBO's operations. Theo Fontaine was the mayor of East Windsor and likely held some political pull. The reference to the election of 1935 suggests that Odette was not interested in undermining the federal Liberals' chances in the area by antagonizing Fontaine. That the board changed its approach to the hotel within six months of the election, combined with Trottier's own recommendation against the continued operation of the hotel, suggests that the Liberals, having swept the elections in all of the local ridings and with a considerable majority in the House, were not so keen to maintain such disreputable hotels. Indeed, after the election, the board decided to close a few of the more troublesome Belle River hotels; both the Taylor and Log Cabin Hotels lost their authorities, the latter in spite of the local council writing with a request to keep it open. That Fontaine applied for a summer authority might suggest that he had been informed by the individuals supporting his application that such an authority was a more palatable way for the board to deal with the hotel. As a resort town, Belle River did not need fully functioning hotels all year, so it was more reasonable to license a number of summer hotels, premises that critics would not see as being necessary during the winter. Reaume's endorsement of Fontaine's second application, in spite of the number of hotels in the town, seems innocuous, but it illustrates the value to the board of a good hotel building and the board's own short memory when dealing with hundreds of hotel issues every week. It might also suggest that the power of local politics continued – there was a provincial election in August 1937.

(Dys)functional Favouritism

Smith's assertion that politics and favouritism would undermine the effectiveness of the board's work spoke a language of authority built on the developing discourse of objective bureaucracy best represented by Max Weber's concept of bureaucratization. The ideal-typical bureaucracy, like the professional society, placed itself above the petty bickering of politics and aspired to construct an administration based on objective implementation of regulations, impersonal rules, and a division of labour that combined central control with individual expertise at the periphery.[64] Yet the activities of inspectors like Norman Ratz and Alfred Larocque demonstrate how the ideal of the bureaucracy was undermined more specifically by the realities of clientelism and patronage in 1930s Ontario. For the board to be effective, the periphery needed more oversight than the central administration was able to give, and the central administration itself was still, to some extent, locked in a pre-Weberian world of patronage and favours.

Certainly, there was considerable appeal in the attempts at objective enforcement of the rules. The ideal of objectivity enabled the board to present the image of an impartial, uninfluenceable decision maker, which used a sort of amoral calculation to make decisions about the placement, management, and discipline of hotels. Smith's assertions about the injustice of granting authorities to people simply because they were "good people" suggest this ideal. It was this impersonalization of rules, one of Weber's fundamental components of the modern bureaucracy, which was especially valuable in a highly politically charged environment such as 1930s Ontario. As Christopher Dandeker explains, "for Weber, impersonal rules are abstract, 'rationalized' principles, typically intentionally established, and apply to a specific delimited range of phenomena."[65] Moreover, such rules, being specific and objective, reinforce the authority of a select group of rule makers and enforcers. Here, the bureaucrats, although under siege by their political superiors, hold considerable power. Deploying a language of objective calculation – the calculus of need – could strengthen the board's ability to maintain its authority over the decisions about who could have the privilege of selling beer. At the same time, broader appeals to the behaviour or character of troublesome hotel proprietors could strengthen the bureaucratic arguments against granting an authority because politicians, then as now, were concerned with "optics."

Yet although Smith may have had to do the bidding of certain politicians when faced with considerable pressure, he and most especially William Mair, the assistant director of hotels, were also able to circumvent politics by using the mechanisms of the bureaucracy to deal with situations that had the potential to be politically touchy. In March 1936, for example, Smith was approached by Frederick Avery, MLA for Lincoln, who asked that an authority be given to the Dwarf Village Inn outside of the town of Jordan. Mair wrote to inspector Wilson Wylie asking him to make a report that reiterated the unsuitability of the hotel: "Mr Smith suggests that you visit the premises and point out the reason why the Board cannot consider the proposition."[66] Here, Mair was asking not for a decision on the inspector's part but for Wylie to reiterate the decision that had already been made based on problems with the physical layout of the hotel. Having done this, Wylie reported to the board that there were more than physical problems. He noted suspicions that the new proprietor, with whom he was unfamiliar, was using the hotel's light-beer permit to sell regular-strength beer and that there were considerable political machinations behind the application.[67] But publicly, by detailing the physical unsuitability of the establishment, the board could avoid submitting to the exigencies of politics. The proprietors, whose ability to follow the board's rules was suspect, would have a hard time contesting more concrete issues of physical layout. It was three years before they applied again for an authority.[68]

As the Dwarf Village example suggests, the board could also use its rules and its administrative complexities to shield it from revealing the true reason it did not want an authority granted. In 1935 the Armigari Hotel in Fort Erie applied for an authority. Noting that the hotel did not have enough rooms to meet the board's rules, Mair informed the proprietor that he could not have an authority. But the proprietor persisted, and when he submitted plans outlining his intended renovation to meet the board's rules, Mair wrote to inspector William Hart telling him that "Mr. Smith would appreciate your going over same and re-drafting them in such a manner that Sabino [the proprietor] will be required to expend a considerable amount of money on the conversion, Mr. Smith being in hopes that by this method Sabino will be compelled to forego his proposals."[69] Here, the regulations regarding layout and architectural suitability were used to manipulate aspiring hotel managers, although the reason that the board did not want this authority to be approved remains unclear. Finally, and most prominently, when the board felt that there was too much protest or that an authority could garner too much negative attention, it could fall back on the calculus of need, declaring simply that there were sufficient authorities for the area even while contemplating others. For example, when the Loon Lake Hotel persisted in asking for an authority, the board said there were sufficient authorities. Not a month earlier, Smith had admitted to a member of the Port Arthur Liberal Association that another hotel authority could be possible with the right establishment and the right kind of proprietor.[70]

Although the objective enforcement of rules – or at least the impression that the rules were being enforced objectively – had the functional value of preserving the board's social authority, patronage and the politics of favouritism were also functional within the control efforts of the LCBO. The regional diversity of the province required many perspectives on the operations of authorized premises. The board required all proprietors to obtain three character references from people who knew them; one had to be from the police and a second from a local politician. Moreover, when investigating applications or the conduct of authority holders, the board would often consult with a local member of the provincial Legislative Assembly or other government figure for a second or third opinion. Although this practice might appear to have been simple partisan politics, it is more properly viewed as evidence of the persistence of a hierarchical system of evaluation based on the guaranteed character of the evaluators. Politicians, respectable business people, and other public figures were simply better suited to interpreting the activities of authority holders and determining the respectability of these individuals than were unknown, everyday correspondents. Respectability was fundamental to the LCBO's operations because "the right person" would run a "respectable" hotel.

The impression that the LCBO was a tool of the Liberal Party meant that hotels whose operations were disreputable could reflect badly on the party and on the LCBO. This was the underlying theme of many criticisms of hotels that the board received. Three residents of the town of Hardrock, in north-western Ontario, wrote to the board advising it against granting an authority to the Hardrock Hotel: "We feel that the liberals or the liberal government is to[o] honest to grant a licence to such a woman she has a very bad reputation and all the family. If the government gives a license to [her] they will be guilty of adultry [sic] and manslaughter and we are not exaggerating if we say murder."[71] A correspondent wrote to Odette in 1934 complaining about the operation of the St. Clair Hotel in Windsor: "I don't know who your inspector around the Border cities is, but whoever he is, he is not thinking much about the future of the Liberal party."[72]

The assumption that poor hotel operations that held authorities from the LCBO could reflect badly on the Liberal Party could also be useful to the board because party loyalty might encourage broader surveillance by partisans. A Liberal ward chairman in Ottawa, commenting on the Carleton Hotel, promised to "keep a watch on this place to see that things were run in a manner that would be creditable to the Board and the Liberal Party in the county of Carleton."[73] Many others simply wrote to condemn authorized premises, citing their partisan connections in order to give credibility to their arguments. A justice of the peace in Geraldton wrote to protest the authority granted to the town's Canadian Legion branch. After providing an outline of the disorderly conduct that went on in the legion's halls, he reiterated his qualifications:

> I am the president of the Geraldton Liberal Association, having held executive office in that organization since it was founded. I am not a teetotaler, neither am I interested in any hotel business. I am definitely interested in good government and democratic ideals, and the proper functioning of the department of justice as it concerns the community in which I have made my home.[74]

A Liberal organizer in the Thunder Bay district wrote in 1937 to warn the board that the poor condition of hotels in Beardmore and Geraldton could reflect badly on the party and "may jeopardize our chances in [the provincial election in] October and undo all the work we have done ... This issue if not settled may prove to be the cause of ending organized Liberalism in a district which has grown in leaps and bounds and prospered under the present administration."[75] Each writer used his or her Liberal credentials to strengthen concerns about the prospects of the party while insisting that the LCBO do something to deal with disreputable hotels in his or her community.

Others used their Liberal credentials simply to bolster their criticisms of the board's actions in general. Mrs. George Mitchell began her letter protesting the authority granted to the Noah's Ark Hotel in Toronto's Danforth area by listing her background in Liberal organizations. Then she complained that the Noah's Ark would attract many "undesirables from down town."[76] Her interest was not partisan but personal since she was a resident, but she used her Liberal background to assert her authority. This was also the case of C.R. Widdifield, who wrote in 1940 to Odette's successor, Arthur St. Clair

Gordon, about his disillusionment with the actions of the board in Waterloo County:

> I well remember that before I went on the platform in the 1937 election campaign that I was instructed that I could say, with confidence, that politics were to be eliminated from the decisions of the Board; however, I find that in my first dealings with the Commission since that time that the local member is instructing Mr. Smith what to do.[77]

This statement is unreliable and unlikely to be true, but of importance here is the place of partisan politics in the public impression of the board's work.

The Limits of Political Influence: Port Arthur

Although politics could have a functional value in the regulatory operations of the LCBO, this fact should not blind us to the ways that partisan favouritism and a reliance on the perspectives of local politicians could restrict the board's field of visibility and interfere with its ability to function as a viable regulatory agency. The need to construct a feasible local public-drinking system required the board to license appropriate and respectable individuals whose premises were suitable for a community's needs. Failing to do this and making decisions that seemed clearly partisan could undermine the board's authority and therefore its ability to do its job. These intertwining discourses of functional and dysfunctional partisanism became resoundingly clear in the case of Donati's Hotel in Port Arthur. In this case, local and provincial politics clashed, and the value of obtaining the opinion of a reputable municipal politician conflicted with the interference of the area's MLA. The board was caught between allowing partisan favours, on the one hand, and adhering to the ideals of justice and the calculus of need, the mainstays of the board's decision making, on the other hand. This case also shows that, contrary to what we saw in Essex County, partisanism was not the only or the strongest force in the operations of the board.

When Charles Donati first applied for a standard hotel licence in 1933, inspector Hart commented on several physical problems that would need to be addressed before the board could consider the hotel for a licence. His evaluation went beyond the physical capacity of the building. He noted that, given the restrictions that had already been placed on beer sales in the area (restaurants had recently lost the right to sell beer, and hotelkeepers were feeling the financial pinch of the Depression), "the granting of [this] ... license would stir up a lot of trouble."[78] Yet Donati was a local business man who had run an apparently successful fruit store out of a part of the hotel premises, and he had the support of a number of prominent business-people, who wrote to the board endorsing the application. L.A. Green, one of the contractors who was working on the renovations, argued that Donati's store was "quite a community gathering place" and that he was therefore a respectable citizen who deserved to have an authority.[79] Donati's barrister also emphasized that the hotel would not be in competition with other hotels since Donati "caters to Italians."[80] He received a standard hotel licence in November 1933.

When the new LCA (1934) came into force, Donati reapplied to the board for an authority, and his application was rejected. He claimed to have spent by this time over $35,000 on renovations to his hotel, at least $10,000 of which had been to conform to the board's rules.[81] The local hotel association wrote a letter supporting Donati's application, noting that his was the only hotel that had received a standard hotel licence but not a beverage room authority.[82] The district inspector of the Ontario Provincial Police said that an authority should be granted, as did the chief of the local police department.[83] One of the hotel inspectors visited the region in November 1934 and observed that he did not see why the hotel had not received an authority.[84] In spite of considerable agitation, and even after Arnold Smith visited Port Arthur and heard many requests that the hotel be granted an authority, even from other hotel owners, no change was made.

Donati was not a perfect candidate for an authority, but his background was not so unusual as to make his application immediately problematic. William Mair noted that prior to 1934 Donati had been suspected of using the light-beer permit as a front for strong-beer sales, a not unusual charge. When he realized that the board was changing its rules in the early 1930s to confine light-beer sales to hotels, Mair explained, Donati began the renovations to his premises to make the place into an acceptable hotel.[85] Several of the correspondents observed that the board's decision not to grant the authority seemed odd and speculated that perhaps the problem was with a conviction Donati had under the old LCA for selling regular-strength beer. Moreover, one correspondent noted, and the LCBO's own inspection confirmed, that Donati had shot a man whom he found in bed with his wife. Interestingly, many of his proponents downplayed the importance of this act as a reflection of Donati's character; after all, they reasoned, the man had been in bed with Donati's wife.[86] So Donati's past, which was cited by several correspondents who wrote in favour of or in opposition to the application, could have been a mitigating factor. Yet as a number of the board's own officials argued, Donati appeared to have changed his ways. Moreover, the LCBO was not above granting authorities to individuals who had acquired a less than pristine reputation under the Ontario Temperance Act or under the old LCA.

These factors, however, did not cause Donati's trouble; his problem lay at the intersection of the personal and political. The local MLA, Charles Cox, who was also the mayor of Port Arthur, repeatedly intervened to challenge Donati's application. In September 1934 Cox wrote to the board that the authority should not be granted, and the board followed his advice.[87] Knowing that the mayor and MLA had argued that local Italians did not want the authority granted, Donati mustered a petition signed by over four hundred people, mostly Italians, who supported the granting of an authority. Donati's parish priest wrote several letters in support of the application and said that when he and Donati had visited Cox to argue their case, Cox insisted that it had nothing to do with him and that the decision "rested entirely with [the] Board."[88] This statement notwithstanding, Donati knew he had to deal with the mayor's opposition to his application. He asked the board whether his case would be helped by getting the Port Arthur city council to support his application even though the mayor did not. Odette agreed.[89] When Donati had such a resolution passed by the Port Arthur council and submitted it to the board with several letters of support from other businesses, the board granted the authority, and put it in the outgoing mail. Cox learned that this authority had been granted, telephoned Premier Hepburn and as explained in the passive voice of Smith, "instructions were given to this Board to cancel the Authority." The mail had not yet left the building, and the envelope containing the authority was intercepted.

Cox's opposition to the authority troubled many of the people involved in this case. According to Donati's priest, who wrote so many letters in support of Donati that he was chastised by his bishop for becoming politically involved, Donati was being used as a pawn in a bigger conflict between the local city council and Mayor Cox, who was purportedly unpopular with many of the local residents.[92] According to another correspondent, Donati was a corrupt Conservative supporter who did not deserve a licence.[93] According to Donati, Cox was being influenced by a woman who worked in Cox's office, whose family was "on very unfriendly terms with me and mine."[94]

Regardless of the cause of the local tensions, of interest here is the board's reaction to and action on the community input. As noted in the previous chapter and earlier in this one, the board was interested both in the reaction of the community leaders to a hotel proposition and in the impact that a hotel would have on the government and the board alike. Local politics were often a deciding factor and directly affected decisions at the provincial level. When the local MLA was not also a member of the municipal council, there was at least some hope of gaining unique perspectives on a hotel proposal, but in the case of Port Arthur, which was not likely unique in blurring the lines between municipal and provincial government, this division was not possible. The MLA's relationship with the municipal council was both intimate and conflicted. So with the Donati's Hotel proposition, we can examine the power of patronage and the board's reaction to it. How did the board's central administrators, some of whom at least gave lip service to acting independently, react to this sort of intervention?

The answer is that the board's administration reacted with a sort of bureaucratic passive aggression. The situation placed the board in a position that undermined its own authority and decision-making ability. So, faced with repeated requests from locals to explain the bizarre decision not to grant Donati an authority and seeing that the decision-making power had been taken out of the board's hands by the premier, Smith wrote an extended memo detailing this situation, which he sent to Premier Hepburn with the following note: "As these letters, under the circumstances, are rather difficult to answer, I am enclosing you herewith [a] memorandum dealing with this whole question, and am returning the letters in case you agree to answer them yourself. If not, I would appreciate your advising me just how you wish them answered."[95] Smith, himself a former politician, had placed responsibility for the decision back in the hands of Hepburn, who had been using the board to surreptitiously push his own personal agenda and to support the agenda of a party member, contrary to the board's own wishes. (Recall that Smith also made a similar request to St. Catharines MLA Frederick Avery when Avery interfered with a board decision.) The records are quiet on Hepburn's reaction to this letter, but for the next few months Cox seems to have been more amenable to the application. Yet it remained ungranted, and two months later, when the board's chief inspector visited the city and spoke to Cox, the MLA continued to express his opposition to the authority. As inspector John Pitt observed, "Nearly all whom I interviewed told me that the trouble was between Cox and Donati, and all told me the same story, which was ... that there was a woman at the bottom of it. I think it would be to Mr. Cox's interest not to oppose this application."[96] The records do not indicate much more opposition to the application for an authority, which was granted soon afterward.[97]

The Donati issue illuminates the board's place between partisan politics and the needs of the locality, between the subjective and objective decisions of a liquor control administration. Initially unimpressed with Charles Donati, the board soon realized that the community supported the application and that the proprietor had created a hotel that would likely suit the needs of the board itself. It was a sort of community centre for local Italians that had the support of local government, and the main problem it faced was based on the personal and the political rather than on the pragmatic issues of liquor control. This is not to say that politics were not involved in the board's actions, but that the decision to remove the authority from the mail after a directive from Hepburn should be considered an indication not that the board was actively involved in partisan politics but rather that its staff members were following the orders of their employer. Smith's subsequent letter to Hepburn demonstrates his frustration with the partisan cronyism of Hepburn's decision, and although we cannot know for certain what Hepburn was thinking, the eventual decision to grant the authority suggests that Hepburn himself realized that it was not politically expedient to continue such tactics. Smith's interest in the reputation of the LCBO's administration and his frustration with partisanism demonstrate an attempt at some kind of objective implementation of the rules, however limited in success this attempt might be.

The Port Arthur situation was not singular. Other cases of attempts at political influence that did not work can be cited briefly. William Houck, the MLA for Welland, was routinely denied special favours when he asked for them, even though he cited tremendous community upheaval (which seems to have existed only in Houck's eyes). More significant was the case of the Queensway Hotel in St. Catharines, noted in the previous chapter. When this hotel, a new, modern, fireproof hotel, was built in downtown St. Catharines, it did not receive an authority in 1939 because the city council and many residents (led it seems by the local newspaper) opposed it. Two years later, in the face of increased beverage room traffic in St. Catharines' downtown, the hotel did receive an authority, resulting in, among other things, the local Liberal MLA, Archie Haines, resigning in disgust, claiming that there was a "toll gate" in the LCBO. A "toll gate" was the term used to indicate insider influence, where certain people were given certain privileges. Hepburn, who usually remained silent on these issues, chastised Haines and accepted his letter of resignation, claiming that there was no toll gate but that there was an increased need for beverage room and hotel accommodation – the board was attempting to deal with increased disorder in the city centre due to the insufficient beverage room and hotel space.[98] Haines's integrity was not absolute: he was closely tied to other local hotel owners, who saw the new authority as competition, but he also did try to uphold the principles expressed by the city council. In the end, he ran again as a Liberal in 1943, winning his seat while the party went down to inglorious defeat.

In the 1930s, although provincial politics were undoubtedly still steeped in patronage, a system that many saw to be functional, the LCBO sought to mitigate the negative impact of the overtures for patronage by emphasizing justice and order in its licensing decisions. It was only partially successful. For several of the members of the senior administration, notably Arnold Smith, but also certainly William Mair and John Pitt, the political machinations of their superiors often interfered with the construction and operation of a reasonable and viable liquor control system across the province. Smith especially attempted to impose a non-partisan philosophy on those whose work he oversaw and simultaneously attempted to influence his superiors to de-emphasize both partisan politics and cronyism in their work. As with the case of the Queensway Hotel in St. Catharines, the political situation remained controversial; in that case, the local MLA resigned when the hotel was granted an authority, a decision he did not support. Yet even in that case, the politician's public statement was that he opposed a potentially cronyistic "toll gate," which he argued must have been the reason that the Queensway Hotel had received an authority. Ironically, of interest in this comment is the assumption that some insider was receiving a political favour, when the evidence suggests that, in fact, the board was acting specifically to deal with a regulatory issue, politics notwithstanding. This decision contrasts somewhat with Donati's case, where the pressure from the locality was resisted by a very personally motivated favouritism. The outcome of the Donati case saw the ideal of justice prevail over partisan cronyism; the outcome of the Queensway Hotel incident saw the principle of social order prevail over municipal and provincial partisan politics.

Although Arnold Smith resigned from the board in 1941, it is difficult to determine from the records after his departure whether he had been the main person responsible for the nonpartisan (or perhaps it is better to say "low partisan") perspective of the board. As I discuss in Chapter 9, the priorities of the board shifted somewhat during the war, so from 1941 to 1944 any partisan rhetoric would be joined by an intense nationalism. We do know that Arthur St. Clair Gordon, who succeeded Odette as chief commissioner, was an elected member of the provincial Legislature, so his political interests may have affected his decisions and his instructions to Smith. Yet, at the same time, Gordon was not immediately replaced after the Liberals lost the 1943 provincial election. So there is some evidence that by the 1940s the LCBO's central administration had moved closer to achieving the apolitical state of Weber's ideal-typical bureaucracy. It may have been an unachievable state, and there is no doubt that politics continued to shape the LCBO's decisions, but the construction of a viable liquor control bureaucracy that was motivated by the ideals of disinterested management weakened, if not severed, the strong partisan political links while reinforcing an agenda based on the priorities of the bureaucracy.

6
Restructuring Recreation in the Drinking Space

The physical restructuring of the public drinking space, the hotel's role in the community, and the politics of granting beer and wine authorities all involved negotiation of the proper uses of licensed drinking spaces. So the activities of the board were fundamentally about controlling, or negotiating, what went on inside the licensed establishments. These efforts were tremendously important to the success of the board's operations because, although drunkenness was a problem, there was concern not only over the consumption of beverages but also over the range of other activities that had been traditionally associated with drinking and the drinking space. By the middle of the nineteenth century in Ontario, the relationship between drinking and other forms of recreation had informed much of the rhetoric of the anti-drink movement.[1] Although the physical effects of alcohol were discussed in temperance rhetoric, the target of the temperance jeremiads was often not so much the substance consumed as the other activities that the drinker undertook when under the influence of drink: gambling, whoring, carousing, fighting, smoking, and so on – what John Burnham has labelled so aptly a "constellation of minor vices."[2]

Studying the history of the public drinking spaces of nineteenth-century North America, be they called taverns, inns, saloons, public houses, or pubs, historians have uncovered a variety of social activities accompanying drinking.[3] Some of these activities were what reformers would consider socially destructive, such as prostitution or gambling, which undermined the integrity of the family. Many other pastimes were parts of the texture of social, political, and economic life, making the drinking space often a community centre: political gatherings, sports events, social support, job hunting, meals, and shelter might be found in the numerous and varied public drinking places. When he fell ill in 1855 from, apparently, drinking a glass of cold water, labourer John Blackie found a bed in a local tavern in Toronto.[4] Julia Roberts has demonstrated the essential position of the country tavern within the social life of the community, and Peter Delottinville's excavation of the place of Joe Beef's Tavern in working-class Montreal suggests a similar role for the urban tavern.[5] The drinking space was not only a part of leisure activity; it was a fundamental part of life.

Nevertheless, the activities within the drinking space were increasingly the focus of scrutiny and control. By the end of the nineteenth century, the movement toward "rational recreation" sought to structure leisure time in a way that ensured this time was productive, moral, and shaped by middle-class values. As advocates of what amounts to a radical social change, rational-recreation reformers saw many of the stereotypical activities within the saloon as anathema to social progress. The ubiquitous images of the saloon, presented in bestsellers such as T.S. Arthur's *Ten Nights in a Bar-Room and What I Saw There* as well as in everyday temperance rhetoric, depicted the public drinking place as a cesspool of degradation, not to mention a place where energies, both vital and physical, along with money, were wasted. Rational recreation sought to redirect these energies, encouraging conformity through the guise of self-improvement.[6]

Although rational-recreation rhetoric was generally on the wane by the 1930s, its ideas lingered in the activities of government regulators. Robert Campbell has shown how provincial regulators in British Columbia seriously curtailed what could and could not be done in the beer parlours of Vancouver, seeing games, dancing, and music as likely to "encourage a saloon-like atmosphere."[7] Similarly, the Liquor Control Board of Ontario (LCBO) sought to separate the consumption of alcohol from other forms of leisure pursuit. Notably, it tried to eliminate the association between drinking and the other stars in the constellation of vices. Drinking was to be done in a staid, controlled environment, music was not allowed, most card games were forbidden, spontaneous singalongs were stopped by a visiting inspector, and single women were not supposed to mingle with single men. In effect, public drinking, as a touchstone for other forms of irrational recreation characterized by wasteful energies, was contained and sanitized. Moreover, as James Nicholls notes for England, pub-improvement strategies, made along lines dictated by middle-class ideas of respectability, "opened up a new front line in the battle for control over the working class drinking place."[8] Middle-class respectability, which motivated the rational recreationists' efforts, could remain even after the movement disappeared.

Yet these efforts presented the board with a bit of a quandary: if people wanted to socialize and indulge in various legal pastimes like singing, dancing, and playing games when they drank, being too restrictive would undermine the board's mission to facilitate public drinking so that people would forsake illegal drinking establishments in favour of the licensed beverage room. For this work to succeed, the board needed to strike a balance between a completely sanitized drinking space and the morally degraded and socially disordered stereotypical pre-prohibition saloon. This was necessary for two main reasons. First, it was intended to keep the drinkers going to licensed establishments rather than to illegal (and therefore uncontrolled) "blind pigs" or "speakeasies." Second, more pragmatically but less often clearly stated, the board recognized the need to permit the hotels to remain solvent. No matter how preferable legal drinking might be, if the local authorized hotel went out of business, the only resort for the socializing citizen-drinker was to patronize the illegal establishments. Consequently, the creation and enforcement of rules about what could take place in the drinking space did not just involve the LCBO dictating and the drinkers or establishment owners concurring. Rather, the process entailed a series of multidimensional discussions, debates, pressures, and evaluations in which ideas of local context and social order were paramount. These elements involved various configurations of binary pairings – proper and improper, legal and illegal, permissible and impermissible – but also more nuanced discourses of control and the exercise and reiteration of biopower. In the efforts to shape the activities within the beverage room, the LCBO and other interested parties re-evaluated the relationship between alcohol consumers and the proper behaviour that made them respectable citizen-drinkers.

This chapter examines the reconstitution of entertainment within the drinking space in Ontario. Although it attempted to separate drinking from other forms of entertainment, the LCBO found that to contain drinking within a controlled space, it needed to permit, to a certain degree, other leisure activities that would make the legal, licensed drinking space attractive to drinkers. After examining the various ways that hotel proprietors attempted to build clientele and the LCBO's reactions to these efforts, the chapter examines the most notable area of negotiation: the introduction and regulation of music and dancing within the drinking space. Dancing, especially, was a unique case. As a part of rational recreation, it had elements of physical activity and healthy socialization. But simultaneously, concerns over the jazz culture and "modern" youth culture that emerged in the 1920s meant that dancing could be something of a supernova in the constellation of vices, leading the way into other forms of excess, most notably sexual misbehaviour but also the potential for class or ethnic miscegenation, drug taking, gambling, and new, post-prohibition dangers, such as surreptitious drinking of hard alcohol and drunk driving. So dancing was Janus-faced, and after the first few years of its attempts to permit dancing in hotel spaces, the board found that there were too many abuses and too many opportunities for rule violation and immorality. It then reconsidered its rules and deployed stricter criteria along class-based lines for permitting the intersection of dancing and drinking.

The 1934 Liquor Control Act's (LCA) public-drinking provisions were designed clearly (yet not blatantly) to eradicate specific unsavoury practices relating to pre-prohibition saloon operations, and they touched directly on more egregious forms of entertainment. Section 79 (2) forbade authority holders from permitting "any gambling, drunkenness or any riotous, quarrelsome, violent or disorderly conduct [to occur,] ... any slot machine or gambling device to be placed, kept or maintained," or "any person of notoriously bad character to remain."[9] The latter provision likely referred subtly to prostitution, although it also permitted inspectors to keep an eye on any "bad elements" who frequented the beverage room. These limited proscriptions empowered the board to enact a variety of rules, often in direct response to activities taking place in various hotels. The regulations would be created by the LCBO's central administration and passed by the governor-in-council, a process that circumvented the need to go back to the provincial Legislative Assembly each time a new rule was made but also one that, according to the LCA, would imbue the regulations with legal force.[10]

Almost immediately, the board created a variety of regulations, which it modified as circumstances and experience necessitated. Consolidated annually in a *Digest of Rules, Orders, Regulations and Legislation* and distributed to hotel proprietors, these regulations outlined in some depth the expectations of proper comportment within hotel beverage and dining rooms. The first post-LCA (1934) version of the *Digest* expanded the list of activities that would not be tolerated in the beverage room. Literally at the top of the list of suspect activities to be prohibited were "music, singing, dancing, disorder, quarrelling, profane or obscene language or misbehaviour." The list that was included in Section 79 of the LCA was expanded to include "any person who is suspected of being on the premises for some improper purpose." All beverage rooms were to be closed by 11 p.m., but dining rooms would be allowed to remain open until midnight.[11] The potential for beverage room customers to move from the beverage room to the dining room at 11 p.m. for a last call was specifically addressed in the rules governing dining rooms, which forbade hotels to sell beer and wine without a suitably large food order, or "guest check" (originally 25 cents, not including the cost of beer), or to reopen their dining rooms from 11 p.m. to midnight "for the sole purpose of selling Beer and Wine with meals."[12] In its first written regulations affecting the activities of people within the public drinking space, then, the LCBO reiterated a discourse of social order that connected disorderly drinking to a broad array, or "constellation," of troublesome activities.

This decision to isolate drinking from other forms of socialization, except dining, was soon found to be inadequate. The imaginary sterile drinking place, in which patrons did nothing more than, to paraphrase Campbell, sit down and drink their beer, did not suit the expectations of drinkers and proprietors.[13] In the first few years of the LCA (1934)'s operation, the LCBO's inspectors spent considerable time and effort policing the attempts by proprietors to introduce a variety of types of entertainment into their establishments. Singing, music, dancing, cards, and gambling – indeed, virtually all of the activities prohibited in the 1935 *Digest* – were some of the forms of recreation that proprietors, either wittingly or (less likely) unwittingly, permitted in their establishments.

Innovative attempts to inject some entertainment while also encouraging people to stay in the hotel were not viewed kindly by the LCBO. When the inspector learned that the Hotel Howard in Fort Erie let patrons roll dice for "ducks, geese and turkeys as prizes," he put an end to the practice immediately.[14] The Golden Hotel in Tecumseh attempted to draw customers with door prizes and was similarly reprimanded.[15] Some proprietors were persistent. In April 1939 Toronto's Ridley Arms Hotel had a "tea cup reader" in its dining room and was told not to do it again. A week later, they featured a crystal-ball reader in "an Egyptian costume."[16] The proprietor of the Bon Villa Hotel in Niagara Falls tried a variety of entertainment ventures to lure customers. One week, the hotel featured "Madame Vendus ... [who] purports to foretell the fortunes of patrons." The next week it brought in tap dancers.[17] Even something as seemingly innocent as playing a radio in the beverage room so that the customers could listen to baseball's World Series was refused in the case of the Station Hotel, near Welland.[18] The board looked askance at blatant attempts to encourage people to stay in order to drink.

One of the main types of leisure activities that the board's inspectors or police discovered in beverage rooms was gambling in a variety of forms. Gambling was a persistent target of the rational recreationists, who saw it as an unfortunate accompaniment to drinking. Some research has confirmed that gambling was indeed a common element within the drinking environment.[19] Gambling played many roles in working-class culture, from providing a pleasurable pastime to offering the hope of relief from financial desperation. The board received many stories from police, inspectors, and the general public about gambling activities taking place in beverage rooms. In 1937 the Ontario Provincial Police reported on a proposed hotel in Sandwich, near Windsor, arguing that the place "was no doubt a dive operated not only for the illegal use of liquor but perhaps also for gaming."[20] The same year, the Belmont Hotel in Port Colborne was suspected of harbouring "a person of no visible means of support and of whom it was said was using the rooms for the purpose of gambling." On further discussion, Arnold Smith learned that the man "conducts poker games." He was asked to vacate his rooms, although three months later he was reportedly still there.[21] In 1934 the inspector in Welland crawled through a window in the basement of the Roma Hotel to find evidence that gambling had taken place.[22] Even "friendly" games of cards were not only forbidden but actually illegal. When the police "paid a visit" to two Ottawa clubs, the Bridge Club and the Association Athletique Montagnard, they found "a friendly game of poker ... where very little money was involved."[23] Both clubs were charged with being in violation of the Liquor Control Act and had their beer authorities suspended. The suspensions were lifted after the management of the clubs, insisting they had not realized that they were violating any laws, promised not to let it happen again, although in the next few years both clubs committed repeat offences.

Like games of chance, suggestions of bookmaking also appeared, resulting in the suspension of authorities and in prosecutions. In March 1936 the proprietor of the British American Hotel in Windsor was convicted of running a betting house. Police found a battery of telephones and betting slips in the proprietor's room. He contended that they "pertained to his private active interest in racing as an owner and trainer of horses," but the magistrate retorted, "I believe you were maintaining a common betting house."[24] In 1939 the police began "a drive on the handbooks" in Windsor and, according to one somewhat credible correspondent, closed down a betting house next door to the Ambassador Hotel, "materially effecting [sic] the beverage business" of the nearby Ambassador and Woodbine Hotels. According to the correspondent, a disbarred lawyer who purportedly had lost a lot of money, the result of the raid was that the Woodbine Hotel established "a wide open book"[25] – that is, a bookkeeping operation that everyone in the beverage room knew about.

Any mention of gambling would usually receive immediate attention from the board. In any report or letter sent to the board that contained the word "gambling," it would likely be circled or underlined in the central administration's ubiquitous red pencil, and a letter of some sort would be sent out immediately. In letters of complaint, gambling became a sort of trope for more general immoral activity. In an anonymous letter that was later determined to be baseless, the proprietor of Ottawa's Palace Hotel was accused of "running a Game of Quits at the rear of the building the loser paying the drinks,"[26] and an anonymous complaint about the Border Cities Polish Canadian Club called the place a "terrible gambling house."[27] "A citizen" wrote to the LCBO in 1942 complaining that the owner of Welland's Colonial Hotel held "a dice and poker game ... nearly every night till [sic] all hours of the mornings."[28] In these and other instances of letters accusing an establishment of gambling, the central administration immediately insisted that the local inspector investigate the charges and report back.

Most letters with accusations such as those above were found to be untrue, but of importance here is the meaning behind the repetition of this imagery. Anonymous correspondents who wrote to the board complaining of activities in local, licensed establishments were suspected of being either temperance advocates or, more often, local competition, either other hotels or illegal drinking establishments that may have been finding that the legitimate establishments were cutting into their profits. Yet significantly, all appear to have believed that using images of illicit gambling in association with drinking would damage the reputation of the beverage room. And they were right. By creating suspicion of gambling, they drew on the very constellation of vices that informed the dominant cultural metaphors of problem drinking. What they may not have counted on was that the board looked at most anonymous letters, or letters whose author could not be found, as suspicious and unlikely to be credible. So the opponents of authorized beverage rooms, be they temperance advocates or competing "blind pigs," deployed traditional imagery in their drive to discredit legitimate public drinking spaces. They put pressure on legal drinking spaces by exploiting the board's need to create respectable space. Yet this same guiding principle, the need for respectable space, in combination with the board's attempts to enforce its rules judiciously, meant that it investigated with rigour but some skepticism complaints of blatant rule transgression.

Although most gaming activities were censured by the board as clear instances of gambling, this was not to say all gaming was forbidden. Of importance was the connection between gaming and drinking; the two activities needed to be kept separate. When the proprietor of Ottawa's LaSalle Hotel renovated his basement "such as to provide room for patrons to participate in a game called 'sand bag throwing,'" the board permitted the activity, although Smith rejected inspector Alfred Larocque's rather bizarre suggestion that the room be turned into a beverage room so that patrons could drink while playing. Since games were being played, no beer could be served.[29]

Another notable form of gambling, and far less easy to conceal than card games or dice, was the use of mechanical gambling devices, especially slot machines. Just as new technology permitted gambling in the American saloons, so too did this technology appear in Ontario's hotels.[30] According to some authorities, slot machines were invented in the 1890s but became increasingly popular in the 1930s.[31] This popularity has been attributed to the invention of much lighter and quieter machines, but likely the desperation of the Depression drove people to see gambling as a possible route to some financial relief.[32] Slot machines appeared especially popular in Essex County and Niagara, border communities that were susceptible to the influence and expectations of American visitors.[33]

The term "slot machine" was given to any device that required the user to place coins or slugs in a slot, so it could apply to machines such as vending machines and other games that gave no prizes, like early pinball games. Slot machines were licensed in many municipalities across the province, mostly as simple amusements, and were legal so long as they either were games of skill or did not pay off in actual money or prizes. Yet even if the slot machine paid off with nothing more than slugs, the machines were part of a subculture of gambling. Toronto's Police Court often heard stories of patrons or undercover police officers who played the games and could exchange a certain number of slugs for gum, cigarettes, or money. This practice was illegal. In one of many slot machine cases tried by the Toronto Police Court, P.C. Deans, the officer working the slot machine beat, reported how, after winning slugs in a restaurant's slot machine, he asked the waitress to exchange his slugs for cigarettes. She said she was not allowed to do that. But after Deans continued to play for a bit, she looked at him and said, "I guess you're all right" and made the exchange.[34] In many of these trials, the defendants might attempt to argue that the games were not games of chance (which were illegal) but rather games of skill. By 1935 authorities across the province had begun to crack down on slot machines, and critics argued that the devices were a drain on the financial and moral resources of the poor. As Suzanne Morton has explained, in the 1930s slot machines and other games with minimal payoffs were an especially attractive form of recreation and gambling for poor people and were lucrative for the vendor.[35]

This growing moral panic around gambling and the high visibility of slot machines in general, combined with the traditional association of drinking with gambling, led LCBO inspectors to view the presence of such devices in hotel beverage rooms as problematic, irrespective of the grey legal area slot machines occupied. Betting on the outcome of games, whether they be games of chance such as dice or of skill like many card games and sports, was a mainstay of the pre-prohibition saloon culture.[36] Allusions to this activity could result in immediate action from authorities. For example, in a somewhat sensationalized story, the *St. Catharines Standard* reported on a police raid on a local hotel in 1928. Listening beneath the window, the police purportedly heard one patron say, "let's shoot the dice and see who will buy the next drink."[37] The police broke down the door. Given the LCBO's recognition of the unsavoury link between any game of chance and drinking, when board officials discovered "slot machines" or "machines of the slug variety" or even machines that proprietors argued were simple vending machines, they ordered them removed, and they suspended or threatened to suspend the hotel's beer authority.

When found to have a slot machine on their premises, hotel proprietors attempted to downplay its significance, claiming they did not consider it to be an illegal gambling machine but rather a vending machine or innocent entertainment. Investigating the New Statler Hotel in St. Catharines, inspector Wilson Wylie reported that although the proprietor "has always insisted that it was simply a source of amusement to patrons," his inspection had determined that the machine "is used for gaming purposes, the method being that a number of men put up a sum of money with the highest scorer to buy the drinks."[38] Such activities were reflections of pre-prohibition saloon practices, but without drinking involved, they were not necessarily illegal.

When provincial police found that the Erie Downs Golf Club had slot machines on its premises, they pushed for a conviction, but the local magistrate "does not find that they are used for gaming purposes."[39] Similarly, Harry Hamilton, proprietor of the Log Cabin Hotel in Belle River, near Windsor, argued that the slot machine he had in his establishment was simply a "licensed vending machine" and that most local hotels used them.[40] Pleading ignorance, Hamilton promised to remove it immediately. Eldon Scratch, the proprietor of the Grand Central Hotel in Windsor, argued that his town licensed slot machines. Having just purchased the hotel, he claimed that the previous owner had paid a $100 licence fee and "was under the impression that this [fee] legalized" the slot machine.[41] Like Hamilton at the Log Cabin, Scratch pleaded ignorance and claimed he had not intended to renew this licence. When Riverside's Island View Hotel was found to have two slot machines in operation in 1936, the proprietor, Albert Hebert, was told to remove them. He complied, writing to the board, "we have removed our vending machine," which suggests that even if he did not actually believe it was simply a vending machine, he was letting the illusion of innocence persist.[42]

The apparent confusion between gambling machines and vending machines, between illegal and legal devices, appears to have been rooted, at least partly, in the fluid and often subjective judgments of the LCBO staff members themselves. Their assessments often contradicted contemporary popular culture and local regulations. Although communities might license certain types of machines or other public entertainments in public places, the LCBO, an agency of the provincial government, was not bound by the spirit of such laws. A machine might be legal, but to the board it was inappropriate in a licensed drinking space. Legitimacy at one level did not mean that the LCBO had to permit the behaviour in the spaces it authorized to sell alcohol; in this way, the board's regulations were often more rigorous than the parameters set out by law.

This regulatory independence was especially valuable when the board had to determine what to do about relatively new games that occupied a grey area of legality. The use of both keno and bingo was especially problematic for the board. In keno, which was not unlike many modern lotteries, players would purchase a ticket that had a list of numbers; the player would mark the numbers he or she hoped would be drawn, and prize values corresponded to how many correct numbers the player had predicted. Bingo was essentially the same as it is today. Both games were relatively new to Canada. Although keno's name was European in origin, the game originated in China and may have been brought to North America by Chinese labourers; the birthplace of bingo is less clear, but it is believed to have been brought to Canada by returned soldiers after the First World War.[43] The foreign origins of the games seem never to be mentioned in the board's records, so it is unlikely that its opposition to them was based in racialized notions of deviance.

The similarity between keno and bingo made them simultaneously popular with the public but problematic for the board. Both games were necessarily activities for large groups, which meant they were fundamentally social. Either game itself could be the single focus of a group event, or it could be one of a number of games played on a social night out. This social characteristic in itself was not problematic, but since winners were determined by luck rather than skill, the games could easily be defined as gambling. Most commentators (and often laws) distinguished between gambling and other games by the skill level needed to win. Winning by pure luck was considered morally questionable. So games of chance held in large groups were often frowned on by social and moral commentators. Yet at the same time, both were popular among respectable organized groups and were often held for charitable purposes.[44] Suzanne Morton explains that bingo quickly became popular in church fundraising activities, laying the groundwork for a century of jokes about ministers, church ladies, and little balls.[45]

The relative newness and popularity of keno and bingo resulted in a good deal of scrambling by the board to determine the nature of games being held in hotels. In 1937 Essex County inspector U.G. Reaume noted that several hotels in his district "have been in the habit of holding Keno parties around this season of the year, supposedly for charitable purposes." This appears to have been considered a legitimate use of keno, but Reaume began to receive reports that some of the hotels were actually holding the keno games "for their own gain to bolster up their business." He named specifically the Island View Hotel in Riverside but noted that he had observed a trend among hotels to take up the sorts of entertainments that the board was allowing at one hotel and try these games themselves: "When one hotel hears of another having a Keno they also want to have one and they offer any excuse for that purpose." To deal with the problem, he requested that the chief commissioner send a press release to the local newspaper explaining that the board was against keno games.[46] The article appeared in early December.[47]

Yet this prohibition did not hold. A year later, the same hotel asked to be allowed to host the local Booster Club's annual keno. Reaume argued that this should be permitted, using a subjective evaluation of the merits of the organization: "The club is doing very good work in the Town and is worthy of consideration. I would recommend that permission is given to them and I will see that no beverage is served in the dining room, where the keno will be held."[48] A few months later, the Highway Hotel in Windsor asked Reaume whether they could hold a keno party under the auspices of the "Macedonian Political Organization." Reaume noted that since the request came close to the date of the event, there was no chance to call it off. He told the hotel management that "in future they should give the Board at least ten days' notice ... I told them if they wanted to take a chance and hold the entertainment without the Board's permission in writing they should see to it that no beverage is sold in the dining room during the time of the entertainment."[49] The mention of ten days' notice and the suggestion that the board was granting permission to such events again suggest that the board had developed a new practice regarding keno since the year previous. Although there is no record of this policy change, this appears to be a case of a blanket prohibition being replaced by something more moderate. The outcome appears to be that, when it came to such charitable activities, the board usually permitted them to be held but made sure that drinking was not a part of the festivities. It did, however, keep a close eye on the activities since hotels were not supposed to use them purely to boost their own revenues.

It was the profit motive that caused the most concern for the board. As Reaume's comment about keno games illustrates, inspectors and the board's central administration were cautious about the profit motive of proprietors. Profit undermined disinterested management. Holding events that would draw patrons into the hotel so that they could then partake of alcohol to boost profits was not an acceptable business strategy in the board's view. The proprietor could sell alcohol but not draw people in with various activities simply to get them to buy booze. This approach would both reconnect alcohol to dubious leisure activities and simultaneously be a way of keeping people at the hotel for long stretches of time, during which they could continue to consume alcohol and get drunk. So socially organized games of chance on their own held a danger both of moral corruption and simultaneously of social disorder. Linking such games with drinking held additional danger for two reasons: first, it was reminiscent of the pre-prohibition link between drinking and gambling; second, it indicated a proprietor's own tendency to seek to increase booze sales by luring patrons into the hotel. Although it might be good business to keep patrons at the hotel for long stretches in order to increase the amount of money they spent, a proprietor who wanted to boost his or her own profits through any form of social activity that kept patrons drinking in the hotel was demonstrating questionable moral judgment, however sound his or her business acumen.

The clever hotel proprietor would tap into social trends to draw in customers, so although keno, bingo, and various forms of innovative social activities could appeal to a broad range of people, the golden egg was laid by dancing and music. With music and dancing, the board confronted an activity whose moral status was not as clearly delineated as was gambling and gaming in a drinking space. Here, we find a considerable amount of debate and negotiation over what sort of entertainment could happen in hotels. Although the pre-prohibition saloon was a place where music might have been played, the idea of heterosocial dancing did not fit easily into the conceptualization of this mythic space and therefore was not necessarily anathema to orderly drinking behaviour. The issues relating to the combination of drinking and music or dancing were complex. Drinking as a single social activity had to be isolated from other potentially dangerous activities, but music and dancing could fit within a bourgeois conception of a respectable night on the town. Since the LCA did permit beer and wine to be consumed with meals and since many restaurants and other establishments also held "dinner dances," the LCBO had to wrestle with repeated requests for permission to have music in the dining room, with or without dancing. The negotiation of these new connections between music, dancing, and drinking was informed by the need to avoid pre-prohibition saloon immorality but was driven by modern ideas of leisure and recreation. Indeed, rational recreation itself embraced the value of dancing within a controlled and strictly supervised environment, and the LCBO's "Standard Hotels" supposedly epitomized such a public space. So when developing its rules on dancing and music in public drinking spaces, the LCBO opened the door to a broader place for drinking within the context of a specific form of recreation, one ostensibly controlled and under strict surveillance but not always conducted in an ideal manner.

Although many studies have looked at the dance crazes of the jazz age, often through the lens of the sensationalized speakeasy culture of prohibition, there has been much less attention to the development of dance hall cultures in Canada during prohibition. And few have considered at the link between dancing and drinking in this time. Dancing was often condemned by rational recreationists as immoral or a precursor to immorality. Many religious groups, such as the Baptists, roundly condemned dancing, but as Catherine Gidney has shown, young Baptists in the 1930s found dance pavilions (like the ones in the Niagara region's Port Dalhousie) to be an ideal location for respectable courtship.[50] Similarly, many young working-class men in American cities set up social clubs specifically to meet girls and often spent a good amount of the clubs' savings to renovate the spaces and make them attractive to potential partners.[51] This youth culture was a major source of concern for middle-class, middle-aged Canadians, and many worried about the "youth dance craze," which would lead to "debauchery and degrading circumstances."[52]

Yet dancing was not exclusively the domain of the young, nor were dancing and drinking exclusively considered a bad thing. David Gutzke has shown how, in 1920s Britain, reformist and opportunistic brewers began to build dance halls to capitalize on the new public interest in dance.[53] These establishments were connected to the reformed pubs and drew not on a youth-oriented fixation with jazz culture but on a middle- and upper-class Edwardian and Georgian interest in the public dance. Although Gutzke does not talk about rational recreation, it is reasonable to assume that, for these reformers, dance in a controlled and bourgeois environment could be a part of a broader rational-recreationist agenda. Reacting to Gutzke's assertion that pub improvement was a strategy of British progressives, James Nicholls argues that this was a middle-class attempt at colonization of the working-class drinking space.[54] Whichever perspective you accept, the relationship between middle-class respectability and certain forms of acceptable dancing persisted.

This contrasting view of dancing represents a bifurcated appreciation of the connection between music and dancing and the consumption of alcoholic beverages. This potentially salacious pairing is threaded throughout the board's documentation from its inception in 1927. Prior to the LCA (1934), the "Report of Restaurant Light Beer Permit Holder," which inspectors completed for each establishment, included the question "Is there a dance hall or pool room connected with the Restaurant by any covered passageway or way of internal communication?"[55] The connection of dancing with billiards and the interest in the physical proximity between these activities and a place that sold beer, even the relatively weak light beer, suggest a concern over the potential mingling of alcohol with these other forms of recreation.

Soon after the LCA (1934) became law, the board was faced with increased demands to allow dancing in hotels. If it chose to forbid outright this popular activity, it risked driving people to patronize illegal drinking establishments or to drink illegally in legal dancing establishments. But if rules were not established for the practice, the board would lose control (not an ideal situation for a "Control Board"). So it established parameters. Music and dancing in beverage rooms were strictly forbidden, but they were allowed under certain conditions in dining rooms. Many proprietors attempted to introduce some kind of musical entertainment in the beverage room and were always censured for doing so. Visiting during the day, inspector Wylie found a piano in the ladies and escorts' beverage room of the Trennick Hotel in Niagara Falls. The manager explained that the piano "was placed in this room to provide necessary music to a tap dancing class or school," but Wylie ordered the piano to be removed.[56] The Hotel Grimsby, in the town up the highway from Wylie's home in Jordan, had employed a tap dancer accompanied by "a three piece orchestra discoursing third rate jazz music ... in the front window of [the] Hotel ... The obvious reason for the innovation would be to direct all and sundry that there was in the village a real live tavern."[57] He worried that such a display would provide temperance forces with evidence of the terrible impact of the LCA on a small town, and his use of the term "tavern" suggests the distasteful and morally questionable (but socially alluring) connection between music, dancing, and drink. Moreover, his characterization of the band's music as "third rate" suggests that a first-rate band might have been acceptable and that the proprietor's interest was not to draw in patrons of the musical arts but patrons of the zymurgistic. In Waterloo County inspector Norman Ratz reported that the Embassy Hotel in St. Agatha was using the dining room as a ladies and escorts' beverage room. Although this practice could be acceptable, the dining room also had a music box and piano, which would "encourage the odd party to dancing."[58] Unlike Wylie's concerns about the Hotel Grimsby, Ratz explained that he had received little criticism about this hotel's operation, although within the month the board received a number of complaints about drinking and dancing parties at this hotel and wrote to the manager to remind him to behave.[59]

As the example from the Embassy Hotel in St. Agatha suggests, the dining room was subject to more regulatory flexibility than was the tightly controlled beverage room environment, but it too had fundamental prerequisites. Dining was a priority. In June 1935 inspector John Pitt wrote to Smith after an inspection of the Keewatin Hotel in Ottawa. The managers of this hotel, he noted, "do not operate the Dining room, but use it for Beverage purposes and allow dancing and music."[60] Similarly, in August 1935 the proprietor of Toronto's New Strathcona Hotel asked permission to allow dancing. Initially, he wanted to change the ladies' beverage room into a dining room for the purpose, but this was not permitted. Then he hoped to move the dining room to the main floor and, owing to the small size of the hotel, allow dancing in one room and dining in the other. His several attempts to rearrange the hotel to accommodate dancing were a direct result of local competition. Three hotels were close to the New Strathcona, and as inspector John Kidd explained, if they don't all have dancing, "they will starve to death." Possibly out of exasperation with the demands for dancing in inappropriate spaces, inspector Kidd wrote in his monthly report that "some definite regulation governing dancing in Hotel Dining Rooms should be immediately considered by the board, or we will be accused of playing favoritism."[61]

Kidd's concern may have been unique to Toronto, which had many hotels relatively close to each other, but the lack of specific guidelines for hotels was not unnoticed in the central office. A few months before Kidd's report on the New Strathcona, Arnold Smith travelled to Essex County to deal with the persistent demands for dancing privileges in area hotels. Essex County's hotel proprietors felt considerable pressure from the many roadhouses across the Detroit River. On 8 July 1935 Smith met with Essex County hotel owners at the elite Norton Palmer Hotel in Windsor to explain the new rules. These rules, an expansion of the rules in the *Digest,* were designed to ensure that the dances would be the privilege only of diners. Each patron would have to have a seat at a table and buy a meal of at least 25 cents. The order would have to be written on a "duplicate, serially numbered food check," which the patron would have to keep as "proof that he is entitled to utilize the privileges of the Dining Room, and to dance." These rules were encapsulated in a form letter that was sent to each proprietor whose hotel was granted the privilege of having dancing in its dining room. The letter concluded with the emphatic reminder that "it is to be distinctly understood that under no circumstances is a patron to be served or allowed to purchase Beer or Wine unless seated at his proper table, and that none other than bona-fide Dining Room patrons be allowed the privilege of dancing on the premises."[62] Just as drinking in beverage rooms was to be strictly controlled, so too would dancing in dining rooms, which, although permissible, would require constant vigilance on the part of the proprietor.

In theory, dancing could be a straightforward and unproblematic issue. Immediately after Arnold Smith's visit to the city, W.D. Roach, manager of Windsor's Arlington Hotel, wrote a detailed letter requesting the continuation of dancing privileges. He explained that dancing at his hotel was an economic and social boon to everyone involved. The letter is worth quoting at length to explore the discourse of respectability he presented:

> We believe that the Arlington dining room is one of the finest in the County of Essex ... We can accommodate one hundred guests comfortably, and the appointments in the dining room are the very best. Both [inspectors] Mr. Pitts [sic] and Mr. Hanrahan have seen it and spoke very highly of it.
>
> ... As illustrating the class of our patrons, we have to say that tomorrow evening ... the young ladies in the office of the Canadian Chrysler plant are joining with the young ladies from the Detroit Chrysler plant in a special dinner dance party in our dining room. The local branch of the Metropolitan Life Insurance Company has had two or three dinner parties there, also the Maccabees, a branch of the Oddfellows, the Ex-Army and navy men's club, a local ladies' fraternity and local bridge clubs, etc.
>
> ... Our orchestra is engaged by the week, and as you might surmise, there are all sorts of rumors with respect to dancing in the hotel dining room. We are very well pleased with our orchestra and do not wish them to become alarmed and start looking elsewhere for employment. For that reason we would appreciate advice from you as soon as possible that we may continue as at present.[63]

To the manager of the Arlington Hotel, which was generally a well-run establishment, the privilege of dancing was justified by his hotel's role as a highly regarded community institution. This respectability was demonstrated by the clientele the hotel hosted, which included office workers from major local businesses as well as members of local service clubs. The mention of both women's and men's clubs reinforced the sheen of respectability since it would be unlikely in the discourse of the time for decent women to patronize a disrespectful establishment. Moreover, the mention of the need to keep the orchestra employed suggests a level of quality in the form of entertainment the dances provided. Not just any musicians would do, Roach was suggesting.

Roach was not tilting at windmills in his letter; he was probably aware of the problems the board had found in many hotels. Across the province, the board's inspectors had judged many hotels to be too small for dancing or music; there was inadequate space to dance, and music played in one part of the hotel could be heard in the beverage rooms. For example, St. Agatha's Embassy Hotel was told to remove the nickelodeon in its dining room because, since the proprietor rarely served meals, the machine "would be running ... for the benefit of his Beverage Room patrons."[64] Windsor's proximity to Detroit had caused many problems with American visitors. Americans in beverage rooms of Ontario border cities fuelled concern over social order because, prior to the Second World War, they could be perceived as a morally dangerous influence.[65] Moreover, Windsor's hotel dinner-dance business was competitive; on 8 July 1935, immediately after Smith's meeting on dining and dancing, the proprietor of the St. Clair Hotel in Windsor wrote to the board explaining that his hotel served "over thirty full course meals a day and cater to the very best clientele ... but if it were not for the dancing I am afraid I would lose all of my business as I would be the only hotel on the river road that did not have music and dancing."[66] His request was denied because he had no space for dancing indoors and had been holding the dances outside. He went out of business in October. So Roach's letter, expressing the respectability of his establishment, can also be seen as representing an attempt to improve his business's financial prospects in a competitive market. Geographically distant from the main part of town, Roach's hotel may have been intended to function as a viable alternative to the sometimes seedy waterfront hotels, many of which attracted an "over the river" clientele.

This discourse of respectability implied in the well-run hotel dinner dance stood in stark contrast to a more crucial site of moral panic: the dance hall. Carolyn Strange has observed that in Toronto "the dance hall was arguably the most contentious site of alleged immorality, and it was the most strictly regulated commercial amusement."[67] Some inspectors invoked the image of the immoral dance hall when discussing requests for dinner-dance privileges. In 1935 the proprietor of Ottawa's Grads Hotel asked whether he could turn a large, vacant room into a banquet hall, noting that he was unable to accommodate local organizations because they wanted to have music and dancing during their banquets. Inspector Larocque advised the proprietor to write to the board for permission to have banquets "but not for the privilege of running a dance hall, I am certainly opposed to that."[68] When St. Catharines' New Statler Hotel asked to have a music machine in its dining room, inspector Wylie reported that there was "no intention to run a dance hall or to conduct organized dances, the intention being to run a dining room service which will afford an opportunity to patrons between the course of the meals to indulge themselves in a little tip toe." Wylie was cautiously optimistic about this request: "My own experience in this district in the matter of hotel dancing leads me to the conclusion that it may be all wrong or again all right, its value being set by the manner of conduct and the care of the Licensee."[69] The New Statler had caused the board some problems under earlier management, but after a rough start the new manager, Philip Kamin, proved himself to be an ambitious and respectable proprietor, who was generally able to carry off a suitable dining room dance.

It does not take a genius to figure out many ways to attempt to circumvent these rules, and the proprietors made innovative attempts to adapt the rules to suit their clientele and build their business. In contrast to Roach's assertion of his hotel's respectability, also in July 1935 Elias Doumani, the proprietor of Windsor's British American Hotel, complained when the board denied him dancing privileges. William Mair, the assistant deputy commissioner of hotels, bluntly replied, "[I] cannot understand why you should be surprised ... in view of the fact that the writer personally found that your dining room was not being operated during a period which is generally regarded as the meal hour period."[70] Doumani was opening his dining room only to accommodate dancing, contrary to what the board expected a rule-abiding hotel to do. In Fort Erie, inspector Wylie arrived at the Colonial Hotel in August 1935 and "was surprised to find an Orchestra of five pieces installed and a dance in progress ... in spite of written instructions ... that no dancing could be permitted." Despite chastising the proprietor, he did note that "the company was quite orderly and no drunkenness or rowdyism [was] apparent."[71] So one strategy for circumventing the board's rules was simply to ignore them.

Another strategy was to appear to serve meals while simply not doing so. The stipulation that the guest check had to amount to at least 25 cents could be considered a mandate for a form of cover charge, except that the board required food to be served. So in several hotels, food was available, but it was cheap and generally went uneaten. In 1938 the Mather Arms Hotel in Fort Erie asked to have a dance in its dining room "with sandwiches laid out on tables around the dance floor." Inspector Wylie discouraged the dance but learned afterward that it had gone ahead. At least this hotel's management admitted that it would be serving only sandwiches, which the board did not consider a full meal according to the spirit of the regulations. When police visited Ottawa's Victoria Hotel in April 1943, they found "sandwiches, which were not being consumed, spread all over the tables ... [in the kitchen] we saw a pile of sandwiches all of one kind made up of bread and pressed ham." Such sandwiches would be available at a restaurant, the inspector argued, for at most 10 cents each.[72]

To the LCBO, the ideal situation was one in which dinner and dancing were the primary attractions, with alcoholic beverages being simply a casual addition to the entertainment. The profit motive was acceptable so long as the proprietor was not attempting to make drinking the focus. After all, the LCA itself was designed to permit drinking as an adjunct to staying in a hotel, where the dining room and beverage room were but two of the conveniences of the visit. Yet it became almost immediately clear that this ideal was rarely achieved. Alcohol was simply too lucrative to be a secondary enterprise. Hotel managers were unapologetic about this fact; they needed to stay afloat, and alcohol helped them to do so. This perspective was fundamental to the LCBO's regulatory strategy. In the Depression, the threat to withdraw a hotel's authority was a threat to the hotelier's livelihood. Yet the lucrative nature of the authority was also important for maintaining order of another kind. Social order was predicated on establishing controlled and somewhat modest public drinking. So although the board asserted that it did not accept the financial need for an authority as justification for granting one, the board simultaneously saw the importance of nurturing, or at least accommodating, hotels in areas where, otherwise, thirsty locals would visit an unregulated liquor dealer or, worse still, bring their own liquor to public events, such as dances.

So in its regulation of the events in a hotel, the board had to balance the need to construct a viable public drinking space against the attraction of the illegal bootleggers. It realized that it needed to support hotel proprietors' efforts to make their businesses successful, as long as the financial success did not supersede the morally acceptable and orderly character both of the hotel's activities and of its customers' behaviour. The Depression had significantly reduced the tourist trade in Ontario, and the end of prohibition in the United States had the potential to turn the lucrative trickle of American tourists who had been coming to the province to buy alcohol (so-called "drink tourists") into a potential flood heading the other way. Neighbouring states had changed from more abstemious to much more liberal in their treatment of liquor. Essex inspector Reaume argued in 1936 that "we have a situation here along the Border" because many young people crossed the border to go dancing. This financial imperative was not only about potential customers going "across the line."[73] The proprietors of the Queen's Hotel in Ayr, a small village near Kitchener, asked permission to resume dancing in their hotel specifically because of the need to attract outsiders: "I hope [the suspension of dancing] will not be for too long as I have to have something to draw a few people from outside there is not enough revenue from the village."[74] But the suspension held. The Royal Hotel in Niagara Falls made a straightforward appeal to economics when asking for dancing: "Times have not been too good for us financially in the hotel business and with winter coming on we feel that granting us this permission will enable us to keep things going."[75] The Arlington Hotel, also in Niagara Falls, argued in January 1936 that "business is very slack at this time of year [and] a small additional revenue from this source [dancing] would greatly help to meet expences [sic]."[76] The request was denied. The manager of the Garden City Hotel in St. Catharines referred to trends in local leisure activities when he asked to expand his beverage room: "No doubt you realize that this city is but a one night city as far as the beverage room is concerned and therefore on Saturday night we must try and get what business we can."[77] The request was refused but not because the board did not accept his reasoning: his hotel was found to be registering unmarried couples and illegally altering the registration book – both of which actions violated the Hotels Act – and was accused of a variety of other immoral activities. Its authority was suspended for several weeks at the end of 1936, and the manager, who was leasing the hotel, left the business in early 1937.[78]

The desperation for business, and clever business strategy in general, often challenged the dictates and expectations of the Liquor Control Board and the liquor law. Advertisements for dancing events were strategically sound business investments but also minefields of regulatory transgression. Many times, hotel management would put an ad in the newspaper only to be criticized by the board for the ad's content. The regulations forbade mention of the availability of alcohol in a hotel, yet many hotels would advertise dancing and then allude to "drinks." The Lincoln Hotel in the Lake Erie resort town of Crystal Beach went much further when it included the phrase "Having a government authority to sell Real Canadian Beer and Ale on tap or bottle under Liquor Control Board of Ontario."[79] This wording violated the rules, which allowed only the phrase "proprietors of beer and wine under authority of the LCBO" in relatively small letters on signs attached to the building. When the Airport Inn in Walkerville advertised a Halloween party in 1939, it included a mention of door prizes. Smith wrote to clarify the policy: "In addition to prohibiting any reference to the sale of beer and wine in newspaper and other forms of advertising by Authority holders, the Board do not permit the advertising or giving of inducements to the general public in connection with any entertainment held in Authorized premises."[80] The British American Hotel put an ad in the *Windsor Daily Star* promoting "Dancing tonight with the Canadian Mountaineers Star Radio Orchestra."[81] Smith wrote to inspector Reaume criticizing, it seems, the inspector's permissiveness: "I ... may say I certainly do not approve of this type of advertising, in fact I do not approve of small hotels having dancing at all, as it is merely a means of bolstering up Beer sales and I certainly would prohibit this advertising of dancing in these hotels."[82] Here, the problem of small hotels having dancing and the issue of advertising converged into general discontent with the situation in Essex County.

Dining and dancing may have appeared to be lucrative prospects, but many hotels soon found that dancing did indeed result in problems of their own. Niagara inspector Wylie, commenting on the practice of dimming the lights in the dance hall at the Embassy Hotel in Port Dalhousie, explained the reasons for his concerns, as though the administration was not aware of the potential problems. The issue, to Wylie, was the inability of the proprietor to see what was going on:

> It is more than a suspicion that the darkness lends itself to pocket flask drinking and other practices which the Board frowns upon and I am not aware that there should be anything in a regular dance that could not be as well done and bring its measure of pleasure to patrons in the same degree were the lights turned on.[83]

Several hotels faced the censure of the board after people who had been drinking at their beverage rooms and were clearly heavily intoxicated got in car accidents. Not a few cases of underage drinking hit the news, and some local papers, which may have been of more dry sensibilities, like the *St. Catharines Standard* and the *Toronto Star,* printed sensationalized stories about such activities from across the province.

The board faced so many problems in controlling dancing in hotels that in 1936 it decided to roll back altogether the permission to have dancing. In April chief commissioner Odette explained that the board was investigating floorshows in local hotels: "If this style of entertainment is being used to draw business in beer selling – merely to bolster up the beverage room business – we will crack down on it and crack down hard."[84] Apparently, dancing in general had been under scrutiny. A week before Odette's announcement, in response to Emile Normand's request to have dances in his Duke Hotel in Ottawa, William Mair had explained that "the board are now taking this stand in all sections of the Province and Hotels formerly permitted this form of entertainment are being denied same in future."[85] These directives rolled out across the province over the next year and caused considerable consternation among hotel proprietors who had previously used dancing to attract patronage. Oscar Lepine of Ottawa's LaSalle Hotel was disappointed to learn that "the Board have decided to curtail entertainments of this nature in Hotels and in the case of your Hotel the permission formerly given is hereby withdrawn."[86]

Although no internal memo appears to have survived that outlines the specific reasoning behind the reduction of dancing, there are some tantalizing hints. As noted earlier, inspectors had railed against the idea of hotels operating "dance halls," the implication being that the "dance hall" was a problematic institution. This perception was not restricted to the LCBO's staff. In May 1936 Rev. A.B. Penman of Lindsay was quoted by the *Toronto Star* as being opposed to dancing. This declaration from a Baptist reverend would not be especially remarkable if not for the contrast he offered between dance halls and beverage rooms. "Illegitimacy in Toronto has increased

60 per cent in the last ten years, and I place the responsibility on the dance hall, ahead of the beer parlor," he explained to his congregation.[87] The implication of the immorality of the dance hall and the unsavoury connection between dancing and beverage rooms appeared in a letter that Arnold Smith wrote in 1938 to the lawyer for the Seacliffe Hotel in Leamington:

> When dance halls are run in connection with Hotels it is the beginning of trouble and that is one of the main reasons they [the board] have consistently refused to allow dancing in connection with Hotels in smaller places. In fact in the city of Toronto there are only six hotels where dancing is allowed and in the City of Ottawa the Chateau Laurier is the only place that is allowed dancing.[88]

As Mair explained to a disgruntled hotel proprietor in McKenzie River, in north-western Ontario, the board had determined that "the practise resulted in criticism of the system in general."[89] Odette's statement about floorshows included the assertion that, even if floorshows were found to be acceptable, the board would not "countenance the employment of young girls in such shows," suggesting that activities of questionable morality and the act of consuming alcohol remained strongly discursively linked. The board ended hotel dancing to ensure the perceived integrity of the system. The connection between drinking and dancing would, for the moment, reduce the perception that the authorized standard hotel was a place of social disorder.

Not surprisingly, hotel managers were not impressed. Waterloo County inspector Ratz complained to the administration that he was facing considerable criticism over the decision because a few places had been permitted to continue to have dancing, and several hotel proprietors assumed that Ratz was playing favourites. H.A. Sielig, proprietor of the Dominion Hotel in St. Jacobs, claimed to have spent over $1,000 to build a dance hall next to his hotel and complained to the board that he had a dance hall licence and wanted to continue dancing, just as nearby hotels had been allowed to do. Ratz asked Smith to send a firm letter advising Sielig "to take care of his own premises and not to bother so much about [the towns of] Breslau and Conestoga."[90]

Nonetheless, the dining room did not become as sterile an environment as the beverage room was supposed to be. Music was still permitted but only as background music and as long as it was not audible in other parts of the hotel. In response to a letter from J.W. Connell, managing director of the Hotel Association of Ontario, Mair explained that "the board have no objection to the installation of a radio in the dining room in a Hotel where full course meals are served, providing the music is permitted during the regular meal hours, i.e., Between 12 noon and 2 p.m., and 6 and 7:30 p.m."[91] Dancing to this music, however, was forbidden, at least temporarily.

Just as the prohibition on keno was soon eased, so too was the board once again beginning to authorize dancing in dining rooms by the end of 1936. But now the circumstances were different. When the Belmont Hotel in Port Colborne asked to have a grand (re)opening in December 1936 with an "orchestra and local talent," P.G. Newall, clerk of the Hotels Department, outlined the rules: the orchestra was allowed; the "local talent" was not. "The service of beer, of course will be denied patrons of this dining room during the dancing and the charge per person of $1.50 must be assessed."[92] A month later, the hotel made another request to have a dinner dance, this time "in connection with an organization." Inspector Wylie told the proprietor that he suspected the request would be denied "on the grounds that the charge must be substantial and not simply a fish and chip affair."[93] The higher price of the meal would encourage a better clientele, or at least discourage trouble. When the hotel asked to have a New Year's dinner in December 1938, Wylie observed that it could be acceptable because "the dinner will be one dollar per plate ... I believe the price of the dinner will debar those who might come with the intention of having a rough time."[94] Although it may have just been Wylie's bias, the increased price of the dinner did appear to the central administration to be a valid way of keeping trouble at bay. The "rough time" would be avoided by allowing only people who could afford such an expensive meal to have the privilege of dancing.

Along with usually requiring a larger dinner check, when the board began to reintroduce dancing in hotel dining rooms, it took the approach that the dances had to be held by local organizations rather than by the hotel itself and also that drinking and dancing had to be separated. In this way, the board could enforce another level of disinterested management of the proprietors. This was achieved in two ways. First, when hotels held dinner dances and served alcohol, the expectation was that the food and drink would draw patrons; in contrast, banquets and charitable activities held by other organizations imposed another layer of responsible management and another respectable group governing the behaviour of participants. Executive members of social clubs, it seems, would be expected to look out for the reputation of their organization and therefore ensure the respectable comportment of all. Meanwhile, the hotel management would not be able to simply pack in the dancers with impunity in order to maximize profits. The profit motive was, therefore, further diminished. When the Leamington Hotel asked for permission to have banquets for good causes, the inspector gave the example of "next Friday ... they have a request from a local organization to hold a banquet ... for the benefit of a young married man with a family who is afflicted with cancer."[95] The respectability of the social club was important and could reinforce the proper surveillance of the activity. When the Hollywood Hotel in Windsor was given permission to have a banquet for the Macedonian Political Organization, Reaume explained to Smith that the organization appeared to be quite respectable: "None of them are on relief ... [and] they all help each other."[96] Second, when a hotel held a dinner and dance under the auspices of a community group, the board insisted that the dinner beer and wine service would have to be stopped when the dancing and other entertainment began. When Reaume met with one of the directors of the Hollywood Hotel to discuss the party by the Macedonian Political Organization, he outlined the criteria for such an event: "I explained ... that no beverage is to be served in the room during the time of their entertainment, and he assured me that he would see to it that none is served."[97] Similarly, in September 1937, when the proprietor of the Embassy Hotel requested permission to have a dinner dance for the Athletic Association of the Guaranty Silk and Dye Company, Smith told him that "beer and wine might be served at the dinner but as soon as the dancing commenced no beer could be sold in the dining room and that any beer which was sold must be sold in the regular Beverage Room."[98] He told the proprietor, Gordon Brisson, that future banquets would be dealt with on their merits and after observation of the manner in which this banquet was conducted.[99] The Embassy's requests after this were for banquets under the auspices of other organizations. By changing the rules about dinner dances, the board reiterated the importance of disinterested management in the conduct of hotel business related to drinking and reinforced its central role in shaping public order in the province.

In reinforcing this connection between the respectability of community organizations and the value of a hotel's public spaces to these organizations, the board both recognized the importance of a hotel within its community and deployed multiple forms of surveillance of the hotel's patrons. The appeal of profit in a wet dinner dance was too much of a temptation for many small, struggling hotels to resist, and the strategies that proprietors attempted, from simply making a show of having a meal to admitting people who would not be eating dinner there, resulted in the board pushing against this trend because of the disorderly situations that arose. Its decision to permit banquets and other functions to be held in the dining rooms was a sort of compromise based on traditional notions of the function of a hotel in a community, one that reiterated and even increased the types of oversight placed on the drinking spaces. Here, the respectable social organizations operated as guarantors of order, sort of as organizational chaperones. The hotel management would still be required to seek permission from the board to have dinner dances and banquets, and the managers would still be required to watch the patrons, but at the same time the community organizations would also keep an eye on their patrons and control access to the space. Since these events were either fundraising activities or closed, members-only events, the participation in the events would be further controlled. The profit motive was not entirely divorced from the procedures, but the board needed to reconstruct the hotel's traditional place as community centre, which would support the business of the hotel in more respectful and socially orderly ways. As Arnold Smith explained to William Robinson, proprietor of the Mather Arms Hotel in Fort Erie,

> The Board Realize that a properly run hotel is an asset to a community, and if the Hotel has the proper facilities the Board are Anxious to encourage the holding of social affairs in said hotels so that the proprietor may benefit by the service of meals etc. When a banquet is being held beer may be served to the guests during the banquet, but after the meal is finished and dancing or cards are played in the dining room the service of beer is then confined to the beverage room.[100]

The hotel was, in many small communities, the only place that had public space for activities. As noted above, the proprietor of the Trennick Hotel explained that there was a piano in the ladies' beverage room because a local tap dancing class used the room as a practice space. Whether this explanation was true is immaterial; what matters is that having a tap dance class in this semi-public space was considered a viable explanation. As had been the case for decades, in many small towns in Ontario, the hotel remained the main meeting place of the community.

There are a few caveats we must remember when considering the way the LCBO regulated the dancing and other entertainment in Ontario's standard hotels. First, it was mainly concerned with the intersection between alcohol and entertainment. Many hotels, most notably the larger ones in urban centres, had dance halls or banquet rooms that were not licensed. Other hotels were located close to unlicensed dance halls. About these places, the LCBO could do little. Certainly, the central administration did voice concern at times about the proximity of a hotel to a dance hall, but apart from insisting that the proprietor be careful not to serve people to excess and telling inspectors to keep a close eye on the place, the board had no jurisdiction over establishments outside of its purview. The board was concerned more about the intersection between drinking and dancing in smaller hotels, where it was very difficult to isolate music and dancing from alcohol consumption, than about the existence of dance halls in larger urban hotels. In smaller hotels, even if a hotel had a dance space in which drinking was not permitted, it was not difficult for patrons to drink in the beverage rooms before heading down the corridor to dance. Normally, such behaviour was policed by inspectors, who told the proprietors to be careful, but the board did see its authority as one that, at times and in appropriate conditions, could transcend the normal boundaries between drinking and nondrinking spaces. It was here that the board was especially vigilant. In 1937, having been told that she was not allowed to have dancing in her hotel, Mrs. Dumouchelle of Windsor's Southwood Hotel argued that since she had paid local licence fees for dancing and music, she should be allowed to run dances. Smith replied that "while the proprietress of this hotel may have secured a dance permit from some branch of the government, this only allows her to conduct a dance in her hotel, providing there is no objection from this department, but the mere fact that a license ... is issued does not allow dancing in that hotel if this Board prohibits it."[101]

This analysis is not intended to suggest that Ontario became a quiet, serene place under the auspices of the LCBO. As noted earlier, dancing was popular, and the board had no jurisdiction outside of the licensed drinking spaces. Raucous dances, where patrons brought their own flasks and drank surreptitiously, were outside the purview of the LCBO. Someone holding such a dance might be chastised by the board and may even lose his or her personal liquor permit, but these cases appeared in the public hotel records only when the person in question had some association with a hotel. Moreover, as will be discussed in Chapter 9, when the war began and the demographic and economic shifts that accompanied it fundamentally altered the social possibilities for recreation, the board increasingly allowed public dances and parties in hotels.

The LCBO's approach to entertainment within the drinking space belied a binary perspective regarding activities beyond drinking. The board needed its hotels to remain solvent and recognized the challenges that the depressed economy presented for hotels. Entertainment to entice clientele was a good way of establishing financial solvency. Yet at the same time, the board had to enforce a notion of controlled public drinking; it was responsible to the government, but more important, in its own estimation, was the need to be responsive to public opinion. In seeming to permit activities that hearkened to pre-prohibition excesses and in seeming to license establishments of dubious reputation, the board risked being perceived as permitting disorder and thereby throwing into question its ability to manage the contested area of legal drinking. It therefore meted out the privilege of dancing cautiously, seeing it both as a practice that could attract much negative publicity and as a desirable pastime that could be responsibly managed. Its decision in 1936 to temporarily suspend all dancing in hotels allowed it to reassert its authority over recreation in hotels and remind proprietors to try to keep control. When dancing was reintroduced, the restrictions suggest that the board had backed off from a relatively liberal approach to dancing in licensed premises. The board's emphasis on the requirement for a higher food check and its allowance of dances that were under the auspices of independent community organizations suggest that its attempt to permit an expanded but still highly circumscribed notion of leisure within the drinking space was not entirely successful. The board had held out the expectation of imposing the values of rational recreation on the leisure spaces of those who wanted to have "a rough time," but it determined that such hopes were generally misguided. Although, no doubt, people continued to dance and proprietors continued to bend the rules, the board became increasingly restrictive, limiting even further the opportunities for recreation in licensed premises.

7
Women, Children, and the Family in the Public Drinking Space

In May 1939 Rev. Dr. George A. Little told the Woman's Christian Temperance Union in Welland that the opening of beverage rooms for women and the introduction of mixed-sex drinking constituted "the greatest social disaster that liquor has brought to Ontario."[1] Doubtless, the ladies in the audience agreed, and for good reason. Among the dominant arguments of the temperance movement for more than a half-century had been that women were the moral guardians of the nation and that the drinking woman was debased. The woman drinker was considered by this movement to be a great social disgrace.[2] For at least a half-century, women had been at the forefront of this movement. As we saw in the case of St. Catharines' Rosdol Inn, they could quickly be mobilized to oppose the extension of alcohol into enclaves of middle-class life. For the provincial government actually to sanction women's drinking by creating a space for it, they argued, was for the authorities to open the door to social disaster. After all, as Mariana Valverde has shown, the morally upright mother was a central trope in the social-purity movement: the mother of the race had to be free, but alcohol bound her.[3] By the 1930s, then, for at least two generations, the temperance movement had built its rhetoric on the bifurcated place of women and drink in society: either a woman was free of drink and therefore morally pure, or she was a drinker and therefore debased, representing a fundamental danger to the modern state. If women drinkers presented such a danger to the family and society and if women in public drinking spaces were moral wretches, why not just ban them from the beverage rooms altogether? The Liquor Control Board of Ontario (LCBO) had a lot to explain.

The explanation was that, contrary to the temperance rhetoric and the images to which the temperance movement clung, not only did women want to drink, but the respectable woman and the drinking woman were also not mutually exclusive. This was not new information, but in a political system that had, until the 1920s, been increasingly sensitive to temperance rhetoric and in a society in which eugenic and social-Darwinist rhetoric saw danger all around, this was a relatively new admission.[4] Yet the image of women in drinking spaces was not a historical aberration. As historians have begun to explore in more depth the nuances of drinking cultures, they have revealed a multifaceted relationship between women and drink.[5] In the pre-industrial household, women were traditionally the "brewsters," with the English term "brewster" being specifically gendered female (whereas men were "brewers").[6] Julia Roberts's study of taverns and inns in colonial Canada West suggests a complex delineation between male and female "spheres" within these heavily domesticated social spaces.[7] Although the saloon was predominantly a social space for men, Madelon Powers has demonstrated that in a section of the saloon that was separate from the male drinking space, women often ate, drank, and purchased alcoholic beverages to take away. This was pre-prohibition behaviour that, in the eyes of the temperance movement, was an indication of the debasement of women, but Powers shows that it was a part of everyday saloon life for respectable working women in urban America.[8] Whereas Powers has discussed women drinkers generally in the drinking space, others have specifically examined women workers there. Both Clare Wright and Diane Kirkby have shown that women had many roles within the Australian tavern.[9] In Britain the temperance movement's perception of the debased role of women in drinking spaces stands in stark contrast to the efforts by progressive brewers, who saw the presence of a female landlady as an important part of the reform of the pub. Not necessarily proof that the "separate spheres" had broken down, the brewers' strategy of putting women in pubs was specifically because of the maternal, calming effect women were thought to have on the drinking space.[10] As these studies have suggested, the negative connection between women and drinking, fundamental to the gendered temperance discourse of the nineteenth- and early-twentieth-century temperance movement, was a distortion; the connection between women and drinking was far too complex to be reduced to a simple dialectic.

With women having such a multifaceted place in the early-twentieth-century drinking space, it is not surprising that women's relationship with drinking was increasingly heavily contested. Robert Campbell has argued that liquor regulation authorities and many male customers sought to exclude women from the beer parlours of Vancouver. He notes that "some women wanted in," whereas others "believed that a parlour was no place for a woman." The divisions between the sexes, the creation of separate spaces for men and for women with or without escorts, and the prevalent assumption that a single woman drinking in a beer parlour "risked being treated as a prostitute" were all features of the public drinking environment and of the combination of drinking and sexuality in post-prohibition Vancouver.[11] This equivocality reflects the social reality of the times. Having known more active public lives during the war, women were loath to return to the home and so-called traditional roles. The challenge to traditional gender roles is represented in the "flapper" archetype; prohibition added to the problems this archetype represented. So short skirts, surreptitious drinking, and smoking in public – all forged in the crucible of prohibition-era socialization – took women literally and metaphorically far outside the traditional and respectable domain of the home. These popular images represented but did not typify women's lives, especially not the lives of working women, whose financial means placed significant limits on their ability to indulge in this increasingly consumerist society. Yet at the same time, the expansion of the consumer society drove new images and expectations of women in social life. As Carolyn Strange writes of Toronto, "Whether flocking to lakeside amusement resorts or window shopping along Yonge Street, [working women's] unselfconscious public presence was a vivid reminder that they did not adhere to the traditional norms of restraint imposed upon single women."[12] Moreover, young working women, who were paid low wages by contemporary standards, were industrious enough to permit themselves paid amusements.[13] So, although the temperance movement and evangelicals railed against women in the public space and against the dangers that alcohol and public life could present to young women and hence to society as a whole, women were advancing their interests, indulging in various forms of public life, and thereby challenging traditional views of their social role.[14]

These perspectives inform our understanding of the changing public-drinking landscape in 1934, when the government introduced public drinking to Ontario. In early 1934, after the LCA (1934) became law, but before the Liberals won the provincial election and implemented the act's new provisions, the *Toronto Star,* a Liberal newspaper with strong dry leanings, published an article entitled "Temptation for Girls Seen with Wine in Restaurants." It quoted a speech by the aforementioned Rev. Dr. Little, who painted a troubling picture of the degradation that licensed beverage rooms and restaurants would cause: "At the old bars you didn't often see women but women will go to the beverage room and we will again see the degrading spectacle of women leading other women home who are more drunken than themselves." Meanwhile, the restaurants would be a more subtle temptation: "Picture your daughters coming out of the theatre with their escorts and having a list of wine and cocktails presented to them."[15] The danger ranged from the spectacle of drunken women drinking with other women to the more troubling image of young girls with their escorts being tempted with alcohol. That their daughters were on a date, itself a pastime fraught with sexual opportunity and tension, was not likely lost on the audience. Here, the pure but vulnerable woman often mingled with the degraded woman, and the threat arose from the fact that the former could so easily fall into the role of the latter. When the *Star* printed a story about a woman seen in a hotel lobby giving her child "sips of beer," when Rev. Dr. Little lamented that Torontonians "spend more money on beer than bread," and when, six months after the LCA (1934) came into force, returned missionary Rev. E.C. Hennigar told the Ontario Temperance Federation that the morals of young men were just as high as ever but that there had been a "slump in the morals of young girls," they were reinscribing the tropes of the past, with the added recognition of the increasingly troubled times of the Depression, all framed by what they saw as the debacle of government-sponsored drinking.[16]

Yet the temperance movement's rhetoric was not the only influence on the LCBO's work. The board wanted to create orderly and legal drinking spaces where drinking and social behaviour could be kept under control in a staid and well-managed environment. To do this, the LCBO needed to listen to the needs and expectations of the managers and customers of the drinking spaces. Temperance forces might put pressure on the provincial government and could even campaign to have districts voted dry, but they were not customers of these drinking spaces and should therefore not be considered the only, or even the most significant, voice influencing the LCBO's activities. So, although the vocal critics of alcohol perpetuated the image of the debased woman in the saloon, the administration of the LCBO understood that women wanted to drink and also that women played an essential role in the management of the hotel. The Drys placed persistent pressure on the administration of the LCBO but were not alone. Customers and beverage room management also participated in the redefinition of the drinking space. They spoke of a more inclusive, diverse place of women and public drinking, one that recognized not only that women could bring respectability to the drinking space but also that the drinking space was a heterosocial one and that women should not be denied the privilege of having a drink.

The point of this chapter is twofold. First, it explores the place of women in hotel beverage rooms. By their words and actions, they carved out a separate space for mixed-sex or even women's single-sex drinking. They publicly challenged the notion that the drinking woman was something of a deviant. So by the Second World War, when the LCBO began to contemplate a change to the public-drinking arrangement, the idea of women drinking in public was not so unpalatable; the LCA (1946) included specific provisions for women's drinking spaces, something the LCA (1934) did not include. Second, the chapter argues that commensurate with the emergence of a respectable woman drinker was the increased importance of the woman vendor. The LCBO saw women's role in the management of the authorized hotels as useful for creating a moral atmosphere in which moderate, orderly drinking could take place. In doing so, it reinforced a paternalistic notion of the relationships between women and men and of women's proper role as a maternal force within a home-like environment. To the board, the sexualized woman was anathema to this image, although ironically women's sexuality and respectability might be central to the operations, and often the success, of the hotel beverage rooms.

Soon after the LCA (1934) came into operation, the board confronted the need for gendered provisions in its operations. Within a month of issuing the first hotel beer authorities, the board began to order Toronto hotels to separate the sexes. In August 1934 chief commissioner Edmond Odette announced that hotels would have to create separate beverage rooms for men and women. He argued that women "shouldn't be allowed to go into men's beverage rooms but they will be allowed to take their male escorts into this women's beverage room." The decision was received with "considerable satisfaction" by the organized hotelmen of the city: "While these changes will add considerable expense, the hotelmen are prepared to co-operate with the liquor commissioner."[17] The hotelmen appear to have found women in their establishments to be a problem. In September 1934 they adopted a code of conduct in their hotels. When interviewed by the *Star,* a waiter in one hotel explained that "the women give us the worst trouble, and we do not encourage them to come into our beverage room, even when accompanied."[18] Although presented as an issue of women drinking, it appears that the issue was about mixed-sex drinking among a certain "class" of people. In January 1935 Odette explained that he had ordered separate beverage rooms for men and women in only "some hotels ... it depends on the district and the class of clientele of the hotels involved." He argued that if the separation were total, "it would not be possible for a man and his wife to drink together except in a dining room where they would have to buy food as well."[19]

Generally, the creation of the distinct "men's" and "ladies and escorts'" drinking spaces has been seen as resulting from a patriarchal, perhaps misogynistic perception of the dangers of single women in a bar full of drunken men. Women, single men, and drink were a potent combination. Inspector George Hanrahan, who registered at the notorious Royal Cecil Hotel in Toronto, made clear associations between drink, lax management, and misbehaviour: "This place, I would say is the gathering place of a number of men and women of low moral mentality, and character. Drinking of beer gives them the medium to satisfy their inclinations. The conduct of those in charge and their attitude gives passive assent to the same."[20] Although for many observers women in public drinking spaces were morally suspect, probably prostitutes, or at the very least "loose," Hanrahan suggested the equal culpability of men and women and of poor management. Management, of course, was key to this equation. When hotel proprietors held entertainments, the female dancers and singers were closely scrutinized by officials, who often suspected the moral integrity of such shows. For example, when plainclothes police officers entered the British American Hotel in Windsor to watch a floorshow put on by "two girls," they noted that "there was nothing immoral in these dances" but that "if we had not been recognized this show may have been different." Commenting on this report, inspector U.G. Reaume wrote cryptically, "we suspect what kind of party it was."[21] The hypersexualized environment of the licensed hotel space needed to be kept under close watch.

Some stories of prostitution demonstrate a long-term association between hotels and resident prostitutes. Investigating an authority application in 1934, the Royal Canadian Mounted Police reported that a Fort William hotel was nothing more than a disorderly house, with "girls" brought from Winnipeg to work in the hotel restaurant, but only one working at a time. At other times, "these girls were prostituting themselves and paying part of the proceeds to" the proprietor's wife.[22] The hotel did not receive an authority until the management changed hands. Less directly implicated in prostitution but still tainted by association was the Belmont Hotel in Port Colborne. In 1938 inspector Wilson Wylie became suspicious of the activities of a "girl" living in the hotel. She was reportedly without any means of financial support, "indiscreet in her associations," yet continued to pay her bills. The proprietor of the hotel claimed that "her mother pays" and that he could not be charged with any violation. After investigating further, Wylie learned that there were in fact two girls working as prostitutes in the hotel and that their mother, Mrs. H., "has quite a record in Port Colborne in boot legging activities so much so that she has had to move out and is presently domiciled in a northern town and I suspect living under the same conditions as she encouraged in Port Colborne."[23] Although the hotel manager made arrangements for the girls to leave the hotel, he attempted to put a good spin on the situation, noting that "they were of loose characters but confined their attention to only social superior clients."[24] The associations here were not directly between drinking and prostitution but between the hotel accommodation and sex for money.

Identifying the direct connections between prostitution and drinking is more difficult because the lines become blurred between sexual promiscuity and prostitution in the drinking space. Yet a woman who registered at a hotel with a man who was not her husband (an illegal act), although not necessarily a prostitute, could provoke the same kind of condemnation of a hotel as women who exchanged sex for money. When visiting Toronto's Ambassador Hotel in November 1936, LCBO inspectors overheard a conversation in the overly dark dining room "between lady and man ... that the man should keep his hands off her leg, and the language used was bad, waiter told them to get the hell out, lady and man went to office talked a while and proceeded upstairs with another man joining the party."[25] The connections between excessive drinking and sexual danger were also well known; a police officer in Ottawa observed a man escorting an extremely drunk woman into the lobby of the Grand Hotel, where "she was placed in a chair and sat in a slumped position. I saw the man approach the hotel register and sign." The officer found that the man and woman were not in fact married; he was from Hull, Quebec, and she from Ottawa.[26] The proprietor of the hotel, which the inspector noted was generally well run, claimed it was the error of a "negligent night clerk ... Needless to say this proprietor is very much upset over the matter, as he is not the type of man to induldge [sic] in such business, and he has immediately taken steps to replace this negligent attendant by a more dependable man."[27]

As these examples illustrate, whether part of a cash transaction or not – and the LCBO records do not indicate when cash exchanged hands – sex between unmarried individuals was seen as a major problem in hotels. The provincial Standard Hotel Registration of Guests Act made it an offence for a hotel to allow "any untrue statement as to the name or place of residence of the guest" to be entered into the hotel's register.[28] The legislation targeted both hotel management who allowed false registration and guests who falsely registered. Moreover, it forbade a man from procuring or attempting to procure a room "for himself and any woman whom he falsely holds out to be his wife," and it mandated that women who allowed themselves to be misrepresented could also be charged.[29] Hence inspector John Pitt's concern over the activities at Ottawa's Beechwood Hotel: "Too many signatures in Register Mr and Mrs to suit me and no supervision over Guest rooms there should be a woman employed at all times to supervise the conduct of the hotel end of the business I have never seen a woman in this hotel on any of my visits as it serves no good purpose."[30] Pitt recommended against the licence being renewed. In the effort to reconstruct a more socially acceptable space for drinking, so the argument went, such activities should be eliminated from the drinking space.

Although prostitution and sexual misbehaviour were undoubtedly taking place in hotels, the extreme solution of simply banning women from the drinking spaces would never have taken hold because many women wanted to be there. Soon after the advent of "beer by the glass" drinking in Ontario, the LCBO received a number of requests from proprietors or female patrons to carve out separate women's beverage rooms. This was neither because men did not want women in their spaces nor because the proprietors were concerned about prostitution. This space was requested because women wanted a place to drink unharassed by men. The manager of the Hotel Grimsby asked for permission to "prepare a Ladies Beverage room, as a great number of ladies do not want to go in the same room as the men."[31] The manager of the Caverly Hotel in Niagara Falls did not wait for permission. Responding to customers' requests, she began to use her hotel's dining room as a ladies' beverage room since "many lady patrons prefer the atmosphere of the dining room to that of general beverage room." Unfortunately, to achieve this division, the proprietor had to violate the board's provisions by "supplying a cheese sandwitch [sic] which the consumer has not ordered and probably does not want." Inspector Wylie was sympathetic to the intention but not to the "subterfuge of the cheese sandwitch." He told Mrs. Caverly that she should create a ladies' beverage room that was separate from the dining room.[32] Soon after being granted an authority for his hotel in Nipigon, Ontario, Thomas Keating requested that the board authorize him to sell beer in his hotel's sample room. He explained, "I want to use it for a Man comming [sic] along with his wife and for the Ladies as well to use." For Keating it was good business to give women such a space, but it was also a request made in xenophobic, paternalistic protection since "it would be better to seat them in this room away from the Foreigners who come in at the weekends."[33] The demands of customers and hotel managers stand both in contrast to the concerns of the temperance movement and simultaneously in concert with them. Both wanted to separate the sexes, but some hotel proprietors were reacting to the wishes not of temperance opposition but of the drinkers.

Building the Ladies' Beverage Room

The decision to mandate separate men's and women's beverage rooms, thereby establishing a "ladies'" beverage room (officially, it was the "ladies and escorts'" beverage room, but both terms were used interchangeably), presented many headaches for the board and for hotel management. Most of the hotels that received beer authorities on the passing of the LCA (1934) had been hotels for years, if not decades, and it often took considerable architectural innovation and expense to create another beverage room space. A number of hotels began to accommodate the provision for a ladies' beverage room by opening a room upstairs in which women and their escorts could be served beer.[34] Such a reconfiguration had practical and moral problems. First, the room was often small and noisy as well as close to sleeping quarters, presenting the possibility that patrons could move the party into more intimate quarters, opening the danger of prostitution or at least sexual impropriety.[35] Second, the room was not always near a washroom or was near the washrooms that were to be used by bedroom customers.[36] And third, beer had to be carried by waiters from the taproom on the main floor to the ladies' beverage room, which meant having beer carried through public corridors, an arrangement that was unacceptable because the LCBO sought to remove drinking from public view. So although the board's own rules permitted individuals to rent a room and drink there, when proprietors freed up some bedrooms for the use of drinking parties, the implications caused the board considerable concern.[37]

The upstairs ladies' beverage room was one problem; "overflow rooms" were another.[38] Often proprietors sought to augment space in the ladies' beverage room by allowing it to "overflow" into the dining room. Although in some communities (such as rural parts of north-western Ontario) and specific hotels, the ladies' beverage room was barely used, in other places a ladies and escorts' beverage room might become the main location for drinking and thus full to capacity. The board recognized that to forbid such overflow was to place both an unnecessary hardship on the proprietor's business and to open up the possibility that people would choose illegal drinking activities, including heading to a local "blind pig," drinking harder liquor in unlicensed parts of the hotel, or even just taking bottles on the road. At least in a beverage room, there was the possibility of surveillance and control.

Indeed, the very public nature of the ladies' beverage room may have been the reason for its success. This room was both a space for women to drink, alone or with male companions, and a controlled, monitored, and most importantly, separate environment. The board criticized proprietors when inspectors found that a ladies' beverage room was accessible only by passing through another room, like the men's beverage room or the dining room, or alternatively, that other rooms were accessible only via the ladies' beverage room, thus creating an opportunity for unescorted men to linger while passing through. Similarly, Arnold Smith told the manager of the Log Cabin Hotel in rural Essex County that "strict supervision must be kept at all times to see that dining-room guests stay with their own parties and that no 'picking up' of girls is permitted by male guests."[39] In Port Arthur's Kimberly Hotel, the doors to the two beverage rooms faced each other, "permitting unobstructed view and allowing for easy contact between patrons."[40] The hotel was reconfigured to meet the approval of the board, with the new layout giving "better supervision and [it] will have [a] service room between the Beverage rooms."[41] This panoptic notion of the hotel layout may have appealed to women as well. By separating the beverage rooms, making them accessible through a common hotel entrance, and keeping an eye on the individual entrances of each room, the board attempted to ensure that the ladies' beverage room in an authorized hotel premises facilitated a safe night out.

We cannot, however, assume that every woman was looking for an orderly, chaperoned evening. To do so would be to embrace rather than scrutinize the paternalistic discourse of the time. Rev. Dr. Little's prediction of "the degrading spectacle of women leading other women home who are more drunken than themselves" suggests that women drinking was a problem, but it also indicates a homosocial dimension of women's drinking.[42] Moreover, some women liked to party as much as some men. During police raids at hotels, usually when searching for after-hours drinking, police usually found men and women drinking together. Additionally, LCBO inspectors would enter hotels after midnight and often find the places lousy with men and women. Inspectors also commented at times on women who were found drunk and incoherent. For example, when Hamilton's inspector Joseph Cheeseman paid a visit to the Belmont Hotel in Port Colborne in 1939, he reported seeing an "elderly lady who was wandering about the street in front of Hotel," and while he was watching her, "she collasped [sic]. I helped her to her feet again and started her down the street ... It was pitiful to see her staggering and collasping [sic]."[43] In the lobby of the Ohio Hotel in Fort Erie, inspector Wylie found "a young woman considerably under the influence." The proprietor insisted the woman had come into the hotel in this condition and had not been served.[44]

While women and their escorts were filling the ladies' beverage rooms, single men were also hoping to get in. Many times inspectors, correspondents, or the police reported on cases of single men trying to mingle with women in the ladies' beverage room.[45] Visiting the Tusco Hotel in Toronto in December 1936, inspectors Pitt, O.M. Rombough, and Reaume observed twenty-two men and five ladies in one of the four ladies' beverage rooms, which were simply small converted bedrooms.[46] When inspector George Skuce asked the bartender of the Avenue Hotel in Fort William why he was serving unaccompanied men in the ladies' beverage room, the man replied that he did not want any trouble. Skuce reported, "I told him he was getting into it."[47] Inspector M.C. MacDonald despaired of the condition of the Kimberly Hotel in Port Arthur, noting that "the ladies' beverage room is used pretty much as a 'hang out' for dissolute characters. Men frequent this portion of the hotel, without escorting ladies, almost as freely as they enter the men's beverage room, in spite of the fact that I warned the proprietor's wife to put a stop to this practice."[48] The American Hotel in Sandwich, Essex County, had a "low partition" between the two beverage rooms, which the inspector noted had to be changed because there was "no privacy whatsoever."[49]

Cases of men trying to get into the ladies' beverage room demonstrate an aspect of public drinking that often goes unrecorded: if men were trying to get in, there must have been a good number of single women in these spaces. If the ladies and escorts' beverage room had been full of heterosexual couples, there would have been much less impetus for single men to try to mingle. Groups of single women have an uncanny ability to attract single men. The manager of the Dunkirk Hotel in Ottawa recognized this problem with single women and informed the board that, along with refusing unescorted men, he would not let "unescorted ladies" into the ladies and escorts' beverage room: "I have found that in other hotels their trouble[s] have been with unescorted women."[50] To him, men were the main clientele; he saw no need for or value in a space for single women who wanted to drink. Eventually, he converted his ladies' beverage room back into a bedroom, a move with which, uncharacteristically, the board concurred because he had so few female patrons.[51] As noted earlier, the manager of Toronto's elite Royal York Hotel argued that he did not want to create a men-only beverage room. He argued that "the possibility of ladies accompanying their male escorts in our beverage room tends to increase the tone of business and I feel that it would not be a good feature if we were compelled to maintain a room specially for the use of male customers."[52] Clearly, the idea of a men-only beverage room evoked the image of a low-class saloon, which, in this elite hotel, simply would not do. For his part, the manager of the Lincoln Hotel in Crystal Beach found that women were most definitely interested in drinking. He explained to the board that he was going to have a hard time keeping "ladies out of the Men's room when their room gets filled up."[53]

The idea of "ladies and escorts" created some confusion regarding the appropriate ratio of women to men in the ladies' beverage room. As noted above, inspectors found twenty-two men and five women in the Tusco Hotel, a ratio of four men to every woman. It was obviously a situation in which the notion of the "lady and escort," based on the idea of a couple out for a drink, was undermined. In 1935 the manager of the Wheat Sheaf Hotel in Toronto asked what he should do about "a party of five men 'escorting' one woman." He had refused the group service in the ladies' beverage room but wanted a clear decision from the board.[54] Smith decided that he could see

> no reason why a party of five men escorting one woman should not all be classed as "escorts" and permitted the use of the Ladies beverage room. No hotel proprietor could be expected to [require] a party legally constituted to break up and use different Departments of the Hotel, provided that in the opinion of the Hotel keeper their use of the Ladies' beverage room would be in accordance with the proper conduct of such Department.[55]

Leaving the decision to the proprietor's judgment suggests a bold confidence on the part of the board. Yet two years later, a hotel in St. Catharines was informed that, "should one lady come into your hotel in company with more than two male escorts, we believe she should be allowed to have one escort in the ladies' beverage room, and the balance be directed to the men's beverage room."[56] We can only speculate about the reasons behind this different policy decision: perhaps the board was more familiar with the Wheat Sheaf in Toronto and had confidence in the proprietor's ability to manage any trouble; perhaps in the intervening two years its view of groups of men with one woman had changed through experience. Nevertheless, this change of heart does suggest a tightening of the rules and increased restrictions on the connections between drinking and socialization, something explored in more detail below.

In some locations, the ladies and escorts' beverage room rapidly became the main social space for heterosocial interaction. Men like the five escorts of the one woman in the Wheat Sheaf were likely entering the ladies' beverage room looking to meet single women. In Crystal Beach, the Lincoln Hotel's situation of having the ladies' beverage room full and women trying to enter the men's beverage room reiterates the popularity of heterosocial drinking and the idea of the drinking space as a viable arena for socialization, whether one was meeting new people or going out with already familiar friends. Yet it is unclear whether women welcomed or expected such attention and, if they did, whether they were going to these beverage rooms solely to meet men or for a night out with female friends. The examples of women requesting a separate space do suggest that some women wanted to drink apart from the rabble in the men's beverage room, but we cannot draw any definite conclusions about the intentions of the single women in the ladies' beverage rooms.

Phony Women and Competing Discourses of Respectability

Uncovering the social respectability of the woman drinker is difficult since we rarely have an opportunity to hear the voices of the drinkers themselves, unfiltered by the self-imposed constraints one might place on oneself when communicating with a regulatory agency such as the LCBO and certainly unsanitized by the bureaucratic rhetoric of inspectors. Yet it is possible to disentangle some ideas about respectability in the contrived representations of drinking spaces. Here, we look to the tool of discourse analysis to uncover some aspects of the ideas behind women's public drinking that may otherwise remain hidden. Let us consider, then, the competing discourses presented in the complaints to the board made by supposedly respectable women.

The first of these discourses is the familiar family-centred rhetoric of the temperance movement, which was transposed into complaints about the activities in certain hotels. The progressive bias toward women as agents of social advancement had its pedigree in the temperance movement and its emphasis on women as the centre of the family and the moral compass for the civilized world. This was the language of the post-prohibition temperance movement's leadership, who were fighting a rearguard action in a battle that had turned against them. These erstwhile reformers drew their rhetorical weapons from the armoury of the pre-prohibition movement. Here, the beverage room was just the saloon in a different form and drew in unsuspecting innocent men and women, who were subsequently debased and whose families suffered. In letters to the LCBO, this discourse was persistent. One writer complained that the Rex Hotel in Port Arthur sold "all the liquor wide open ... my husband hauls wood with a truck and we have six children and as soon as he makes some money he goes to the Rex Hotel and spends it all."[57] The Commercial Hotel in Port Colborne had its detractors, one of whom ("Mrs. A. Jones") wrote, "I was in the Commercial at one time a certain woman came in for her husband and who had not been home for 3 days and he was sitting drinking with our so called known woman that hang out at these hotels."[58] Prostitution, drinking, and family decline went hand in hand in such letters.

Most notable is that, as with the complaints discussed in the previous chapter, many of the letters of this kind were found to be fakes. The one from "Mrs. A. Jones" was determined not to have been written by anyone of this name. It is immaterial whether they were written by temperance agitators or, more likely, by local bootleggers who found that legitimate beverage room sales were cutting into their profits. The point is that this metaphor – the poor harried wife whose husband spends all of his money in the beverage room to the detriment of the innocent wife and children – spanned generations. Indeed, that bootleggers were using such metaphors suggests that the bootleggers thought the story of a family destroyed by liquor would grab the attention of the board more than something less sensational. In such letters, paternalism is implied in the gaze of liquor control authorities.

Yet this fictitious trope of the harried wife and mother competed with another trope: the respectable drinking woman who was troubled by the behaviour of her local hotel. Indeed, "Mrs. A. Jones" was patronizing the hotel when she saw the mythical, pathetic wife of the whoring male drinker. She was not alone. Consider a not-atypical letter written to the LCBO in 1937 regarding the activities in the two licensed hotels in Dunnville. The letter was likely written by a bootlegger or "blind pig" operator and followed the common pattern of positioning the author as a respectable drinker who was not opposed to public drinking but was offended by the activities of specific drinking places. Of note here is that the author signed the name "Mrs. Wilson." Here was an image of the respectable woman drinker, challenging the idea that all drinking women were disrespectful. "Mrs. Wilson" argued that, although she and her husband "enjoy a bottle of beer just as well as anyone," what she saw happening at these hotels was disgraceful: "You will see men walk in the ladies beverage room with no ladies and sit down also girls are served that I know are only 18 and under and people are served even when they are rolling about on the tables surely that is against the law." "She" reiterated that, unlike the members of the Woman's Christian Temperance Union, she was not against the beverage room but insisted that such behaviour was disruptive: "We are entitled to a little [quiet] drink without seeing such conditions as that."[59]

That this letter was likely written by a competitor of the hotels is significant. Instead of representing "herself" as a teetotalling moral guardian of the community, this author chose the image of a woman drinker. If the image of a woman drinker had functioned only as a metaphor for debauchery, the author likely would not have chosen a drinking woman as his fictitious correspondent. The reference to a woman who enjoyed going out for a drink, then, suggests that the woman who drank was not necessarily a problem. Women's drinking was normalized; and the woman drinker could then act as an improving influence on the men. The progressive bias of the pub reformers in Britain, who viewed women's very maternal nature as a positive influence in the drinking space, appears in the LCBO records as well.

So now we see two competing discourses: the classic temperance argument about drink debasing the family and the woman being a victim of this debasement; and the emergence of a respectable woman drinker, such as "Mrs. Wilson" or "Mrs. A. Jones," who observed and reported on problems in the beverage rooms. Both were likely the creation of competitors of the legal drinking space; and both manifested simultaneously conflicting and complementary discourses. When we peel away the differences, what remains is a dominant discourse of respectability. The respectable lady drinker and the respectable lady abstainer both wrote about disrespectable behaviour in the beverage room. The correspondents saw disorder as the feature that would motivate the LCBO to act against a hotel, and often this disorder was also connected to women behaving badly in the beverage room. Yet at the same time, the very existence of the "Mrs. Wilson" and "Mrs. A. Jones" characters meant that it was possible for a woman to drink in a hotel beverage room and still remain both respectable and a capable critic of disrespectful behaviour. To the individuals who wrote these letters, this was a viable and potent image. Since they were writing to the LCBO in an attempt to undermine the board's own legalized drinking space, they would have been careful to write in a way that appealed to the board. So in the perception of the bootlegger, who was channelling dominant values of respectability, a woman could be simultaneously a drinker and a moral guardian of the home.

This image decidedly undermines the dominant idea that respectable women would never patronize beverage rooms at this time. Given how women's social world had expanded and how popular images of the era showed more middle-class women drinking in public, it is difficult to accept the assertion of the temperance movement that "respectable women did not drink." Except for hotels like Toronto's Royal York and Ottawa's Chateau Laurier, whose clientele was clearly "exclusive" and whose management was eager to exclude people who did not belong, it is difficult in many of these cases to identify the social class from which the women in question were drawn. It is therefore inadequate to assume that all of these women were drawn from the groups who traditionally would have been drinking in public.

Children

Since a woman's respectability was fluid, depending on the value system and gaze of the observer, we need to look beyond simple assertions of respectability and consider the activities that touched on the common values of all who observed. Social commentators of all political stripes sought to ensure that women were capable of fulfilling their motherly role so that their children were raised properly. For this reason, it is useful to consider how the LCBO managed the relationship between women, alcohol, and children. For nearly a century, the temperance movement had linked drinking to the decline of the family and the degradation of children. As noted in Chapter 3, hotels that were close to schools or other areas with a high concentration of children often faced opposition to their applications for authorities, both from the community and from the board itself. For many temperance and evangelical organizations, any connection between a child and drinking was cause for concern. Yet, since many historians have identified the evangelical temperance movement as middle-class in orientation and perspective, it is difficult to tease out the working-class views of women drinking and childrearing. Both Joy Parr and Joan Sangster have argued that, although class and gender were interlaced motivations for resistance, women's maternal nature was fundamental in arguments for improved conditions and rights for women workers.[60] Did concerns about women drinkers and their inability to raise children span class divisions, or did working-class people have a different view of women and drinking?

The dominant cultural expectation was that, class notwithstanding, a woman's role included childrearing; but did it *exclude* drinking, and did it include the need to isolate a child from the drinking space? The working-class perception of a drinking mother and her ability to raise a child is difficult to evaluate and has not been explored in any detailed way.[61] Moreover, the middle-class, evangelical temperance movement's voices were loud but narrowly focused. By the 1930s, they were in decline. So when we look at women and drinking in the beverage rooms, we are not necessarily looking at an expression of class consciousness or even class cultural divisions. We are looking at a cultural division based on interest in drinking – sort of a "Drys versus Wets" cultural divide.

In the records of the LCBO, we can see evidence that the dire association between mothers' drinking and childrearing may not have been deeply problematic to many patrons of hotel beverage rooms, the "wet class" if you will. At times, the board's perception of children and drink was concerned with the image of the board and the "optics" of stories linking children and drink. The most extreme cases appeared when children themselves were reported to be drinking alcohol. In September 1934, when Toronto minister J.F. Halliday announced that he had seen a woman giving "sips of beer" to her baby in the lobby of Toronto's Broadview Hotel, chief commissioner Odette promised immediate action.[62] There is no evidence in the LCBO's records of a follow-up. A few days later, the board faced the problem of licensing hotels on Toronto's Centre Island. Looking at the facilities in the Manitou Hotel, inspector John Kidd noted that "it may not be just right to issue a Beverage License for the Island on account of the fact that the Island is the playground for Children and if the elders are allowed free access to Beer there might be a drowning."[63] In November all of the hotels on Centre Island lost their authorities.[64] Although part of the problem had been that most of these hotels were not hotels in any real sense, the connection between adults drinking and children playing was an important consideration. The island would henceforth be dry.

Although Kidd's comment linking drinking to the potential drowning of children was about safety, the relationship between children and drinking was normally constructed as a fundamentally moral issue, one centred on the ability of a parent (especially the mother) to raise a child. In 1937 a correspondent wrote to the board complaining of the danger to the child of one of the employees of Dunnville's Victoria Inn: "Now this child can be seen every night playing in the back of this hotel seeing and hearing the drunks and the terrible language that is around such places." Inspector M.G. Dean visited the place and offered a contrasting picture: "The little girl is well clothed, attends public school, and also attends Sunday school on Sundays. As far as this little girl hearing drunks and terrible language referred to in the letter ... I would say the complaints are positively untrue."[65] The correspondent's association between a child near a licensed premises and improper parenting was exploded by Dean's investigation. Nothing further was done.

The child in this story was the daughter of a female employee, but the board was more concerned when customers brought their own children to the hotel. When questioned about the baby reportedly given beer in Toronto's Broadview Hotel, Odette explained that "you can't bar them ... If the parents want to take their children into a dining room, and to have a beer or wine on their table, that is a matter for their own judgment."[66] However, children were absolutely not allowed in beverage rooms, parental supervision notwithstanding. In March 1935 inspector George Hanrahan visited the Drake Hotel in Windsor, finding at 11:30 p.m. "two small children ... seated, one on a chair and the other in the lap of a lady whom I judge was its mother." Both were under ten years old.[67] Ottawa inspector Alfred Larocque reported that a four-year-old child accompanied three women in the ladies and escorts' beverage room of the Pacific Hotel.[68] Many parents seem to have had no qualms about bringing their children to the beverage room while they drank, but as Odette insisted, this was absolutely forbidden.

Other parents simply left their children outside. In 1935 a correspondent complained that the Queen's Hotel in Dunnville allowed people to leave their children outside the hotel while they were inside drinking.[69] Although the veracity of this particular letter is questionable, this trend is not. A police officer visiting the Cameron Hotel in Toronto "found a child between the age of four and five in the Rotunda, the mother of the child being served in the beverage room, and when the matter was drawn to the attention of the waiter and the Proprietor, they apparently could see nothing the matter."[70] A proprietor who did see something the matter, Eugene Sullivan of Toronto's Maple Leaf Hotel, wrote to the board in 1941 asking how to stop patrons from "bringing their children of tender age ... and leaving them in the lobby while they are drinking in the beverage room." The board gave no advice but informed Sullivan that he had to "see to it that the practice is discontinued immediately."[71] In contrast, one afternoon in January 1943, inspector Harry Simington visited the Shamrock Hotel in Toronto, finding two women in the ladies' beverage room with a baby buggy beside them: "I went over and had a look and to my surprise did not find a baby ... [but] a load of groceries."[72]

Odette's insistence that they could do nothing to stop parents from having alcohol at their table in the dining room appears to have changed over time. A young child was found in the dining room of Parr's Hotel in Windsor in 1939, "apparently with her parents, enjoying the music and singing while patrons were drinking." The board found this situation unacceptable. Contrary to Odette's statement in 1934, by 1939 "no person under twenty-one years of age is permitted in any room where beer is being served."[73] Again, the issue appears to have been the outside perception of this situation. Odette's insistence that the board could not stop parents from having a drink while dining with their children may not have been politically astute. The policy change reflected the continued problematization of any association between children and alcohol.

The connection of children with the beverage room was troublesome to the board, but these examples suggest that for many women it was a normal part of life. It is difficult to determine whether the rhetoric of the temperance movement reflected general values, whether those who did bring their children into beverage rooms were deviating from a general cultural norm, or whether the value system was rooted in a bourgeois conceit that still insisted that women's social world revolved around the home. Nevertheless, given the inclusion of children in the drinking spaces of some ethnic clubs and in beverage rooms, it is possible that for many people the proximity of children to alcohol was not problematic. Odette's argument that the board could not stop families from having a drink when dining with children in hotels suggests that the problem was not alcoholic beverages but the moral environment of the dedicated drinking space. Yet the inspectors' subsequent concerns over children outside of beverage rooms and over the child sitting with his or her parents in a dining room suggest that the discourse of deviance embedded in these activities was about shaping parental behaviour. Apart from the unproven story in the *Toronto Star* about the woman giving beer to her infant, none of the inspectors reported young children drinking alcohol. Moreover, the differentiation between the dining room and the beverage room seems in some ways artificial. Both were heavily controlled. The ladies' beverage room appears to have served, at times, as an informal ladies' club. Moreover, if women in the hotel could mitigate unruly behaviour in the drinking establishment, could not children as well? So the issue here was about proper parental behaviour and about a bourgeois, state-centred idea of the relationship between alcohol and the family. In effect, the board's interest was to reinforce a gendered notion of women by enforcing an idea of the way that women acted toward their children. This form of control was an extension of biopolitics, controlling the way women behaved by controlling their ideas about their children's bodies.

We can see this extended biopolitics in the way the board viewed hotel staff or management who had children in the hotel. The story of Dunnville's Queen's Hotel, where the young girl was playing in the backyard every night, provides a useful example. Here, the board responded to a complaint about the way a child was being reared. When the inspector learned that she was well clothed and went to Sunday school every week and that the main reason she was at the hotel was that her mother was working, he determined that the mother was doing her maternal duties as best she could. Good parenting and what we might anachronistically label positive family values appear to have been valid mitigating discourses in hotel operations. Applying to run the Log Cabin Hotel in Belle River, J.E. Couture deployed such a discourse when he explained to the board that his interest in moving to the area and in running the hotel was the benefit of his children. He had run a hotel in Blind River, in northern Ontario, but "because the education facilities there were not any too good, I decided to sell the hotel and bring my children down here ... Belle River is an ideal place for me to bring up my family and I can assure the Board that if they grant me authority, that the place will be run properly."[74] Unfortunately for Couture, this argument did not sway the board; the Log Cabin had been a problem for too long, and as noted in Chapter 4, its time as an authorized premises had come to an end.

Women Working in the Licensed Hotel

Couture's argument refers to the other type of women in licensed premises: women hotel workers. Although women were not allowed to serve beer or wine in hotels until well into the Second World War, they occupied a variety of roles within the hotel operations. Hotels in the communities under examination involved women in almost every aspect of their operations, including as proprietors, owners or co-owners, and management. I now turn to considering how the board viewed the various roles of women workers in the hotel space. This examination is not exclusively about the regulation of beverage room spaces, but since the LCBO's hotel-licensing function emerged from its role in liquor licensing, the operations of hotels and the sale of alcoholic beverages within these spaces were fundamentally interconnected.

Many hotels were owned or managed by women. As Table 2 indicates, out of 1,381 applications for a Standard Hotel licence examined between the 1920s and 1944, for which there was a single applicant whose gender is clear and for which a decision is clear, 180, or 13 percent, were filed by women.[75] Among all of these applications, those made by women were accepted in a higher proportion than those made by men.[76] Men's applications failed in 25.9 percent of the cases, whereas women were rejected in 18.9 percent of the cases. Moreover, applications by women represented about 9.9 percent of all applications rejected but 14 percent of those accepted. These statistics mask the fact that, whereas a woman who applied was usually a widow, a man who applied was often representing a married couple who would operate the hotel together. At the same time, the numbers mask the relatively rare occasion when a woman may have applied instead of her husband because her husband was considered unsuitable or was not yet a "naturalized" Canadian and therefore ineligible for the privilege of a beer and wine authority.

As noted in the introduction to this chapter, women had a long history of work in what we might call the hospitality industry. Traditionally, women had owned and operated hotels, taverns, or inns, so it is not surprising that they continued to operate these places after prohibition ended. Several times in 1930, the *Canadian Hotel Review and Restaurant* printed articles by women extolling the importance of women's role in the hotel. Mrs. K.C. Horton,

Table 2

Gender of applicants for hotel licences, 1920s-44

	Accepted	Rejected	Total
Men	890	311	1,201
Women	146	34	180
Total	1,036	345	1,381

Source: Archives of Ontario, Liquor License Board of Ontario, Establishment Files, RG 36-8, and Standard Hotel Case Files, RG 36-1.

manager of the Antlers Hotel in Mena, Arkansas, explained to the Arkansas Hotel Association that women may be more suitable to hotel management: "Being by nature domestic, she finds it easy to combine her household duties with business; and she is resourceful enough, when occasion demands to fill in from cook to chambermaid, from waitress to porter. Most men would find this hard to do." More than just possessing handy domestic skills, Horton argued, a woman was more temperamentally suited to hotel management, especially in smaller hotels: "Woman is by nature more tactful, tidy, fastidious and painstaking. She will attend to the small things that make her hotel a home for the traveling public. She understands human needs better than men, and takes a personal interest in the comfort of her guests."[77] Clare Wright found this was the case in a large proportion of hotels in Australia, where women often ran the establishments. As already noted, women's maternal presence was considered a good influence in "improved" pubs of interwar Britain.[78]

The LCBO recognized and embraced the role of women in many aspects of hotel management; and there is some evidence that the board preferred a hotel where a woman was involved in the management. Horton indicated that a single man would not be able to look after the housekeeping, something inspector U.G. Reaume observed when investigating improprieties at the Log Cabin Hotel in Belle River. He noted that the proprietor "is a bachelor and has no one to look after the housekeeping."[79] It may be for this reason that, as noted above, when J.E. Couture wrote to the board requesting an authority two years later, he specifically mentioned he had moved to the town for the sake of his children. The Ormond Hotel in Thorold faced censure because the manager lived apart from the hotel and left a single man to run the business. Inspector Dean recommended that the manager be "compelled to move his family and live in the Hotel."[80] This situation may have been more about the proximity of the proprietor to his hotel than about the need for a family, but the presence of a family in a small hotel was important. The manager of the Castor Hotel in Ottawa was a bachelor, but at least he was "living on the premises with his mother and four sisters."[81] Part of the reason for the rough character of the Kimberly Hotel in Port Arthur was that the proprietor's wife was in a sanatorium sick with tuberculosis.[82] When she came back, inspector George Skuce reported that "things are better when she is around."[83] In 1940, after the female manager of the Savoy Hotel in Dunnville died, her unmarried son took over. Inspector Dean wrote to the board with his concerns: "I consider it will be necessary to have a married man and his wife living at this Hotel and look after its management if not it will have a tennancy [sic] to get out of controll [sic]."[84] The lack of a woman's touch explained why Ottawa's Elmdale Hotel was "in poor condition, gives no real service, every room a Beverage Room, no dining room service and nothing to eat in the place." The inspector described it as "another one of those Hotels where no woman is to be found" and recommended the licence be cancelled. It was.[85]

Whereas single men were potential trouble, single or widowed women were rarely considered to be problematic. Possibly the most remarkable case of a hotel with a woman proprietor was the Capital Hotel on Rideau Street in Ottawa. As indicated on the initial application for an authority in 1934, the applicant and proprietor of the hotel was twenty-two-year-old Tessie Weiss. Both of her parents lived in the hotel, and her father was listed as the manager, but Tessie was the proprietor. This may have been a case of a Canadian-born daughter of immigrants being a citizen and therefore permitted to hold an authority, or it may have been an arrangement the Weiss family chose because of perceived or real experience with anti-Semitic attitudes of government regulators, but whatever the circumstances, it remains intriguing. The arrangement was so unique that inspector Larocque was confused in his letters to the board, referring to the manager as her husband, not her father, and when discussing the operations of the hotel, he referred to "him" rather than "her." The hotel appears to have been quite well managed and had very few problems with disorder.[86]

Single young women like Tessie Weiss were rare in hotel proprietorship; more often, a woman proprietor was a widow or a wife whose husband either worked in the hotel or worked elsewhere. When investigating the Erie Lane Hotel, which had been violating many of the board's rules, inspector Wilson Wylie learned that "whilst the wife ... is the nominal licensee to all intents and purposes the Husband ... is the controlling factor." This arrangement was necessitated "by reason of his reputation," but Wylie was not pleased with this deception.[87] In contrast, when a letter of complaint about the operation of the Royal Oak Hotel in Toronto noted that "a woman was running the ... hotel," inspector George Kennedy interviewed the proprietor and his wife and concluded that "they are both competent persons."[88] When Michael Kliski took over the lease of the Alexandra Hotel in Toronto, all of his documentation included his and his wife Stella's names, indicating the firm familial partnership in the operations.[89] Gender relations could lead to expectations of behaviour. The female manager of the Silver Dollar Hotel in Hespeler wrote to the town's mayor to complain about the behaviour of the local chief of police, who felt he could "barge in any time like a roaring bull." She criticized this behaviour by reiterating expected gendered propriety: "I am just a woman proprietor ... I had expected him to come in like a gentleman."[90] Her insistence on gentlemanly behaviour in a woman's premises reflected her own notion of respectability and the moderating influence that a woman could have on a man's activities.

The board appears to have accepted the idea of women as a positive influence in the management of hotel beverage rooms, but this image was not always maintained by the women. In May 1935, while visiting the Woodbine

Hotel, inspector Hanrahan found the wife of the proprietor "seated at a table with three men, this in the men's beverage room." He was troubled by the impression this behaviour could create since she "is a very fine woman and does not seem to realize the bad impression created."[91] More troubling were cases where women were not following their expected domestic duty. Inspector John Pitt commented that the proprietor of the Royal Hotel in Niagara Falls was a "decent sort of a fellow" but was hampered by his inexperience and "by not having the right kind of wife as she is not cut out for the hotel business."[92] Much more worrisome was a letter about the manager of Windsor's Ambassador Hotel:

> The only words that the woman knows that runs the Ambassador Hotel is GOD DAM IT. Christ Sake. And the most frequent the dirty word SON OF A BITCH ... This womans [sic] dirty tongue is knwn [sic] by every person that ever went into her hotel ... I told her that I entended [sic] writing to you about her I was told to go to hell and you also.[93]

The complaint certainly got the board's attention, but on investigation Reaume found that the letter was a forgery and that the proprietor was "a good Christian woman and attends church regularly."[94]

One key difference between women in Ontario's hotels and those in Britain's reformed pubs was that the former were forbidden by the board to work in the men's beverage room. Even when the woman owned the hotel, she was not allowed to enter the men's beverage rooms at all. This was exclusively a male environment. The bad impression created by a woman sitting with three men in the men's beverage room, even a "very fine woman," suggests that the association between a male drinking space and women in that space was one of sexual impropriety. Yet the rule was also tremendously impractical. The board forbade women even to act as cashiers in the beverage room, which would have just involved handling money, not beer. The reason for this decision is unclear but seems to have rested on traditional associations regarding women in men's drinking spaces; it may also have been a result of men's expectation of a homosocial environment in the men's beverage room. As will be discussed in Chapter 9, women could not serve beer at all until the middle of the Second World War, when labour rules were changed to allow women to serve beer in the ladies' beverage room. They could, however, stand outside of the men's beverage room keeping an eye on who went in, watching who was registering for rooms, and monitoring activities in the dining room or ladies' beverage room.

To this paternalistic rhetoric, we should add one more image: the struggling woman hoping to support her family by running a hotel. It was this image that female hotel proprietors and their male supporters often used as grounds for special consideration when applying for an authority or when explaining their deviation from the rules. They drew on the sorts of arguments that Horton made and that were reinforced by the LCBO's own assumptions about the woman as an ideal housekeeper, caregiver, mother, and all-around good influence. We have already seen, in Chapter 2, how Mrs. Labelle's request in 1929 to be allowed to have a private New Year's party in her hotel in Niagara Falls inspired a kindly, paternalistic response from then director of hotels William Dingman. Yet, when he learned that Labelle had ended up abusing the privilege, using it to have a wide-open drunken party, Dingman's response was equally paternalistic. He advised her that the best way of keeping her standard hotel licence was "by being a real good girl and absolutely observing the law, and keeping clear of doubtful acts of any kind whatever."[95] Yet the paternalism often resulted in genuine assistance to a struggling proprietor. When an officer of the Ontario Provincial Police found liquor being sold in the Prince of Wales Hotel in St. Agatha, he observed that since "this woman is a widow and is having a hard time to make ends meet ... I believe a warning should be sufficient for her this time."[96] The paternalistic approach to granting licences to women could become a liability for applicants when they were found to be violating the rules because paternalism hinged on a power relationship in which the patriarchy looked out for the wellbeing of the weak, innocent, and disempowered woman.

The paternalistic view of women, in which their proper role as a moral example and positive influence coexisted with the image of women as sexually dangerous, constructed a discourse in which the latter reinforced the need for the former. So despite admitting the pragmatic necessity of allowing women to drink in hotel beverage rooms, the LCBO reiterated a paternalistic, bourgeois discourse that placed the married, middle-class woman (or at least a woman who articulated middle-class respectability) in the role of moral helpmeet and leavening influence on the male beast. This is the sort of role that Mrs. Horton saw as suiting women in a hotel:

> Women managers of the smaller hotels become the "mothers" of those who abide with them and are often addressed as such. A tired traveling man is certain of a quick smile of sympathy from this understanding "mother" of the public. She deals with this stream of human souls with a finesse and sympathy that no man understands. Her life is a busy routine, but she finds the happiness of usefulness mingled with the cares. Men in a way have a broader outlook on life and expect greater returns from the business world.[97]

The LCBO based its evaluations of an individual's suitability as a hotel proprietor on such paternalistic assumptions, as did the progressives in Britain who sought to reform the drinking establishments by creating a homier environment in which drinking was not the only, or even the main, attraction in a pub.[98]

In the end, when evaluating the relationship between women, the LCBO, and the hotel drinking environment, only one thing is clear: the real and metaphorical connections between women and public drinking were as complex and diverse as the women who frequented these places. Single women, married women, and respectable and disrespectable women drank in public. Certainly, women in beverage rooms could be immoral prostitutes, or they could be moral, upstanding women keeping an eye on things. But these were not the only two roles they could fill. Accepting the "woman as whore or woman as angel" dyad ignores the very complexity that I am trying to emphasize. Although the discourses represented by these two female stereotypes helped to shape ideas of how women should fit within the authorized hotel, they were challenged not only by the apparent fact that respectable women wanted to drink but also by the fact that drinking in public did not necessarily debase them. So women in beverage rooms might be wives out for a drink with their husbands, or single women looking for good, clean, if slightly inebriated, fun, or women looking for a male-free environment, or even women looking for a complete, sexually experimental bender.[99] This diversity likely explains why the LCBO would not ban women from beverage rooms. Just as creating entirely unfriendly beverage rooms would have driven drinkers back to bootleggers, removing women would have done the same – because, as we have seen, where women went to drink, men were sure to follow.

8
"Their Medley of Tongues and Eternal Jangle": Regulating the Racial and Ethnic Outsider

In 1939 John W. MacKenzie, the superintendent of Bankfield Consolidated Mines in Geraldton, wrote to Edmond Odette, chief commissioner of the Liquor Control Board of Ontario (LCBO), asking him to permit beer sales in a new veterans' club in the northern boom town:

> A club of our own ... where they could assemble and partake in peace of such amenities of life as the club could offer would be much preferable to forcing these men to frequent the beer halls, for in new mining towns like Geraldton the clientele of the tap rooms includes many races and nationalities who have no interests in common with the return[ed] soldier ... Such premises, with their medley of tongues, the general atmosphere and eternal jangle, are not places where our returned men should be driven for their recreation and association.[1]

Deploying sophisticated language, MacKenzie's letter drew on a number of discourses that were quite common at the time and might appeal to the LCBO. To him, white, native-born Canadians naturally wanted and deserved a place of refined respite from the troubling polyglot cacophony of the current drinking space, which was nothing more than a chaotic "beer hall." He presented the idea that the club was intended for the noble soldiers who fought for king and country. Considering much of what has been written about the often tense relationship between native-born Canadians and the "ethnic" newcomers, one might expect the clear ethnocentric and elitist bias in this letter to have resonated positively with the board's central administration.[2] It did not. The LCBO did not grant a licence to create a new club that would be dedicated to white Anglo-Canadian veterans. They would have to mingle with the masses.

The LCBO's rejection of MacKenzie's request seems contrary to much of the history of ethnocentricism in Canada, but it was consistent with the board's primary mandate: preserving social order. A major aspect of the board's mission was to ensure order by limiting the number of places where alcoholic beverages could be served. In Geraldton, licensing another drinking place, irrespective of the perceived needs of the white Canadian veterans, would create more opportunities for drinking. It would violate the idea of control ensconced in the board's very name. Besides, the board knew that white Anglo-Canadian soldiers were no less troublesome than the multicultural masses MacKenzie described. The ethnocentric argument fell on deaf ears because ethnicity was not a prime category of restriction for the liquor control authorities in Ontario.

MacKenzie's expectation of ethnocentric privilege illustrates the themes of much of what has been written about ethnic relations in early-twentieth-century Canada. In the first few decades of the century, concerns about the direction in which the nation was heading, combined with growing labour radicalism and so-called imported dangers of European extremism, Bolshevism, anarchism, and fascism, led to fevered discussions about ethnic out-groups and new, potentially dangerous foreigners.[3] Studies of nation-building efforts, the reaction of white Anglo-Canadians to increasingly diverse immigration, and more recently studies of the immigrant experience and the history of ethnic communities have opened a broad understanding of the multi-ethnic character of Canadian history.[4] Donald Avery has noted that concern over white immigrants from eastern and southern European countries was assuaged with the knowledge that "time and Anglo-Canadian institutions ... would ultimately erase these differences and facilitate the absorption of all-white immigrants into the Anglo-Canadian community."[5] Nevertheless, many agencies attempted to speed along the processes. Most studies that include a consideration of immigrants' encounters with agencies working toward assimilation have looked at ethnic groups as immigrant groups, focusing on their relationship with government immigration officials and social reformers, such as Home Mission Societies of evangelical churches and groups like the Woman's Christian Temperance Union that did temperance work among various ethnic and racial groups.[6] Once arrived, however, and established within the country, the individual of different ethnic background interacted with a variety of hegemonic institutions designed to construct or preserve some "imagined" sense of Canadianness, or at least Britishness.[7] How, then, did discourses of ethnicity and nationalism function within other hegemonic bureaucracies?

As an agency that sought to establish new norms of proper behaviour, the LCBO was one of these agencies. The board sought to (re)construct manageable drinking spaces and common ideas of proper and improper consumption of alcohol, which in turn created new "truths" about the relationship of the individual and the alcoholic beverage. These ideals manifested themselves in a new, ideal type of drinker, one who adhered to the values of responsible citizenship. This citizen-drinker understood the importance of moderation, dissociated him or herself from the moral hazards of the pre-prohibition saloon culture, and drank his or her beer in a respectable way.[8] Since Anglo-Celtic ethnicity was assumed to be a part of the profile of the citizen-drinker, ethnic difference needed to be managed in a sensitive but ultimately inclusive way. Rather than simply excluding ethnic and racial groups from the privilege of drinking, the board granted them the same privileges as native Canadians, although it would be difficult to argue that they were treated equally. The board scrutinized the racially and ethnically different applicant and consumer more closely.[9] The discourse of difference that emerged was one that could function within the paradigm of the somewhat homogenized citizen-drinker. Difference was not a problem as long as it did not upset the social order. Yet at the same time the LCBO was not willing to push the boundaries of interracial and interethnic communication. It tolerated ethnocentric prejudice and did not force native Canadian proprietors to serve customers whose backgrounds they felt made them undesirable in their hotels.

This chapter examines how the ideas of ethnicity and race affected the LCBO's regulation of public drinking. The analysis is necessarily in two parts: the first section looks at the reaction of the board to racial difference, notably people of African descent and native North American Aboriginal people (referred to as "Indians" in the records); and the second section considers the interaction of ethnic-immigrant outsiders with the board's regulatory activities.[10] The second section is the more sizable, simply because the board had more dealings with ethnic social groups than with Black or Aboriginal people. Although the ideas about ethnic outsiders expressed by native-born Canadians or residents of British ethnic heritage adhered to a classic ethnocentric discourse, the LCBO's central administration was motivated by a vision of social order that was less hung up on blatant ethnocentricity. Instead of discriminating based on ethnic origins, the LCBO permitted ethnic groups to have beer drinking in their clubs and hotels as long as they adhered to the board's ideas of social order. Its hegemonic vision was intended not only to encourage an ideal of moderation that would ensure social order but also to permit activities that, although not necessarily consistent with the board's ethnocentric view of proper behaviour, were not going to undermine social order. When the Second World War began and concerns arose over the loyalty of individuals from several ethnic communities in Ontario, the board's central value of social order ensured that increased surveillance of such individuals and groups was consistent with the public interest. Yet again, as a bureaucracy focused on managing a specific type of behaviour and social space, the LCBO limited its own work to ensuring social order. Although it was aware of the need for surveillance of potential "enemy aliens," it left wartime security to other agencies.

Visible Race and Drinking

Attention to racial difference was deeply entrenched in Canadian society. Often in the LCBO's records, with few exceptions, racial differences occupied the periphery of the regulatory gaze but the centre of a discourse of deviance. The federal Indian Act (1876) forbade the sale of liquor to Aboriginal residents, those who were known as "status Indians." "Non-status Indians," those who had satisfied various qualifications that included relinquishing traditional Aboriginal culture, became "enfranchised" and were legally allowed full rights of citizenship. Yet as Mariana Valverde and as Scott Thompson and Gary Genosko have observed, the board's application of the law to "Indians" went beyond legal definitions to consider more racially stereotyped uses.[11] Robert Campbell notes that, as with Aboriginal people in the United States, the issue of Aboriginal Canadian drinking centred on the "firewater myth."[12] Described by Joy Leland, this was the idea that Aboriginal people were more prone to become habituated to drink and that they became extremely violent when they drank.[13] There was considerable confusion among the population regarding which people of Aboriginal birth were and were not allowed to drink. Even though the rules of enfranchisement would normally have permitted drinking and despite the fact that children of white men and Aboriginal women (often called "half-breeds") were legally not Aboriginal, the LCBO often cast the net of discrimination, and therefore of prohibition, wider than did the Dominion law.[14] Indeed, the prohibition of alcohol for Aboriginals was so culturally entrenched that the indictment list used by the LCBO to record names of people who were not allowed to purchase alcohol was known as the "Indian List." Since others have dealt more extensively and quite well with the relationship between Aboriginal people, drinking, and the state,[15] this chapter considers only briefly the experience in the communities under examination, paying attention to the various ways the law was interpreted and applied.

Although non-status Aboriginal people were "enfranchised" and legally permitted to drink, this exception was applied inconsistently. Proprietors and the LCBO inspectors were not certain of all of the rules, and as noted above, the LCBO's rules were more exclusionary than the Dominion law (although, as Valverde notes, even the law moved the "boundary of indianness back and forth").[16] Thus, for example, in a circular to vendors noting that the Dominion law forbade Aboriginal people from drinking alcohol, the board observed that this should include those continuing to live the "Indian way of life."[17] Further subtleties were also troubling. For example, in 1941 the proprietor of the Esquire Hotel in St. Catharines asked about serving to Aboriginal people enlisted in "His Majesty's Forces." He was unsure what to do but was under the impression that "such person having his Franchise Card is entitled to be served in the Beverage room" and asked for a description of the card so that he would know what to look for. The board did not contradict this assumption, simply replying with the requested information.[18] In other cases, the enlisted status of an Aboriginal person may not have mattered. In 1937 inspector George Skuce reported on trouble with an Aboriginal man who had been arrested when he became violent after being refused beer service at the Beardmore Hotel. Even though the man "is a returned man [an ex-soldier] but not living the life of an Indian," the proprietor refused to serve him, saying "it didn't matter what he was he wasn't going to allow him around the place." Whether this prohibition was because the man had Aboriginal ancestry or was just a "bad character" is unclear.[19]

The legal subtleties of the "status" or "non-status Indian" designation were blurred when all Aboriginal people were painted with the same exclusionary brush. When an inspector found that a hotel was catering to Aboriginal people or that there were Aboriginal people in the vicinity, he would reiterate the need to exclude them and to keep an eye on the premises. Hotels in north-western Ontario were especially problematic to the board, both because there was a proportionally larger number of Aboriginal people in the area and because the inspector did not visit many remote areas as often and as easily as he might visit urban centres. The National Hotel in the remote town of Allan Water had been a trouble spot for the LCBO owing to its proximity to the Hudson's Bay Company and to the fact that the hotel proprietor, Dallas Gastmeier, also ran the general store and reportedly spoke four Aboriginal languages. Aboriginal trappers would meet and do some trading in the hotel. The Ontario Provincial Police described it in the early 1930s as "a rooming house instead of a Hotel," but nevertheless it did receive a Standard Hotel licence prior to 1934.[20] In 1937 the proprietor applied for a standard hotel licence and beer authority. Investigating the location, inspector Skuce reported, "I have never seen much around the place but Indians." He consulted with the local Indian agent, the government official who administered the Indian Act in the district, who agreed that "it would be a dangerous proposition to have a hotel at that point."[21]

Gender and intermarriage added to the complexity of the regulatory challenges. In 1943, using a common slang for Aboriginal women, inspector M.C. MacDonald (Skuce's replacement) reported that there were a lot of "Indians, especially Squaws," frequenting Nipigon's Ovilio Hotel. One of the three Aboriginal women whom he found in the ladies and escorts' beverage room was married to a white waiter. The confusion arose because "there has been so much intermarriage between Whites and Indians that it is practically impossible to know where to draw the line in cases of this kind." This situation with Aboriginal people drinking and the confusion between status and non-status Aboriginals led him to encourage a more concerted effort to exclude them from the drinking space. In consultation with local police, he advised the three hotels in town to "work together in refusing to serve beer to Indians or others who are troublemakers there."[22] Similarly, in Fort William a waiter at the Avenue Hotel served beer to "two white men accompanied by two Indian women ... [and] did not realize until [the police constable] arrived that the women were half-breeds. Their make-up was so perfect and deceiving that the waiter did not detect them at first sight as being Indian women."[23] The proprietor insisted that he never allowed Aboriginal people "near the Hotel" and argued that, given how quickly the police arrived after the women were served, someone "tried to get me in the wrong."

In the northern parts of the province, inspectors, police, and proprietors may have been on the lookout for Aboriginal people in beverage rooms, but in areas where Aboriginal people were not such a large demographic group, it may have been easier for them to blend in and be served. In 1939 a waiter at the Gregory Hotel in Toronto served four glasses of beer to two men. After a few minutes, two other men came in and drank the additional two beers. When these men called for another round, the waiter "upon looking over his guests discovered one of them a [sic] Indian. He refused to serve the table unless the Indian would go out." The Aboriginal man was soon arrested for drinking beer, and the other three men were charged with assisting him "to secure beer."[24] The LCBO inspector noted that if the waiter had followed the rule stipulating that only one beer could be served to an individual at a time, this would not have been a problem. Also notable here is that the waiter did not recognize the ethnicity of the Aboriginal man until he came to the table and "looked him over."

At the same time, the story illustrates that non-Aboriginal people were not necessarily concerned with the drinking of Aboriginals. As Campbell has noted for Vancouver, some Aboriginal people might have been accepted as "white" in areas where there was less official vigilance and more camaraderie between Aboriginal and non-Aboriginal residents.[25] We see this in some of the stories involving Aboriginal people in Ontario hotels. For example, friendly drinking was likely the cause of a tragic story of a nineteen-year-old Aboriginal man, Maurice Trimble, who drowned while working on a fishing boat on Lake Nipigon, near Beardmore. He had been drinking with two friends, a white man and one the police described as "breed" (probably meaning half-breed). The two latter men had been served at the National Hotel in Beardmore, and Trimble, who had not entered the hotel, apparently got drunk on rye whisky with his friends after they left. He went missing while the boat was on the water and was presumed drowned.[26] The police saw this as an example of the National Hotel's bootlegging activities, not as an issue of Aboriginal drinking, since Trimble's friends seem to have bought the bottle of rye there.

The complexities of regulating or restricting Aboriginal people were different from those of regulating or restricting the two other main visible racial groups in the province: people of African or Asian ancestry. The challenges with regulating Aboriginal people emerged from the difficulty some people had in identifying them, from their complex legal status with respect to the consumption of alcohol, and from varying views of Aboriginal people throughout the province. Residents of African and Asian descent faced no specific legal prohibitions with respect to drinking alcohol; they did, however, face considerable cultural challenges. Board officials and the general public drew on common stereotypes and racial discourses when evaluating or describing the activities of African and Asian residents. They were scrutinized more closely by both board officials and the general public than were white people. They also appear in a different way in the LCBO records. Whereas, as discussed below, individuals who claimed distinct European ethnic origins often self-identified within this ethnic group and sought privileges or special consideration owing to this cultural distinctiveness, residents of Asian and African descent, with few exceptions, usually appear as unique individuals seeking privileges not for their ethnic cohort but for themselves as private citizens. The exceptions to this general trend were found in two Windsor establishments, a social club and a hotel, that were explicitly identified by the patrons and management as catering to "coloured" residents. Their experiences are discussed later, but first I will consider the treatment of Asians and Africans within the heterogeneous social space of the hotel and social club.

Residents of Asian descent appear rarely in the LCBO records. In the records of the six communities under examination, of the 1,266 distinct authority applications investigated by the LCBO between 1927 and 1944 for which ethnicity is identifiable, fifteen applicants were Chinese.[27] Ten of these applicants received authorities, and the five refusals may have had nothing to do with race. It appears that at least one of these applicants was not "naturalized" and therefore ineligible for authority-holder status, and several other applications were for places that did not conform to the definition of a standard hotel. Occasionally, Chinese residents appear as staff in licensed spaces, sometimes in relatively influential positions. The St. Catharines Club, an elite businessman's social club, was reported in 1937 to have a "steward or manager [who] is a Chinaman."[28]

The only Asian people who appear in the LCBO records under examination were described as Chinese, and it appears that the descriptions and assumptions about these individuals reiterated Chinese stereotypes. The "Chinaman" at the St. Catharines Club was mentioned only because the club had been found to have slot machines on its premises; the inspector noted that the steward "does not appear to be vested with authority for control." In other words, the slot machines were not his fault. This qualifier is notable since it suggests that the contrary case would be assumed: that the Chinaman was the deviant. This sort of rhetoric, which expected but did not find deviance in Chinese residents, reappears both in the LCBO's inspectors' reports and in letters to the board. An applicant complained to the board about the inadequacy of some of the establishments that had received authorities in Windsor, singling out the Chinese-run St. Clair Hotel as an example of poor premises: "How come a dinky little Chinese Lunch-room like the St. Clair Lunch ... is able to get a beer and ale authority while first class restaurants owned and operated by white people are not?"[29] Evaluating the application for an authority for the Imperial Hotel, which was owned by King Lee, Windsor inspector U.G. Reaume noted that "Lee is a Canadian citizen. Personally, I have known him for over 25 years ... I honestly think that King Lee is an honest Chinese and that the hotel would be properly conducted."[30] By the 1940s, applicants for authorities were often subject to a detailed "bond report," which often dug into an applicant's salacious background. In 1943 a report about Sam Quan (not his real name), who applied to run the Wyandotte Hotel, also in Windsor, described him as having good habits even though he was known to have lived with "various white women and at one time had two of them." This transgression notwithstanding, the report also noted that "he associates with a good grade of Chinese and is one of the leaders in the Chinese community."[31] Quan had previously been the manager of another hotel in Windsor and was considered a respectable citizen. The authority was granted.[32] In all of these instances, Chineseness appears as an indicator of expected deviance, even though, in the last two examples at least, the absence of unsavoury behaviour in Chinese individuals was what set them apart from expected characteristics.

Such positive evaluations of Chinese applicants stand in stark contrast to the inspections of Chinese-run establishments that emphasized filth and disgust. As noted in Chapter 3, in the first few months of the operation of the Liquor Control Act (1934), many restaurants applied for authorities, with proprietors hoping to convert a few adjacent rooms into slapdash bedrooms so that they could conduct a thriving restaurant business augmented by a beer and wine authority. Several of these restaurants were run by Chinese people. In Niagara Falls, the Annex Café was found to be "a well known Chinese Restaurant and has never pretended to give hotel service." Although the dining room was of an acceptable appearance, the "Kitchen, bedrooms, and beds [were] dirty and filthy. Could not imagine this place being patronised by hotel guests." The proprietors had convinced the owner of an adjacent store to put his name forward as a "cover name to secure authority."[33] Inspector Frank Ferguson, on visiting the Imperial Hotel in Windsor, described it as "the worst sham and the most disgraceful place it has been my misfortune to inspect." Although in Ferguson's estimation the place was nothing more than a restaurant, with filthy windows and little hotel accommodation, it was also staffed by "two Chinese," and in his report this discursive linkage between the filth of the space and the race of the staff is notable. Just as in the other cases, inspectors who visited establishments that were nothing more than Chinese restaurants often noted the ethnicity of the management to punctuate the impression of filth. Although it is speculative, this discursive linkage between Chinese people and filthy hotel operations may have been clear enough that the simple association between a restaurant and Chinese people would be reason for concern. So, when an anonymous complaint promised to "acquaint you with a few facts" about the operation of Allen's Hotel in Jellicoe and specifically noted that the hotel's restaurant had been leased by "two Chinese," the correspondent may have simply been implying the inadequacy of the restaurant facilities.[34]

Whereas Chinese people normally appeared in the LCBO records as staff or potential managers of hotels and dining rooms, residents of African descent usually appeared as two types of customers: troublemakers or those discriminated against based on their skin colour. The reports of disruptive Black people followed the familiar discourse of the hypersexual or physically violent Black individual. A correspondent complained that the Embassy Hotel in Toronto employed "a negro porter who wanders around the place asking respectable women if they wont [sic] go out with him or if they wont [sic] take him to their room. He must think he's in the African Jungle."[35] This letter was discredited. Similarly, an anonymous correspondent wrote to the board in 1940 about the conduct at the Erie Hotel in Niagara Falls:

> Last August [1939] during the horse race period a negro and a white woman occupied room #14. During the day time the negro had gone to the race tracks and had brought many men down in the evening who had lined up in the corridor and awaited their turn to get in contact with the white woman in her room.[36]

The idea of the hypersexual Black person often intersected with the stereotype of the violent Black man. It was manifested most clearly and in blatantly racist terms by Hamilton inspector Joseph Cheeseman, who, on a visit to the perpetually problematic Alexandra Hotel in Toronto, described the following scene:

> At 10.30 PM ten coloured men came into Beverage Room and believe me they were sure big and black and appeared to have full charge of Beverage Room Even the white patrons appeared more nervous when the black men came in. From then on until I left it was more of a burlesque watching the darkies going from there [sic] table to the door leading to the Ladies Beverage Room and placing their fingers to their nose at the patrons. They would then come back too [sic] their tables and in a few minutes a female would come from Ladies to Gents Beverage Room and stand until big nigger

> would get up from table and have a few minutes conversation. Nigger would then go outside and come in through Ladies Beverage Room.[37]

The big Black man, threatening both physically and sexually, was a repeated trope in the language of race. Although this sort of blatant racist language was rare in the LCBO's inspectors' reports, it is no surprise that some inspectors held these views.

In an environment infused with such a dominant discourse of the violent, hypersexual Black resident, it should not seem strange that the board also received correspondence from residents of African descent who complained of blatant racial discrimination in hotel beverage and dining rooms. In 1935 Tony Angelo reported that the Columbia Hotel in Toronto had refused to serve friends of his, a mixed-race couple, "on account of the lady['s] husband being [a] coloured gentleman." Asserting that his friend was a respectable citizen, Angelo asked, "why should he be denied the privilege of a glass of beer when he comes home from work and also be made a fool of in a public place where there should be no concerning about anyone's colour or nationality?"[38] Similarly, in 1935 inspector George Hanrahan reported that Dr. Taylor, "a prominent colored citizen of Windsor," told him that another "colored" man had been "used with some discourtesy" at the Grand Hotel in Windsor. This patron had been served beer in "a very small glass," and when he complained, the hotel told him that "they could serve any sized glass they wanted and refused to give him a glass of the ordinary size." Both Hanrahan and Taylor presumed that the hotel was attempting to get the customer "disatisfied [sic] so as he would not enter the place again."[39] When in 1941 two soldiers from the Medical Corps of the Royal Canadian Air Force entered the Royal Oak Hotel in Toronto, one of the men, a Black man named Morisette, was refused service. William Mair, who took the complaint and asked general inspector Harry Simington to investigate, described Morisette as "a coloured chap but appears to be of very high type." The waiter had explained that he would not serve them specifically because Morisette "was colored," and when they had appealed to the manager, he had "informed them while backing away that the uniform did not mean anything."[40]

Although Mair took a personal interest in this latter case of discrimination, the first two examples appear to have been viewed as unavoidable conditions of life in Ontario. The board responded with polite disinterest and marginalized the importance of the complaints. Rather than Arnold Smith or William Mair responding to these reports, P.G. Newall, the chief clerk of the Hotels Department, signed the letters. Newall told Angelo that, although the discrimination was "unfortunate ... the Board are not empowered to force any Authority Holder to cater to any individual class or creed of persons, it being the Authority Holder's privilege to refuse service at his own discretion."[41]

Similarly, he told Hanrahan to explain to Dr. Taylor that "there is nothing in the Act or Regulations by which an Hotel proprietor can be forced to cater to any class or creed." He went on to express the board's regret that this incident had taken place but noted, "we are powerless to act as an intermediary." He suggested that "the parties concerned seek some other means of accommodation ... either secure their supplies and consume them at home, or seek accommodation at an hotel catering to coloured people."[42] The lower administrative status of the letter writer, combined with the standardized language ("class or creed"; "powerless" or "not empowered"), suggests the diminished priority of such discrimination. Dealing with racial exclusion was not a regulatory priority.

The board may have seen such discrimination as a necessary evil for the sake of social order, which could be shattered by racial tensions in hotels. When a racially motivated fight began outside of the Alexandra Hotel, which had resulted after a white man named Low continued to make "disparaging remarks about coloured people," inspector John Pitt suggested that the manager keep Low off of the premises.[43] In early 1941 a correspondent named Petgrave (who appears to have been of African descent) wrote to the board complaining about a number of hotels that had "banned colored people simply because a few have become intolerant." She or he mentioned specifically the Paramount Hotel, which, although not blatantly banning Black people, had banned "[Black] women folk from partaking of some refreshment ... simply because two or three women have behaved in a disorderly manner." Petgrave characterized this exclusion as "one of the most scathing indictments ever to be meted out to a race of people save that as done to the Jews in Germany or other parts of a Hitler dominated Europe."[44] In response, Smith explained that proprietors were constantly facing pressure from the board to keep their establishments orderly, "with the result that some hotel keepers in their anxiety and desire to operate in an orderly manner, pleasing to the board, sometimes may take action which gives rise to further complaint."[45] Despite promising to investigate the complaint, he did not indicate that such exclusion was problematic; on the contrary, he appears to have viewed such management of hotel customers as a reasonable reaction to disorder. When, two years later, Petgrave wrote to complain again about the Paramount Hotel, she or he argued that the exclusion of Black people was disproportionate to their involvement in altercations: "It is a well known fact that other minority groups have caused disturbances in these places, yet have never been collectively treated in such a manner." Petgrave finished with a plea for justice: "There are several hotels in Toronto that claim they reserve the right to give service to whom they please, yet those that are directly affected are colored people, and are not one wit [sic] responsible for being colored than are people who are white responsible for being so."[46]

Several aspects of these stories require analysis. Foremost, these later stories of exclusion came during wartime, and they received greater attention – from more important members of the administrative hierarchy – than had the earlier letters of individual discrimination. So, although the board's response was essentially the same and generally gave the impression that it was powerless to force proprietors to serve customers whom they did not wish to serve, claims of racial discrimination appear to have risen in importance. Mair's letter to Simington, concerned that a Black serviceman faced discrimination, may have been about soldiers being disrespected as much as it was about racial discrimination. Mair was a veteran of the Great War and may have felt especially strongly about this issue. Smith's response to Petgrave's complaints, meanwhile, suggests that the board saw such issues as being of increased importance. His response, however, reiterated the need for social order over social justice. Just as Newall had advised Dr. Taylor that to avoid discrimination Black people should simply go elsewhere, so too did Smith advise Petgrave five years later. Petgrave's complaint in 1943 fell on deaf ears.

In its interaction with racial minorities, then, the board reproduced a discourse that essentially marginalized the racial outsider. Irrespective of the social status of the complainant, Black people would continue to occupy a liminal space in the board's regulatory activity. Racial discrimination, although an issue that deserved some sympathy, was not important enough to merit any kind of concerted action by the board. Such action would create conditions of disorder rather than a more orderly drinking environment.

Given this reiteration of the regulatory priority of social order, it is useful to consider the board's interactions with the two establishments that fulfilled Newall's suggestion that segregated drinking was ideal. In Windsor a hotel and social club were operated by and for the residents of African descent. The Walker House and the Frontier Social Club were located a few buildings apart from each other on MacDougall Street in downtown Windsor. The hotel had been licensed since 1927, and in 1934 when it applied for an authority, the privilege was granted with little comment. In contrast, the club first applied for an authority in August 1936, and despite a respectable sounding board of directors and a letter from the club's manager, Clarence Monroe, explaining that "apart from this club the colored population of this district has no recreational centre," its initial application was refused. The board had decided that there were enough clubs in Windsor to suit the population, a circumstance that Monroe pointed out "does not apply to the colored population ... they have no club with a license to serve beer."[47] A year later, after inspector Reaume recommended that the place receive a licence, observing once again that "this is the only colored club in the city" and that the club was genuine, the board granted the beer authority.[48]

In general, it seems that the board's central administration treated each of these establishments with the same regulatory expectations that they would impose on other licensed premises. A lack of cleanliness and tidiness was a problem for the Walker House, something that the inspector observed had not been a problem under the "old management." When the Frontier Social Club received its authority, the board required it to serve only bottled beer, a provision that Smith explained was a standard policy that had come into force during the period when the club received its authority. This was an issue of concern: Monroe noted that the club's members were not wealthy and could not afford the price of a bottle of beer, which had to be 15 cents per bottle to compete with the prices at other hotels.

From its inception, the club justified its claims for special regulatory consideration in terms of its racial distinctiveness. The issue of the price of a bottle of beer, for example, was framed by Monroe not only as an issue of cost but also as one that respected the value of the club to its members, who were not welcome elsewhere:

> All places in Windsor sell Beer bottled at fifteen cents. As an instance, if one of our members is coming to the club and has only twenty cents, he expects to get two glasses, but when he finds he can only purchase a bottle and it costs him fifteen cents, he doesn't want it. Not because it's too much money but he can get twice as much for twenty cents some place else, where he does not really wish to go. How would you like to go in a place where you know you are not wanted? That is the reason we applied for an authority so our members would have the same feeling as anyone else would have.[49]

The issue of beer prices, in turn, related directly to the club's ability to remain open. The board generally did not approve of clubs using beer revenue to support their operations. Yet in the case of the Frontier Social Club, beer sales were explicitly needed to support the operations of the club. Reaume wrote to Smith in the spring of 1938 expanding on the issue of beer sales: "It is impossible for them to put men to work looking after the club premises unless the club receives more revenue and they feel that if they had draught beer they would be able to get more of their members to patronize the club." The club could not raise its price of beer since it had to remain competitive with the nearby Walker House, which sold its bottled beer for 15 cents.[50]

Smith was critical of these comments. Drawing on the ideal of standardized rules, he reiterated the board's policy that "authorities are not issued to clubs for the maintenance of club quarters. The sale of beer is merely a privilege in connection with the other activities of the club." He observed that if the Walker House was selling beer at 15 cents, this must be a viable price, and he maintained that if he permitted the Frontier Social Club to have draught beer, every other club that had been required to sell only bottles would ask for the privilege of selling draught beer. However, he was sensitive to the needs of the club and decided to give it draught beer for a month, "but if it turned into a draft beer proposition [i.e., operating solely to sell draught beer] the right will promptly be recinded [sic]."[51] His concerns about fairness to all clubs and his dissection of the special pleading made by Reaume and Monroe indicate Smith's dedication to some kind of bureaucratic objectivity, tempered by the unique situation in which this club found itself.[52]

Whereas the Frontier Social Club's main interaction with the board concerned conditions around its beer-selling privileges, the Walker House presented a much more consistent regulatory issue. As noted above, inspectors criticized its lack of cleanliness, something that was attributed to there being "no woman to look after the general housekeeping."[53] The hotel's licence was suspended until the board received assurances that this condition would improve, and it did. Yet a lack of cleanliness was not the only problem. As with many other hotels, the Walker House was found to have continued beer sales after midnight, a direct violation of the regulations. When the board suspended the hotel's authority in May 1937, the proprietor sent a letter of apology claiming that he had been sleeping and that when he awoke after midnight, he immediately tried to clear the hotel of drinkers. He added that he had worked for the Liberal Party since 1887, and he promised to behave after this time.[54] All of these explanations were in themselves not remarkable and followed a standard pattern of proprietor-board interaction. The authority was reinstated a few days later.[55]

Yet the Walker House was clearly a hotel for residents of African descent, and the racial distinctiveness of the proprietor and the patrons was threaded throughout both official correspondence and letters from the general public. In 1936 a correspondent wrote to complain about the conditions at the hotel, claiming that "they have gambling up stairs and have white girls and married women hanging around for business which is a colored hotel and also sell on Sunday or any time of the night and keep theas [sic] girls at night."[56] When this complaint was investigated, the inspector learned from the manager that "at times he had been running over time but that he absolutely denies having any white girls on the premises ... and that no gambling of any kind is allowed." Reaume promised to keep an eye on the place.[57] Other reports mention the racial aspect of the hotel's operations, at times balancing the language of tolerance with that of racism. For example, when visiting inspector Harry Edgecombe reported on the hotel in early May 1937, he observed that "the general interior of the building is about the same shade as the color of the owner and would cost considerable money to properly furnish and redecorate ... I suppose colored people must have some place to congregate and enjoy themselves and I understand [the proprietor] Mr. Smith runs it very well."[58] This grudging acceptance of the "need" for such a hotel was combined with a racial slippage between a filthy hotel interior and the skin colour of the proprietor. Both were mediated by an assessment of the proprietor's own capability to manage the premises.

It is difficult, however, to separate generalized racial discourse from that uttered by specific people on the board's staff. Whereas Reaume, the local inspector, who seemed well acquainted and friendly with the hotel management, tended not to make racially charged statements, Edgecombe, an outsider, who was on a somewhat routine visiting inspection, was less circumspect. Later that month, he and Reaume visited the Walker House after midnight and found the place "in full swing." Although the conditions were generally similar to those found in "white" hotels that were operating after hours, comments on the racial character of the patrons permeated the report:

> We found the beverage and Dining rooms well filled with colored patrons, beer being in evidence on all tables but saw no food. Several of these colored gents and ladies were fairly well lit up, singing, laughing and apparently having a very pleasant time. Mr. Smith [proprietor] started for the Tap room and I followed him but he managed to get the lights out and door locked before I reached it but I made him open it up and found Smith Jr. behind the bar serving beer, two bottles of beer with caps off and glasses in a tray on the counter waiting to be served and four colored men drinking beer and playing cards at a table in front of the bar.

After ordering that the hotel be cleared immediately, Edgecombe offered a sympathetic observation: "It was [a] rather unfortunate call for them as it is the only colored hotel in the city but I believe an indefinite suspension might have a good moral effect upon other hotels who might be doing the same thing."[59] Edgecombe's repeated use of the adjective "colored" in his damning report indicates an additional negative weight placed on the actions of the management.

Yet the racial discourse that oppressed could also be used as a tool of resistance or self-elevation by those being oppressed. After Edgecombe and Reaume's visit, as discussed above, the board suspended the Walker House's authority. This resulted in the proprietor John A. Smith's letter noting his connection with the Liberal Party, as discussed in Chapter 5. Not discussed in that chapter were the racialized explanations and leverage that the proprietor used in offering his special pleading. Born and raised in Niagara Falls, John A. Smith was associated with several prominent Liberals in that town. He had lived there until he came to Windsor "to take over this hotel," probably in 1934. Not only had he been a member of the Liberal Party since 1887, but as discussed in Chapter 5, he noted that after the most recent election, "I would have had an appointment in Niagara Falls if I hadn't of

[sic] been coloured. All the rest of the boys that I worked with all got their appointments and something to do."[60] He then reiterated the need for the hotel, framing it in terms of regulatory efficacy and racial intolerance: "As you know this is the only coloured Hotel in Windsor where our people can come and enjoy themselves as the white Hotels won't serve them as they draw the colour line and they haven't any alternative but to go to some bootlegger."[61] Four days after penning this letter, John Smith received his reinstated authority.

These two cases demonstrate the difficulty in forming any clear conclusions regarding the way that the LCBO addressed the licensing of racially distinct establishments. What seems clear is the highly subjective nature of the evaluation of the racial social space. When considering most non-"coloured" establishments, the board and its inspectors attempted to deploy some kind of objective criteria, but when evaluating the Walker House and the Frontier Social Club, they employed language permeated with the discourse of race. Much of this was offset by assertions that coloured people deserve their own place to socialize, but the presence of these qualifiers seems to have reiterated the racial discourse. All of this, of course, is not surprising. The 1930s were far from a time of racial tolerance, and that the board reinforced a need for unofficial but sanctioned segregated social spaces is in keeping with general governmental action. That the LCBO was an agency with a principal mandate to preserve social order reinforced the need for such segregation: to do otherwise might be to invite racial violence and social disorder. As discussed below, the board reiterated such concerns when dealing with ethnic difference, but the room for the language of tolerance and the willingness to embrace cultural differences were more overt. The appearance and behaviour of racially distinct groups were more difficult to fold into the hegemonic norm.

The Medley of Tongues

Ethnic tension was not absent from the work of the LCBO, but it did not comprise a dominant discourse of exclusion from the privilege of a beer authority. In the vast correspondence the board generated between inspectors and the central administration, between politicians and administrators, or with the general public, ethnicity was clearly present. When a hotel proprietor applied for an authority, inspectors usually visited the premises and evaluated the proprietor's likelihood of following and enforcing the rules. The ethnicity of the proprietor would often be mentioned, but it was usually combined with a qualifier that mitigated potential concern. Inspector George Skuce noted that the proprietors of the Algoma Hotel in Jellicoe, in the Thunder Bay district, "are Finnish peoples but very willing to co-operate in anything I ask them to do."[62] Given the district, where many of the new immigrants were men working in the resource industry who might therefore have been generally associated with boisterous and troublesome activities, Skuce viewed ethnic outsiders as potentially problematic but recognized the pliability of these respectable hotel proprietors. Finns were considered especially troublesome.[63] More equivocally, when inspector John Pitt evaluated the proprietor of the King George Hotel in Crystal Beach, he noted that "this man ... may be all right but I am a little suspicious of these foreigners especially in a place like Crystal beach."[64] Although ethnic background was worth noting, inspectors often mentioned proprietors' ethnic backgrounds as a way to illustrate that they were, ethnicity notwithstanding, solid citizens who could be trusted with running their hotels. Both of the hotels noted above received authorities. Ethnicity was not a category of exclusion, but it did need qualification.

Although the board may not have made it a practice to exclude applicants based on ethnicity, nativism and ethnic difference were rife in many complaints sent to the board. For example, if a nonethnic club were denied a licence to sell beer, whereas a local ethnic club received the privilege, native-born people might express indignation based on the idea that native-born Canadians deserved special treatment. John W. MacKenzie's letter on behalf of Bankfield Consolidated Mines in Geraldton is an indication of this nativist tendency. Likewise, the predominantly working-class Talbot Club of Windsor had a barrister write to the board arguing that his clients "certainly are entitled to [a licence] just as much as any organization of Germans, Polish or Italians or any other nation who have already received authorities."[65] Proprietors of hotels also used ethnicity as a point of complaint. One Niagara-on-the-Lake proprietor who grew frustrated when her authority was delayed based her complaint on her sense of nativist privilege: "I was born in this town, as was my mother and my people for four generations back are all Canadians ... If I was an Italian or Polack I perhaps would be granted a license."[66] The proprietor of the French Canadian Club of Windsor was less inflammatory when he argued that "the French Canadian's [sic] of Windsor should be granted the same privileges of dispensing beer and wine in their clubs as Alien born who operate clubs in Windsor."[67] Windsor's National Veteran's Social Club was more diplomatic but displayed similar prejudice when it observed that since a number of authorities had been granted to "our foreign friends," it seemed only reasonable that a group of men "who went forth to fight for the democracy which we should enjoy" should receive a similar privilege.[68] Just as MacKenzie's nativist justification in Geraldton had been unacceptable, so too was the one for Windsor's National Veteran's Social Club.

Native-born Canadians' concerns were rooted in a sense of nativist privilege, which was offended because the beer and wine authority represented a form of official sanction or recognition of an ethnic outsider's credibility and, in some ways, right of citizenship. It is useful to remember the importance of the board's terminology. Since the liquor licence was an "authority" and since establishments granted an authority were "authorized," the proprietor became an ostensible agent of the LCBO. Although the responsibilities of the proprietor were considerable, it was also true that the proprietor was charged with enforcing rules that reiterated a specific national identity. So when native-born applicants saw outsiders receive such a privilege, they began to question why outsiders might be permitted this type of state-sanctioned – dare we say, hegemonic – role, whereas "true" Canadians were denied it. Yet the board was concerned about orderliness and respectable behaviour, not about ethnocentric privilege. When inspector Hanrahan, of Essex County, was confronted by one of the members of the Talbot Club about the fact that a local German club had received an authority, whereas the Talbot Club's authority would not be renewed, the inspector simply replied that "if all clubs were run like the German club I wouldn't have any trouble."[69] Clearly, the behaviour of the proprietors and the patrons, not the ethnicity, was far more crucial to this inspector. Indeed, when an applicant complained to Arnold Smith, "I feel that a Jew or a Greek can get more consideration than I can," Smith replied sharply, "this Board is not in any way interested in a man's nationality and do not grant authorities because of a man's religion or nationality nor do we on the other hand hold that against him."[70]

The Ethnic Social Club

As Hanrahan's reference to the German club indicates, much of the interaction between the board and self-identified ethnic groups was through the operation of ethnically oriented social clubs. The Liquor Control Act (1934) carved out a special place for clubs "incorporated or organized and operated in accordance with the regulations [and not] ... operated for pecuniary gain."[71] It made provisions for "any of the established war veterans' organizations in Canada which the Board may recognize" and for "any of the established labour organizations."[72] These provisions were intended to allow beer to be sold in places where various other activities took place. The board repeatedly asserted to club management that drinking was to be a sort of courtesy extended to patrons, not something that should be the major focus of a club's operations. Moreover, just as hotels were supposed to derive most of their revenues from non-alcohol-related operations (i.e., room rentals and dining room operations), the club should not have to rely on revenue from beer sales to maintain its operations. Also, club authorities were relatively inexpensive. Whereas a hotel proprietor paid from $100 to $300 per year (the fee increased during the 1930s), a social club's licence was $100, and labour union and veterans' clubs paid $50.[73] Hotels, but not clubs, also had to pay monthly gallonage fees. Yet because a club was not required to have bedroom or dining services, for many entrepreneurial citizens, a club licence could be a way of surreptitiously creating a drinking space without the bother of all those other things like food and bedrooms. Consequently, the regulation of clubs provided many headaches for the LCBO. So the board quickly became quite wary of any club applications.

Many ethnic-oriented clubs applied for beer authorities, and the board spent a good deal of time investigating their operations. In 1939 the LCBO had an inspector from a different region investigate, surreptitiously, the activities of all of the clubs in Windsor. He reported on the Italo-Canadian Political Club's activities, which were more typical of those found in a bad hotel beverage room:

> Women having to be helped from the Club to the Taxi Cabs on Account of being intoxicated, Neighbors being awakened out of their sleep on account of the Noise, One Man who has 2 Motherless children and not a Member was allowed to get intoxicated and the two Children would go to the Club and call their Father at the door, who would be shoved out to the children in this condition.[74]

Windsor hotelier W.D. Roach wrote the board in 1935 complaining that competition from the local German club, the Ostschwaben Alliance of America and Canada, was severely damaging his business. "It is nothing more nor less than a saloon," he argued.[75] The board had its own suspicions, meanwhile, and warned the club's manager to make sure he was selling to bona fide members of the club or their guests "in accordance with the general usage of clubs."[76] The inspector, counting the number of kegs of beer that the club went through in a month, did the math and knew that it was highly unlikely that "any club that sold 58 [half barrels] in one month ... could not have been restricted to selling to members only." But when warned about the inspector's suspicions, the proprietor replied that "German people are heavy beer drinkers."[77]

As this example suggests, ethnicity did present a category of evaluation and explanation but not necessarily one of exclusion. The only facet of the Liquor Control Act that indicated ethnic bias was the provision that only native or naturalized Canadians could receive an authority. The remainder of the LCA (1934) was sufficiently vague that any number of behaviours that seemed normal to some groups, like the supposedly heavy drinking of German immigrants, could be deemed problematic by the board. Consequently, the board's inspectors were expected to make judgment calls on the specific contexts of a supposed transgression.[78] In an early examination of the Ostschwaben Alliance, inspector Hanrahan noted that "it is typical of [Germans] ... to keep within their group for the enjoyment of their social life" and that if there were a hotel where "persons of their race could gather there would no longer be need of giving an authority" to the club.[79] Similarly, inspector Norman Ratz of Waterloo County justified the Austrian Club's need for a beer licence by saying, "I can readily appreciate how they feel as regards having beer in their club, to the Austrian German, beer is as essential for everyday living, as milk is to the Canadian, and since they live in a strange country, speaking a dialect distinctly different than most Germans they feel themselves out of place in a public beverage room."[80] Here, creating a space for ethnic minorities was the issue, but even within this homogeneous ethnic environment, specific norms of the new country had to be observed.

The dynamics of control and permissiveness are illustrated well with the example of the Austrian Club in Waterloo. When the club applied for an authority in 1937, inspector Ratz endorsed the application, drawing on ethnic stereotypes to inform the language of respectability, mixed with recognition of the unique requirements of this ethnic group:

> As a group they are industrious, thrifty and law-abiding citizens, who left their homes because of the unrest in Central Europe, and the horrors of war which they endured during the Great War ... A great many of them have become Canadian Citizens and express themselves quite freely as having no particular desire to return to their native land ...They are almost as a unit in helpfulness to one another, and maintain a common fund to help the sick and needy, and in a general way avoid becoming wards of the community.[81]

The central administration was not initially convinced that the club authority was a good idea and decided to grant it only when several prominent local individuals vouched for the club's members. It placed restrictions on the membership. Women would not be allowed as members, membership had to be kept to fewer than one hundred, and only full, not "associate," memberships would be permitted.

It would be inaccurate to assume that such regulations were placed on the Austrian Club by virtue of the ethnicity of the applicants. Many clubs faced similar restrictions, and it appears that the board was tightening its control over all clubs owing to their tendency to attempt to use the beer authority to compete for the business of hotel beverage rooms. Kitchener's Sachsen-Schwaben Club, which claimed a membership of Yugoslavian, Romanian, and Hungarian immigrants, had just recently seen its authority suspended for two weeks because it had been allowing the general public to attend dances and had been selling two classes of membership, one for $1 per month and one for 50 cents per month (with varying levels of sick benefits).[82] These sorts of violations, which were not confined to ethnic clubs, had made the board hesitant to grant any club authorities, and by 1937, when the Austrian Club made its application, the board had reduced to a trickle the number of new authorities it was granting to hotels or clubs. Few clubs had received authorities after the initial flurry of applications from July to October 1934. Before the fiscal year-end of 31 October 1934, the board received 124 applications for or inquiries about club licences, granting 89 and rejecting 35 (a success rate of 72 percent). In contrast, in the fiscal year of November 1934 to October 1935, the board received 63 applications and granted only 25 licences, a success rate of 40 percent. The numbers diminished significantly after that. Thus the stipulations that the LCBO set for the Austrian Club are most accurately viewed as an attempt to limit significantly any increase in the opportunities to drink in Waterloo.

Within six months, the Austrian Club was lobbying heavily to permit women to join their husbands in the club space.[83] The club's executives, through their lawyer, argued that they had conducted their organization respectfully and had demonstrated their ability to stay within the law; relaxing the strict regulations, they suggested, would not be unreasonable. The crux of the argument illustrates the central place of clubs in the lives of this particular ethnic group:

> The premises occupied by the Club are a centre for the social activities of the members. They keep pretty well to themselves, and are all reputable citizens highly regarded in the community. There is considerable resentment on the part of the wives of the male members on account of the fact that they are not permitted to join their husbands in their social activities at the Club and the Club members themselves cannot see where any harm would result from enlarging its membership along the lines asked for.[84]

In spite of this appeal to respectability and tradition, and regardless of receiving a letter of support from the mayor of Waterloo, the board remained adamant that women should not become members.[85]

To the supporters of the Austrian Club, the club's request did not seem out of line with what other clubs were receiving in the area. It was asking that it receive the same sorts of privileges as the Sachsen-Schwaben Club. One writer argued that the Sachsen-Schwaben's members were both male and female and had equal access to the same beverage room, although this was not accurate. As noted earlier, the Sachsen-Schwaben Club had experienced problems that made it a poor point of comparison for the Austrian Club. A better comparison was made by inspector E.A. Berges, who replaced Ratz in 1939. He noted that the Concordia Club, a German club but one patronized mostly by younger, Canadian-born members, had been permitted to have dances and to sign in guests on Fridays and Saturdays. He observed that, in contrast, the Austrian Club's members were middle-aged and had wanted to have fewer heterosocial activities. This comparison, which provided an example of a reasonable way of integrating men and women into club activities, appealed to the board's need to ensure social order. After reviewing the specifics of the club's modified request, the board altered the parameters of the authority to permit dances twice a month and a specified list of occasional heterosocial activities.[86] Whether the club continued to observe these restrictions is impossible to determine since a year later, along with all other German clubs in the region, it was forced to close owing to wartime concern about associations of German people.[87]

As the Austrian Club's experience illustrates, although the board permitted a place for ethnic groups, it did not necessarily permit a continuation of Old World drinking behaviour. What appears to have been seen as a natural community space for the ethnic group was usually restricted to men by the board. Thus, when the local inspector kept finding that the Hungarian Self-Culture Society in Welland was serving women and had women on its membership rolls, the board rescinded its authority.[88] Similarly, the proprietor of a club of Windsor Hungarians, the Independent Mutual Benefit Society, had been "under the impression that [women] have the same rights to enjoy the privilege of having beer as the men members." He was consequently informed that this was not the case.[89] Inspector Reaume entered the Ostschwaben Alliance one night to find "the place filled [with] ... approximately, 40 women and about 100 men ... singing German songs ... to music from a five piece string orchestra accompanied by a piano."[90] Inspector Pitt was horrified in 1935 to find "men and women drinking with babes in arms not over three or four months old" in the beverage room of the Polish War Veteran's Association in Windsor.[91] Notable here is that repeatedly the ethnic clubs, which seemed to function as social centres, were being shaped along the lines of the norms of the host country, where this communal beer-hall configuration presumably contradicted Ontarians' sense of respectability.

Just as the board investigated ethnic clubs on their merits as clubs rather than as ethnic out groups, so too were these clubs not necessarily representative of their ethnic community. Expecting the behaviour of one small group to represent the values of the entire community is problematic; several historians have recently demonstrated how ethnic immigrant groups were divided, often between religion and politics.[92] Several times, the board had to deal with controversy within an ethnic community or across communities of immigrant groups. So it would be inappropriate to assume that the drinking cultures revealed in the investigations of ethnic clubs indicated a homogeneity of behaviour for individual ethnic groups. In a number of cases, complaints came from other members of the same ethnic group. Complainants were concerned about the effect of certain activities on the morality of their children and on the peace of their neighbourhoods. The pastor of the Hungarian Evangelical Lutheran Church in Windsor wrote to the board in 1935 that the club license for which the Windsor and District Hungarian Society had applied should not be granted. His argument was that since, in the depths of the Great Depression, the morale of unemployed Hungarians was already very low, "they should not be exposed to more temptations than they already have." He concluded by noting that he was anxious to "protect the good name of the Hungarian people."[93] A group of Hungarian ministers also protested the activities of the Hungarian Independent Mutual Benefit Society, noting that "the liquor traffic has become a menace to the youth of the community ... Much good will be derived from such a revoking as it will protect the morals of our youth."[94] That these requests came from religious leadership is notable. Was the club replacing the church as the social centre? Or was this an instance of the values of the host country being adopted by another great hegemonic institution: the church?

The proximity of a licensed club to a church could create considerable tension, and interethnic conflicts were not unusual. The pastor of the Ukrainian Catholic Church, which was located next door to the Border Cities Polish Canadian Club in Windsor, argued that whenever an event such as a parish supper took place at the church, "there was always an intercourse between the church and the club ... In other words, persons not members of the club were being sold beer in the club room."[95] The unlicensed Ukrainian Labor Temple was across the street from the Roumanian Beneficial and Cultural Society of Ontario in Windsor. The Labor Temple's secretary argued to the board that such proximity could "cause us and the public patronizing our hall many difficulties, quarrels and possibly fatal accidents."[96] A similar protest was lodged in Fort William, where the Finnish Pentecostal Church, which was across the street from an Italian branch of the Canadian Legion, stated that "you can help us and the Church in this by not granting them a license."[97] In all cases, the complainants expressed their concern that drinking was incompatible with good behaviour, regardless of the place of drinking in the ethic group's culture.

So although ethnicity mattered, ethnicity as a category of exclusion was subsumed by an indigenous notion of respectability. Ethnic clubs that could impress the board's inspector and receive positive character references had a better chance of receiving an authority than did others. I have already noted the language of respectability that Ratz used to endorse the application of the Austrian Club and that others used to evaluate the character of ethnic Canadians who applied for authorities. Certainly, the language could be patronizing, but it also employed concepts that were ideal to the board's mandate of social order. Members of the club were respectable, good community members, and the reference to their unwillingness to become wards of the community spoke to an ethic of financial independence: all good, British values. In 1934 inspectors Hanrahan and Pitt recommended that all Polish authorities in Windsor not be renewed but that the Polish War Veteran's Association should receive one instead. They noted that this group "was a very worthy organization, doing charitable work ... and that the others do not have the backing of the Polish people."[98] Hanrahan further noted that the Polish People's Home Association consisted of "a very good class of people" who were "lending their efforts to moral and educational uplift."[99]

The interconnected language of respectability and social order was pervasive in these applications and evaluations, and it was not only the inspectors who employed it when recommending an establishment receive an authority. When the Hungarian Self-Culture Society in Welland lost its authority in 1937, barrister R. Boak Burns wrote to the LCBO asking that it be restored. He observed that the Hungarian people in that city "are without a doubt, the best of the non Anglo-Saxon groups" and requested a degree of leniency:

> The majority of the members are of the labouring or heavy manual class, and there are few especially of the older members, that are completely educated in our way, and a large majority although naturalized, have very little knowledge of the English language ... [their] idea of a club and the use they make of it were certainly different from such as our own.[100]

His request, and those of other members of the community, did not sway the board's decision, although given that Welland had just experienced several years of labour tension that many believed was the result of immigrant radicalism, there may have been more to this refusal than the records suggest.[101] Similarly, a Fort William alderman characterized the Italian Society of that city as

> composed of the outstanding Italian residents of Fort William, and its efforts have been, ever since it was formed, to instruct the Italians who come to this City in British institutions and in what is required of British subjects and I think I am safe in saying, it has met with fair success along these lines. It has carried on extensive relief and educational work in the foreign section of the city and it has taken part in supporting all municipal works and schemes of this city.[102]

Such good works from such upstanding people, who were endeavouring to improve the lot of their ethnic group and were undertaking the same hegemonic efforts as other British institutions, deserved to be supported. Unfortunately for this club, the board did not agree, and the Italian Society did not receive a beer authority. It would have to continue its sober activities, soberly. Given that these applications were made in the spring of 1937, when the board had significantly limited new club authorities, these clubs were likely victims of bad timing rather than of any ethnic discrimination at the board.

Radicalism and the Fear of Disorder

Ethnicity might have been easily related to respectability, but in the political atmosphere of the 1930s it could also be related to disorder. As several historians have demonstrated, the growth of industrial cities and the expansion of the resource-extraction industries in Canada during the first quarter of the twentieth century had created a need for immigrant labour that resulted in the sort of multicultural communities MacKenzie railed against in his letter from Geraldton.[103] Many of these immigrants were seen as the cause of much of the labour unrest that these booming areas faced. The economic uncertainty of the 1930s created and exacerbated tensions, which were fuelled as well by growing fears of anarchists, communists, and as the decade ended, Nazis and fascists. Each of these groups was considered to have subversive elements ensconced in the ethnic subcultures of people whom the Canadian government had encouraged to immigrate in the years following the Great War. Whereas the United States had embarked on immigration restriction, the Canadian government had encouraged immigration for much of the 1920s, notably for workers in resource extraction (such as in northwestern Ontario) and industry. Many of these workers ended up in factories in growing industrial cities like Windsor and Toronto.

There were two key ways that radical politics among ethnic groups entered into the LCBO's records. First, some ethnic groups were considered key to keeping radicalism at bay insofar as they reinforced the values of British/Canadian culture, as indicated in some of the letters mentioned earlier. These groups needed to be favoured and encouraged. Second, other groups were considered to be hotbeds of radicalism. In both instances, the concern over radicalism was often expressed in letters from the general public. The LCBO, meanwhile, reacted to evidence of radicalism with cautious vigilance. By the beginning of the Second World War, the board was one part of a larger surveillance machine that was intent on keeping the country safe from the ethnic enemies. However, despite using its mechanisms for surveillance activities, the board did not turn its authority-granting power into a tool of national security.

The connection between ethnicity and radicalism was familiar to the LCBO throughout the 1930s. The board's role was to protect the social order by enforcing proper drinking behaviour, so it did not tie the receipt of an authority to potential subversive activities, be it to prevent them or to stop them. In 1935, when the board decided against granting an authority to the Hungarian Self-Culture Society in Welland, a member of the society's executive wrote to the board that "this society had been largely responsible for checking the further advancement of radicalism in this city." He argued that a comfortable and enjoyable clubhouse with a beer authority would permit the members to continue to carry on such good work.[104] The argument fell on deaf ears. Similarly, a barrister supporting the application of an Italian workingmen's club called the Port Colborne Social Club argued that failure to grant an authority could in fact create radicalism. The board had made specific note of the inadequate clubrooms, and the barrister found this to be troubling:

> They cannot understand why this should be a bar to securing a license ... It gives them the idea that the securing of a license appears to be a rich man's privilege, and the only reason that they cannot get a license is because they are labouring men. This is the sort of thing which produced communism and discontent among such people and I respectfully submit that everything in reason should be done to counteract the fermenting of such discontent.[105]

Again, this petition was unsuccessful. The LCBO did not seem to consider this sort of argument to be a valid reason for contradicting its own parameters for club authorities.

The argument that a beer authority would act as some sort of prophylaxis against radicalism was rare. Prior to the Second World War, intimations of the threat of radicalism usually came from people who opposed the granting of a license to a club. Essex County, especially Windsor, saw most of this sort of argument, and the proximity to Detroit might have been the reason.[106] For example, in 1938 a petition to the LCBO commissioner from three pastors of a local Hungarian church cited complaints from "law-abiding citizens relative to anti-government agitation of communistic tendencies" taking place at the Hungarian Independent Mutual Benefit Society.[107] Following up on a complaint from a local Ukrainian church, inspectors Hanrahan and Pitt reviewed the Border Cities Polish Canadian Club's activities, noting that "paid agitators are brought from Detroit to address club gatherings and their utterances are of the Red and Communistic type, down with church, government etc."[108] The club's authority was not initially renewed, but a few months later the board sent the club a new application form and subsequently granted a new beer authority.

The nature of complaints from the general public against ethnic clubs demonstrates how deeply embedded in the national psyche were concerns over radicalism. Whereas complaints (often signed anonymously) against nonethnic clubs or hotels often included sensationalized accounts of lewd behaviour, heavy drinking, lascivious entertainment, and other forms of immorality, complaints against ethnic clubs often included charges of political radicalism and anti- or nonreligiosity. For example, the Border Cities Polish Canadian Club was the target of a letter ostensibly (but unlikely) from "ladies of Catholic Church" that claimed the club had "plenty cominnist [sic] in there" and that its members were also anti-religious: "When you past [sic] there [sic] hall they laugh and say look crazy church people go to church."[109] A few years later, another series of letters about the same club was sent to the board. It is likely that these letters were from a local bootlegger who was upset with competition. They accused the club of harbouring "Commints" and claimed, "they don't believe in church or priest."[110] Notable about these letters, regardless of their veracity, is that the correspondent felt the most important factor about these "Commints" was their nonreligiosity. Inspector Reaume seemed to concur with this dubious source, reporting that "over sixty per cent of their members are 'Reds,'" but he did not mention religion.[111] Yet, although inspectors found such "communistic" tendencies worth noting, they did not view these as reasons for the club to be refused a licence.

Although observations of radical tendencies appear to have had little impact on whether the board granted a licence to a club, when the Second World War began in 1939 the importance of such observations changed. Germans, Austrians, and Italians (as well as other "Germanic" groups) and Japanese could be labelled enemy aliens, and the LCBO's activities turned to surveillance measures more integrated with other security branches of the provincial and federal governments.[112] According to Toronto's *Globe and Mail,* government began its crackdown on ethnic clubs in Waterloo County.[113] As soon as the war began, the city councils passed a motion urging the Germanic clubs to close. Soon afterward, the Concordia Club and the Sachsen-Schwaben Club ceased operations. The Austrian Club, which in its correspondence to the board had repeatedly asserted its allegiance to Canada (and renamed itself the Austrian-Canadian Club in 1939), was closed by May 1940.[114] After the federal government made the decision to intern Italians in June 1940, the board withdrew the licences of four Italian clubs, effectively shutting them down.[115] When the Border Cities Italian Club sought to reopen in 1942, inspector Reaume noted that "this community would not stand for re-opening of an Italian club during this war," a sentiment that may indicate concern over the club but might also suggest that granting an authority would cause disorder and problems in the community, especially given that such clubs were the targets of militant anti-Axis violence during the war.[116]

The board's reaction to the concerns over radicalism was patriotic but does not appear to have been excessive. Throughout the province, practically every German and Italian club and hotel proprietor was subject to a background check by the Royal Canadian Mounted Police (RCMP). Rarely did these background checks turn up suspicious activity, but the RCMP officer replying to the LCBO's information request always noted that a report turning up no subversive activity "should, however, not be taken as an assurance of the loyalty of the individual in question."[117] The reactions to these background checks demonstrate a good deal about the board's position on a person's past. When investigating the proprietor of the Roma Hotel, which was renamed the Welland Hotel on the outbreak of hostilities, Smith noted that the proprietor had a bad reputation, likely because he had once shot and killed his wife. Smith observed that they were not interested in "what occurred in a man's past, and would not consider cancelling the Authority for the reasons given." Instead, "the only reason we would wish to withdraw an Authority or License issued by this Board, would be if a man were anti-British in his leanings."[118] Given that the board observed but did not react to concerns over radicalism in the pre-war period, this statement suggests that once the war broke out, the LCBO's interest in the morality of the nation shifted to an interest in its security.

Yet these stated concerns were not always followed with action. There were a number of instances when security concerns became a central issue to the LCBO during the war, but rather than cancel authorities, the LCBO simply passed on the information. Along with the RCMP, the LCBO conferred with the Ontario Provincial Police (OPP), and in June 1940 an OPP inspector argued strongly against the granting of any licences to "enemy aliens," noting that one part of Windsor, where the "Polish Falcons" had hoped to establish a club, "is a hotbed of aliens and in my estimation should be the last place ... to issue a permit." He took a consciously law-and-order perspective, arguing that "it would be in the best interests from the standpoint of law enforcement to refuse permits to organizations other than those comprised of British and Canadian subjects."[119] The Falcons did not receive a permit. More perplexing for the board were establishments that already had licences. The OPP and RCMP were clear in their interests, noting that the Windsor and District Hungarian Society should have its licence withdrawn, "thereby eliminating another nest for prospective fifth columnists."[120] It was, according to the anonymous report, a centre of Nazi sympathy. The Order of the Sons of Italy in Windsor, meanwhile, as with many other Italian establishments, was considered to be housing a school where the children of Italian immigrants were taught "the tenets and principles of Fascism."[121] Initially, the board did not cancel this club's authority, but eventually, as noted above, it rescinded four Italian clubs' authorities in Windsor after the RCMP reported its concerns.

When the LCBO evaluated and regulated the actions of racial and ethnic groups, social order remained its main concern. The board's willingness to give the Frontier Social Club special treatment and its leniency with the Walker House were both framed within the need to allow segregated space for people of African descent in order to avoid social disorder. This is also how it explained the exclusion of Black patrons by some white hotel proprietors, which it permitted in spite of some notable opposition by these people of colour. The vividness of concerns with racial issues was muted when the board addressed the licensing and management of distinct ethnic-outsider groups. As long as ethnic groups were seen to adhere to the LCBO's vision of social order, their activities were legitimate and generally accepted. The ideal ethnic club was one in which drinking was not a main goal, so groups whose members' activities centred around drinking would receive much more scrutiny than those who were doing other things, like offering mutual support in economically troubled times.

Threaded throughout all of these examples is the balance between, on the one hand, racialized and ethnocentric discourses of intolerance and, on the other, the blatant, bureaucratic language that asserted some need to enforce a unified, standardized vision and system of governance. Racial and ethnic difference was a salient issue, but rather than just leading to intolerance and exclusion, it created a need for awareness and some leeway in the cultural activities of the individuals under scrutiny. Nevertheless, the racialized tropes of the sexual and violent Black person, combined with concerns over miscegenation when "white girls" were suspected to be mingling with Black men, permeated the board's treatment of people of African descent. The stereotype of the unclean Chinese restaurant was rare but persistent in the regulatory discourse. The ethnic stereotypes of the heavy-drinking German, the troublesome Finns in north-western Ontario, and the mixed-sex social behaviours of many eastern and southern European residents were frequent images but not necessarily always issues of concern. As discussed in the next chapter, the war placed the board in a different relationship with respect to policing outsiders, one in which the board was content to play a secondary role. Throughout its interaction with different ethnic and racial groups, the board scrutinized ethnic difference but did not necessarily discriminate against it. There seems to have been a persistent recognition of the value of tolerance as long as the outsiders governed themselves and their relationship with the state according to the board's directives.

9
Public Drinking and the Challenges of War

The onset of the Second World War brought significant economic and social changes to Ontario. From a period of depression and high unemployment, all of Canada shifted to high employment and increased disposable income within a few months. These changes were accompanied, however, by an increased scarcity of many consumer items and by the centralization of control over prices, distribution of resources, and eventually, management of staffing. The Dominion government, under the authority of the War Measures Act and the exigencies of the wartime emergency, began to have a more significant impact on the work of the Liquor Control Board of Ontario (LCBO) and on the social and recreational lives of Ontarians. So the LCBO had to balance the needs and demands of the national wartime economy against the requirements of the federal government, with the situation affecting communities differently. Added to its normal work was an increase in the board's potential as a surveillance body that could keep an eye on possible dissidents and anti-British activities. This chapter examines several of the key issues faced by the LCBO and hotel proprietors during the war. Its end date, however, is not 1945, when the war ended, but rather 1944, when the hotel-licensing operations of the LCBO were transferred to a new agency, the Liquor Authority Control Board. Although the discussion in previous chapters includes events and activities that occurred during the war, this chapter looks at issues that were unique to the wartime situation.

Increased incomes, along with more people employed in key wartime industries, produced a concomitant increase in the patronage of hotels. Figure 5 illustrates the change in employment in nonagricultural industries from 1941 to 1951. Of particular note is the inset graph, which shows the trends in payroll and employment from the 1920s through to the end of the war, illustrating clearly the rapid increase in wages during this period. Hotels, as places of both recreation and accommodation, reaped the benefits but also felt the pressure of demographic and financial change. A 1942

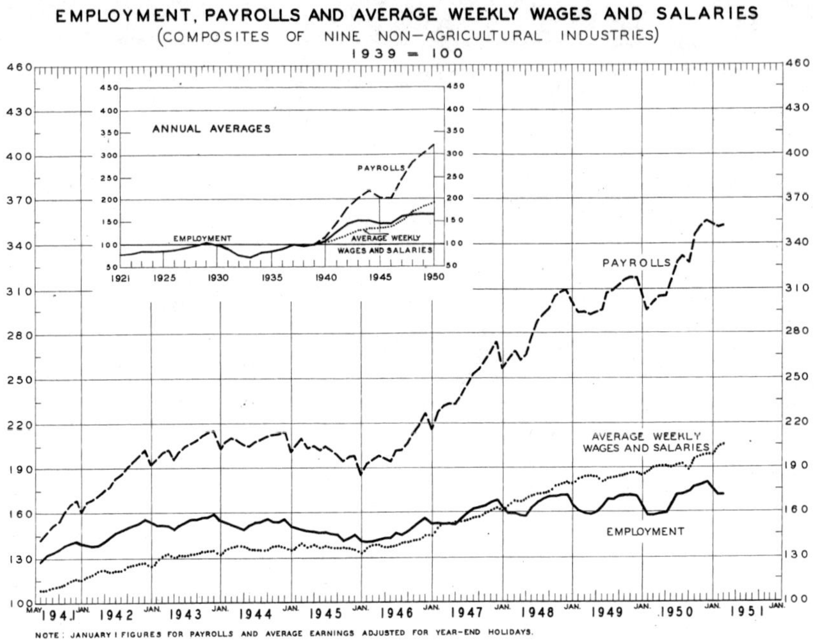

Figure 5 Employment and wage figures with inset chart of longer-trend increases. *Source:* Dominion Bureau of Statistics, *Employment, Payrolls and Average Weekly Earnings, 1939-1946, with Index Numbers of Employment, 1921-1938* (Ottawa: Dominion Bureau of Statistics, 1946), 2.

editorial in the *St. Thomas Times-Journal,* reprinted by the *Toronto Star,* told of a visitor to one of Toronto's hotels who noticed fifty-three women and eight men standing in a queue for the hotel's ladies and escorts' beverage room, with no similar queue for the men's room.[1] When the fire chief and sanitary inspector of Fort William complained to the proprietor of the St. Louis Hotel that his hotel was too full and reprimanded him for including cots in the basement to accommodate workers who had no place else to go, the proprietor replied that "if they can get a place for these men to go he would be more than pleased."[2] Nearby, the Weyland Hotel benefited from the increased customers living in wartime housing the government was building nearby. As a result, "in the evening the men and their ladies come to the hotel for some beer." The proprietor, Baretta Bernardi, asked in September 1942 for permission to expand the dining room and use it for an overflow beverage room.[3] In the Thunder Bay district, the economy of the town of Longlac, which had experienced the booms of Depression-era mining and road building followed by declines, was improving once again.[4] As a result, the Longlac Hotel was "naturally receiving a larger patronage," and the inspector listed many complaints about the hotel that he had received from local residents. These problems ranged from the poor state of toilets to soldiers taking beer out of the hotel.[5]

Wartime industrial expansion placed additional emphasis on the local hotel as a site for workers' socialization. Inspector Vern Buchanan supported the request for dancing at the Ontario Hotel in St. Catharines, noting that it was across the road from a large factory, had recently expanded its dining room to accommodate workers, and "serves a real need by keeping the dining room open until midnight."[6] With longer shifts in factories, the employees at Fleet Aircraft in Fort Erie requested that the board allow the local Fort Erie Hotel to continue dancing after midnight. Smith was equivocal in his reply: he did not refuse the request but stated instead that the "continuance of dances into Sunday morning would not be appreciated" and that it was "undoubtedly contrary to certain laws of the Dominion of Canada."[7] Since it was not a request to continue to sell liquor after hours, the LCBO did not absolutely refuse to grant permission.

Smith's hesitancy in the Fort Erie Hotel request may have resulted from his understanding of the situation in border cities. With Canada on a wartime footing, both hotel proprietors and inspectors argued that it was important to try to keep Canadian money in the country and attract Americans. Although this rhetoric was not missing during the Depression, it seems to have become more urgent once the country was at war. For example, in September 1939, within days of war being declared, the proprietor of the Bridge Ave. Inn in Windsor asked for permission to have dancing and music in her hotel: "We are losing so much good Canadian business as it only takes six minutes to go across to Detroit and we feel that at this time every bit of money should be spent in Canada. Will you gentlemen please help us in every way possible."[8] The board granted permission three weeks later. Similarly, in June 1940, when the proprietor of the Royal Hotel in Niagara Falls, who had been denied permission to have dancing several times prior to the war, requested again to have a music box in the dining room, he (through his barrister) couched the appeal in the language of wartime economics:

> 1. The fact that by its retention and operation there, it is retaining a large number of Canadians in the City, who but for the fact that they can get music on this side of the River, would cross to the other side where they can get such entertainment, and this retains money in Canada, which otherwise would be lost to the Country.
> 2. The fact that by having music in our dining room attracts Americans not only to go where there is such music, but to remain and to spend money, chiefly foreign currency, here which otherwise they would not so spend.[9]

Table 3

Summary of wartime increases in beverage-alcohol taxes and duties

Excise Act	*Increase*
Spirits distilled in Canada	From $4 to $7 per proof gallon
Canadian brandy	From $3 to $6 per proof gallon
Beer or malt liquor	From 22¢ to 30¢ per gallon
Malt domestic or imported	From 6¢ to 10¢ per pound
Malt syrup suitable for brewing beer (domestic)	From 10¢ to 15¢ per pound
Malt syrup suitable for brewing beer (imported)	From 16¢ to 21¢ per pound
Special War Revenue Act	*New taxes*
Wines except sparking wines	Tax of 15¢ per gallon
Champagne and other sparkling wines	Tax of $1.10 per gallon

Source: "Text of Budget Speech Regarding Tax Changes," *Globe and Mail,* 13 September 1939.

It was not only self-interested hotel proprietors who saw the benefits of keeping Canadian money at home and luring American money to support the war. Niagara inspector Buchanan argued on behalf of the proprietors of the Dwarf Village Inn, near Jordan, that their hotel was "a real attraction for American tourists ... at a time when every effort is being made to attract American tourists to spend every dollar possible in this country."[10] When the owner of the steamship SS *Pelee,* which travelled from Sandusky, Ohio, through Pelee Island to Leamington, Ontario, asked for a beer and wine authority, Essex County inspector U.G. Reaume agreed, noting that "the large percentage of customers would be American ... We are making every effort to secure American money and this would be a good way to help the cause along."[11] In these places, then, the hotel functioned as a centre of socialization and revenue generation, both of which supported the war effort.

This revenue was not insubstantial. Within a few days of declaring war, the Dominion government introduced an emergency budget that increased taxes and imposed a number of new taxes to generate revenue. Table 3 lists the changes to the various forms of government revenue that pertained to alcohol. The Excise Act increased taxes on alcohol from roughly 30 percent to 100 percent, and a modified Special War Revenue Act added increased taxes on wines to a list of previously existing taxes on luxuries, including alcohol. Increases in Dominion excise taxes meant an increase in gallonage fees and revenues for the Liquor Control Board and a corresponding increase in the provincial government's percentage of profits from liquor sales. Table 4 shows the increase in revenues from alcohol sales, and Table 5 gives total

Table 4

Revenue from alcohol sales, 1937-45

	1937-38	1938-39	1939-40	1940-41	1941-42	1942-43	1943-44	1944-45[a]
Spirits[b]								
Domestic	$13,825,094[c]	$13,672,892	$14,257,133	$17,124,821	$22,003,923	$26,933,355	$31,008,797	$25,200,541
Imported	$5,690,553	$5,687,072	$5,333,753	$5,934,703	$6,916,911	$7,453,911	$9,152,275	$7,876,868
Total	$19,515,648	$19,359,964	$19,590,885	$23,059,524	$28,920,834	$34,387,264	$40,161,072	$33,077,408
Wine								
LCBO domestic	$1,470,895	$1,496,981	$1,672,474	$2,000,957	$2,161,094	$2,774,557	$2,085,189	$2,369,193
LCBO imported	$621,415	$555,288	$553,170	$611,370	$471,636	$647,344	$413,040	$431,623
Wineries	$1,886,530	$2,025,700	$2,278,768	$2,636,514	$2,903,584	$3,177,122	$3,246,070	$2,504,792
Total	$3,978,840	$4,077,970	$4,504,412	$5,248,841	$5,536,314	$6,599,024	$5,744,300	$5,305,608
Beer								
LCBO domestic	$1,136,143	$928,262	$927,426	$1,099,143	$1,372,422	$1,533,670	$1,153,193	$2,333,746
LCBO imported	$85,902	$79,565	$76,735	$76,963	$89,858	$117,659	$95,343	$134,483
Breweries[d]	$26,289,136	$25,192,225	$28,435,820	$34,599,090	$45,548,177	$50,523,429	$48,647,605	$61,034,601
Total	$27,511,181	$26,200,053	$29,439,980	$35,775,196	$47,010,457	$52,174,758	$49,896,141	$63,502,830
Total sales	$51,005,669	$49,637,986	$53,535,277	$64,083,560	$81,467,605	$93,161,047	$95,801,513	$101,885,847

a For fiscal years ending 31 March.
b All spirits had to be purchased at LCBO stores. Wine and beer could be purchased at wineries and breweries or at LCBO stores.
c Decimal amounts have been removed by rounding.
d Includes breweries and brewery warehouses, a retail business operated by most breweries.

Source: Ontario, Liquor Control Board of Ontario, *Annual Report*, Sessional Papers (1938-46).

Table 5

Sales of spirits, wine, and beer in gallons, 1937-45

	1937-38	1938-39	1939-40	1940-41	1941-42	1942-43	1943-44	1944-45[a]
Spirits[b]								
Domestic	1,239,164	1,230,708	1,115,419	1,236,128	1,576,144	1,664,789	1,591,793	1,209,400
Imported	327,971	328,311	274,158	284,584	335,057	326,724	349,838	308,667
Total	1,567,135	1,559,019	1,389,577	1,520,712	1,911,201	1,991,513	1,941,631	1,518,067
Wine								
LCBO domestic	704,834	723,169	765,595	872,877	820,680	973,167	633,284	698,507
LCBO imported	69,071	59,364	58,554	62,333	49,851	75,105	43,901	44,782
Wineries	861,846	934,361	998,100	1,101,193	1,054,881	1,040,949	864,060	880,883
Total	1,635,751	1,716,894	1,822,249	2,036,403	1,925,412	2,089,221	1,541,245	1,624,172
Beer								
LCBO domestic	702,741	573,551	572,474	677,068	846,566	938,778	678,310	1,366,943
LCBO imported	23,057	21,733	21,283	21,327	24,290	28,192	21,641	29,888
Breweries[c]	25,096,435	24,141,817	26,756,549	30,626,640	37,640,744	40,650,522	37,807,947	45,785,337
Total	25,822,233	24,737,101	27,350,306	31,325,035	38,511,600	41,617,492	38,507,898	47,182,168

a For fiscal years ending 31 March.
b All spirits had to be purchased at LCBO stores. Wine and beer could be purchased at wineries and breweries or at LCBO stores.
c Includes breweries and brewery warehouses, a retail business operated by most breweries.
Source: Ontario, Liquor Control Board of Ontario, *Annual Report*, Sessional Papers (1938-46).

Figure 6

Changes in liquor sales, in dollars, 1937-45

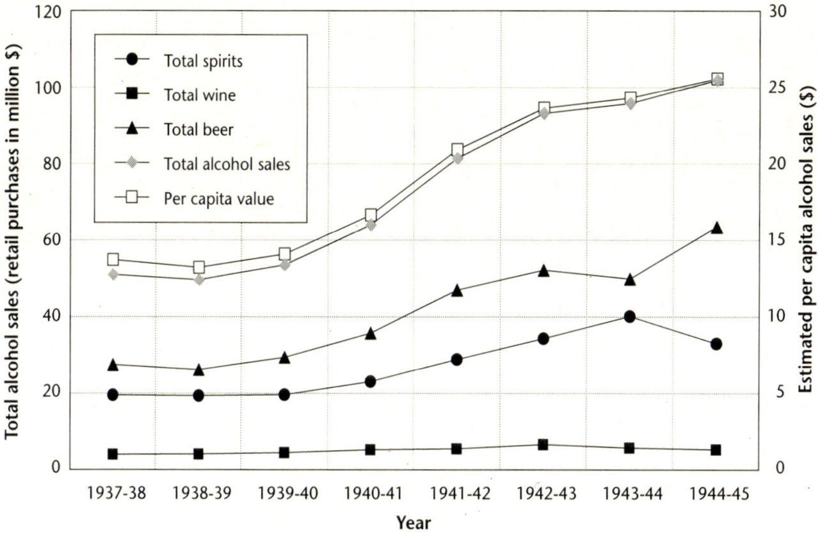

Note: Based on fiscal years ending 31 March.

gallons sold. Figure 6 and Figure 7 chart this data, respectively. To illustrate that the increase was not due to a significant change in population purchasing liquor, Figure 6 also charts the increased sales of alcohol per capita.[12]

The increase in taxes immediately affected the drinking habits of Ontarians. The significant increase in the price of spirits, up by about 50 cents per forty-ounce bottle, caused an immediate shift toward beer, which increased about 2 cents per quart bottle.[13] Initial estimates suggested that liquor sales had declined by 40 percent.[14] Indeed, the change was so significant that in December 1939 the LCBO announced a drop in the price of domestic spirits. This decision was in response to the Quebec government's decision to drop the price of a forty-ounce bottle by between 40 and 50 cents in order to offset the sticker shock caused by Dominion excise increases. It would also address the increase in bootlegging, which Ontario premier Mitchell Hepburn, in the aftermath of the Dominion's emergency budget announcements, had predicted would be the effect of the increased federal taxes.[15] Contrary to its neighbour to the east, Ontario dropped the price of forty- and twenty-six-ounce bottles by only 25 cents.[16] The actual effect of this policy change is difficult to gauge. As Figure 7 and Table 5 demonstrate, the sales of spirits immediately declined for the first fiscal year, whereas beer sales continued to increase. Although the provincial government observed that the increase in taxes may have resulted in a decline in liquor sales, the drop

Figure 7

Changes in liquor sales, in gallons, 1937-45

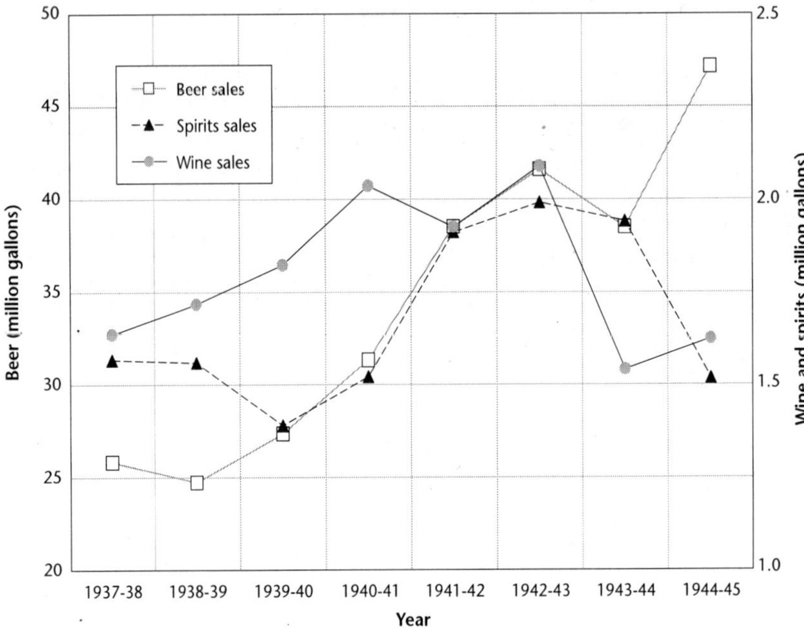

Note: Based on fiscal years ending 31 March.

in prices may have mitigated this reduction somewhat; liquor sales between 1939 and 1940 did not, in fact, drop by 40 percent, although the annual numbers may mask the fact that half of that fiscal year occurred prior to the declaration of war and subsequent tax increases.

Temperance Voices

With the war came renewed ammunition for the temperance cause. Many writers to newspapers, the LCBO, and the premier's office argued that liquor consumption was not conducive to military success. Although the war may have resulted in increased revenues for hotels, in the eyes of the temperance advocates, these profits were tainted. To the traditional images of the degradation of the family, social disorder, and moral decline in general, members of the temperance movement added specifically war-related arguments: national efficiency, resource depletion, and the problems with soldiers drinking.

From the outset of the war, temperance forces drew on issues relating to national efficiency and the prevalence of alcohol. Dr. John Coburn, field secretary to the Board of Evangelism and Social Services of the United Church, called distillers, brewers, and hotelkeepers "allies of Hitler" in a speech to the Huron County temperance federation in October 1939.[17] A correspondent to the *Globe and Mail,* signing her name "A mother of sons," quoted former British prime minister David Lloyd George, who had said during the First World War that they were fighting three enemies, "Germany, Austria and Liquor, and the worst is liquor." Arguing that "the greatest enemy Canada has is the liquor business," she called on "the best people in Canada" to implore the government to ban liquor from all places where soldiers were being trained.[18] Rev. Gordon Domm of Toronto's Bathurst Street United Church similarly channelled Lloyd George when he told a crowd that liquor "pathetically and disgracefully weakens the war effort in terms of money squandered together with human resources and morale."[19] Yet another pastor in Oakville preached that the total suppression of the liquor trade was necessary "if the peak of efficiency is to be reached in the struggle in which our nation is now engaged."[20] For the temperance movement, the wartime emergency made extremely strict regulation, if not total prohibition, of liquor a national necessity.

Yet the government's connection between alcohol taxes and the war effort seems to have undermined these arguments, further fuelling dry opprobrium. The executive of the Ontario Temperance Federation publicly encouraged the government to look "to other sources of taxation attended with less injurious results to our national strength." It explained that although liquor may bring in some revenue, its cost was "up toward $200,000,000," a figure with an unstated source.[21] The Kingston Presbytery sent a resolution to Hepburn urging the government to "consider immediately the restriction and ultimate suppression of all traffic in intoxicating liquors." Although this group's scope was the entire trade, many other temperance organizations focused on the public consumption of drink. The Salvation Army wrote to the government asking that the sale of alcohol be permitted only for medical purposes and be discontinued in "taverns, beer rooms, wine-shops and other like places."[22] In the autumn and winter of 1940-41, several church groups wrote to the premier with the following request: "Knowing our Prime Minister's sincere desire for the successful promotion of our province's war effort we petition his government asking for the curtailment of hours of sale in beverage rooms and urge that a greater restriction apply on Saturdays."[23]

Along with the problems of the economic dependency on liquor, many temperance forces noted how the liquor industry drew valuable resources from the nation's war effort. Many of them pointed to the misdirection of commodities, including grain and sugar, along with human resources, which, as the war continued, increasingly became a crucial component of the wartime economy. To its calculation of the financial cost of the liquor trade, the Ontario Temperance Federation added the fact that the industry resulted in "the destruction of valuable foodstuffs."[24] Since the war effort reached into the homes of every Canadian, the redirection of family resources into liquor was seen by some as particularly egregious. Not one month after war was declared, a correspondent to the *Globe and Mail,* "RHS," presented a gendered impression of the impact of the war on the family. When she had tried to buy sugar for canning her peaches, the vendor told her, "The war must be won – no sugar." After some investigation, she determined that the distilling industry was still using sugar. She surmised, "The logic would be that booze guzzling is a he-man, war winning activity that should be encouraged, while peach canning or fruit-preserving is an effeminate peacetime proposition that does not really matter in a national emergency."[25]

At the beginning of the war, the temperance arguments were routinely rebuffed by the government. In November 1939 a group of temperance workers, led by A.J. Irwin of the Ontario Temperance Federation, met with Hepburn and LCBO chief commissioner Arthur St. Clair Gordon to request that the government place restrictions on liquor sales "comparable to or approximate to those found necessary in the Great War." Among their demands were severely restricted hours for beverage rooms and prohibiting all soldiers from buying liquor by placing them on "the Indian list." Hepburn argued that such restrictions were not prudent and that "if the individual ... wants liquor, he is going to get it some way." He admitted that the government was considering earlier closing times for beverage rooms but noted that even such changes could be troublesome, "lest, under such policy, the traffic be driven underground into the hands of the bootleggers again, where it was difficult to convict."[26] Although he did not mention the increased revenues to the government, Hepburn did note that, contrary to the fears of the temperance delegation, liquor sales had fallen in the past year, likely due to increased prices. The premier preferred legal means to illegality and argued that government control was far superior to overly restrictive practices.

Although Hepburn's observation that higher prices reduced consumption implied that he saw this as a beneficial outcome, any assurance felt by the Drys was dashed two weeks later. As noted above, in the middle of December 1939, the LCBO reduced prices on Canadian-made liquor and wine in consultation with the Quebec Liquor Control Board, mostly in response to its decision to do so. Immediately after the Dominion government's budget announcement in September, Hepburn had predicted that the increased taxes would result in "a sharp increase in bootlegging from the United States."[27] Chief commissioner Gordon explained that, after the increase in government excise taxes, the board had found that "there is increasing bootlegging, illicit manufacture and illegal sale in the Province ... Accordingly, this board has decided to reduce, to the purchaser, the price on spirits manufactured in Canada." The board also extended the closing hours of liquor stores over the Christmas holiday season; in all of these changes, beverage room beer prices and hours of operation did not change.[28] Indeed, soon after the federal budget had increased excise taxes, the LCBO announced that hotel operators would have to absorb the cost of increased gallonage fees (which were charged on a percentage basis); they were not allowed to increase their prices.[29] Just as Hepburn had argued to the Drys that high prices were deterrents to drinking, the price drop was framed as a way of deterring illegal drinking. Again, the board wanted to keep the drinkers under control.

Yet, as the war continued, the provincial government faced increasing pressure to restrict access to alcohol. A good proportion of this pressure came from the Dominion government. On 16 December 1942 Prime Minister William Lyon Mackenzie King gave what would become known as his "temperance address," in which he encouraged provincial governments to restrict opening hours of beverage rooms, an announcement that came not two months after the Wartime Prices and Trade Board (WPTB) had announced tight quotas on the sale of liquor, which I discuss below. These quotas fell within federal jurisdiction because the Dominion government was authorized to manage all resource allocation during the war. Tensions with the federal Liberal government had resulted in Hepburn's abrupt resignation in early 1942, and his handpicked replacement, George Conant, was also somewhat hostile to the prime minister's intervention in provincial affairs. Not surprisingly, then, Conant decided not to follow the Dominion government's entreaties.

In January 1943 the heads of provincial liquor boards across the country met in Ottawa to discuss their responses to the Dominion government's actions. Despite initially supporting King's suggestion to reduce beverage room hours to a maximum of eight hours per day, the Ontario board does not appear to have acted on this endorsement. Since the quotas were the result of a federal wartime order-in-council, the provinces had no way of changing them. Other aspects of King's address were not given the backing of federal law; King had merely requested modification to the rules and regulations of provincial liquor control boards. Most notable in terms of the public perspective is that Conant decided not to reduce the hours of beverage room operation, which King had made a key point of his argument.

The provincial government's decision not to follow Ottawa's lead incurred tremendous opposition from the temperance forces. Many church boards, missionary societies, branches of the Woman's Christian Temperance Union, and private citizens wrote to Conant to urge him to get behind King's temperance address or even to go further. Much of their rhetoric employed standard temperance fare, augmented by arguments about wartime efficiency and moral responsibility to soldiers overseas. For example, the congregation of the United Church in Baltimore, Ontario, noted its "regret that Ontario, alone of all the provinces, has thus far failed to comply with the Prime Minister's request that the sale of liquor be restricted to eight hours per week day."[30] One private correspondent linked the disagreements between governments to the war effort: "By constantly opposing the dominion government we have created a situation that must rejoice the Axis Powers."[31] Many of the letters made arguments that directly contradicted the perspective of the Liquor Control Board and the government that a reduction in the hours of sale and significant restrictions on the sale of liquor would increase illegal drinking. Consider, for example, the telegram from the West Lorne Church of Christ requesting that "the government of Ontario ... put into effect fewer hours of sale of intoxicating liquors as a war measure and also for a more extensive programme to stop bootlegging."[32] Others added the entreaty to restrict liquor advertising, something that the board had been doing since its inception. McPhail Baptist Church apparently believed this message was urgent enough to justify sending a telegram: "In view of the recent action of the Dominion government curtailing the amount of alcoholic beverages released for sale we strongly urge that the provincial government of Ontario drastically reduce the hours of sale[,] eliminate indirect advertising and take steps to prevent bootlegging."[33]

The Effect of Policy Change on the Hotel Business

Federal restrictions affected some fundamental aspects of hotel operations and consequently shaped some aspects of the LCBO's interactions with hotel management. The Wartime Prices and Trade Board (WPTB) and the National Selective Service (NSS), in particular, managed the distribution and use of commodities and human resources. The WPTB was created a week before the country declared war, with the mandate to "set prices and wages, license firms selling consumer goods, prosecute hoarders, and manage the distribution of scarce items."[34] Its first task was to discourage hoarding by assuring Canadians, who feared impending shortages, that supplies of many products remained good. Indeed, within a few days of the outbreak of war, Ontario newspapers reported people laying in large supplies of liquor, although this was done more likely to avoid the impending increase in prices than to deal with expected shortages.[35] A division of the federal Department of Labour, the NSS was created in March 1942 to deal with the shortage of workers in wartime industry.[36] As a part of its mandate, it prioritized forms of civilian work, decreeing that it was illegal for healthy men between seventeen and forty-five to work in nonessential occupations. Both the WPTB and the NSS significantly affected the operations of hotels and the LCBO's regulation of them.

As the war continued and resources became increasingly scarce, the WPTB tightened access to a broad array of commodities. The most notable restriction affecting hotels was the establishment of a quota system for beer distribution. In November 1942 the Dominion government issued the Wartime Alcoholic Beverages Order, which restricted quantities of beer available from

1 November 1942 until 31 October 1943. This quota system affected hotels, clubs, and private individuals alike.[37] Its impact on sales can be seen in the last three points of Figure 7, notably in the reduction in beer sales and the increase in spirits and wine, which would have been purchased for sale in private residences. For hotels and clubs, the gallonage permitted for beer was calculated as 90 percent of the amount purchased the same month the year before.[38] The one-year proclamation was extended at the end of the first year, and quotas continued to be calculated based on 1940-41 sales. So, for example, in 1943 when the Seacliffe Hotel in Leamington requested an increase in its quota owing to a renovation that had increased the hotel's size, R.A. Gaskin, the assistant director of hotels, explained that this was impossible. "Reference to our record of this Hotel shows that in the month of November 1941, 482 gallons were purchased. Therefore for the present month [November 1943] we have no choice but to allot them this amount less 10 percent. The December 1941 purchases amounted to 437 gallons."[39] Required to enforce the federal regulation, the board had little choice in the amount of beer it could allocate. Even when, in March 1943, it increased the quota to Kingston hotels owing to the increased number of troops stationed in that city, it had to reduce the beer allocation in a different community.[40] The beer-quota system was an ongoing source of federal-provincial tension.[41]

Being retrospective, the beer quota assumed consistent drinking patterns, which several hotel proprietors found unrealistic. The Seacliffe Hotel's experience with its renovations adding capacity to its drinking spaces demonstrates one change that the board could not accommodate. Another was the shifting preferences of customers. Many hotel proprietors found that the type of beer being consumed changed as incomes increased. Rather than the cheaper draught beer, more people, it seems, were ordering bottles. When the proprietor of the Grand Hotel in Bridgewater requested a recalculation of his quota, deputy chief commissioner Roy Elmhirst, who had replaced Arnold Smith in 1941, acknowledged that "the trend over the past few months has been towards bottle beer, due to improved economic conditions, and I think by March we will issue the quotas on a ration, as between bottled and draught beer, so that it will be nearer the present trend of beer consumption."[42]

The quota system resulted in a number of changes in the way that many hotels operated and, ironically, resulted in the sort of hour restrictions that King had requested. With limited amounts of beer, some beverage rooms closed early, many in the early evening, when beer ran out. In 1944 Ottawa's Capital Hotel told inspector Alfred Larocque that it would be serving for three half-hour sessions each day.[43] Others calculated a minimum amount of beer they would need over the course of the week and subsequently restricted sales each day. Still others shifted their opening hours or even kept the beverage rooms closed during the week, preferring to open on the weekends. The management of Toronto's Danforth Hotel, situated near several factories, had received constant complaints from some shift workers that by the time they got off work, all the beer was gone. Consequently, the hotel's beverage room hours were changed to fit the end of shifts. Unfortunately for the workers, this plan was ineffective "because, when we re-opened at 4:00 p.m. every chair in the house was immediately absorbed by patrons from every part of the city and when workers did get in[,] in most cases there was no place to put them or sufficient help to look after them."[44] In the eyes of the LCBO, many of these arrangements, where hours were strictly curtailed and many hotels aimed to maximize beverage room patronage at key times, were acceptable strategies. The Danforth Hotel's experience reflected what happened at many hotels across the province.

Other restrictions also caused regulatory problems. The board required dining room service to be substantial, but at least one hotel reported that it was having trouble with its food orders. The manager of Niagara Falls' Elliott Hotel explained that "our dining room has never been closed but was limited to serving sandwiches and short orders ... I will be glad to start serving full course meals as soon as I am able to have my food quota increased."[45] Most hotels, meanwhile, attempted to close their dining rooms and faced censure from the board. Ultimately, recognizing the significant financial challenges, and impracticality, of requiring dining rooms to be open all day, the board permitted hotels to restrict their dining room hours to normal mealtimes. When the Longlac Hotel was criticized for not running its dining room, district inspector M.C. MacDonald explained to the board that "until the war is over, and conditions change, it would seem to be almost impossible to enforce this regulation, as things are."[46] When the Erie Hotel in Fort Erie was censured for not serving regular meals, the proprietor, Michael Kozak, explained that this was not due to a lack of food as much as a lack of staff: "We have at all times served meals and sandwiches when asked to do so. It is very hard for my wife because we just cannot get help but we will continue to give service in our dining room to the best of our ability."[47]

Kozak's explanation alludes to a far more extensive problem in hotels than the shortage of products: the significant shortage of staff. The board accepted the excuse of John Rumig, proprietor of the Imperial Hotel in New Hamburg, when he wrote to explain that, "on account of shortage of help, I have been compelled to discontinue service in my dining-room, except for breakfast, which I am able to handle myself ... I intend to continue to rent rooms and shall re-open the dining-room, as soon as the labor situation improves."[48] When the proprietor of the Mettawas Inn in Kingsville (Essex County) faced censure from the town council for not running his dining room, which the council complained was dearly needed in the area, the proprietor explained that he simply could not find a chef.[49] Hotels that were expected to have "full service" saw the wartime situation significantly affect their ability to do so, and the board was generally accepting of the exigencies of such situations.

The shortage of staff led to a significant alteration in at least one aspect of the board's policies: the addition of women to the serving staff in ladies and escorts' beverage rooms. As noted in Chapter 7, before the war, only men were allowed to serve beer in beverage rooms, even in the ladies and escorts' beverage room. The staffing shortage changed this situation. By 1941, especially in the Niagara region and Essex County, hotel proprietors were either employing women in beverage rooms without permission or requesting permission to do so. Inspectors were initially not impressed. In May 1942 the inspector rejected the request by the Royal Hotel in Fort Erie to have women serve:

> The manage[ment] tell me they have a very hard time to get the porper [sic] help. I have every reason to believe that at times they have ladies work in there [sic] beverage rooms, however I did not see this condition, I do not know why it is that these people in Fort Erie all complain about help and have to have ladies to work in the ladies beverage rooms.[50]

Also in May, while inspecting the Anglo-American Hotel in Niagara Falls, inspectors Harry Simington and Vern Buchanan "found two ladies working in the ladies beverage room ... [the manager] told me the[y] only worked in the ladies beverage room." When Simington told the manager that "he could not have a lady work in the beverage room ... he made an excuse that it was the dining room."[51] When the Esquire Hotel in St. Catharines asked for permission to do likewise, the board's explanation was that "the law does not permit such a procedure and we have no right to permit such a request."[52]

Soon afterward, these constraints were removed. In June 1942 the Dominion government created the women's division of the National Selective Service, paving the way for an increased presence of women in the workplace. The National Selective Service created specific rules around the advertising and hiring of staff, requiring that most "help wanted" ads had to be vetted and approved by the local NSS office. Although it is unclear whether the NSS made specific provisions regarding women in the hospitality industry, it appears that, by the middle of June 1942, the board had begun to permit women to serve beer in dining rooms and in ladies and escorts' beverage rooms. As Ruth Roach Pierson argues, women's work during the war was often an extension of the domestic sphere.[53] Correspondingly, by the middle of 1942 the LCBO was permitting hotel management to employ women in an expanded role but in as limited a manner as possible.

In making this change, the LCBO interlaced ideas about the dangerous connections between women and alcoholic beverages and ideas about women and wartime security to create an arguably misogynistic approach to women's work in the beverage rooms. In keeping with its mandate of centralized control, the board required hotel proprietors to request from the board (and likely also from the NSS) permission to employ women in these spaces; in keeping with wartime paranoia about the potential danger of women in public social spaces, these proprietors had to submit "medical certificates" for each woman. Such certificates were not new: the Liquor Control Act (1934) had required all employees in hotels to submit a medical certificate, apparently as a part of a tuberculosis-control measure (but one for which there is little evidence of compliance). The women's medical certificates, however, often documented only check-ups for venereal disease. In October 1943 Windsor's Drake Hotel submitted records of health tests for each waitress in its ladies and escorts' beverage room; some of these were tests for syphilis.[54] Other hotel proprietors who wanted to employ women submitted similar records, with at least one being for tuberculosis.[55] Although many inspectors reported that the medical tests were done, we cannot be certain of the contents of all of the tests because most results were not kept in the LCBO's files.

As a result, more hotels employed women, even though the board remained reluctant to grant permission. Corresponding with Pierson's argument that women's wartime participation was reluctantly embraced as only a temporary measure, these women would ideally be part-time employees, filling in gaps between times when men could work. For example, the Europe Hotel in East Windsor reported that it had five women waitresses, who "have been serving in the beverage room during the day and they have some factory workmen to wait ... at night."[56] When inspector Simington found that the proprietor of Leamington's Auto Stop Inn was allowing his daughter to serve in the men's beverage room and "a young lady" to serve in the ladies' beverage room, he complained to the manager. The manager, who "seemed to be sincere," explained that it was "owing to the shortage of help and [that] they were only open for such a short time that it was impossible to get a man to do this work."[57] He was told to cease the practice immediately. Jennifer Stephen has argued that part-time day work, the "housewife's shift," was intended to involve in wartime production women who otherwise would not be able to work. So although this innovation was intended to expand the industrial activities, it may have also shaped the approach to women working in nonessential areas, like hotels.[58]

Along with increased incomes and the concomitant problems with staffing shortages, the war brought some hotel proprietors added responsibility to the community. The proprietor of Fort William's St. Louis Hotel, as noted earlier, explained his reasons for crowding men into cots in the basement as fulfilling a community need. This often happened in some of the more remote parts of the province, notably in places like Beardmore and Longlac, where increases in wartime resource extraction led to a renewed economic boom. Other hotel managers recognized that their hotel's space could make a positive contribution to the war effort. Many hosted (or claimed to host) fundraising events or socials for soldiers. In October 1940 the proprietor of the Dominion Hotel in St. Jacobs offered space in his hotel "gratis" for the use of the Red Cross to hold a dance. The board granted the special permission for this dance.[59] In 1943 the proprietor of the Beardmore Hotel asked whether she could extend the opening hours of her beverage room to hold a fundraiser for the Red Cross. This permission was granted.[60] The proprietor of Toronto's Avion Hotel explained that the singing an inspector had heard in his hotel was the result of a social organization "singing their good byes" to soldier relatives. As he said, "frankly we are sometimes at a loss to stop these little family gatherings."[61] As during peacetime, the space available in the hotels was ideal for such events and could reinforce the important place of the hotel within a community.

Yet just as during peacetime the hotel proprietors could claim that their space was for the use of community organizations while merely organizing events to make money from beer sales, this also happened during the war. The Ulster Arms Hotel in Toronto played host to an organization it described as the Medical Corps Club, which the board suspected was simply "a beer sales promotion scheme with no other apparent object in common." The proprietor had a history of attempting to create "social clubs" that would meet in his premises.[62] When the board told the proprietor to cease these events, the erstwhile club's organizers replied that they were trying to raise money for the war effort. The board persisted in refusing this request.[63] When the board found that the Canadian Legion No. 65 in Toronto was holding regular dances without permission, it told the legion to stop. The legion complained that this decision was not fair. It argued that it was using the dances to raise money and other items for comfort bags to send to soldiers. Although this story seems to have been true, the board continued to forbid the dances since they required the legion to admit many nonmembers. Ultimately, the legion rented a separate hall to organize dance parties without alcohol.[64] So in spite of the wartime exigencies, the board continued to adhere to the spirit, if not the letter, of its own regulations.

The social events were not simply bifurcated between genuine, well-run war efforts and surreptitious frauds. Even the best plans could go awry, especially when soldiers were involved. The Red Cross dance at the Dominion Hotel in St. Jacobs ended up being "a disappointing affair" when two recently enlisted soldiers entered the dance and started a fight, which "turned out to be a free-for-all," and everyone left the dance.[65] The board decided to refuse this hotel's future requests for dances, however well intentioned the hotel might be.

Soldiers occupied a unique practical and rhetorical place in the regulation of beverage rooms. In numbers and comportment, they posed a challenge to social order, yet there was some suggestion that, as soldiers, they should receive special consideration. Certainly, prior to the war, the government was often expected to provide work for returned soldiers. At least one of the board's central administrators, William Mair, had fought in the First World War. Yet the presumed nobility of the returned soldier was not enough to excuse the often socially disruptive activities of currently enlisted men. The traditional bonds of regimental brotherhood presented many opportunities for disorder. We do not know the reason for the fight between the two enlisted men in St. Jacobs, but there were many other instances of soldiers in groups posing considerable trouble for local authorities during or after assembling in hotel beverage rooms.

Any illusions that hotel proprietors may have had that the onset of wartime industry would usher in a golden age for the hotel industry were dashed soon after the declaration of war. In October 1939 the manager of the Alexandra Hotel in Toronto completed construction on a new taproom, which, the inspector noted, would help in management of patrons. He added that "the soldiers have added a little to their troubles."[66] Two years later, a complaint sent to the board by "Mrs. Taylor" of Niagara Falls observed that the Empire Hotel "cant [sic] be a decent public house ... [because] they always have six or seven soldiers in the place where ladies drink."[67] Police reports could be especially salacious. In September 1941 the Ottawa Police Department submitted a report to the LCBO of the outcome of its raid on the Grad's Hotel. When the police officers arrived at 3:10 a.m., they broke up a craps game in the men's beverage room. They then proceeded to check the bedrooms:

> In room 101 ... we found a soldier in bed in a very intoxicated condition but he had no companion ... in room 105 ... we found a member of the RCAF [Royal Canadian Air Force] and [another man] in company with two local girls of questionable character, all in bed undressed, in room 110, rented to [two married couples] ... we found in one bed an army officer and a local girl both undressed, while in the other bed we found another army officer and a local girl both undressed with evidence of drinking having taken place.[68]

These were not atypical discoveries in hotels across the province, although it was not usual for police to give a room-by-room account of their raid. In this case, the police report noted that there had been several complaints about the operations of the Grad's Hotel, so the officers may have been especially thorough.

Moral issues were not the only problems in hotels. The camaraderie of the military personnel could exacerbate tense situations. In February 1942 inspector George Skuce reported that the St. Louis Hotel in Fort William had "a little truble [sic] with a local soldier boy last night they knew he was under age and refused to serve him. He got the captain and he ordered them to serve him but they still refused."[69] In Ottawa, inspector Alfred Larocque reported that the Association Athletique Montagnard had been having problems with "men in uniform [who] make their presence felt in greater number than usual." The club's members and executive were trying to screen these patrons in order to ensure that only individuals with membership cards were admitted, but the soldiers were indignant. They "argue that their uniform is sufficient qualification to admit them anywhere, and I have heard some express the determination to come back in greater number and force their way in." Larocque concluded that the best solution would be to cease dancing for the duration of the war "since that form of amusement is the main attraction for soldiers and airforce [sic] men."[70] When this was done, the club management reported that "members of the armed forces attempting to force their way in without membership cards have drifted elsewhere."[71]

The solution Larocque offered, cancelling permission for dances, was one major strategy the board employed to break up heavy concentrations of soldiers looking for a good time, but it could lead to other problems. Inspector John Kidd noted that after Toronto's Piccadilly Hotel cancelled dancing at the beginning of 1941, the soldiers flocked to the Carls Rite Hotel. It had become "the only place down town where dancing was allowed." Kidd was philosophical about the situation: "It is quite natural for soldiers to patronize a hotel where there is music and if they cluster around, they will not move so readily as civilians will, when requested." He noted that controlling these crowds was made more difficult "due to the lay-out of the premises," with the dining room on the mezzanine but toilets on a different floor. His solution was a simple change in the layout: the proprietor needed to increase the number of lavatories on the mezzanine level, thereby keeping dancers from other parts of the hotel.[72] The layout was also a problem with the once venerable Leonard Hotel in St. Catharines. After a military patrol visited the hotel and complained about its lax management, Roy Elmhirst wrote to the hotel's management urging them to remodel the "badly run down" beverage rooms. He noted that that "the present set-up makes it difficult to handle the crowds."[73] In these cases, the onus for change in the behaviour of patrons was placed squarely on the hotel management.

Yet cancelling dances and expensive remodelling were not the only solutions to troublesome servicemen. The most radical option was placing the hotel "out of bounds." This order, handed down from the local command, was often applied to specific military units and could be made for any number of reasons. The LCBO did not have to enforce the order in any discernible way, and usually the information appeared as a comment in an inspector's report. After a newly enlisted soldier was knifed at Port Arthur's Kimberly Hotel, the police and military authorities placed the hotel out of bounds. The knifing was not the only impetus for the order; inspector M.C. MacDonald learned that "the medical authorities are tracing venereal disease to frequenters of this hotel."[74] In contrast, after the police and local military authorities in Port Arthur decided to place several hotels out of bounds in July 1940, the commanding officer told inspector MacDonald that although the proprietor of Donati's Hotel "is an Italian, he conducts such a decent, well managed hotel, that he was not listed among those out of bounds."[75] Given the trouble other hotels had with groups of soldiers clustering in their beverage rooms, this decision, for Charles Donati, may have been a mixed blessing. In the case of the underage soldier whose captain ordered the St. Louis Hotel to serve him beer, the captain threatened to "make the hotel 'out of bounds.'"[76] Skuce decided to speak to the commanding officer about this threat.

Although this last case suggests that the "out of bounds" designation was a detriment to business, many hotel managers sought this designation precisely to keep the soldiers away. In early 1940, two days after Toronto's Picadilly Hotel had been placed out of bounds, dancing was cancelled. Inspector Kidd explained that the management wanted dancing reinstated since, for those two days after the hotel was declared out of bounds, there had been "a marked improvement in the conduct of the place." Kidd recommended that the hotel institute a cover charge "in order to control the class of trade" and that it remain out of bounds for the time being.[77] Many other hotel managers also found the "out of bounds" designation to be the ideal solution. The Imperial Hotel in Crystal Beach and the Spadina and Avonmore Hotels in Toronto were all placed out of bounds at the request of the proprietor.[78] In October 1941 the manager of Niagara Falls' Empire Hotel noted that he had "considerable trouble with the soldiers," who had damaged the property and driven away the civilian patronage. He had managed to have the South Alberta Regiment placed out of bounds but asked for the order to be extended to all regiments of the army, reasoning that such an order would help staff to avoid the complications of "being able to serve one and not the other."[79] Although a potentially radical solution, the "out of bounds" order permitted perplexed hotel proprietors to eliminate the problems associated with soldiers in their premises.

Of course, not all proprietors saw soldiers as a problem. Although they may have caused some disorder and trouble with management, many hotel proprietors ran operations that had always had an especially sordid reputation. For them, soldiers were just an additional source of revenue. Indeed, many courted the soldiers, and the newspapers, especially the more salacious tabloids, were filled with the results. Inspector Larocque reported that at Ottawa's Lord Elgin Hotel the management was being too lenient with soldiers, including rowdy officers:

> In the course of my visits there at nights, in the Ladies and Escorts beverage room, I observed Army Officers under the influence of Liquor being served beer in that condition also some soldiers ... I am of the opinion that attendants, instead of trying to deal leniently with him in particular, should of [sic] ejected him at once. The soft pedal was applied too generously.[80]

Similarly, inspector Simington was critical of the management of the aforementioned Piccadilly Hotel after spending some time there one evening in July 1942. Recall that it had been made out of bounds in 1940 but that dancing had been reinstated on request. The records do not record when it was put back "in bounds," but by the summer of 1942, it was full of enlisted men once again. Simington reported in a detailed memo what he found to be scandalous behaviour of various enlisted men:

> About 11:45 there were two sailors and a couple of Norweign [sic] Airmen and in the presence of a number of women they used such language that I would hesitate to repeat it to the writer [sic] of this memorandum. They were using words familiar to sailors on Active Service. I spoke to the Manager about his disgraceful episode and when he tried to stop it the boys called him names similar to the type of cursing they had been using ... However I, personally, chatted with the sailors and at heart they were not bad boys but they were let run wild in the early part of the evening.[81]

As the hotel began to close, the situation quickly deteriorated, with over one hundred enlisted men pouring onto the street, and soon several fights broke out. The manager spoke to Simington, expressing his shock and concern but arguing that other hotels were just as bad. Simington replied, "I was not interested in other hotels at that moment but only interested in the manner in which his hotel was conducted." When the manager asked what the inspector would do, he replied that he "would only report to the Board exactly what I saw," clearly a not-too-veiled threat.[82] These and many other examples tell of soldiers acting disgracefully and proprietors either allowing them to do so or unable to stop them. Only observations and interventions by the board's staff that drove changes in the proprietors' activities – along with threats of drastic actions, most likely authority suspension or having a hotel declared off limits – would get the proprietors' attention. However, since the Piccadilly Hotel had been declared off limits before, the threats appear to have been of limited effectiveness; the board could not be everywhere, and some places remained very difficult to handle.

Although these broader surveillance and social-control networks enabled the LCBO to do its work of overseeing drinking facilities, the board's system of oversight also enabled other agencies to keep an eye on the people. The need to deal with troublesome soldiers required the LCBO to work closely with both military and civilian police forces, and the mechanism of the "out of bounds" designation tied the board closely to military surveillance. In effect, the board functioned as a surveillance operation irrespective of its liquor control mandate. Most notable with respect to the activities of potentially subversive foreign-born residents is that the board provided assistance to security services in keeping tabs on outsiders. In this work, the board acted as a second set of eyes rather than doing any primary policing of potential enemy aliens.

As noted in Chapter 8, scrutiny of foreigners was not new in 1939. The Liquor Control Act (1934) restricted the privilege of holding a beer authority to born or naturalized British subjects. Many identifiable foreign-born ethnic groups had sought to license their own social spaces. Often these requests were treated with what we might now call cultural sensitivity. To this ethnic scrutiny was added, prior to the war, the concern over radicalism, communism, Bolshevism, and anarchy.[83] The board was concerned to ensure that the licensed social clubs were not hotbeds for radicalism, and on rare occasions it would communicate with other authorities, notably the RCMP, to check the background of an individual who had applied for an authority. The war increased the frequency of such checks. Germans, Austrians, other "Germanic" groups, and after June 1940, Italians could be labelled "enemy aliens." The LCBO's activities began to include moderate surveillance measures in conjunction with other security branches of the provincial and federal governments.

In spite of the often virulent anti-Italian and anti-German sentiment voiced by many Ontarians, the LCBO appears to have approached the issue of ethnicity and security with a good degree of temperance. Whereas it was legally obligated to close the clubs of German and Italian nationals, when it came to hotels, the board was less concerned with the ethnicity of a proprietor as long as the premises were operated properly. Recall that Donati's Hotel in Port Arthur was considered so well run that it was one of the few hotels not placed out of bounds by the military authority, a decision that explicitly included a reference to Donati's Italian heritage. Possibly the most vivid example of this sort of administrative leniency was in the story of Angelo's Hotel and Restaurant (also called Angelo's Restaurant), an Italian restaurant in Toronto that had managed to restructure itself as a hotel in the early years of the LCA (1934). In June 1940, after the government had declared war on Italy, the hotel management ran an ad in the local paper that attempted to address nativist concerns and those of its clientele. The ad referred to the restaurant's "Canadian-born proprietor," reminded the reader that his family had been in Canada for 60 years and had supported several charities, and "would appreciate the continued patronage of all fair-minded and loyal Canadians."[84]

Angelo was interned soon after for "suspected alien activity," but the Custodian of Enemy Alien Property did not take over the premises, and it was not shut down. The management was allowed to continue to operate the hotel, and inspector Kidd reported to Smith that the place had always been well run, that 99 percent of customers were English-speaking, and that "the trade was representative of the business men and women of Toronto."[85] During his internment, Angelo was allowed to continue some of the basic administration of the hotel, such as signing his application for renewal of the Standard Hotel licence and authority. The controllers for the Custodian of Enemy Alien Property, Price Waterhouse and Company, informed the board in March 1941 that Angelo's stepson had been permitted to continue operating the restaurant and that "he is responsible to the Custodian for his interest therein." The letter concluded with what appears to be a directive to the board: "We would, therefore, appreciate your co-operation in arranging for the renewal of the hotel's Authority Privileges."[86] Apparently, the respectable nature of the business and the Dominion agency's imposition on the board's jurisdiction combined to alleviate any potential problems the proprietor may have had. Angelo was released from internment in April 1941.[87]

The LCBO was generally clear on its subordinate role within the security hierarchy. It functioned not as a major enforcer of security regulations but as an informant and observer. It ensured that proprietors were not violating the laws under which the LCBO operated, and when there was suspicion of activity beyond the scope of the LCA, the board either passed on information or simply considered what potential illegal activity meant to the board's oversight of hotel operations. For example, when Max Schultz (not his real name), a Niagara Falls proprietor of German background, was suspected of Nazi activity, the board contacted the RCMP to ask whether it thought the board should grant the man an authority. The RCMP's commanding officer was equivocal, saying the Dominion government did not have any hard evidence against Schultz. When he was arrested and convicted for some suspicious activity related to letters he sent to Germany from Niagara Falls, New York, the board did not immediately suspend his authority. They contacted Schultz to see whether he planned to transfer his authority. It seems the board thought that the illegal activity had been the result of a misunderstanding; Schultz claimed he had gone to the United States just to send a letter to his mother-in-law in Germany, something that was impossible to do from Canada during the war. The local inspector was sympathetic, arguing that the authority should be retained since Schultz ran the hotel well. Two years later, however, Schultz was arrested for much more suspicious activity. Police found Canadian army uniforms and Nazi paraphernalia hidden at his hotel. This time, the board cancelled the authority outright. A new proprietor took over several months later.[88]

The Second World War introduced a number of changes in the operation of the LCBO and created a situation in which these changes led to additional modifications in the board's operations and ultimately to a restructuring of the board itself. Increased disposable income among patrons, declining supplies of beer, and a tightly regulated workforce created notable changes in the operations of public beverage rooms and subsequently drove changes in the way the LCBO operated. During the war, its records became much less detailed, something that may have been partially the result of its own resource limits or a result of the changing workload of inspectors. Paper shortages at the board's offices often necessitated writing on both sides of a page, and it is not unreasonable to assume that inspectors might have chosen instead to reduce their comments. The new "Authority Holder's Monthly Conduct Report" form was also restructured to reduce the amount of space for an inspector's comments, thereby reducing the amount of subjective data the central board would process. Much of the work of the inspectors became a matter of counting (tables, chairs, patrons), calculating (gallonage, revenues, food), and reporting this data back to the board using the standardized forms. Although there is no way to determine the exact reasons behind these changes, the inspectors would have had an additional workload dealing with the increase in disorderly or problematic hotel premises, and they were also the board's main contact for proprietors who wanted to complain about things like beer quotas and staffing shortages. Likely, then, their work changed, and the field of visibility of the LCBO shifted with it.

The irony of wartime affluence and wartime scarcity should not be understated. A decrease in beer supplies and an increase in disposable income shifted the nature of public drinking. More often, beverage rooms would close for specific times of the day (often during dinner hour), so when they reopened, people would flood the premises, drink all the beer they had in stock, and then move on. This form of what might be called binge drinking created issues of public order for the board, but at the same time, the fact that beer supplies were so limited meant that the actual consumption levels for many people would have declined. Tracing the specific ways the wartime economy affected LCBO regulations is difficult. No records were left charting how the war changed the board's view of its work. Although it was connected to a broadening, increasingly funded, and extremely important wartime-security network, the LCBO continued to operate on the fringes of this system. Ironically, the agency of control itself became controlled, with dictates coming down from the Wartime Prices and Trade Board, the RCMP and military police, and other federal agencies.

Conclusion

By 1944 the Liquor Control Board of Ontario (LCBO) had been in existence for seventeen years. Regulatory patterns and a culture of controlled public drinking had been imposed for ten years, and the bureaucracy itself had expanded and, in some ways, if not ossified, certainly firmed up its procedures. The efforts by people like Arnold Smith to reduce the partisan political influence over the board's operations may have eventually borne fruit. When in 1943 the Liberals lost the Ontario provincial election, with the Progressive Conservatives under George Drew forming a minority government, chief commissioner Arthur St. Clair Gordon, a Liberal member of the provincial Legislature, remained in his post until February 1944, and when he left, Premier Drew and Attorney General Leslie Blackwell both voiced fond appreciation for his work.[1] A month later, Blackwell introduced new liquor control legislation that bifurcated the LCBO's operations. The sales and distribution would continue to be the purview of the LCBO, whereas the licensing of public drinking places fell to the new Liquor Authority Control Board of Ontario (LACB), which was renamed three years later the Liquor License Board of Ontario (LLBO).

The LACB was legally constituted to be a three-person board, which was required to hold open meetings at which each applicant for an authority presented his or her case and community members could contest or support the application. That the number of board members was ensconced in the law indicates the degree to which the government wanted to reduce the potential for opportunistic meddling by the sitting government; both previous Liberal and Conservative governments had played with the numbers of commissioners, at times placing the board's power into the hands of one, politically connected, person. The Drew government clearly traced a sharp distinction between the old and new systems, with the latter distancing the distribution of liquor licences even further from government interests. This air of openness replaced the often mysterious machinations and perceptions of "toll gates," or partisan decision making. The distinction was not lost on commentators, with the *Globe and Mail* calling the move "a step in the right direction of eliminating patronage."[2] The new chair of the LACB, Walter Robb, was a Conservative who, despite assertions of impartiality, is said to have remained in close contact with the Drew government: "This image of independence served Drew's desire to retreat from [former premier Mitchell] Hepburn's overt use of patronage but did not lessen the licensing system's potential to reward the party faithful in less public ways."[3] However, the singular fixation on partisanism expressed here by Sharon Jaeger and elsewhere by others blurs the story I have tried to tell, where party affiliation may have helped in some ways but where running an orderly establishment was paramount.

Compared to the changes of 1934, these modifications to the liquor control system passed with relatively little fanfare. Many newspapers gave the story scant attention, which is notable. Although the war may have been on the minds of everyone, liquor issues still remained good fodder for sensationalized stories and inflammatory editorials, so the limited newspaper attention to the creation of the LACB and to the public's reaction (or nonreaction) demonstrates how fundamentally different the social landscape had become. In ten years, the LCBO had become a complex bureaucracy that governed, in an increasingly technocratic manner, a simple biological activity that could have considerable political and emotional impact – the ingestion of alcoholic beverages. The change in the way Ontarians perceived their relationship with alcoholic beverages, the biopolitical process, was complex and diverse. The board reconstructed physical space, deploying ideas that merged pragmatic issues of hotel management with surveillance of the behaviour of drinkers. It paid attention to the needs of the community, balancing concerns over political backlash with the need for legal, regulated public drinking establishments to undermine illegality. In efforts at bureaucratic detachment from blatant party machinations, it attempted to reduce overt partisan patronage and to construct a less subjective, more bureaucratic system of oversight. Its politics were bureaucratic, ensuring the authority of the board by balancing the voices and needs of dry and wet constituents. Likewise, it constructed a more pluralistic drinking space, where women and ethnic minorities could have their social spaces. It may also have allowed for spaces for people of different sexual preferences, although this did not come out in the records. Both Steven Maynard and David Churchill have discussed the use of the beverage room space for homosexual sociability in Toronto.[4] I found no evidence of this in the pre-war period, but this is not to say that it was not there. This is another limitation of the fields of visibility of the LCBO records. In creating these new drinking spaces, the LCBO erected a system in which the citizen who wished to consume beverage alcohol in public could do so as long as it was in a properly constructed space and under the benign eye of a duly authorized individual. This citizen-drinker's responsibility was to behave.

So although the political rhetoric surrounding the LACB was about a break from the sins of the previous administration, I argue that the liquor legislation of 1944 and the system it engendered were built on the fundamental changes that the LCBO had established in its first seventeen years. It is unlikely that in 1934 an open system of application and consultation with the voices of dissention would have been anything more than a logjammed system of histrionics and grandstanding (from both sides). Citizens held too many divergent ideas about what constituted proper drinking, and about whether alcoholic beverages should even be consumed, to make such an open consultative process viable. And the temperance movement remained strong and vocal. But by 1944, things had changed. Temperance sentiment had declined. In April 1944 the *Toronto Star* reported that a Gallup poll demonstrated that "anti-prohibition sentiment" was at an all-time high and growing, with 73 percent of polled Ontarians opposing any kind of prohibition.[5] Moreover, and possibly related to this ideational shift, the LCBO had established a new baseline of expectations for behaviour in public spaces. The province had moved further away from the previous decade's emotionally charged rhetoric of evangelical temperance and community destruction. Administrative imperatives drove the LCBO's growth as it sought to affirm its authority while negotiating regulations, facilitating and controlling the public consumption of alcoholic beverages, and thereby restructuring fundamentally the way Ontarians viewed their relationship with liquor.

This last point leads us to consider, however briefly, the perspective of the drinker him- or herself. As I noted in the introduction, by relying on the records of the board, however detailed and rich they are, we are forced to see the situation from the perspective of the bureaucracy. Our field of visibility, like that of the board, is limited, possibly more so, by the recordkeeping decisions made at the head office, the type of (occasionally coded) language used, and the conscious or unconscious decisions to limit certain information. Nevertheless, with the caveat that this study has a tendency to "speak like a state," it is useful to consider what the drinkers were doing in the face of government control. After all, my conception of the "citizen-drinker" is necessarily an idealized trope, used as a way of characterizing the LCBO's vision of its regulation of public drinking, which shaped the board's regulatory activities.

Throughout these records, we repeatedly find Ontarians' attempts to modify, if not completely violate, the regulations of the board. These efforts, sometimes blatant but more often surreptitious, demonstrate the limits of new forms of control and the persistence of earlier, more traditional ideas about public drinking. The expectations of drinkers whose experience with public drinking stretched to the pre-prohibition period were certainly not fulfilled in the much more austere and sterile social environment of the post-prohibition beverage room. Moreover, we can surmise that younger residents, whose habits of social drinking may have been developed during prohibition – when drinking was an underground activity and therefore unfettered by state control – would have found the new rules particularly onerous. So the ideal of a well-controlled beverage room environment contradicted many of the expectations of the patrons, and the addition of the physical and behavioural effects of alcohol made for more intense contradictions between sober behaviour and drunken revelry. Hotel owners, as I noted when discussing recreation, attempted numerous entertainment innovations to attract patrons and often ran afoul of the board or the police or other authorities. As a result, we see a persistent resistance to the vision of a controlled drinking environment promoted and enforced by the LCBO. The board's ideal of the citizen-drinker continued to brawl with the reality of the drinking citizen.

Such persistent resistance could undermine my suggestion that the LCBO successfully reshaped the drinking environment of the province and facilitated the internalization of state control, a fundamental component of biopolitics. It suggests that the LCBO was akin to the boy with his finger in the dike, holding back but not reducing the pressure against its work. In fairness, we cannot gauge with any hope of accuracy the level to which individuals internalized ideas about self-control when drinking. Although we can see the *attempts* to restructure the drinker's relationship with his or her body when drunk and the way the state controlled the drinking environment and certain drinking practices, we cannot confidently demonstrate that by 1944 people had internalized a new form of self-governance. What we can see, however, is how forms of behaviour that deviated from newly established norms were constrained within a state-governed drinking environment. And the LCBO was successful in achieving one of its key goals, that of creating controlled and state-supervised public spaces as alternatives to the illegal "blind pigs" and bootleggers. The attempts to circumvent the rules within the space of the beverage room were tacit recognitions of the validity of this space and of drinkers' hopes to violate the rules within the proper drinking environment. Although it is true that the LCBO records do not cover illegal drinking spaces and that we cannot conclude illegal drinking was eliminated, we can look at the wild success of packed-to-the-rafters beverage rooms during the war to see that many residents accepted their legitimacy and the constraints this space forced on their behaviour.

Today, I contend, we have tantalizing suggestions of how effective the state was in reshaping, over time, our ideas about proper drinking behaviour.

I offer these as suggestions, not as concrete proof. Common beliefs about where and when drinking should take place illustrate the power of government rules to enforce ideals of propriety. Drinking in the morning (before 11 a.m. in Ontario and at other times elsewhere) is construed as a deviant behaviour. (Consider that when the province allowed bars to begin serving one hour earlier during the FIFA World Cup games held in South Africa in 2010, it was front-page news, complete with "person on the street"–style interviews asking people's opinions of this contentious policy.) In Ontario and in most provinces, drinking outdoors in public spaces such as parks, beaches, and the street is likewise considered anti-social and problematic. Regardless of the surreptitious bottles of wine at picnics, beer cans on the beach, and mickeys of peach schnapps at the high school prom (I'm assuming my experience was not unique), the instinctive understanding is that these behaviours are not just illegal but actually deviant in a more fundamental way. This was not always the case, nor is it everywhere the case, as illustrated by the experience of my British friends in Banff, Alberta, mentioned in the Preface. Such behaviour is socially and culturally constructed through the mechanisms of the state. In his work on the growth of the American medical profession, Paul Starr uses Max Weber's term for the power to define fact and value – "cultural authority" – in order to scrutinize the power of physicians. Cultural authority is distinct from social authority in that the latter gains its power only through force of law, whereas the former is more subtle, an internalization of cultural understanding. Although the LCBO and the liquor laws it enforced were and are based on social authority, the citizen's instinctive reaction to violations of what are, ultimately, very arbitrary rules about where and when one can drink a beer illustrates that a more subtle process took place. It suggests the effective cultural authority of the post-prohibition drinking system. This cultural authority may not have been firmly entrenched by 1944, but by that time, having reconstructed the drinking environment of the province, the LCBO had laid the foundation for beliefs about public drinking behaviour that were fundamentally different from those of the pre-prohibition era. It set the groundwork for a liquor control regime that, for many twenty-first-century Ontarians, seems increasingly bizarre, abstemious, and archaic. At one time, the regime was not perceived in this way but was regarded by many as the best hope for the reintroduction of liquor to the province. Just as long as its residents continued to try to control themselves.

Appendix: The Communities

The six communities in this study were chosen for a variety of demographic and geographic reasons. They reflect a diversity of factors, and although it would be impossible to have any sample of the regions of the province reflect accurately the full diversity of the province's industrial, economic, geographic, and social makeup, I did pay attention to the need to explore regions far beyond the centre of the government's bureaucratic universe, Toronto. The study includes communities at the borders and the centre of the province, urban and rural locations, and established and rapidly growing populations. Such a division is unavoidably messy. For example, when studying Essex County, towns and villages bordering this community were not included. This would normally not be problematic, except that Edmond Odette, the chief commissioner of the board from 1934 to 1939, was from Tilbury, just outside of Essex County.

Essex County

Essex County is in the far south-western section of the province. It is surrounded on three sides by water: Lake Erie to the south, the Detroit River to the west, and Lake St. Clair to the north. The city of Windsor is in the north-western corner of the county, directly south of Detroit. The original European settlers were French, but by the middle of the nineteenth century more Anglo Europeans and Americans had moved into the area. Essex County was also a major end point for the Underground Railroad and, as a result, by the 1930s had a relatively large proportion of residents of African descent, many of whom could trace their roots to escaped slaves.

By the 1930s the county's economy was based on several key industries. A large proportion of its industrial base was in manufacturing, notably the automobile industry. Adjacent to the city of Windsor was Ford City, named after the automobile manufacturer whose factories employed the residents. Next to Ford City was Walkerville, named for Hiram Walker, who had founded his distillery in the area in 1858. Outside of the cities, two major industries contributed to the economy: agriculture and tourism. Summer homes, cottages, hotels, and yacht clubs, especially around the south shore of Lake St. Clair, saw a significant influx of tourists, many of whom were wealthy Americans from across the river, on an annual basis. This was also a feature of the area to the south of the county. With Pelee Island, the southernmost point in Canada, immediately south of Essex County, both Leamington and Kingsville were destinations for American day trippers from across the lake. Several ferries operated in the area, taking people from Sandusky in Ohio to Essex County. Partially due to the economic exigencies of the Depression, on 1 July 1935 the cities of Windsor, Walkerville, Sandwich, and East Windsor amalgamated into the city of Windsor, necessitating, among other things, a renumbering and renaming of several streets.[1]

Niagara Region

The name "Niagara region" is an anachronism since the region did not exist as a political entity until 1 January 1970, when Lincoln and Welland Counties, as well as a number of municipal governments, were amalgamated. Geographically, however, the region is distinctive, bounded by Lake Ontario to the north, Lake Erie to the south, and the Niagara River to the east. The region's industry was similar to that of Essex County, with a few notable exceptions. It too was a major manufacturing centre, something facilitated by the existence of the Welland Canal, a major component of the St. Lawrence Seaway. Ethnically, it was heavily British, with a good number of both Dutch families, many of whom farmed the fertile and relatively flat areas below the escarpment, and French families, who also had deep roots in the area. Also an end point of the Underground Railroad, the region had a strong African heritage, although a proportionately smaller African Canadian population than Essex County.

The canal was itself a major industry, distinguishing the region from Essex County, but there were two other major differences in the economy of the Niagara area. The first was the agricultural industry and, most notable in a study of liquor control, the burgeoning grape and wine industry. The second difference, of course, was and remains the tourism industry, especially with regard to Niagara Falls. As the only region in the study that contained one of the Seven Wonders of the World, the Niagara region saw a tremendous influx of tourists into the area every year.[2] This circumstance, combined with Niagara Falls' relative proximity to the city of Toronto, whose residents were often lured there on day trips across the lake, meant that the operation of hotels and of places of recreation was significant to the local economies.

Waterloo County

Waterloo County sits in the centre of the region known as south-western Ontario. In the 1930s it contained one major city, the former city of Berlin, renamed "Kitchener" during the First World War, and the smaller city of Galt (now part of Cambridge). Like Essex County and the Niagara region, Waterloo County's economy was a considerable mix of industry (including furniture making and rubber) and agriculture. As in other areas, the Depression hit these industries hard. Furniture manufacturing, for example, dropped from just over $11 million in 1928 to just over $1 million in 1932.[3] What set this area apart from the other communities in this study was its significantly different demographic makeup. As suggested by Kitchener's earlier name and by the names of some of the smaller towns in the county (including New Hamburg, Heidelberg, Strasburg, Manheim, and Prussia), a large proportion of the community's residents were of German, Austrian, or other "Germanic" origins. Prior to the First World War, for example, over 70 percent of the residents of the city of Kitchener reported their ethnic heritage as German. This figure had declined by the time of the 1921 census, owing partly to self-reporting and partly to a reduction in German immigration. However, during the 1920s and 1930s, new "Germanic" groups, notably Romanians (also known as "Saxons") and Yugoslavians (called "Swabians"), arrived in the area.[4] Versions of these ethnic divisions gave the name to Kitchener's Sachsen-Schwaben Club.

Thunder Bay District

The area defined as the "Thunder Bay district" stretched along much of the northern shore of Lake Superior and deep into the remote northern part of Ontario. Although the bulk of the population of the Thunder Bay district was concentrated in the towns of Port Arthur and Fort William, the district contained many towns of differing sizes, many of which were tied to the resource-extraction industry. As a result, the actual demographics of the region are difficult to chart. As demonstrated in Table 6, the area was considerably more mixed in ethnic composition than were the other communities in this study, with a larger proportion of eastern European cultures represented across the district. With an economy based primarily on resource extraction and agriculture (along with associated industries such as shipping), the Thunder Bay district was hit hard by the Depression. The sole exception was the mining industry, which faced a substantial boom, a minor gold rush, in the middle of the 1930s.[5] Several towns experienced booms due to the mining speculation and rapid road building of the Depression, which produced what amounted to relief-work projects for many men in the 1930s.[6] Consequently, towns that boomed for a few years declined rapidly soon afterward. Another industry of the district, but much less significant, was based on tourism of a more rugged nature than that found in the southern communities. Finally, like the Niagara region, the area west of Port Arthur had its own falls, the Kakabeka Falls. Unfortunately for the owner of the Kakabeka Inn, the township in which the falls are located was dry and remained so throughout the period under study.

Ottawa

On the border with Quebec but having roots in the logging industry, the nation's capital of Ottawa was also a place of complex demographics. Although the resource-extraction days were mostly over, the city's proximity to the less settled areas to the northwest along the Ottawa River and to the northeast in the Gatineau Hills, combined with the appeal of the nation's capital as a centre for tourism, meant that Ottawa's population was mixed and ever changing. Its residents included the rich and powerful elites of the government, along with visiting dignitaries. The Chateau Laurier and Lord Elgin Hotels were jewels in the crown of the hospitality industry. Moreover, the expansion of government bureaucracy meant that Ottawa's economy was heavily "white collar." Ethnically too, Ottawa was divided, with a larger number of French Canadians living or working in the area. The French Canadian connection also affected the city's local politics, both formally and informally. As we have seen, the Catholic religious orders, many of which operated schools and convents in the downtown core, were actively concerned with the operation of hotel beverage rooms in the area.

Toronto

It would be impossible to offer a valid thumbnail sketch of the city of Toronto in the 1930s without tremendous distortion. In many ways, Toronto was a combination of most of the demographic peculiarities of the other communities under study. It would probably be more appropriate to describe Toronto as a collection of communities, which in some ways is exactly what it was. Like Windsor, Toronto by the 1930s was a product of several amalgamations, with communities of West Toronto and North Toronto joining the city of Toronto in the decades before the 1930s. At the same time, Toronto's economy was heavily manufacturing-based but also heavily bureaucratic. It was the centre of Canadian commerce and of Ontario's government. It was also a major end point for the journeys of many immigrants to the country. As a result, the city was in one respect heavily white and anglophone but in another respect tremendously ethnically mixed. It really depended on what neighbourhood you were visiting. Consequently, Toronto's politics were often decidedly local, and the Liquor Control Board of Ontario, whose offices were located in the city, paid particular attention to the potential problems that might arise from decisions to grant or not to grant beverage room licences depending on the area of the city in which the hotel was or would be situated. Yet, since Toronto was a centre of commerce and provincial politics, its local politics could also have broader repercussions, with some applicants and interested parties having tremendous political clout.

Table 6

Ethnicity in communities, 1931, as a percentage

	Essex County	Niagara region	Ottawa	Thunder Bay district	Toronto	Waterloo County
English	32.51	39.43	24.59	23.94	44.80	23.48
Irish	12.61	12.18	23.38	10.07	18.11	6.20
Scottish	12.55	14.09	13.47	14.11	17.10	10.23
French	20.68	3.12	29.53	4.97	1.72	1.89
German	4.91	8.72	2.16	1.76	1.48	49.62
Other						
European[a]	14.82	21.28	6.23	41.99	15.85	8.17
Non-European[b]	2.75	1.58	4.28	2.40	2.30	3.66
Indian and Eskimo	0.07	0.17	0.02	2.61	0.04	0.00
Unspecified	1.03	0.47	0.12	0.04	0.35	0.04

a Other British, Austrian, Belgian, Czech and Slovak, Dutch, Finnish, Hebrew, Hungarian, Italian, Polish, Romanian, Russian, Scandinavian, Ukrainian, and other European.

b Chinese and Japanese, other Asiatic, Indian and Eskimo, unspecified, and others.

Note: Some ethnic groupings used in the census are combined because the numbers are very small.

Source: Calculated from "Table 32: Population Classified According to Principal Origins for Municipalities etc.," *Census of Canada* (1931).

Notes

LCBO Establishment Files (RG 36-8) are filed under the name of the hotel at the time the file was created, not by a distinct record number. Consequently, some hotels named in the text of this book are linked to Establishment Files with different names. The hotels listed in the LLBO Standard Hotel Files at the Archives of Ontario, in contrast, are indexed with distinct record numbers (i.e., RG 36-1-0-xxxx). These do not require distinct hotel names. In some cases, usually when the file holds only preliminary documents related to an individual asking about the possibility of opening a hotel, no name was ever given to the hotel. On the rare occasion when I have intentionally changed the name of the hotel, it has been to obscure the identities of individuals whose criminal actions are discussed. In these instances, I indicate clearly that the names have been changed.

All relevant LCBO Establishment Files at the Archives of Ontario are kept within the files of the Liquor License Board of Ontario (LLBO), the agency that took over establishment licensing in 1947.

Introduction

1 Domestic wineries had been permitted to sell their products during prohibition but only in large quantities at their own stores. So the vintners may have been excited too.

2 Gerald A. Hallowell, *Prohibition in Ontario, 1919-1923* (Ottawa: Ontario Historical Society, 1972); Craig Heron, *Booze: A Distilled History* (Toronto: Between the Lines, 2004).

3 See Robert Campbell, *Demon Rum or Easy Money? Government Control of Liquor in British Columbia from Prohibition to Privatization* (Ottawa: Carleton University Press, 1991: 22, 32).

4 On British Columbia's liquor control system, see ibid. For other provinces, see Heron, *Booze*. For a contemporary account (as of 1928), see Reginald Hose, *Prohibition or Control? Canada's Experience with the Liquor Problem, 1921-1927* (Toronto: Longmans, Green, 1928).

5 Gary Genosko and Scott Thompson, "Administrative Surveillance of Alcohol Consumption in Ontario, Canada: Pre-electronic Technologies of Control," *Surveillance and Society* 4 (2006): 1-28.

6 "Liquor Control Act," *Statutes of the Province of Ontario* (1927), ch. 70, sec. 2(q).

7 "An Act Respecting the Sale of Intoxicating Liquors in the Province of Ontario," *Statutes of Ontario* (1902), ch. 22. For the results, see several articles in the *Toronto Globe*, 5 December 1902.

8 Hallowell, *Prohibition in Ontario*.

9 The title of Sharon Jaeger's doctoral dissertation captures this dichotomy. See Sharon A. Jaeger, "From Control to Customer Service: Government Control of Liquor in Ontario, 1927-1972" (PhD diss., Department of History, University of Waterloo, 1999).

10 Hallowell, *Prohibition in Ontario;* J.E. Hodgetts, *From Arm's Length to Hands-On: The Formative Years of Ontario's Public Service, 1867-1940* (Toronto: University of Toronto Press, 1995).

11 Heron, *Booze*, 275.

12 Jaeger, "From Control"; Heron, *Booze*.

13 Liquor Control Board of Ontario, *Digest of Rules, Orders, Regulations and Legislation Affecting Standard and Other Hotels* (January 1935), Archives of Ontario (AO), RG 36-5-0-2.2.

14 Foucault never made this statement in English, although it is often attributed to him. He originally referred to "*conduire des conduits*" in *Dits et écrits IV* (Paris: Gallimard, 1994), 237. For a useful commentary, see "The Foucault Blog," http://foucaultblog.wordpress.com/2007/05/15/key-term-conduct-of-conduct.

15 Mitchell Dean, *Governmentality: Power and Rule in Modern Society* (London: Sage, 1999), 10.

16 For the fundamentals of biopolitics, most point to Michel Foucault, *The Birth of Biopolitics: Lectures at the College de France, 1978-1979* (New York: Palgrave Macmillan, 2004). This text is probably not the best source since Foucault was and continues to be debated. One can follow the debate on Wikipedia.com, as the entries for "biopower" and "biopolitics" change regularly.

17 The process is described in excruciating detail by Scott Thompson and Gary Genosko, *Punched Drunk: Alcohol, Surveillance and the LCBO, 1927-1975* (Black Point, NS: Fernwood, 2009).

18 Weber's discussion of bureaucratization was most comprehensive in his posthumously published *Economy and Society: An outline of interpretive sociology,* ed. Guenther Roth and Claus Wittich, trans., Ephraim Fischo et al. (New York: Bedminster Press, 1968).

19 John Markoff, "Governmental Bureaucratization: General Processes and an Anomalous Case," *Comparative Studies in Society and History* 17 (1975): 479.

20 Christopher Dandeker, "Patronage and Bureaucratic Control – The Case of the Naval Officer in English Society, 1780-1850," *British Journal of Sociology* 29 (1979): 301.

21 John Burnham contrasts this idea of prohibition as a failure with an assertion that it was a success owing to the reduction of drinking in post-prohibition America. Nevertheless, at the time, people saw the illegality that was spawned during prohibition, its inability to stop people from drinking, and its demise as indicative of its fundamental failure. See John C. Burnham, "New Perspectives on the Prohibition 'Experiment' of the 1920's," *Journal of Social History* 2 (1968): 51-68.

22 Thompson and Genosko, *Punched Drunk,* offer a detailed commentary on the way that the LCBO's surveillance lay at the heart of government control. But their work tends to fixate on the ideal rather than actual function (or dysfunction) of the control system. It was limited, as is any technology, by what it excluded.

23 Ontario, Liquor Control Board of Ontario, *Second Report,* Sessional Papers (1929) No. 20 (Toronto: King's Printer, 1930), 6.

24 This body was succeeded in 1947 by the Liquor License Board of Ontario.

25 On gay sociability in pre-1930s Toronto, see Steven Maynard, "Through a Hole in the Lavatory Wall: Homosexual Subcultures, Police Surveillance and the Dialectics of Discovery, Toronto, 1890-1930," *Journal of the History of Sexuality* 5 (1994): 207-42. On post–Second World War Toronto, see David S. Churchill, "Mother Goose's Map: Tabloid Geographies and Gay Male Experience in 1950s Toronto," *Journal of Urban History* 30 (2004): 826-52.

26 Jack S. Blocker Jr., *Give to the Winds the Fears: The Women's Temperance Crusade, 1873-1974* (Westport, CT: Greenwood, 1985). The idea of cycles comes from Jack S. Blocker Jr., *American Temperance Movements: Cycles of Reform* (Boston: Twayne, 1989).

27 On Ontario's WCTU, see Sharon Ann Cook, *Through Sunshine and Shadow: The Woman's Christian Temperance Union, Evangelicalism, and Reform in Ontario, 1874-1930* (Montreal and Kingston: McGill-Queen's University Press, 1995); Dan Malleck, "Priorities of Development in Four Local Woman's Christian Temperance Unions in Ontario, 1878-1895," in *The Changing Face of Drink: Substance, Imagery and Behaviour,* ed. Jack S. Blocker Jr. and Cheryl Krasnick Warsh, 189-208 (Ottawa: Les Publications Histoire sociale-Social History, 1997). On the international WCTU, see Ian Tyrrell, *Woman's World/Woman's Empire: The Woman's Christian Temperance Union in International Perspective, 1880-1930* (Chapel Hill: University of North Carolina Press, 1991).

28 Jack S. Blocker Jr., *Retreat from Reform: The Prohibition Movement in the United States* (Westport, CT: Greenwood, 1976); K. Austin Kerr, *Organized for Reform: A New History of the Anti-Saloon League* (New Haven, CT: Yale University Press, 1985). On the Dominion Alliance, see Cheryl Krasnick Warsh, "Dominion Alliance for the Total Suppression of the Liquor Traffic," in

Alcohol and Temperance in Modern History: An International Encyclopedia, ed. Jack S. Blocker Jr., David M. Fahey, and Ian R. Tyrrell, vol. 1, 197-98 (Santa Barbara, CA: ABC-Clio, 2003).

29 See for example, Beat Kümin and B. Ann Tlusty, eds., *The World of the Tavern: Public Houses in Early Modern Europe* (Aldershot, UK, and Burlington, VT: Ashgate, 2002).

30 Julia Roberts, *In Mixed Company: Taverns and Public Life in Upper Canada* (Vancouver: UBC Press, 2009).

31 Perry R. Duis, *The Saloon: Public Drinking in Chicago and Boston, 1880-1920* (1983; reprint, Chicago and Urbana: University of Illinois Press, 1999); Madelon Powers, *Faces along the Bar: Lore and Order in the Workingmen's Saloon, 1870-1920* (Chicago: University of Chicago Press, 1998); Roy Rosenzweig, *Eight Hours for What We Will: Workers and Leisure in an Industrial City, 1870-1920* (London: Cambridge University Press, 1983); Peter Delottinville, "Joe Beef of Montreal: Working-Class Culture and the Tavern, 1869-1889," *Labour/Le Travailleur* 8-9 (1981-82): 9-40.

32 Craig Heron, "The Boys and Their Booze: Masculinities and Public Drinking in Working-Class Hamilton, 1890-1946," *Canadian Historical Review* 86 (2005): 411-52; Heron, *Booze.*

33 As explained by Ryan Potter, "Enforcing National Prohibition along the Detroit River" (MA thesis, Department of History, University of Eastern Michigan, 2000), 1.

34 Among many examples, see Mark Lawrence Schrad, "Constitutional Blemishes: American Alcohol Prohibition and Repeal as Policy Punctuation," *Policy Studies Journal* 35 (2007): 437-63; David E. Kyvig, *Repealing National Prohibition,* 2nd ed. (Kent, OH: Kent State University Press, 2000); Kenneth D. Rose, *American Women and the Repeal of Prohibition* (New York: New York University Press, 1996); Jeffrey A. Miron and Jeffrey Zwiebel, "Alcohol Consumption during Prohibition," *American Economic Review* 81 (1991): 242-47; Hanna Sprecher, "'Let Them Drink and Forget Our Poverty': Orthodox Rabbis React to Prohibition," *American Jewish Archives* 43 (1991): 135-79; Paul Aaron and David Musto, "Temperance and Prohibition in America: A Historical Overview," in *Alcohol and Public Policy: Beyond the Shadow of Prohibition – Panel on Alternative Policies Affecting the Prevention of Alcohol Abuse and Alcoholism,* ed. M. Moore and D. Gerstein, 127-81 (Washington, DC: National Academy Press, 1981); Norman H. Clark, *Deliver Us from Evil: An Interpretation of American Prohibition* (New York: W.W. Norton, 1976); John Kobler, *Ardent Spirits: The Rise and Fall of Prohibition* (Greenwich, CT: Fawcett Books, 1973).

35 See, for example, Pamela E. Pennock and K. Austin Kerr, "In the Shadow of Prohibition: Domestic American Alcohol Policy since 1933," *Business History* 47 (2005): 383-400; David E. Kyvig, "Objection Sustained: Prohibition Repeal and the New Deal," in *Alcohol, Reform and Society: The Liquor Issue in Social Context,* ed. Jack S. Blocker Jr., 211-33 (Westport, CT: Greenwood, 1979); Jay Rubin, "The Wet War: American Liquor Control, 1941-1945," in *Alcohol, Reform and Society,* ed. Jack S. Blocker Jr., 234-58; Ron Roizen, "How Does the Nation's 'Alcohol Problem' Change from Era to Era? Stalking the Social Logic of Problem-Definition Transformations since Repeal," in *Altering American Consciousness: The History of Alcohol and Drug Use in the United States,* ed. Sarah Tracy and Caroline Acker, 61-87 (Boston: University of Massachusetts Press, 2004).

36 Greg Marquis, "'Brewers and Distillers Paradise': American Views of Canadian Alcohol Policies, 1919 to 1935," *Canadian Review of American Studies* 34 (2004): 135-66; Stephen T. Moore, "Bootlegging and the Borderlands: Canadians, Americans, and the Prohibition-Era Northwest" (PhD diss., Department of History, College of William and Mary, 2000); Stephen T. Moore, "Defining the 'Undefended': Canadians, Americans, and the Multiple Meanings of Border during Prohibition," *American Review of Canadian Studies* 34 (2004): 3-36; Potter, "Enforcing National Prohibition."

37 Campbell, *Demon Rum;* Robert Campbell, *Sit Down and Drink Your Beer: Regulating Vancouver's Beer Parlors, 1925-1954* (Toronto: University of Toronto Press, 2001); Robert Campbell, "Profit Was Just a Circumstance: The Evolution of Government Liquor Control in British Columbia, 1920-1988," in *Drink in Canada: Historical Essays,* ed. Cheryl Warsh, 172-92 (Montreal and Kingston: McGill-Queen's University Press, 1993); Robert Campbell, "Liquor and Liberals: Patronage and Government Control in British Columbia, 1920-1928," *BC Studies* 77 (1988): 30-53; Greg Marquis, "'A Reluctant Concession to Modernity': Alcohol and Modernization in the Maritimes, 1945-1980," *Acadiensis* 32 (2003): 31-59; Marquis,

"'Brewers and Distillers Paradise'"; Jaeger, "From Control"; Dianne Kathryn Stretch, "From Prohibition to Government Control: The Liquor Question in Alberta, 1909-1929" (MA thesis, Department of History, University of Alberta, 1979).

Chapter 1: Liquor Control Bureaucracy and the Mechanisms of Governance

1 Scott Thompson and Gary Genosko, *Punched Drunk: Alcohol, Surveillance and the LCBO, 1927-1975* (Black Point, NS: Fernwood, 2009); Mariana Valverde, *Diseases of the Will: Alcohol and The Dilemmas of Freedom* (Cambridge, UK: Cambridge University Press, 1998).

2 Ontario, Liquor Control Board of Ontario (LCBO), *First Report,* Sessional Papers (1928) No. 20 (Toronto: King's Printer, 1930).

3 Ontario, LCBO, *Seventh Report,* Sessional Papers (1934) No. 20 (Toronto: King's Printer, 1935).

4 Deputy chief commissioner Arnold Smith was at times referred to as a second member of the central administration, although this relationship is unclear and not stated in official reports, which were signed exclusively by Odette, in contrast to pre-1934 reports, which were signed by all members of the central administration.

5 Ontario, LCBO, *First Report.*

6 Ontario, LCBO, *Seventh Report.*

7 Ontario, LCBO, *Eighth Report,* Sessional Papers (1935) No. 20 (Toronto: King's Printer, 1936).

8 Julia Roberts, *In Mixed Company: Taverns and Public Life in Upper Canada* (Vancouver: UBC Press, 2009).

9 On the rise of the auto camps and motels in Niagara Falls, see Karen Dubinsky, *The Second Greatest Disappointment: Honeymooning and Tourism at Niagara Falls* (Toronto: Between the Lines, 1999), ch. 5, esp. 130-31.

10 Peter Delottinville, "Joe Beef of Montreal: Working-Class Culture and the Tavern, 1869-1889," *Labour/Le Travailleur* 8-9 (1981-82): 9-40.

11 LCBO, *First Report;* LCBO, *Eighth Report.*

12 The number of rejections is difficult to quantify since some denied applications were actually nothing more than a letter to the board, followed by a cursory, negative inspector's report, or were even just a note in a file saying that someone had expressed an interest in obtaining a hotel licence for a particular building.

13 Dubinsky, *Second Greatest Disappointment,* 131-35, 148-49.

14 Mitchell Dean, *Governmentality: Power and Rule in Modern Society* (London: Sage, 1999), ch. 1, esp. 30-31.

15 Gary Genosko and Scott Thompson, "Administrative Surveillance of Alcohol Consumption in Ontario, Canada: Pre-electronic Technologies of Control," *Surveillance and Society* 4 (2006): 2.

16 "'Headaches and Heartaches on Nov 1,' Odette Promises," *Toronto Star,* 19 October 1934.

17 See Mair to Bloor District Business Men Inc., 20 September 1934, Archives of Ontario (AO), RG 36-8 Bloor Hotel (Toronto).

18 The importance of circulars as forms of centralized control is emphasized by Valverde, *Diseases of the Will;* Genosko and Thompson, "Administrative Surveillance"; and Thompson and Genosko, *Punched Drunk.*

19 I could not find a main file including the content of these circulars. Many of them were taken from copies that appear occasionally in LCBO establishment files.

20 Even more dire was the request that a proprietor surrender his or her authority and order books, which meant the hotel lost the privilege of selling booze.

21 Mair to Macmillan, 19 April 1941, AO, RG 36-8 Variety Hotel (Toronto).

22 J.E. Hodgetts, *From Arm's Length to Hands-On: The Formative Years of Ontario's Public Service, 1867-1940* (Toronto: University of Toronto Press, 1995), 64-5.

23 Margaret Jane Hillyard Little, *"No Car, No Radio, No Liquor Permit": The Moral Regulation of Single Mothers in Ontario, 1920-1997* (Oxford, Toronto, and New York: Oxford University Press, 1998); Xiaobei Chen, *Tending the Gardens of Citizenship: Child Saving in Toronto, 1880s-1920s* (Toronto: University of Toronto Press, 2005).

24 W.C. Mair to Mr. W.B. Common, 30 October 1930, AO, RG 36-1-0-719.

25 Reaume to Smith, 21 April 1937, AO, RG 36-1-0-295.

26 See Patrick Donnelly to Smith, 29 November 1934, and assorted letters to Donnelly, AO, RG 36-1-0-1229.
27 Gordon to Odette, 9 March 1936, and Odette to Gordon, 10 March 1936, AO, RG 3-10-0-488, Premier Mitchell F. Hepburn Private Correspondence, "LCBO Positions."
28 See Ratz to Hepburn, 7 April 1937 and 14 July 1937, AO, RG 3-10-0-702.2 Mitchell Hepburn Private Correspondence, "Liquor Control Board – general."
29 Smith to Larocque, 28 January 1941, AO, RG 36-8 Bridge Club (Ottawa).
30 Although it might also suggest that Larocque was too well connected to be dismissed, the fact that Ratz was not likewise protected by his patronage appointment indicates that the board was not averse to firing someone whose political sentiments had landed them the job.
31 Smith to Fort William BPO Elks, 19 December 1939, AO, RG 36-8 Elks Club (Fort William).
32 Mair to Schmalz, 8 July 1935, AO, RG 36-8 American Hotel (Kitchener).
33 Smith to Skuce, 15 June 1937, AO, RG 36-8 Nipigon Hotel (Nipigon).
34 Smith to Elliott, 12 July 1935, AO, RG 36-1-0-1230.
35 Michel Foucault, *Discipline and Punish: The Birth of the Prison,* trans. Alan Sheridan (New York: Vintage, 1979); Max Weber, *Economy and Society: An Outline of Interpretive Sociology,* ed. Guenther Roth and Claus Wittich, trans. Ephraim Fischo et al. (New York: Bedminster Press, 1968). For additional discussion, see Mitchell Dean, *Governmentality: Power and Rule in Modern Society* (London: Sage, 1999). But see also John Markoff, "Government Bureaucratization: General Processes and an Anomalous Case," *Comparative Studies in Society and History* 17 (1975): 479; Max Weber, "Bureaucracy," in *Economy and Society,* ed. Guenther Roth and Claus Wittich, 856-1005 (Berkeley: University of California Press, 1978).
36 The social problems arising from the implied objectivity of scientific language have been discussed by Max Weber, among others. See Max Weber, "Science as Vocation," in *From Max Weber: Essays in Sociology,* ed. Hans H. Gerth and C. Wright Mills, 129-56 (London: Routledge, 1970); and Max Weber, "Politics as Vocation," in *From Max Weber: Essays in Sociology,* ed. Hans H. Gerth and C. Wright Mills, 77-128 (London: Routledge, 1970).
37 W.C. Mair to Church, 21 November 1934, AO, RG 36-8 Central Hotel (Preston).
38 Doumani to Mair, 18 July 1935, and Mair to Doumani, 19 July 1935, AO, RG 36-8 British American Hotel (Windsor). Mair's title, like several others, changed over the period under study.
39 Mair to Williams, 26 July 1935, AO, RG 36-1-0-306.
40 Several letters, June to July 1942, AO, RG 36-8 Embassy Hotel (St. Agatha).
41 Dean, Inspector's Report, 28 September 1934; Gertrude M. Barrick to Odette, 3 October 1934; and Smith to Thomas J. Darby, 14 January 1936, all in AO, RG 36-1-0-1511.
42 Note in Mair's handwriting, [c. mid-December 1934], AO, RG 36-1-0-604.
43 Mair to MacSween [barrister], 5 January 1935, AO, RG 36-1-0-604.
44 Smith to Central Hotel, 16 April 1935, AO, RG 36-8 Central Hotel (Preston).
45 Church to LCBO, 17 April 1935, AO, RG 36-8 Central Hotel (Preston).
46 C.W. Cox to Mair, 5 February 1936, AO, RG 36-1-0-1107.
47 W.J. Dodds, Chief Constable, to W.S. Dingman, 3 December 1931, and Dingman to Dodds, 10 December 1931, AO, RG 36-1-0-1119.

Chapter 2: The Public Life of Liquor, 1927-34

1 "An Act to Amend the Liquor License Laws," *Statutes of Ontario* (1906), ch. 47, sec. 1(a).
2 "An Act to Amend the Liquor License Laws," *Statutes of Ontario* (1909), ch. 82, sec. 6.
3 Norman Lambert, "Hotel Accommodation Minus the Bar," *Toronto Globe,* 22 January 1916, continued on 24 January 1916 and over the next few weeks. Unfortunately, not all issues have survived.
4 The BLC was created by "An Act to Improve the Administration of the Liquor License Laws," *Statutes of Ontario* (1915), ch. 39. In previous liquor legislation, a three-person Board of License Commissioners was appointed for each municipality. The 1915 law centralized the authority in one board of five people, appointed by the lieutenant governor of the province.
5 "Ontario Temperance Act," *Statutes of Ontario* (1916), ch. 50, sec. 146(5).

6 Karen Dubinsky, *The Second Greatest Disappointment: Honeymooning and Tourism at Niagara Falls* (Toronto: Between the Lines, 1999), 128-38.
7 OPP Report, 14 July 1932, Archives of Ontario (AO), RG 36-8 Royal Hotel (Elmira).
8 E.A. Rae, District Inspector, to Dingman, 26 September 1930, AO, RG 36-8 King Edward Hotel (New Hamburg).
9 District Inspector to Commissioner, OPP, 13 September 1928, AO, RG 36-8 Lafayette Hotel (Ottawa).
10 Inspector's Report, 8 May 1933, AO, RG 36-1-0-723.
11 H.W. Roger to LCBO, 24 June 1927, and Director of Permits to Rogers, 25 June 1927, AO, RG 36-1-0-1496.
12 E.D. Past [?] to Dingman, 13 July 1928, AO, RG 36-8 Fort Erie Hotel (Fort Erie).
13 Dingman to Fort Erie Hotel, 23 May 1929, AO, RG 36-8 Fort Erie Hotel (Fort Erie).
14 W.G. Willson to Dingman, 3 June 1931, AO, RG 36-1-0-1496 Inspector's Files.
15 Thomas W. Oldfield, Constable, OPP, to District Inspector, Niagara Falls, 4 July 1929, AO, RG-1-0-717.
16 Powell to Dingman, 22 May 1930, AO, RG 36-8 Waverly Hotel (Toronto).
17 Director of Permits to Landriau, 31 May 1927, AO, RG 36-1-0-1576. The pun on "sporty" was likely intentional.
18 Arthur Moss, OPP Investigator, to Dingman, 18 July 1928, AO, RG 36-1-0-1576.
19 Pitt to Dingman, 31 October 1928, AO, RG 36-1-0-1575.
20 Dingman to Bailey, 14 May 1930, AO, RG 36-1-0-1792.
21 Dingman to Bailey, 19 June 1930, AO, RG 36-1-0-1792.
22 Ibid.
23 Malone to Dingman, 20 June 1930, AO, RG 36-1-0-1792.
24 Elliott to Dingman, 22 May 1931, AO, RG 36-1-0-1792.
25 Dingman to Bailey, 30 May 1931, AO, RG 36-1-0-1792. This note was included in a memo to Elliott regarding the letter to Bailey (a copy of the letter was sent to Elliott).
26 Oliver to Commissioner, OPP, 10 June 1932, AO, RG 36-1-0-1792.
27 Nugent, Inspector's Report, 10 October 1934, AO, RG 36-8 Kimberly Hotel (Port Arthur).
28 Director of Permits to Burstrom, 7 June 1928, AO, RG 36-8 Kimberly Hotel (Port Arthur).
29 Dingman to William Markey, 27 April 1928, AO, RG 36-8 Jordan Hotel (Jordan).
30 Dingman to District Inspector F.E. Elliott, 13 April 1931, AO, RG 36-1-0-1106.
31 See Scott Thompson and Gary Genosko, *Punched Drunk: Alcohol, Surveillance and the LCBO, 1927-1975* (Black Point, NS: Fernwood, 2009), 167-88; Robert Campbell, *Sit Down and Drink Your Beer: Regulating Vancouver's Beer Parlors, 1925-1954* (Toronto: University of Toronto Press, 2001), 94-105; Mariana Valverde, *Diseases of the Will: Alcohol and the Dilemmas of Freedom* (Cambridge, UK: Cambridge University Press, 1998), 162-68; and Craig Heron, *Booze: A Distilled History* (Toronto: Between the Lines, 2004).
32 Dingman retired in March 1932. See General Manager A.H. Birmingham to E. Heaton, Fire Marshal, 19 March 1932, AO, RG 36-1-0-1223.
33 A.K. Coulthard, Director of Permits, to Inspector Kilpatrick, 29 May 1933, and A.K. Coulthard, Director of Permits, to Inspector Kilpatrick, 14 November 1933, AO, RG 36-1-0-1106.
34 Dingman to [Rossi], 27 February 1930, AO, RG 36-1. File number withheld for confidentiality purposes.
35 W.G. Ingram, OPP Memo, to Director of Permits, 12 March 1930, AO, RG 36-1.
36 Dingman to Dodds, 9 April 1930 AO, RG 36-1.
37 Dingman to S.B.P., 7 May 1930, AO, RG 36-1.
38 S.B.P.'s name was obscured to ensure confidentiality. His reason for leaving is unknown. Since I first read these records, they have gone missing at the Archives of Ontario.
39 Ingram to Dingman, 17 July 1931, AO, RG 36-1.
40 Dingman to [Rossi], 22 July 1931, AO, RG 36-1.
41 J. Nixon, Constable, OPP Report, 14 October 1932, AO, RG 36-1.
42 Mrs. [Rossi] to Dingman, 19 March 1930, AO, RG 36-1.
43 Dingman to Conrad Klein, 28 May 1927, AO, RG 3-8 New Royal Hotel (Galt).
44 Pitt, Report, 24 August 1929, AO, RG 36-8 Commodore Hotel (Windsor), emphasis added to the original report by a second reader, likely Dingman.

45 The law restricted the sale of "non-intoxicating drinks and beers, cigars, cigarettes and tobacco" to standard hotels; see "Liquor Control Act," *Statutes of the Province of Ontario* (1927), ch. 70, sec. 140(7). Dingman does not state which items the hotel was selling.
46 Dingman to Windsor Hotel, 8 February 1929, AO, RG 36-8 American Hotel (Kitchener).
47 Dingman to Zuber, 8 February 1929, AO, RG 36-8 Walper Hotel (Kitchener). Zuber was a well-known hotelier, and any attempt at masking his name would have been futile.
48 Ibid.
49 W.G. Ingram, OPP District Inspector, to Inspector E.F. Elliott, 14 February 1933, AO, RG 36-8 Walper Hotel (Kitchener).
50 Memo for District Inspector from Walter, Provincial Officer, [c. 30 June 1927], AO, RG 36-8 Clifton Inn (Niagara Falls).
51 German and Brooks to Dingman, 21 September 1927, AO, RG 36-8 Clifton Inn (Niagara Falls).
52 Dingman to German and Brooks, 28 October 1927, AO, RG 36-8 Clifton Inn (Niagara Falls).
53 Dingman to German and Brooks, Barrister and Solicitor, 9 November 1927, AO, RG 36-8 Clifton Inn (Niagara Falls).
54 Airey to Dingman, 10 Decembr 1927, AO, RG 36-8 Clifton Inn (Niagara Falls).
55 Unsigned memo to Chief Commissioner, 8 August 1928, AO, RG 36-8 Clifton Inn (Niagara Falls).
56 Mrs. [Labelle] to LCBO, [c. 20 December 1929], AO, RG 36-8 Paris Hotel (Tecumseh).
57 Dingman to [Labelle], 24 December 1929, AO, RG 36-8 Paris Hotel (Tecumseh).
58 Dingman to [Labelle], 26 February 1930, AO, RG 36-8 Paris Hotel (Tecumseh).
59 Dingman to District Inspector Rae, 3 March 1931, AO, RG 36-8 American Hotel (Kitchener).
60 OPP Report, 7 December 1932, AO, RG 36-8 American Hotel (Kitchener).
61 Thomas Innes, Proprietor, to LCBO, 9 November 1927, AO, RG 36-1-0-280.
62 Director of Permits to Innes, 12 November 1927, AO, RG 36-1-0-280.
63 Dingman to J. Gardner, District Inspector, 17 December 1927, AO, RG 36-1-0-262.
64 Ibid.
65 Gardner to Dingman, [rec'd. 20 December 1927], AO, RG 36-8 Island View Hotel (Riverside).
66 Heron, *Booze,* 208, 212.
67 Campbell, *Sit Down,* 18.
68 Heron, *Booze,* 98.
69 For more on the high politics of the situation, see Sharon A. Jaeger, "From Control to Customer Service: Government Control of Liquor in Ontario, 1927-1972" (PhD diss., Department of History, University of Waterloo, 1999), esp. 66-114.
70 "Laborite Protests Banners in Parade," *Toronto Globe,* 16 September 1932.
71 General letter, H.S. Pritchard, Secretary, Moderation League of Ontario, 25 November 1932, AO, RG 3-8-0-226 "Liquor Control – Operation of #1," MS 1748. The league sent this letter to, among others, the advertisers of the *Toronto Telegram.*
72 Henry to H.I. Hellmuth, 26 August 1932, AO, RG 3-8-0-227 "Liquor Control – Operation of #2," MS 1749.
73 H. Mitchell, Secretary, Hamilton District Trades and Labor Council, to Henry, 5 June 1932, AO, RG 3-8-0-227 "Liquor Control – Operation of #2," MS 1749.
74 S.J. Robins, Managing Director, Hotel Association of the Province of Ontario, to Henry, 19 September 1932, AO, RG 3-8-0-227 "Liquor Control – Operation of #2," MS 1749. For an examination of the problems between hotels and other accommodations in the context of Niagara Falls, see Dubinsky, *Second Greatest Disappointment,* 131-35, 148-49.
75 Mike Filey, *I Remember Sunnyside: The Rise and Fall of a Magical Era* (Toronto: Dundurn, 1996), 52; "The Old Mill and Spa History," Old Mill and Spa online, http://www.oldmilltoronto.com/about/history.
76 Venables to Henry, 14 July 1932, AO, RG 3-8-O-227 "Liquor Control – Operation of #2," MS 1749.
77 Jaeger, "From Control."
78 Henry's Secretary to R.A. Stewart, 14 September 1932, AO, RG 3-8-O-227 "Liquor Control – Operation of #2," MS 1749.

79 Spence to Henry, 15 September 1932, AO, RG 3-8-O-227 "Liquor Control – Operation of #2," MS 1749.
80 Henry to Spence, 1 November 1932, AO, RG 3-8-O-227 "Liquor Control – Operation of #2," MS 1749.
81 Pritchard to Henry, 15 December 1932 and 25 November 1932, AO, RG 3-8-0-226 "Liquor Control – Operation of #1," MS 1748.
82 Henry to Rev. F.K. Clysdale, 3 November 1933, AO, RG 3-8-0-343 "Liquor Control – Operation of #2," MS 1756.
83 "Liquor Control Act," *Revised Statutes of Ontario* (1937), ch. 294, sec. 70(1).
84 "Hotels Await Rules on Beer, Wine Sales," *Toronto Star,* 13 July 1934.
85 "No Beer in Restaurants, Hepburn Promises Drys," *Toronto Star,* 22 February 1935.

Chapter 3: Idealistic Form and Realistic Function

1 Inspector's Report, 4 May 1937, Archives of Ontario (AO), RG 36-8 American Hotel (Sandwich).
2 David Gutzke, *Pubs and Progressives: Reinventing the Public House in England, 1896-1960* (DeKalb: Northern Illinois University Press, 2006), esp. chs. 8 and 10.
3 Robert Campbell, *Sit Down and Drink Your Beer: Regulating Vancouver's Beer Parlors, 1925-1954* (Toronto: University of Toronto Press, 2001).
4 Mariana Valverde, *Diseases of the Will: Alcohol and the Dilemmas of Freedom* (Cambridge, UK: Cambridge University Press, 1998), 143-70.
5 I should note that Valverde's discussion includes examples from the LCBO that are quite simply incorrect. In *Diseases of the Will,* 156, she mentions that the LCBO denied the request of Toronto's hotel owners that they be permitted to use dining rooms as overflow beverage rooms. Valverde reasons that "the board held firm to its theory about the incompatibility of food and beer." This was not true. Beer and wine drinking were allowed in licensed dining rooms, and hoteliers were quite often allowed to use their dining rooms as overflow beverage rooms. Second, she argues that "no authority ever devised a legally actionable definition of a meal." Although I cannot comment on whether it was "legally actionable," the LCBO did have a specific definition of what constituted a meal in a dining room. As I discuss in Chapter 6, it deployed this definition when authority holders requested permission to hold dances in their dining rooms; these were allowed only when meals, defined in writing by the board, were served.
6 Michel Foucault, *Discipline and Punish: The Birth of the Prison,* trans. Alan Sheridan (New York: Vintage, 1979), esp. 195-228.
7 Margo Huxley, "Spatial Rationalities: Order, Environment, Evolution and Government," *Social and Cultural Geography* 7 (2006): 774.
8 Ibid., 777.
9 Mair to C.K. Fisken, Deputy Controller of Construction, Department of Munitions and Supply, 23 January 1942, AO, RG 36-8 Duke of Connaught Hotel (Toronto).
10 Quoted in Margo Huxley, "Geographies of Governmentality," in *Space, Knowledge and Power: Foucault and Geography,* ed. J. Crampton and Stuart Elden (London: Ashgate, 2007), 194.
11 Ibid., paraphrasing S. Elden, *Mapping the Present: Heidegger, Foucault and the Project of a Spatial History* (London: Continuum, 2001).
12 Huxley, "Spatial Rationalities," 774.
13 Stevens to Odette, 12 April 1935, AO, RG 36-1-0-604.
14 Report, 11 September 1934, AO, RG 36-1-0-1153.
15 Authority Holder's Conduct Report (AHCR), 13 August 1935, AO, RG 36-8 Chez Lucien (Ottawa).
16 Frank Ferguson, Special Report to Board, 12 March 1937, AO, RG 36-8 American Hotel (Sandwich).
17 Reaume, Inspector's Report, 7 February 1939, AO, RG 36-8 American Hotel (Sandwich).
18 Ratz to Smith, 12 June 1937, AO, RG 36-8 Breslau Hotel (Breslau).
19 Report, 17 October 1934, AO, RG 36-8 Prescott Hotel (Ottawa).
20 Anonymous to Draper, 13 March 1936, AO, RG 36-8 Venezia Hotel (Toronto).

21 Smith to Draper, 26 March 1936, AO, RG 36-8 Monarch Hotel (Toronto).
22 AHCR, 6 November 1934, AO, RG 36-1-0-1230, emphasis added.
23 Ibid.
24 Valverde, *Diseases of the Will,* 143-70.
25 Gutzke, *Pubs and Progressives.*
26 James Nicholls, *The Politics of Alcohol: A History of the Drink Question in England* (Manchester, UK: University of Manchester Press, 2009), 182.
27 Smith to Harbluk, 3 November 1937, AO, RG 36-8 Grandview Hotel (Shuniah).
28 Buchanan to Smith, 23 November 1940, AO, RG 36-8 Metropole Tavern (Niagara Falls).
29 Smith, Memo, 31 May 1937, AO, RG 36-1-0-738.
30 Wylie to LCBO, 29 May 1937, AO, RG 36-1-0-738.
31 Smith, Memo, 31 May 1937, AO, RG 36-1-0-738.
32 Mair to Bloor District Business Men Inc., 20 September 1934, AO, RG 36-8 Bloor Hotel (Toronto).
33 AHCR, 2 March 1937, AO, RG 36-8 Bloor Hotel (Toronto).
34 Downey to Smith, 20 April 1937, AO, RG 36-1-0-1347.
35 See John C. Burnham, *Bad Habits: Drinking, Smoking, Taking Drugs, Gambling, Sexual Misbehaviour and Swearing in American History* (New York: New York University Press, 1993).
36 Smith to Deadey, 11 May 1937, AO, RG 36-1-0-1347.
37 Mair, Memo, 4 July 1938, AO, RG 36-1-0-1347.
38 Downey to Smith, 20 April 1937, AO, RG 36-1-0-1347.
39 An article in *Hush* magazine, 16 August 1941, compared the troublesome Alexandra Hotel to the Royal Cecil, saying that what was going on at the former "makes even the Royal Cecil look to its laurels." See AO, RG 36-1-0-1347.
40 Pitt to Mair, 6 June 1939, AO, RG 36-1-0-1347.
41 "Order Some Hotels to Separate Sexes," *Toronto Star,* 24 January 1935.
42 B.A. Neale to William Common, 11 August 1934, AO, RG 36-8 Royal York Hotel (Toronto).
43 Common to Neale, 13 August 1934, AO, RG 36-8 Royal York Hotel (Toronto).
44 Hanrahan, Report, 30 July 1937, AO, RG 36-8 Kimberly Hotel (Port Arthur).
45 AHCR, 26 November 1937, AO, RG 36-8 Kimberly Hotel (Port Arthur).
46 Inspector's Report, 17 January 1938, AO, RG 36-1-0-1225.
47 Cheeseman to Smith, 17 January 1938, AO, RG 36-1-0-1225.
48 Hanrahan to LCBO, 30 July 1937, AO, RG 36-1-0-1149.
49 AHCR, 28 April 1939, AO, RG 36-8 British American Hotel (Windsor).
50 Simington to Elmhirst, 23 March 1943, AO, RG 36-8 British American Hotel (Windsor).
51 Barnabe to Smith, 5 April 1935, AO, RG 36-8 Gilmour Inn (Ottawa).
52 Smith to Barnabe, 8 April 1935, AO, RG 36-8 Gilmour Inn (Ottawa). See also Mair to Coulson, 19 November 1936, AO, RG 36-8 Alexandra Hotel (Ottawa).
53 Smith to V.T. Pegg, 23 January 1937, AO, RG 36-8 St. Regis Hotel (Toronto).
54 Robinson to LCBO, 18 November 1935, and Mair to Robinson, 20 November 1935, AO, RG 36-8 Pickwick Arms (Fort Erie).
55 Macrae to Smith, 13 June 1935, and Smith to Macrae, 14 June 1935, AO, RG 36-8 Leonard Hotel (St. Catharines).
56 AHCR, 18 March 1937, and Mair to Robinson, 21 March 1937, AO, RG 36-8 Pickwick Arms (Fort Erie).
57 Smith to Macrae, 21 November 1938, AO, RG 36-8 Leonard Hotel (St. Catharines).
58 "The Leonard Hotel," *Canadian Hotel Review and Restaurant* 7, 10 (October 1929): 15-18.
59 AHCR, 12 November 1935, AO, RG 36-8 Grand Hotel (Bridgewater).
60 Teresa Schneider to LCBO, 28 November 1935, AO, RG 36-1-0-1489.
61 Haverluck to LCBO, 20 September 1937, AO, RG 36-8 Savant Hotel (Savant Lake).
62 Haverluck to LCBO, 25 September 1937, AO, RG 36-8 Savant Hotel (Savant Lake).
63 Haverluck to Mair, 26 October 1937, AO, RG 36-8 Savant Hotel (Savant Lake).
64 "Two Firemen Hurt as Clifton Hotel at Niagara Burns," *Toronto Globe,* 2 January 1933.
65 See several letters between the board and the Clifton Hotel in June 1932, AO, RG 36-1-0-717. The fire was well documented in several newspapers.

66 M.C. MacDonald to LCBO, 8 March 1940, AO, RG 36-8 Allen's Hotel (Jellicoe).
67 See several letters, January-February 1943, AO, RG 36-8 Tudor Hotel (Toronto). The hotel burned down on 14 February 1943; see "60 Driven to Icy Streets: Fire Sweeps Tudor Hotel," *Toronto Star,* 15 February 1943.
68 Dingman to Viau, 27 November 1931, AO, RG 36-8 Commercial Hotel (Ottawa).
69 Unsigned Memo to Drayton, 1 April 1932, RG 36-1-0-1223 Inspector's Files.
70 McClenaghan to Henry, 17 October 1933, AO, RG 3-8-0-342 Henry Letters, "Liquor Control: Operation of #1," MS 1756.
71 A.N. Smith to H. Smith, 18 May 1936, AO, RG 36-8 St. Charles Hotel (Ottawa).
72 Mair to Doumani, 28 July 1937, AO, RG 36-8 British American Hotel (Windsor).
73 Reaume to Smith, 6 March 1939, AO, RG 36-8 British American Hotel (Windsor).
74 C.J. Defields, Fire Chief, to Reaume, 24 March 1943, AO, RG 36-8 British American Hotel (Windsor).
75 Owing to wartime scarcity of resources, the work proceeded slowly. The provincial fire marshal, Windsor fire chief, and LCBO officials all expressed sympathy with the situation. Reaume noted that "the work ... has gone on as fast as could be expected on account of the difficulties of securing various mechanics" and then listed what work had been done. See Reaume to Elmhirst, 1 June 1943, AO, RG 36-8 British American Hotel (Windsor).
76 Report, 20 December 1935, AO, RG 36-8 Maple Leaf Hotel (Toronto).
77 Report, 3 January 1940, AO, RG 36-8 Edgewater Hotel (Toronto).
78 Kamin to Smith, 23 August 1939, AO, RG 36-8 New Statler Hotel (St. Catharines); Buchanan to Gordon, 17 March 1941, AO, RG 36-8 Queensway Hotel (St. Catharines).
79 Gutzke, *Pubs and Progressives.*
80 Sean Purdy, "Building Homes, Building Citizens: Housing Reform and Nation Formation in Canada, 1900-20," *Canadian Historical Review* 79 (1998): 498.
81 The quotations are from E.C. Bogart to James McIllmurray, 7 August 1935, AO, RG 36-1-0-1323. See also additional letters in AO, RG 36-1-0-1323.
82 T.A. Ross, Secretary-Treasurer, Beardmore Chamber of Commerce, to Smith, 14 May 1937, AO, RG 36-1-0-1109.
83 Mair to Gould Hotel, 30 November 1935, AO, RG 36-8 Edison Hotel (Toronto).
84 See a long series of letters and reports from 1936 in AO, RG 36-8 Victory Hotel (Toronto).
85 Mariana Valverde, *The Age of Light, Soap and Water: Moral Regulation in English Canada, 1885-1925* (Toronto: McClelland and Stewart, 1991); Richard L. Bushman and Claudia L. Bushman, "The Early History of Cleanliness in America," *Journal of American History* 74 (1988): 1213-38; John Pickstone, "Dearth, Dirt and Fever Epidemics: Rewriting the History of British 'Public Health,' 1780-1850," in *Epidemics and Ideas: Essays on the Historical Perception of Pestilence,* ed. Terence Osborn Ranger and Paul Slack, 125-48 (Cambridge, UK: Cambridge University Press, 1992); John M. Eyler, "The Sick Poor and the State: Arthur Newsholme on Poverty, Disease and Responsibility," in *Framing Disease: Studies in Cultural History,* ed. Charles E. Rosenberg and Janet Golden, 275-95 (New Brunswick, NJ: Rutgers University Press, 1992); Nancy Tomes, *The Gospel of Germs: Men, Women and the Microbe in American Life* (Boston: Harvard University Press, 1998); Suellen Hoy, *Chasing Dirt: The American Pursuit of Cleanliness* (New York: Oxford University Press, 1996). Virginia Smith, *Clean: A History of Personal Hygiene and Purity* (Oxford: Oxford University Press, 2007), notes that the desire for cleanliness is also a biophysical and evolved characteristic.
86 AHCR, 24 August 1935, AO, RG 36-8 Central Hotel (Preston).
87 Smith to Louis Marck, 3 July 1940, AO, RG 36-8 Port Hotel (Port Dalhousie).
88 Valverde, *Age of Light,* 13.
89 Skuce to Smith, 29 October 1935, RG 36-1-0-1124.
90 Nugent, Long Report, 8 October 1934, AO, RG 36-8 Lakehead Hotel (Port Arthur).
91 Ratz to Smith, 12 June 1937, AO, RG 36-8 Breslau Hotel (Breslau).
92 Inspector's Report, 14 June 1937, AO, RG 36-8 Dixie Hotel (Windsor).
93 See "'Headaches and Heartaches on Nov 1,' Odette Promises," *Toronto Star,* 19 October 1934.
94 Sources on the origins of sample rooms are obscure, but an Internet search reveals descriptions of hotels describing a sample room as a place where travelling salespeople could either

store or display their wares. For the most credible source, see "Sample Room," *Oxford English Dictionary* online, Dec. 2011 edition, www.oed.com.

95 Inspector's Report, 19 July 1932, AO, RG 36-1-0-710.

96 Ratz to Klinck, 19 October 1936, AO, RG 36-8 St. Clements Hotel (St. Clements).

97 AHCR, 30 May 1935, AO, RG 36-8 Teal's Hotel (Crystal Beach).

98 Pitt to LCBO, 17 June 1935, AO, RG 36-1-0-116.

99 Skuce to Smith, 29 October 1935, AO, RG 36-1-0-1124.

100 Reaume, Inspector's Report, 24 February 1939, AO, RG 36-8 Highway Hotel (Windsor).

Chapter 4: Hearing the Voices

1 "Promise Still Lower Rates," *St. Catharines Standard,* 11 June 1934.

2 Sandell to Smith, 11 August 1936, Archives of Ontario (AO), RG 36-1-0-622.

3 Isabel Irvines to Mrs. G. Tomey, 19 June 1937, AO, RG 36-1-0-622.

4 Jean Finch, Secretary, to Mrs. Tomey, 19 June 1937, AO, RG 36-1-0-622.

5 W. Sherman, Chief of Police, to Mrs. Sandell, 16 June 1937; E.J.H. Vanston, Manager, Bank of Toronto, St. Catharines, to Smith, 8 July 1937; A.J. Haines to Smith, 8 July 1937; and A.S. Goxing, Alderman, to LCBO, 8 July 1937, all in AO, RG 36-1-0-622.

6 J.A. Russell, Secretary, Official Board, to Mr. Odette, 8 May 1935, AO, RG 36-8 Elliott Hotel (Niagara Falls).

7 Houck to Smith, 8 August 1935, AO, RG 36-8 Elliott Hotel (Niagara Falls).

8 E.J. Anderson, MLA, to Odette, 10 October 1934, AO, RG 36-1-0-1529. Thorold voted itself dry in January 1935.

9 Finnish Pentecostal Church to LCBO, 29 January 1939, AO, RG 36-1-0-1145.

10 Letter from Rev. William Croth [?] to LCBO, 20 March 1935, AO, RG 36-1-0-1479.

11 Mrs. L. Armstrong to Odette, 16 April 1935, AO, RG 36-8 Dorking Hotel (Dorking).

12 See AO, RG 36-1-0-1345.

13 G. Heidman to Odette, 6 April 1935, AO, RG 36-8 Carleton Hotel (Ottawa).

14 F.G. Payne, Secretary, and Geo Payne, President, Church of the Nazarene, to LCBO, 17 November 1934, AO, RG 36-1-0-1283.

15 C.D. Farquharson [on Westminster United Church letterhead] to Odette, 17 August 1934, AO, RG 36-8 Driving Park Inn (Windsor).

16 C. Brown to LCBO, [c. 10 May 1935], AO, RG 36-8 Queen's Hotel (Dunnville).

17 Rev. A.J. Irwin, General Secretary, Ontario Temperance Federation, to A.W. Roebuck, Attorney General, 6 June 1935, AO, RG 36-8 New Statler Hotel (St. Catharines).

18 Irwin to Common, 15 December 1934, AO, RG 36-8 Hespeler Hotel (Hespeler).

19 Irwin to Odette, 26 September 1934, AO, RG 36-1-0-1236.

20 A.J. Irwin to LCBO, 8 November 1934, AO, RG 36-1-0-1259.

21 L.A. Tucker, Comptroller, Brompton Pulp and Paper Co., to J.M. McGeache, Comptroller, LCBO, 1 June 1944, AO, RG 36-8 Red Rock Inn (Red Rock).

22 Alan Digman, Secretary, Bloor District Business Men Incorporated, to Odette, 19 February 1935, AO, RG 36-1-0-1330.

23 J.R. Gourlat to Odette, 28 February 1935, AO, RG 36-1-0-1330.

24 See petitions in AO, RG 36-1-0-111.

25 J. Mansell to Odette, 9 January 1935, AO, RG 36-1-0-1346.

26 His polling found 604 "for," 64 "neutral," 80 "against," and 67 "refusing to sign either way." See Scott to Odette, 10 January 1934 [sic; should be 1935], AO, RG 36-1-0-1346.

27 R.L. Roach to Odette, 23 October 1934, AO, RG 36-8 Stafford Hotel (Toronto).

28 Brooker to Odette, 2 November 1934, AO, RG 36-8 Stafford Hotel (Toronto).

29 Raymond Sauve, Clerk, Village of Belle River, to LCBO, 9 June 1936, AO, RG 36-1-0-288.

30 Mair to Letourneau, 26 March 1936, AO, RG 36-1-0-288.

31 Kittel to Newall and Smith, 11 July 1935, AO, RG 36-1-0-1481.

32 Peter F. Schummer, Wellesley Township Clerk, to William Common, LCBO, 13 December 1929, AO, RG 36-8 St. Clements Hotel (St. Clements).

33 Matt Schummer to LCBO, 18 April 1935, AO, RG 36-8 St. Clements Hotel (St. Clements).

34 Haverluck and Koval, General Merchants, to LCBO, 20 December 1934, AO, RG 36-8 Savant Hotel (Savant Lake).

35 Two petitions signed by 176 people, 14 December 1935, AO, RG 36-1-0-1111.
36 W.M. Egan to Odette, 20 October 1937, AO, RG 36-1-0-1136.
37 Raymond Sauve, Clerk, Village of Belle River, to LCBO, 9 June 1936, AO, RG 36-1-0-288.
38 Harry E. Bondy, Township of Sandwich West, Clerk and Treasurer's Office, to E.G. Odette, 7 April 1937, AO, RG 36-1-0-263.
39 A. Belanger, MLA, to Smith, 6 July 1935, AO, RG 36-8 LaSalle Hotel (Ottawa).
40 Skuce, Report, 20 February 1936, AO, RG 36-8 Kimberly Hotel (Port Arthur).
41 Ratz to Smith, 23 November 1936, AO, RG 36-8 Embassy Hotel (St. Agatha).
42 H.B. Arkell to Hepburn [forwarded to Odette], 22 March 1935, AO, RG 36-8 Ambassador Hotel (Ottawa).
43 Craig Heron notes that the Moderation League began in 1919; see Craig Heron, *Booze: A Distilled History* (Toronto: Between the Lines, 2004), 272. Perhaps Pritchard was referring to the Ontario League.
44 H.S. Pritchard, Executive Secretary, Moderation League of Ontario, to E.G. Odette, 30 August 1935, AO, RG 36-1-0-1341.
45 Ibid.
46 Moderation League to LCBO, 30 September 1935, AO, RG 36-8 Commerce Hotel (Toronto).
47 Mair, Memo, 9 December 1938, AO, RG 36-8 Alexandra Hotel (Toronto).
48 Prichard to Odette, 24 September 1935, AO, RG 36-1-0-1341.
49 Heron, *Booze,* 198.
50 See letters dated 30 August 1935, 1 October 1935, 2 October 1935, 5 October 1935, AO, RG 36-8 Riviera Hotel (Toronto).
51 Inspector's Report, 29 August 1934, AO, RG 36-1-0-265.
52 Larocque to Smith, 10 April 1935, AO, RG 36-8 Ambassador Hotel (Ottawa).
53 Hanrahan, Report, 27 November 1936, AO, RG 36-8 Royal Cecil Hotel (Toronto).
54 T. Garnet Fraser to Odette, 11 September 1934, AO, RG 36-1-0-306.
55 W.L. Houck to Mair, 23 October 1936, AO, RG 36-1-0-719.
56 Margaret Jane Hillyard Little, *"No Car, No Radio, No Liquor Permit": The Moral Regulation of Single Mothers in Ontario, 1920-1997* (Oxford: Oxford University Press, 1998); Xiaobei Chen, *Tending the Gardens of Citizenship: Child Saving in Toronto, 1880s-1920s* (Toronto: University of Toronto Press, 2005).
57 Reaume to Smith, 30 July 1936, AO, RG 36-8 International Hotel (Windsor).
58 "A member of the Methodist Church" to Smith, 24 September 1936, AO, RG 36-8 Venetian Hotel (Niagara Falls).
59 "Fed Up" to Hanrahan, [c. 10 August 1935], AO, RG 36-8 American Hotel (Windsor). Ironically, Clark was often vehemently opposed to the activities of the LCBO.
60 W.C. Clark to LCBO, 2 August 1939, AO, RG 36-8 Austin Hotel (St. Catharines).
61 Cheeseman to Smith, 10 August 1939, AO, RG 36-8 Austin Hotel (St. Catharines).
62 Smith to Avery, 20 May 1936, AO, RG 36-1-0-614.
63 Couthard to Jones, 30 August 1934, AO, RG 36-1-0-1364.
64 McCann to Odette, 19 October 1934, and Odette to McCann, 22 October 1934, AO, RG 36-1-0-1364. A handwritten note by William Mair on the copy of the reply reads, "After discussion the CC says 'definitely no.'"
65 W.C. Mair, Memo, 30 November 1937, AO, RG 36-1-0-1335.
66 President of City Properties Ltd [name obscured] to Smith, 5 November 1934, AO, RG 36-1-0-1322.
67 Smith to City Properties, 15 November 1934, AO, RG 36-1-0-1322. Other protests accompanied the applications for an authority from the Golden House (denied), AO, RG 36-1-0-1283; the Parkdale Hotel (granted), AO, RG 36-8; and the Lakeside Athletic Club (denied), AO, RG 36-1-0-1433.
68 Smith to Odette, 30 December 1936, AO, RG 36-1-0-1335.
69 Odette to Smith, 8 January 1937, AO, RG 36-1-0-1335.
70 W.C. Mair, Memo, 30 November 1937, AO, RG 36-1-0-1335.
71 See picture from *Toronto Star,* 19 June 1940, AO, RG 36-8 Edgewater Hotel (Toronto).
72 "WCTU See Hotel Rise over Its Vain Protests," *Toronto Globe,* 11 August 1939.
73 Inspector's Report, 3 January 1940, AO, RG 36-8 Edgewater Hotel (Toronto).

Chapter 5: "As a Result of Representations Made"

1 N.J. Lacasse to Smith, 15 February 1935, Archives of Ontario (AO), RG 36-8 Baxter Hotel (Ottawa).

2 Smith to Lacasse, 19 February 1935, AO, RG 36-8 Baxter Hotel (Ottawa).

3 J.E. Hodgetts, *From Arm's Length to Hands-On: The Formative Years of Ontario's Public Service, 1867-1940* (Toronto: University of Toronto Press, 1995), 64-5.

4 For an earlier description of the relationship between politics and the drinking space, see Julia Roberts, *In Mixed Company: Taverns and Public Life in Upper Canada* (Vancouver: UBC Press, 2009), ch. 3, esp. 67-72.

5 "Charges Propaganda Bonus Paid Agents by Distillers," *Toronto Star,* 23 May 1934. For more on this scandal, see Records of the Liquor Control Board Inquiry, AO, RG 18-019.

6 Hodgetts, *From Arm's Length,* 212. Of course, this also means that over 50 percent of employees employed under the Conservatives retained their position. Although the numbers are clear, the reasons behind the dismissals are more difficult to confirm. Although they were likely due to patronage, this changing of the guard could have been a part of Hepburn's attempts to remove Conservative patronage appointments from the board's operations at the lower levels.

7 Hepburn to Odette, 15 November 1934, AO, RG 3-10-0-113, Premier Mitchell F. Hepburn Private Correspondence, "Liquor Control Board #1."

8 Mair had been employed with the Board of License Commissioners, which predated the LCBO.

9 Hodgetts, *From Arm's Length,* esp. 163-65, discusses in some detail both the utility to a government of having partisan faithful in positions of trust and how the LCBO could buffer the government from negative publicity.

10 Jeffrey Simpson, *The Spoils of Power: The Politics of Patronage* (Toronto: Collins, 1988); S.J.R. Noel, *Patrons, Clients, Brokers: Ontario Society and Politics, 1791-1896* (Toronto: University of Toronto Press, 1990).

11 Alan Gordon, "Patronage, Etiquette and the Science of Connection: Edmond Bristol and Political Management, 1911-21," *Canadian Historical Review* 80 (March 1999): 1-31.

12 Ibid., 28.

13 John Markoff, "Government Bureaucratization: General Processes and an Anomalous Case," *Comparative Studies in Society and History* 17 (1975): 479; Max Weber, "Bureaucracy," in *Economy and Society,* ed. Guenther Roth and Claus Wittich, 856-1005 (Berkeley: University of California Press, 1978).

14 Sharon A. Jaeger, "From Control to Customer Service: Government Control of Liquor in Ontario, 1927-1972" (PhD diss., Department of History, University of Waterloo, 1999), 89 and n125, citing John T. Saywell, *"Just Call Me Mitch": The Life of Mitchell F. Hepburn* (Toronto: University of Toronto Press, 1991), 175.

15 John A. Smith to LCBO, 29 May 1937, AO, RG 36-8 Walker Tavern (Windsor).

16 Houck to Smith, 20 June 1938, AO, RG 36-8 Metropole Hotel (Niagara Falls).

17 Sacco to Hon. M.F. Hepburn, 22 July 1937, RG 36-1-0-738. Typically, this letter was forwarded to Smith without comment from the premier's office.

18 Kittel to Newall and Smith, 11 July 1935, AO, RG 36-1-0-1481.

19 J. Eassy, Memo, forwarded to LCBO by H.J. Sims, 3 January 1939, AO, RG 36-1-0-1487.

20 Houck to Smith, 26 May 1935, AO, RG 36-8 Teals Hotel (Crystal Beach).

21 Smith to Houck, 28 April 1936, AO, RG 36-8 Teals Hotel (Crystal Beach).

22 Houck to Smith, 8 May 1936, AO, RG 36-8 Teals Hotel (Crystal Beach).

23 Smith to Teal, 9 May 1936, AO, RG 36-8 Teals Hotel (Crystal Beach).

24 J.E. Taggart to Smith, 2 October 1934, AO, RG 36-1-0-107.

25 Anderson to Odette, 10 October 1934, AO, RG 36-1-0-1529.

26 Mr. R.H. Gluns to Edmond Odette, 20 August 1934, AO, RG 36-1-0-261.

27 Various letters, AO, RG-36-1-0-100.

28 Brady Hotel File, AO, RG 36-1-0-1238.

29 J.M, Dalrymple to Odette, 27 August 1934, AO, RG 36-1-0-1364.

30 Coulthard to Jones, 30 August 1934, AO, RG 36-1-0-1364.

31 Smith to Greer, 15 April 1937, AO, RG 36-8 Atlanta Hotel (Toronto).

32 C.W. Wilson to Odette, 29 October 1935, AO, RG 36-1-0-1118.
33 Smith to McMullen, 18 November 1935, AO, RG 36-1-0-1118.
34 Smith to Ratz, 13 November 1936, AO, RG 36-8 Olde Heidelberg Inn (Heidelberg).
35 Smith to Houck, 19 June 1936, AO, RG 36-1-0-1591.
36 Authority Holder's Conduct Report (AHCR), 11 September 1935, AO, RG 36-8 City Hotel (Waterloo).
37 Smith to Odette, 30 December 1936, AO, RG 36-1-0-1335.
38 Odette to Smith, 8 January 1937, AO, RG 36-1-0-1335.
39 Pitt to Coulthard, 1 September 1934, AO, RG 36-1-0-1575.
40 Croll resigned over Hepburn's opposition to industrial unionism. See Robert Bothwell, "David Arnold Croll," in *Canadian Encyclopedia,* http://www.thecanadianencyclopedia.com.
41 Hanrahan to Smith, 9 November 1935, AO, RG 36-8 Walker Road Hotel (Windsor).
42 Trottier to Odette, 22 November 1935, AO, RG 36-8 Walker Road Hotel (Windsor).
43 H.B. McGowan, Secretary, Worker's Ex-servicemen's League, to Hepburn, 22 August 1934, AO, RG 36-8 Plaza Arms Hotel (Windsor).
44 Odette to McGowan, 8 September 1934, AO, RG 36-8 Plaza Arms Hotel (Windsor).
45 Jaeger, "From Control," 88, quoting Saywell, *"Just Call Me Mitch,"* 174.
46 "Fed Up" to Hanrahan, [c. 10 August 1935], AO, RG 36-8 American Hotel (Windsor).
47 Smith to Odette, 5 August 1937, AO, RG 36-8 Dixie Hotel (Windsor).
48 Dan Malleck, "An Innovation from Across the Line: The American Drinker and Liquor Regulation in Two Ontario Border Communities, 1927-1944," *Journal of Canadian Studies/Revue d'études canadiennes* 41, 1 (Winter 2007): 151-71.
49 Herbert Taylor to Odette, 14 August 1934, AO, RG 36-1-0-309.
50 Leo Sylvestre, Barr and Sol, to Odette, 4 September 1934, AO, RG 36-1-0-309.
51 Council of Belle River to LCBO, 11 September 1934, AO, RG 36-1-0-309.
52 Hanrahan to Mair, 22 January 1935, AO, RG 36-1-0-309.
53 Board to Taylor Hotel Co., 23 July 1935, AO, RG 36-1-0-309.
54 Hanrahan to Smith, 3 August 1935, AO, RG 36-1-0-309.
55 T.J. Fontaine to Odette, 8 August 1935, AO, RG 36-1-0-309.
56 Smith to Chief Commissioner, 20 August 1935, AO, RG 36-1-0-309.
57 Mair to Pitt, 11 September 1935, AO, RG 36-1-0-309.
58 AHCR, 16 November 1935, AO, RG 36-1-0-309.
59 Inspector's Report, 25 February 1936, AO, RG 36-1-0-309.
60 Trottier to Mair, 18 March 1936, AO, RG 36-1-0-309.
61 Mair to Taylor Hotel Co., 20 March 1936, AO, RG 36-1-0-309.
62 Inspector's Report, 2 April 1937, AO, RG 36-1-0-288.
63 Theo J. Fontaine to Mair, 31 March 1936, AO, RG 36-1-0-309.
64 Weber, "Bureaucracy," esp. 956-58.
65 Christopher Dandeker, "Patronage and Bureaucratic Control – The Case of the Naval Officer in English Society, 1780-1850," *British Journal of Sociology* 29 (1979): 300.
66 Mair to Wylie, 11 March 1936, AO, RG 36-8 Dwarf Village Inn (Jordan).
67 Wylie to LCBO, 16 March 1936, AO, RG 36-8 Dwarf Village Inn (Jordan).
68 Mair to Cheeseman, 29 September 1939, AO, RG 36-8 Dwarf Village Inn (Jordan).
69 Mair to Hart, 15 May 1935, AO, RG 36 1 0 1505.
70 Smith to Andrews, 9 September 1938, and Smith to W.H. Peach, Secretary, Port Arthur Liberal Association, 16 August 1938, AO, RG 36-1-0-1136.
71 Ed Wiley, Clive Hart, and M. Banon to LCBO, 9 July 1935, AO, RG 36-1-0-1125.
72 T. Garnet Fraser to Odette, 11 September 1934, AO, RG 36-8 St. Clair Hotel (Windsor).
73 C. McCurrie, Liberal Ward Chairman, to LCBO, 7 October 1935, AO, RG 36-8 Carleton Hotel (Ottawa).
74 Leon L. Scher to LCBO, 1 April 1939, RG 36-1-0-1122.
75 Eric Noble to LCBO, [c. 20 August 1937], AO, RG 36-1-0-1108.
76 Mrs. George A. Mitchell to Odette, [c. 16 November 1934], AO, RG 36-8 Noah's Ark Hotel (Toronto).
77 C.R. Widdifield to St. Clair Gordon, 24 April 1940, AO, RG 36-8 New Royal Hotel (Galt).

78 Hart to Birmingham, 16 March 1933, AO, RG 36-8 Lakeland Hotel (Port Arthur).
79 L.A. Greene to Judge McNamara, 29 March 1933, AO, RG 36-8 Lakeland Hotel (Port Arthur).
80 McComber and McComber to Coulthard, 25 March 1933, AO, RG 36-8 Lakeland Hotel (Port Arthur).
81 Charles Donati to Odette, 17 August 1934, AO, RG 36-8 Lakeland Hotel (Port Arthur).
82 John J. Kelly, Secretary, Lakehead Hotelkeepers Association, to Odette, 22 August 1934, AO, RG 36-8 Lakeland Hotel (Port Arthur).
83 W.G. Ingram, District Inspector, to Director of Permits, 19 September 1934, and George Taylor, Chief Constable, City of Port Arthur Police Department, to A.K. Coulthard, 24 September 1934, AO, RG 36-8 Lakeland Hotel (Port Arthur).
84 W.T. Nugent, Inspector's Report, 8 October 1934, AO, RG 36-8 Lakeland Hotel (Port Arthur).
85 Memorandum, Mair to Deputy Chief Commissioner, 14 August 1935, AO, RG 36-8 Lakeland Hotel (Port Arthur).
86 Smith, Memo [c. 30 June 1936], AO, RG 36-1-0-1146.
87 Charles Cox to A.K. Coulthard, 20 September 1934, AO, RG 36-8 Lakeland Hotel (Port Arthur).
88 Smith, Memo [c. 30 June 1936], AO, RG 36-1-0-1146.
89 Donati to Odette, 21 March 1936, AO, RG 36-8 Lakeland Hotel (Port Arthur); Smith, Memo [c. 30 June 1936], AO, RG 36-1-0-1146.
90 Smith, Memo [c. 30 June 1936], AO, RG 36-1-0-1146.
91 Ibid.
92 Murray to Smith, 27 January 1936, AO, RG 36-1-0-1146.
93 J.J. Scarcello to Arthur Roebuck, Attorney General, 23 October 1934, AO, RG 36-8 Lakeland Hotel (Port Arthur).
94 Donati to Hepburn, 16 June 1936, AO, RG 36-1-0-1146.
95 Smith to Hepburn, 30 June 1936, AO, RG 36-1-0-1146.
96 Pitt to Mair, 21 September 1936, AO, RG 36-1-0-1146.
97 The authority was granted on 22 September 1936. See AO, RG 36-1-0-1146.
98 This story unfolded in issues of the *St. Catharines Standard,* July-August 1941, and several other newspapers jumped at the chance to present Hepburn and the LCBO as hypocrites. There is also evidence in three LCBO files: AO, RG 36-8 Harding Hotel (St. Catharines); AO, RG 36-8 Queensway Hotel (St. Catharines); and AO, RG 36-1-0-614. See also *St. Catharines Standard,* August 1939, June-July 1941.

Chapter 6: Restructuring Recreation in the Drinking Space

Acknowledgment: Portions of this chapter originally appeared in Dan Malleck, "Leisure, Liquor and Control: Negotiating Recreation in the Beverage Rooms of Post-Prohibition Ontario, 1927-1939," *Annals of Leisure Research* 11 (2008): 368-85.

1 See Jan Noel, *Canada Dry: Temperance Crusades before Confederation* (Toronto: University of Toronto Press, 1994).
2 John C. Burnham, *Bad Habits: Drinking, Smoking, Taking Drugs, Gambling, Sexual Misbehaviour and Swearing in American History* (New York: New York University Press, 1993).
3 Julia Roberts, *In Mixed Company: Taverns and Public Life in Upper Canada* (Vancouver: UBC Press, 2009); Roy Rosenzweig, *Eight Hours for What We Will: Workers and Leisure in an Industrial City, 1870-1920* (London: Cambridge University Press, 1983); Perry R. Duis, *The Saloon: Public Drinking in Chicago and Boston, 1880-1920* (1983; reprint, Chicago and Urbana: University of Illinois Press, 1999); Madelon Powers, *Faces along the Bar: Lore and Order in the Workingmen's Saloon, 1870-1920* (Chicago: University of Chicago Press, 1998); various articles in several collections, including Jack S. Blocker Jr. and Cheryl Krasnick Warsh, eds., *The Changing Face of Drink: Substance, Imagery and Behaviour* (Ottawa: Les Publications Histoire sociale-Social History, 1997); and Cheryl Krasnick Warsh, ed., *Drink in Canada: Historical Essays* (Montreal and Kingston: McGill-Queen's University Press, 1993).
4 See Jacalyn Duffin, "In View of the Body of Job Broom: A Glimpse of the Medical Knowledge and Practice of John Rolph," *Canadian Bulletin of Medical History* 7 (1990): 9-30.
5 Roberts, *In Mixed Company;* Peter Delottinville, "Joe Beef of Montreal: Working-Class Culture and the Tavern, 1869-1889," *Labour/Le Travailleur* 8-9 (1981-82): 9-40.

6 T.S. Arthur, *Ten Nights in a Bar-Room and What I Saw There* (London: Houlston and Stoneman / W. Tweedie, 1854). For a summary of this work, see http://www.encyclopedia.com/doc/1O123-TenNightsinBrrmndWhtSwThr.html.
7 Robert Campbell, *Sit Down and Drink Your Beer: Regulating Vancouver's Beer Parlors, 1925-1954* (Toronto: University of Toronto Press, 2001), 36.
8 James Nicholls, *The Politics of Alcohol: A History of the Drink Question in England* (Manchester, UK: University of Manchester Press, 2009), 182.
9 "Liquor Control Act," *Revised Statutes of Ontario* (1937), ch. 294, sec. 79(2).
10 Ibid., ch. 294, sec. 11(1).
11 Liquor Control Board of Ontario, *Digest of Rules, Orders, Regulations and Legislation Affecting Standard and Other Hotels* (January 1935), 14-15, Archives of Ontario (AO), RG 36-5-0-2.2.
12 Ibid., 8.
13 Campbell, *Sit Down.*
14 Authority Holder's Conduct Report (AHCR), 14 October 1937, AO, RG 36-8 Ohio Hotel (Fort Erie).
15 Hanrahan to Smith, 20 December 1935, AO, RG 36-8 Golden Hotel (Tecumseh).
16 AHCR, 4 May 1939, AO, RG 36-1-0-1339.
17 AHCR, 21 October 1936, and Mair to Mrs. Hattie McNaughton, 29 October 1936, AO, RG 36-8 Bon Villa Hotel (Niagara Falls).
18 AHCR, 1 September 1936, AO, RG 36-8 Station Hotel (Crowland).
19 Duis, *Saloon,* 238-49; Powers, *Faces along the Bar,* 137-62; Suzanne Morton, *At Odds: Gambling and Canadians, 1919-1969* (Toronto: University of Toronto Press, 2003).
20 OPP Report, 28 December 1937, AO, RG 36-1-0-256.
21 Smith to Adams, 4 November 1937, and AHCR, 21 February 1938, AO, RG 36-8 Belmont Hotel (Port Colborne).
22 Inspector's Report, 27 September 1934, AO, RG 36-8 Niagara Hotel (Welland).
23 Inspector's Report, 27 February 1937, AO, RG 36-8 Bridge Club of Ottawa (Ottawa); Larocque to Smith, 11 February 1937, AO, RG 36-8 Association Athletique Montagnard (Ottawa).
24 Newspaper clipping, [c. 7 March 1936], AO, RG 36-8 British American Hotel (Windsor).
25 L.H. to Reaume, 24 May 1939, AO, RG 36-8 Woodbine Hotel (Windsor). Since the individual in question claimed to have broken the law but was not a public figure (unlike the proprietors, whose correspondence was done in an official and therefore public capacity), I have obscured this correspondent's name in accordance with my Access to Information agreement with the Archives of Ontario.
26 Anonymous to LCBO, 29 August 1937, AO, RG 36-8 Palace Hotel (Ottawa).
27 Anonymous to LCBO, 21 September 1938, AO, RG 36-8 Border Cities Polish Canadian Club (Windsor).
28 "A citizen" to LCBO, 25 June 1942, AO, RG 36-8 Colonial Hotel (Welland).
29 AHCR, 15 November 1938, and Smith to Larocque, 17 November 1938, AO, RG 36-8 LaSalle Hotel (Ottawa).
30 Morton, *At Odds,* 50.
31 Ken Durham, "History of Slot Machines," GameRoom Antiques, 1996, http://www.gameroomantiques.com/HistorySlot.htm.
32 On gambling and financial desperation, see Powers, *Faces along the Bar,* 143-45; and Morton, *At Odds,* 23-39.
33 Dan Malleck, "An Innovation from Across the Line: The American Drinker and Liquor Regulation in Two Ontario Border Communities, 1927-1944," *Journal of Canadian Studies/Revue d'études canadiennes* 41, 1 (Winter 2007): 161.
34 "No 1. Police Court," *Toronto Star,* 19 October 1936.
35 Morton, *At Odds,* 49-62.
36 Powers, *Faces along the Bar,* 138-62.
37 "Police Raid at Welland," *St. Catharines Standard,* 14 September 1928.
38 Wylie to LCBO, 15 August 1936, AO, RG 36-1-0-616.
39 AHCR, 7 September 1936, AO, RG 36-8 Erie Downs Golf Club (Fort Erie).
40 Hamilton to LCBO, 21 December 1937, AO, RG 36-1-0-288.
41 Eldon Scratch to LCBO, 20 December 1937, AO, RG 36-8 Grand Hotel (Windsor).

42 Albert Hebert to William Mair, 2 March 1936, AO, RG 36-8 Island View Hotel (Riverside).
43 The history of keno seems to have been written by online gaming sites, so it is a little difficult to trace; see James Langtry, "The History of Keno," Keno.cd, 18 January 2006, http://www.keno.cd/keno-history.html. On bingo, see Morton, *At Odds,* 92.
44 Morton, *At Odds,* 23-39; Powers, *Faces along the Bar,* 137-62.
45 Morton, *At Odds,* 23-39.
46 Reaume to Smith, 27 November 1937, AO, RG 36-8 Island View Hotel (Riverside).
47 "More Kenos Being Held," *Windsor Daily Star,* 6 December 1937.
48 Reaume to Smith, 27 October 1938, AO, RG 36-8 Island View Hotel (Riverside). These records are stuck in with the files of the Grand Hotel, Windsor.
49 Reaume to Smith, 28 December 1937, AO, RG 36-8 Highway Hotel (Windsor).
50 Catherine Gidney, "'The Dredger's Daughter': Courtship and Marriage in the Baptist Community of Welland, Ontario, 1934-1944," *Labour/Le Travail* 54 (2004): 121-50.
51 Randy McBee, "'He Likes Women More Than He Likes Drink and That Is Quite Unusual': Working-Class Social Clubs, Male Culture, and Heterosocial Relations in the United States, 1920s-1930s," *Gender and History* 11 (April 1999): 84-112; Suzanne Wasserman, "Cafes, Clubs, Corners and Candy Stores: Youth Leisure-Culture in New York City's Lower East Side during the 1930s," *Journal of American Culture* 14 (1991): 43-48.
52 Cynthia Comacchio, "Dancing to Perdition: Adolescence and Leisure in Interwar English Canada," *Journal of Canadian Studies* 32 (Fall 1997): 5.
53 David Gutzke, *Pubs and Progressives: Reinventing the Public House in England, 1896-1960* (DeKalb: Northern Illinois University Press, 2006), 166-69.
54 Nicholls, *Politics of Alcohol,* 182.
55 See, for example, the report in AO, RG 36-1-0-1498 Derby Inn (Crystal Beach).
56 AHCR, 26 April 1938, AO, RG 36-8 Metropole Hotel (Niagara Falls).
57 AHCR, 10 November 1937, AO, RG 36-8 Grand Trunk Hotel (Fort Erie); AHCR, 21 December 1935, AO, RG 36-8 Hotel Grimsby (Grimsby).
58 Ratz to Smith, 21 January 1938, AO, RG 36-8 Embassy Hotel (St. Agatha).
59 LCBO to Bruder, 8 February 1938, AO, RG 36-8 Embassy Hotel (St. Agatha).
60 Pitt to Smith, 17 June 1935, AO, RG 36-8 Russel Hotel (Ottawa).
61 AHCR, 18 September 1935, AO, RG 36-0-1-1318.
62 This was printed in a form letter sent to all hotels that were granted permission to have dinner dances. See, for example, the copy of Mair to Williams, 11 July 1935, AO, RG 36-8, St. Clair Hotel (Riverside).
63 W.D. Roach to Smith, 9 July 1935, AO, RG 36-8 Arlington Hotel (Windsor).
64 Ratz to Smith, 19 October 1939, AO, RG 36-8 Embassy Hotel (St. Agatha). See also AHCR, 10 November 1937, AO, RG 36-8 Grand Trunk Hotel (Fort Erie).
65 Malleck, "An Innovation," 164-66.
66 Williams to Smith, 8 July 1935, AO, RG 36-1-0-306.
67 Carolyn Strange, *Toronto's Girl Problem: The Perils and Pleasures of the City, 1880-1930* (Toronto: University of Toronto Press, 1995), 157.
68 Larocque to Smith, 19 December 1935, AO, RG 36-8 Grads Hotel (Ottawa).
69 Wylie to LCBO, 20 September 1935, AO, RG 36-1-0-616.
70 Mair to Doumani, 19 July 1935, AO, RG 36-8 British American Hotel (Windsor).
71 AHCR, 2 August 1935, AO, RG 36-1-0-1507.
72 Police Report, 10 April 1943, AO, RG 36-8 Victoria Hotel (Ottawa).
73 I discuss this issue in depth in Malleck, "An Innovation."
74 Ingham to LCBO, 19 June 1936, AO, RG 36-8 Queen's Hotel (Ayr).
75 Wraight to LCBO, 15 September 1936, AO, RG 36-8 Royal Hotel (Niagara Falls).
76 Heinzman to LCBO, 11 January 1936, AO, RG 36-0-1-719.
77 Cecil R. Day to Mair, 20 November 1936, AO, RG 36-8 Garden City Hotel (St. Catharines).
78 See various items, November-December 1936, AO, RG 36-8 Garden City Hotel (St. Catharines). The lease was transferred in January 1937.
79 Newall to Buck, 2 July 1936, AO, RG 36-8 Lincoln Hotel (Crystal Beach).
80 Smith to Sexton, 6 December 1939, AO, RG 36-8 Airport Inn (Walkerville).

81 Advertisement, *Windsor Daily Star,* 14 May 1936.
82 Smith to Reaume, 18 May 1936, AO, RG 36-8 British American Hotel (Windsor).
83 AHCR, 14 September 1935, AO, RG 36-8 Embassy Hotel (Port Dalhousie).
84 "Won't Have Shows Help Beer Selling" *Toronto Star,* 17 April 1936.
85 Mair to Normand, 9 April 1936, AO, RG 36-8 Duke Public House (Ottawa).
86 Smith to Lepine, 29 April 1936, AO, RG 36-8 LaSalle Hotel (Ottawa).
87 "Blames Dancing for Girls' Ruin," *Toronto Star,* 12 May 1936.
88 Smith to W.H. Furlong, 23 April 1938, AO, RG 36-8 Seacliffe Hotel (Leamington).
89 Mair to McComber and McComber, 4 August 1936, RG 36-0-1-1141.
90 Ratz to Smith, 10 June 1936, AO, RG 36-8 Dominion Hotel (St. Jacobs).
91 Mair to Connell, 8 May 1936, AO, RG 36-8 Canada Hotel (Ottawa).
92 Newal to Adams, 4 January 1937, AO, RG 36-8 Belmont Hotel (Port Colborne).
93 AHCR, 21 January 1937, AO, RG 36-8 Belmont Hotel (Port Colborne).
94 Wylie to LCBO, 15 December 1938, AO, RG 36-8 Belmont Hotel (Port Colborne).
95 AHCR, 27 July 1938, AO, RG 36-8 Leamington Hotel (Leamington).
96 Reaume to Smith, 19 December 1938, AO, RG 36-8 Highway Hotel (Windsor).
97 Reame to Smith, 19 December 1938, AO, RG 36-8 Highway Hotel (Windsor). This letter discussed activities at the Hollywood Hotel, which was a different establishment from the hotel in this file.
98 Smith to Wylie, 28 September 1937, AO, RG 36-8 Embassy Hotel (Port Dalhousie).
99 Ibid.
100 Smith to Robinson, 16 March 1937, AO, RG 36-8 Fort Erie Hotel (Fort Erie).
101 Smith to Kennedy, 16 December 1937, AO, RG 36-8 Southwood Hotel (Windsor).

Chapter 7: Women, Children, and the Family in the Public Drinking Space

1 "Most Dangerous Drink on the Market," *St. Catharines Standard,* 31 May 1939.
2 Cheryl Krasnick Warsh, "Oh, Lord, Pour a Cordial in Her Wounded Heart: The Drinking Woman in Victorian and Edwardian Canada," in *Drink in Canada: Historical Essays,* ed. Cheryl Krasnick Warsh, 70-90 (Montreal and Kingston: McGill-Queen's University Press, 1993).
3 Mariana Valverde, *The Age of Light, Soap and Water: Moral Regulation in English Canada, 1885-1925* (Toronto: McClelland and Stewart, 1991). I have borrowed the "mother of the race" phrase from Valverde. Although she was speaking more broadly about discourses of womanhood, the concerns over the fate of the race were deeply imbued in temperance rhetoric; see Mariana Valverde, "'When the Mother of the Race is Free': Race, Reproduction and Sexuality in First-Wave Feminism," in *Gender Conflicts: New Essays in Women's History,* ed. Franca Iacovetta and Mariana Valverde, 3-26 (Toronto: University of Toronto Press, 1992).
4 Angus McLaren, *Our Own Master Race: The Eugenic Crusade in Canada* (Toronto: McClelland and Stewart, 1990); Valverde, *Age of Light.*
5 Madelon Powers, *Faces along the Bar: Lore and Order in the Workingmen's Saloon, 1870-1920* (Chicago: University of Chicago Press, 1998); Clare Wright, *Beyond the Ladies Lounge: Australia's Female Publicans* (Melbourne, Australia: Melbourne University Press, 2003).
6 "Brewster," *Oxford English Dictionary,* 2nd ed. On women in early modern drinking spaces, a good collection is Beat Kümin and B. Ann Tlusty, eds., *The World of the Tavern Public Houses in Early Modern Europe* (Aldershot, UK, and Burlington, VT: Ashgate, 2002).
7 Julia Roberts, *In Mixed Company: Taverns and Public Life in Upper Canada* (Vancouver: UBC Press, 2009), 140-44.
8 Powers, *Faces along the Bar,* 32-35.
9 Wright, *Beyond the Ladies Lounge;* Diane Kirkby, *Barmaids: A History of Women's Work in Pubs* (Cambridge, UK: Cambridge University Press, 1997).
10 David Gutzke, *Pubs and Progressives: Reinventing the Public House in England, 1896-1960* (DeKalb: Northern Illinois University Press, 2006), 51, 125, 178-79.
11 Robert Campbell, *Sit Down and Drink Your Beer: Regulating Vancouver's Beer Parlors, 1925-1954* (Toronto: University of Toronto Press, 2001), 74-75.
12 Carolyn Strange, *Toronto's Girl Problem: The Perils and Pleasures of the City, 1880-1930* (Toronto: University of Toronto Press, 1995), 6.

13 Strange discusses this in various places; for specific strategies of single working girls, see ibid., 116-17. On the strategies and challenges of working-class housewives, see Cynthia Wright, "'Feminine Trifles of Vast Importance': Writing Gender into the History of Consumption," in *Gender Conflicts: New Essays in Women's History,* ed. Franca Iacovetta and Mariana Valverde, 229-60 (Toronto: University of Toronto Press, 1992); and Katrina Srigley, "Clothing Stories: Consumption, Identity, and Desire in Depression-Era Toronto," *Journal of Women's History* 19 (2007): 82-104. Also, see several chapters in Cheryl Krasnick Warsh and Dan Malleck, eds., *Consuming Modernity: Changing Gendered Behaviours and Consumerism, 1919-1945* (Vancouver: UBC Press, forthcoming).

14 The literature on this is vast. For sources, see Ann Heilman and Margaret Beetham, eds., *New Woman Hybridities: Femininity, Feminism, and International Consumer Culture, 1880-1930* (New York: Routledge, 2004); B. Solande, *Becoming Modern: Young Women and the Reconstruction of Womanhood in the 1920s* (Princeton, NJ: Princeton University Press, 2000); Cynthia Comacchio, *The Dominion of Youth: Adolescence and the Making of Modern Canada, 1920-1950* (Waterloo, ON: Wilfrid Laurier University Press, 2006); Liz Conor, *The Spectacular Modern Woman: Feminine Visibility in the 1920s* (Bloomington and Indianapolis: Indiana University Press, 2004); Laura L. Behling, "'The Woman at the Wheel': Marketing Ideal Womanhood, 1915-1934," *Journal of American Culture* 20 (Fall 1997): 13-32; and Srigley, "Clothing Stories."

15 "Temptation for Girls Seen with Wine in Restaurants," *Toronto Star,* 17 April 1934.

16 "To Investigate Claim Infant Given Beer," *Toronto Star,* 10 September 1934, clipping in AO, RG 36-8 Broadview Hotel (Toronto); "Spend More Money on Beer than for Bread," *Toronto Star,* 22 January 1935; "Great Slump Seen in Girls' Morals," *Toronto Star,* 22 February 1935.

17 "Odette Promises Island Beer, Women to Get Own Rooms," *Toronto Star,* 10 August 1934.

18 "Striving to Keep Licenses Hotelkeepers Adopt 'Code,'" *Toronto Star,* 13 September 1934.

19 "Order Some Hotels to Separate the Sexes," *Toronto Star,* 24 January 1935.

20 Hanrahan to LCBO, 27 November 1936, RG 36-8 Royal Cecil (Toronto).

21 Department of Police, Windsor, Report, 17 January 1939, and Reaume to Smith, 27 February 1939, AO, RG 36-8 British American Hotel (Windsor).

22 Police Report, 12 September 1934, AO, RG 36-1-0-1117.

23 Authority Holder's Conduct Report (AHCR), 21 February 1938, RG 36-8 Belmont Hotel (Port Colborne).

24 Wylie to LCBO, 25 February 1938, RG 36-8 Belmont Hotel (Port Colborne).

25 Report of Inspectors Cheeseman and Edgecombe, 27 November 1936, AO, RG 36-8 Alexandra Hotel (Toronto).

26 Ottawa Police Report, 28 January 1937, AO, RG 36-8 Grand Hotel (Ottawa).

27 AHCR, 28 January 1937, AO, RG 36-8 Grand Hotel (Ottawa).

28 "Standard Hotel Registration of Guests Act," *Revised Statutes of Ontario* (1937), ch. 295, secs. 2(1) and 3.

29 Ibid., ch. 295, sec. 4.

30 AHCR, 25 November 1936, AO, RG 36-1-0-61.

31 Gordon Hannah to Couthard, 16 August 1934, AO, RG 36-8 Grimsby Public House (Grimsby).

32 AHCR, 13 October 1934, AO, RG 36-8 Caverly Hotel (Niagara Falls).

33 Thomas Keating to LCBO, 27 August 1934, AO, RG 36-8 Nipigon Inn Hotel (Nipigon).

34 Inspector's Report, 27 December 1934, AO, RG 36-8 Imperial Hotel (Niagara Falls); AHCR, [c. 2 May 1935], AO, RG 36-8 Empire Hotel (Niagara Falls); George Hanrahan to LCBO, 30 July 1937, AO, RG 36-8 Rex Hotel (Port Arthur).

35 Unsigned Report, May 1935, AO, RG 36-8 Empire Hotel (Niagara Falls).

36 AHCR, 8 October 1934, AO, RG 36-1-0-719.

37 AHCR, 13 June 1936, AO, RG 36-8 Ritz Hotel (Port Colborne).

38 Mariana Valverde states that the LCBO never allowed dining rooms to be used as beverage rooms, suggesting a rigid and ideological rather than a functional approach to regulation by the board. In fact, the LCBO often permitted hotel proprietors to use their dining room as an overflow beverage room, usually for ladies and escorts. The problem for the LCBO was that although music and even dancing might be permitted in the dining room, these activities had to stop if the dining room was used as an overflow beverage room.

39 Smith to Brophy, 19 December 1939, AO, RG 36-8-0-288.

40 Hanrahan to LCBO, 30 July 1937, AO, RG 36-8 Kimberly Hotel (Port Arthur); Mrs. Wilson to LCBO, [rec'd. 13 January 1937], AO, RG 36-8 Savoy Hotel (Dunnville).

41 AHCR, 26 November 1937, AO, RG 36-8 Kimberly Hotel (Port Arthur).

42 "Temptation for Girls Seen with Wine in Restaurants," *Toronto Star,* 17 April 1934.

43 Cheeseman to Smith, 3 November 1939, AO, RG 36-8 Belmont Hotel (Port Colborne).

44 AHCR, 18 March 1937, AO, RG 36-8 Ohio Hotel (Fort Erie).

45 MacDonald, Memo, [c. 3 July 1940], AO, RG 36-8 Kimberly Hotel (Port Arthur); Smith to G. Dan, 14 August 1939, AO, RG 36-8 Erie Hotel (Windsor); OPP Report, 8 April 1935, AO, RG 36-8 Embassy Hotel (St. Agatha); AHCR, 29 October 1937, AO, RG 36-8-0-1112. Mrs. Taylor wrote about the disgraceful situation of soldiers entering the ladies' beverage room without women; see Taylor to LCBO, October 1941, AO, RG 36-8 Empire Hotel (Niagara Falls).

46 Pitt, Rombough, and Reaume to Smith, 7 December 1936, AO, RG 36-8 Tusco Hotel (Toronto).

47 AHCR, 29 October 1937, AO, RG 36-1-0-1112.

48 MacDonald, Memo, [c. 3 July 1940], AO, RG 36-8 Kimberly Hotel (Port Arthur).

49 H.E. Edgecombe, Inspector's Report, 4 May 1937, AO, RG 36-8 American Hotel (Sandwich).

50 Ash to Smith, 24 April 1937, AO, RG 36-8 Dunkirk Hotel (Ottawa).

51 Smith to Ash, 27 January 1938, AO, RG 36-8 Dunkirk Hotel (Ottawa).

52 B.A. Neale to William Common, 11 August 1934, AO, RG 36-8 Royal York Hotel (Toronto).

53 Buck to LCBO, [c. July 1936], AO, RG 36-8 Lincoln Hotel (Crystal Beach).

54 James Hammall to Smith, 16 November 1935, AO, RG 36-8 Wheat Sheaf (Toronto).

55 Mair to Hammall, 29 November 1935, AO, RG 36-8 Wheat Sheaf (Toronto).

56 Newall to Sheehan, 22 March 1937, AO, RG 36-8 Franklin Public House (St. Catharines).

57 Mrs. M.D. to Coulthard, 29 December 1932, AO, RG 36-8 Rex Hotel (Port Arthur).

58 Mrs. A. Jones to LCBO, 30 May 1940, AO, RG 36-8 Belmont Hotel (Port Colborne).

59 Mrs. Wilson to LCBO, [rec'd. 13 January 1937], AO, RG 36-8 Savoy Hotel (Dunnville).

60 Joan Sangster, *Dreams of Equality: Women on the Canadian Left, 1920-1950* (Toronto: McClelland and Stewart, 1989), 15; Joy Parr, *Gender of Breadwinners: Women, Men and Change in Two Industrial Towns, 1880-1950* (Toronto: University of Toronto Press, 1990), 96-119.

61 In the 1870s the Knights of Labor did assert a teetotal agenda that sought to boost the respectability and finances of the working class. See Gregory S. Kealey and Bryan Palmer, *Dreaming of What Might Be: The Knights of Labor in Ontario, 1880-1900* (New York: Cambridge University Press, 1982), esp. 220-37, which describes elections that included labour-temperance alliances.

62 "To Investigate Claim Infant Given Beer," *Toronto Star,* 10 September 1934, clipping in AO, RG 36-8 Broadview Hotel (Toronto).

63 Inspector's Report, 17 September 1934, AO, RG 36-8 Manitou Hotel (Centre Island, Toronto).

64 "Beverage Room Doors Shut as 21 Minus Authorities," *Toronto Star,* 1 November 1934.

65 T.A. Slater to LCBO, [c. 2 December 1937], and Dean to LCBO, 8 December 1937, AO, RG 36-8 Victoria Inn (Dunnville).

66 "To Investigate Claim Infant Given Beer," *Toronto Star,* 10 September 1934, clipping in AO, RG 36-8 Broadview Hotel (Toronto).

67 Hanrahan to Smith, 20 March 1935, AO, RG 36-8 Drake Public House (Windsor).

68 AHCR, 3 March 1936, AO, RG 36-8 Pacific Hotel (Ottawa).

69 C. Brown to LCBO, [c. 10 May 1935], AO, RG 36-8 Queen's Hotel (Dunnville).

70 Mair, Memo, 20 April 1939, AO, RG 36-8 Cameron Hotel (Toronto).

71 E. Sullivan to Mair, 9 April 1941, and Mair to Sullivan, 10 April 1941, AO, RG 36-8 Maple Leaf Hotel (Toronto).

72 Simington, Memo, 28 January 1943, AO, RG 36-8 Shamrock Hotel (Toronto).

73 Smith to Parr, 11 August 1939, AO, RG 36-8 Detroit Hotel (Windsor).

74 J.E. Couture to LCBO, 7 February 1942, AO, RG 36-1-0-288.

75 These numbers refer to applications made after 1 May 1927. They exclude applications both for incorporated hotels and for clubs.

76 Sometimes the application's status is unclear, most especially when another application followed soon afterward.

77 Mrs. K.C. Horton, "Men or Women for the Small Hotel," *Canadian Hotel Review and Restaurant* 8 (July 1930): 26.
78 Wright, *Beyond the Ladies Lounge;* Gutzke, *Pubs and Progressives.*
79 Reaume to Smith, 29 May 1940, AO, RG 36-8 Log Cabin Hotel (Belle River).
80 AHCR, 12 February 1936, and Mair to Felice, 19 February 1936, AO, RG 36-1-0-1529.
81 Inspector's Report, 6 January 1939, AO, RG 36-8 Castor Hotel (Ottawa).
82 AHCR, 14 August 1937, AO, RG 36-8 Kimberly Hotel (Port Arthur).
83 AHCR, 26 October 1937, AO, RG 36-8 Kimberly Hotel (Port Arthur).
84 Dean to Smith, 20 June 1940, AO, RG 36-8 Savoy Hotel (Dunnville).
85 Pitt to Smith, 17 June 1935, AO, RG 36-8 Elmdale Hotel (Ottawa).
86 See records in AO, RG 36-8 Capital Hotel (Ottawa). Interestingly, when Tessie got married in 1938, the authority was transferred to her father. Tessie Weiss may have married Max Zelikovitz; these are the names on the Max and Tessie Zelikovitz Centre for Jewish Studies at Carleton University in Ottawa.
87 AHCR, 2 February 1939, AO, RG 36-8 Erie Lane Hotel (Fort Erie).
88 George Kennedy to Coulthard, 13 September 1934, AO, RG 36-8 Royal Oak Hotel (Toronto).
89 See application dated 24 December 1935 and associated files in RG 36-1-0-1225.
90 Mrs. D.N. McDonald to Mayor Shaw, 25 November 1934, RG 36-1-0-1485.
91 Hanrahan to Smith, 1 May 1935, AO, RG 36-8 Woodbine Hotel (Windsor).
92 Inspector's Report, 13 July 1931, AO, RG 36-8 Royal Hotel (Niagara Falls).
93 A. Cameron to LCBO, 3 January 1938, AO, RG 36-8 Ambassador Hotel (Windsor).
94 Reaume to Smith, 7 January 1938, AO, RG 36-8 Ambassador Hotel (Windsor).
95 Dingman to [Labelle], 26 February 1930, AO, RG 36-8 Paris Hotel (Tecumseh).
96 OPP Report, 16 May 1930, AO, RG 36-8 Prince of Wales Hotel (St. Agatha).
97 Horton, "Men or Women," 26, 48.
98 Gutzke, *Pubs and Progressives.*
99 The LCBO records are entirely silent on the possibility that women in these spaces were looking to pick up other women, but it is likely to have also been the case. Although there may have been lesbian clubs and known lesbian spaces in some of these communities, their presence is absent from the LCBO files of the communities I examined.

Chapter 8: "Their Medley of Tongues and Eternal Jangle"

Acknowledgments: Portions of this chapter appeared in Dan Malleck, "'Their Medley of Tongues and Eternal Jangle': Liquor Control and Ethnicity in Ontario, 1927-1944," in *The Real Dope: Social, Legal and Historical Perspectives on the Use and Regulation of Drugs in Canada,* ed. Ed Montigny, 123-47 (Toronto: University of Toronto Press, 2011).

1 John W. MacKenzie, Supt Bankfield Consolidated Mines, Ltd, to Odette, 10 March 1939 AO, RG 36-1-0-1122.
2 The term "ethnic" is problematic. I am using it loosely to define members of society who are not native-born. They may have been new immigrants or second- or third-generation immigrants. The issue is who was defining them. For the most part, this study looks at individuals of non-Anglo-Celtic ethnicity who self-identified as such, notably people who congregated in ethnic social clubs, but it also includes notions of ethnic "otherness" that were defined by individuals who considered themselves native Canadians.
3 See Donald Avery, *Dangerous Foreigners: European Immigrant Workers and Labour Radicalism in Canada, 1896-1932.* (Toronto: McClelland and Stewart, 1979); Donald Avery, *Reluctant Host: Canada's Response to Immigrant Workers, 1896-1994* (Toronto: McClelland and Stewart, 1995); Kay Anderson, *Vancouver's Chinatown: Racial Discourse in Canada, 1875-1980* (Montreal and Kingston: McGill-Queen's University Press, 1995); and Franca Iacovetta, Paula Draper, and Robert Ventresca, eds., *A Nation of Immigrants: Women, Workers, and Communities in Canadian History, 1840s-1960s* (Toronto: University of Toronto Press, 1998).
4 See, for example, Dirk Hoerder, *Creating Societies: Immigrant Lives in Canada* (Montreal and Kingston: McGill-Queen's University Press, 1999); Vadim Kukushkin, *From Peasants to Labourers: Ukrainian and Belarusan Immigration from the Russian Empire to Canada* (Montreal and Kingston: McGill-Queen's University Press, 2007); and Carmela Patrias, *Patriots and*

Proletarians: The Politicization of Hungarian Immigrants in Canada, 1923-1939 (Montreal and Kingston: McGill-Queen's University Press, 1994).

5 Avery, *Reluctant Host,* 10.

6 See Sharon Ann Cook, *Through Sunshine and Shadow: The Woman's Christian Temperance Union, Evangelicalism, and Reform in Ontario, 1874-1930* (Montreal and Kingston: McGill-Queen's University Press, 1995); Mariana Valverde, *The Age of Light, Soap and Water: Moral Reform in English Canada, 1885-1925* (Toronto: McClelland and Stewart, 1991); and Barbara Roberts, "'A Work of Empire': Canadian Reformers and British Female Immigration," in *A Not Unreasonable Claim: Women and Reform in Canada, 1880s-1920s,* ed. Linda Kealey, 185-201 (Toronto: Women's Press, 1979).

7 The most cited reference to this idea of "imagined" nationhood, of course, is Benedict Anderson, *Imagined Communities: Reflections on the Origin and Spread of Nationalism,* rev. ed. (London: Verso, 1983). On normalization, I draw on the work of Philip Corrigan, notably Philip Corrigan and Derek Sayer, *The Great Arch: English State Formation as Cultural Revolution* (London: Blackwell, 1985), but also Philip Corrigan, "Viewpoint: Power/Difference: Some Elementary Forms of a Post-'sociological' Modernity: Further Remarks on Moral Regulation Celebrating the End of *the* 'Stratification Paradigm,' *the* 'Logic' of 'Society' and All That," *Sociological Review* 39 (May 1991): 309-34. For an interesting take on another government policy that might appear mundane but functioned as a hegemonic institution, see Sean Purdy, "Building Homes, Building Citizens: Housing Reform and Nation Formation in Canada, 1900-20," *Canadian Historical Review* 79 (September 1998): 492-523.

8 Mariana Valverde examines the notion of citizenship and liquor control in her "meta-analysis" of liquor control histories in North America, which requires more data. See Mariana Valverde, *Diseases of the Will: Alcohol and the Dilemmas of Freedom* (Cambridge, UK: Cambridge University Press, 1998), 143-70.

9 In this chapter, I distinguish between ethnic groups and racial groups. The term "ethnic groups" refers to Europeans of various linguistic and cultural backgrounds, often immigrants or their children, who assembled in identified social clusters, whereas the term "racial groups" refers to people of colour (i.e., African Canadians, Asians, and Aboriginal Canadians) who were not necessarily new to the country but whose physical features distinguished them from white residents. Language is tricky here. The language of the day usually used "coloured" for African Canadians, "Asiatics" or "Chinese" for Asians, and "Indians" for members of Canada's First Nations.

10 Using appropriate terminology can be a challenge. I use "Black," an admittedly troublesome term, to apply to all individuals labelled in the records as "coloured," "negro," or "African." The term "Aboriginal," meanwhile, refers to Aboriginal North Americans who were, according to federal law, barred from consuming alcohol.

11 Valverde, *Diseases of the Will;* Scott Thompson and Gary Genosko, *Punched Drunk: Alcohol, Surveillance and the LCBO, 1927-1975* (Black Point, NS: Fernwood, 2009). This prohibition remained until the Indian Act was significantly revised in 1951.

12 Robert Campbell, *Sit Down and Drink Your Beer: Regulating Vancouver's Beer Parlors, 1925-1954* (Toronto: University of Toronto Press, 2001), 92-93.

13 On the firewater myth and its implications for Aboriginal people, see Joy Leland, *Firewater Myths: North American Indian Drinking and Alcohol Addiction* (New Brunswick, NJ: Rutgers Center of Alcohol Studies, 1976); and Peter Mancall, *Deadly Medicine: Indians and Alcohol in Early America* (Ithaca, NY: Cornell University Press, 1995).

14 For a good discussion of the application of the law, see Thompson and Genosko, *Punched Drunk,* esp. 167-88.

15 Robert Campbell, "Making Sober Citizens: The Legacy of Indigenous Alcohol Regulation in Canada, 1777-1985," *Journal of Canadian Studies* 42 (Winter 2008): 105-26; Thompson and Genosko, *Punched Drunk,* 167-88; Valverde, *Diseases of the Will,* 162-68.

16 Valverde, *Diseases of the Will,* 166.

17 Quoted in Thompson and Genosko, *Punched Drunk,* 176.

18 Gordon to LCBO, 18 August 1941, and Mair to Gordon, 21 August 1941, AO, RG 36-8 Esquire Hotel (St. Catharines).

19 Authority Holder's Conduct Report (AHCR), 4 December 1937, AO, RG 36-8 Beardmore Hotel (Beardmore).
20 OPP Report, 12 May 1931, and OPP Report, 20 May 1933, AO, RG 36-1-0-1108.
21 Skuce to Smith, 24 May 1937, AO, RG 36-1-0-1108.
22 MacDonald to Elmhirst, 29 May 1943, AO, RG 36-8 Ovilio Hotel (Nipigon). See also Authority Holder's Monthly Conduct Report (AHMCR), 27 May 1934, AO, RG 36-8 International Hotel (Nipigon).
23 James McCranor to Commissioner, Royal Canadian Mounted Police, 20 April 1936, AO, RG 36-1-0-1112; McCranor to Newall, 16 June 1936, AO, RG 36-1-0-1112.
24 AHCR, 17 June 1939, AO, RG 36-8 Gregory Hotel (Toronto).
25 Campbell, *Sit Down,* esp. 79-105.
26 OPP Report, 30 July 1940, AO, RG 36-1-0-1108.
27 The 1,266 applications do not represent distinct buildings but rather applications by different proprietors than those indicated the previous year. This number does not include clubs or hotels owned by corporations because these applications did not necessarily indicate the ethnicity of the applicant, which was technically the club or corporation.
28 AHCR, 14 January 1937, AO, RG 36-8 St. Catharines Club (St. Catharines).
29 T. Garnet Fraser to Odette, 11 September 1934, AO, RG 36-8 St. Clair Hotel (Windsor).
30 Reaume to Smith, 14 August 1937, AO, RG 36-8 Imperial Hotel (Windsor).
31 See Bond, Report, 16 November 1943, AO, RG 36-8 Wyandotte Tavern (Windsor).
32 The sale was permitted but did not go through. The board's new rules about transfers during the war placed an added expense on the vendor, and ultimately both vendor and purchaser changed their minds. See Martin and Laird to LCBO, 15 December 1943, AO, RG 36-8 Wyandotte Tavern (Windsor).
33 Inspector's Report, 27 November 1934, AO, RG 36-1-0-711.
34 "A Citizen" to "Chief License Inspector," 18 June 1935, AO, RG 36-1-0-1132.
35 "Ruth Robertson" to Mair, 30 January 1940, AO, RG 36-8 Embassy Hotel (Toronto).
36 "A Canadian Citizen" to LCBO, 18 February 1940, AO, RG 36-1-0-719.
37 Cheeseman to Smith, 27 January 1938, RG 36-8 Alexandra Hotel (Toronto).
38 Tony Angelo to Hepburn, 17 July 1935, AO, RG 36-8 Columbia Hotel (Toronto).
39 Hanrahan to Smith, 12 August 1935, AO, RG 36-8 Grand Hotel (Windsor).
40 Mair to Simington, 6 September 1941, AO, RG 36-8 Royal Oak (Toronto).
41 Newall to Angelo, 20 July 1935, AO, RG 36-8 Columbia Hotel (Toronto).
42 Newall to Hanrahan, 14 August 1935, AO, RG 36-8 Grand Hotel (Windsor).
43 Inspector's Report, 14 July 1938, AO, RG 36-8 Alexandra Hotel (Toronto).
44 V.I. Petgrave to Gordon, 8 February 1941, AO, RG 36-8 Paramount Hotel (Toronto).
45 Smith to Petgrave, 24 February 1941, AO, RG 36-8 Paramount Hotel (Toronto).
46 Petgrave to Gordon, 14 August 1943, AO, RG 36-8 Paramount Hotel (Toronto).
47 Clarence Monroe to Odette, 11 March 1937, and Mair to Monroe, 15 March 1937, AO, RG 36-8 Frontier Social Club (Windsor).
48 Inspector's Report, 11 September 1937, AO, RG 36-8 Frontier Social Club (Windsor).
49 Clarence Monroe to LCBO, 24 January 1938, AO, RG 36-8 Frontier Social Club (Windsor).
50 Reaume to Smith, 3 May 1938, AO, RG 36-8 Frontier Social Club (Windsor).
51 Smith to Reaume, 6 May 1938, AO, RG 36-8 Frontier Social Club (Windsor).
52 It appears that the club continued to be allowed to sell draught beer, although little mention was made. Inspector Reaume commented that the club was well run and that it was using approved draught glasses. See AHMCR, 3 December 1940, AO, RG 36-8 Frontier Social Club (Windsor).
53 John Pitt, Inspector's Report, n.d., AO, RG 36-8 Walker Tavern (Windsor).
54 Memorandum Re. Walker House – Windsor, 27 May 1937, and John A. Smith to LCBO, 29 May 1937, AO, RG 36-8 Walker Tavern (Windsor).
55 Mair to J. Smith, 2 June 1937, AO, RG 36-8 Walker Tavern (Windsor).
56 J.A. Johnson to "Lickour Control Bord," 2 July 1936, AO, RG 36-8 Walker Tavern (Windsor).
57 Reaume to Smith, 8 July 1936, AO, RG 36-8 Walker Tavern (Windsor).
58 Inspector's Report, 8 May 1937, AO, RG 36-8 Walker Tavern (Windsor).

59 AHCR, 22 May 1937, AO, RG 36-8 Walker Tavern (Windsor).
60 John A. Smith to LCBO, 29 May 1937, AO, RG 36-8 Walker Tavern (Windsor).
61 Ibid.
62 AHCR, 25 February 1936, AO, RG 36-1-0-1131.
63 Ian Radforth, "Finnish Radicalism and Labour Activism in the Northern Ontario Woods," in Iacovetta, Draper, and Ventresca, eds., *A Nation of Immigrants,* 293-315.
64 Inspector's Report, 20 June 1931, AO, RG 38-1-0-1496.
65 A.F. Gignac to Odette, 8 December 1934, and J.H. Clark to Odette, 11 December 1934, AO, RG 36-1-0-1661.
66 M.H. to LCBO, 17 August 1934, AO, RG 36-1-0-617.
67 Raoul Renaud to "Sinclair" [sic] Gordon, [rec'd. 25 July 1940], AO, RG 36-8 French Canadian Club of Windsor (Windsor).
68 William Bethell to Odette, 17 July 1935, AO, RG 36-1-0-1665.
69 Milton E. Peck, Affadavit, 11 December 1934, AO, RG 36-0-1-1661.
70 Smith to McMullin, 18 November 1935, AO, RG 36-0-1-1118.
71 "Liquor Control Act," *Revised Statutes of Ontario* (1937), ch. 294, sec. 75(1).
72 Ibid.
73 See, for example, Reaume to Smith, 29 December 1939, AO, RG 36-1-0-278.
74 M. Watson to Smith, 1 August 1939, AO, RG 36-8 Italo-Canadian Political Club (Windsor).
75 W.D. Roach to Smith, 3 August 1935, AO, RG 36-1-0-1653.
76 Mair to Reaume, 27 November 1936, AO, RG 36-1-0-1653.
77 AHCR, 18 January 1938, AO, RG 36-1-0-1653.
78 In Toronto the board's central administrators might visit establishments in question, whereas this rarely happened outside of the provincial capital.
79 Hanrahan to Smith, 3 September 1935, AO, RG 36-1-0-1653.
80 Ratz to Smith, 11 February 1938, AO, RG 36-8 Waterloo Club (Waterloo). In the LCBO Establishment Files (RG 36-8) at the Archives of Ontario, the files for the Austrian Club (which changed its name to Austrian-Canadian Club) are included in the files for the Waterloo Club, a different establishment.
81 Ibid.
82 AHCR, 28 November 1937, and Ratz to Smith, 31 May 1937, AO, RG 36-8 Sachsen-Schwaben Club (Kitchener).
83 AHCR, 4 October 1938, AO, RG 36-8 Waterloo Club (Waterloo).
84 A.W. Boos to Smith, 14 December 1938, AO, RG 36-8 Waterloo Club (Waterloo).
85 McKerzie to J.A. Smith, 20 June 1939, AO, RG 36-8 Waterloo Club (Waterloo). This letter from the mayor to hydro commissioner J.A. Smith was forwarded to the LCBO on 20 July 1939.
86 Smith to Austrian-Canadian Club, 2 August 1939, AO, RG 36-8 Waterloo Club (Waterloo).
87 Berges to Smith, 27 May 1940, AO, RG 36-8 Waterloo Club (Waterloo).
88 See various records in AO, RG 36-1-0-1537.
89 Reaume to Smith, 4 December 1937, and Smith to Hungarian Independent Mutual Benefit Society, 8 December 1937, AO, RG 36-1-0-1652.
90 Reaume to Smith, 7 March 1938, AO, RG 36-1-0-1653.
91 John Pitt to Mair, 23 November 1935, AO, RG 36-8 Polish War Veteran's Association (Windsor).
92 See Patrias, *Patriots and Proletarians;* Orest T. Martynowych, *Ukrainians in Canada: The Formative Period, 1891-1924* (Edmonton: Canadian Institute of Ukrainian Studies, 1991); and Lubomyr Luciuk and Stella Hryniuk, *Canada's Ukrainians: Negotiating an Identity* (Toronto: University of Toronto Press, 1991).
93 J.L.E. dePapp to Mair, 9 June 1935, AO, RG 36-8 Windsor and District Hungarian Society (Windsor).
94 Petition to Edmond G. Odette, 24 March 1938, AO, RG 36-1-0-1652.
95 Hanrahan to Smith, 5 November 1934, AO, RG 36-8 Border Cities Polish Canadian Club (Windsor).
96 Emanuel Michailuk to LCBO, [c. 4 September 1934], AO, RG-36-1-0-1657.
97 Finnish Pentecostal Church to LCBO, 29 January 1939, AO, RG-36-1-0-1145.

98 Unsigned note, [c. October 1934], AO, RG 36-8 Polish War Veteran's Association (Windsor).
99 Hanrahan to Smith, 19 November 1934, AO, RG 36-8 Polish People's Home Association (Windsor).
100 R. Boak Burns to LCBO, 20 April 1937, AO, RG 36-1-0-1537.
101 See Carmela Patrias, "Relief Strike: Immigrant Workers and the Great Depression in Crowland, Ontario," in *A Nation of Immigrants,* ed. Iacovetta, Draper, and Ventresca, 322-58; and Patrias, *Patriots and Proletarians.*
102 Frank Cherry to Smith, 26 May 1937, AO, RG 36-1-0-1115.
103 Avery, *Dangerous Foreigners;* Avery, *Reluctant Host;* Nancy Forestell, "Bachelors, Boarding-Houses and Blind Pigs: Gender Construction in a Multi-ethnic Mining Camp, 1909-1920," in *A Nation of Immigrants,* ed. Iacovetta, Draper, and Ventresca, 251-90; Hoerder, *Creating Societies;* Kukushkin, *From Peasants to Labourers;* Patrias, *Patriots and Proletarians;* Barbara Roberts, *Whence They Came: Deportation from Canada, 1900-1935* (Toronto: University of Toronto Press, 1988).
104 HSCS [Hungarian Self-Culture Society] to Smith, 23 April 1937, AO, RG 36-1-0-1537.
105 Robert Forsyth to Commissioner, 21 January 1935, AO, RG 36-1-0-1534.
106 Donald Avery notes that there were many concerns over the cross-border activities of radicals during the Depression. See Avery, *Reluctant Host,* 108-25.
107 Petition to Edmond G. Odette, 24 March 1938, AO, RG 36-1-0-1652.
108 Pitt and Hanrahan, Report, to LCBO, [c. 1935], AO, RG 36-8 Border Cities Polish Canadian Club (Windsor).
109 Anonymous to LCBO, [c. 1935], AO, RG 36-8 Border Cities Polish Canadian Club (Windsor).
110 "Catholic Women Society" to LCBO, 21 September 1938, AO, RG 36-8 Border Cities Polish Canadian Club (Windsor).
111 Reaume to Smith, 22 March 1937, AO, RG 36-8 Border Cities Polish Canadian Club (Windsor).
112 Japanese were labelled "enemy aliens" in the records examined, but I did not find any indication of Japanese people being excluded. This was probably because only a few Japanese people had come under the LCBO's regulatory gaze.
113 "Nazi Roundup Said Started at Kitchener," *Globe and Mail,* 4 September 1939, AO, RG 36-8 Concordia Club (Kitchener).
114 Berges to Smith, 27 May 1940, AO, RG 36-8 Waterloo Club (Waterloo). On the renaming of the club (which the board noted should not mean that individuals of non-Austrian origin could become members), see Smith to Thiele, 9 March 1939, AO, RG 36-8 Waterloo Club (Waterloo).
115 V.A.M. Kemp, Superintendent, Commanding "O" Division, RCMP, to Smith, 28 June 1940, AO, RG 36-8 Italian War Veteran's Association (Windsor); Gordon to Smith, 18 June 1940, AO, RG 36-8 Border Cities Italian Club (Windsor). On internment, see Franca Iacovetta, Roberto Perin, and Angelo Principe, eds., *Enemies Within: Italian and Other Internees in Canada and Abroad* (Toronto: University of Toronto Press, 2000).
116 Reaume to Elmhirst, 23 June 1942, AO, RG 36-8 Border Cities Italian Club (Windsor).
117 This was a standardized form letter. See, for example, V.A.M. Kemp, Superintendent, Commanding "O" Division, RCMP, to Smith, 26 June 1940, AO, RG 36-8 Drake Public House (Windsor).
118 Smith to Officer Commanding, RCMP, 20 June 1940, AO, RG 36-8 Niagara Hotel (Welland).
119 Phil Walter, District Inspector, to F.E. Elliott, LCA Investigation Branch, 6 June 1940, AO, RG 36-1-0-1655.
120 Copy of OPP Report [by an anonymous investigator], 5 November 1940, AO, RG 36-8 Windsor and District Hungarian Society (Windsor).
121 James Clark to Odette, 22 July 1938, AO, RG 36-8 Order of the Sons of Italy (Windsor).

Chapter 9: Public Drinking and the Challenges of War

1 "An Unedifying Spectacle," *Toronto Star,* 3 September 1942.
2 Authority Holder's Monthly Conduct Report (AHMCR), 26 April 1941, AO, RG 36-8 St. Louis Hotel (Fort William).
3 Bernardi to LCBO, 17 September 1942, AO, RG 36-8 Weyland Hotel (Fort William).

4 See Appendix.
5 MacDonald to Gaffney, 23 February 1941, AO, RG 36-8 Longlac Hotel (Longlac).
6 Buchanan to Mair, 20 August 1942, AO, RG 36-8 Golden Pheasant Hotel (St. Catharines).
7 Smith to Storm, 21 October 1940, AO, RG 36-8 Pickwick Arms (Fort Erie).
8 Lond to LCBO, 14 September 1939, AO, RG 36-8 Bridge Ave. Inn (Windsor).
9 Charles Black to LCBO, 8 June 1940, AO, RG 36-8 Royal Hotel (Niagara Falls).
10 Buchanan to Smith, 3 February 1941, AO, RG 36-8 Dwarf Village Inn (Jordan).
11 Reaume to Mair, 14 April 1941, AO, RG 36-1-0-305.
12 The per capita amount is based on an estimated provincial population derived from the Statistics Canada national population estimates. Since the Ontario population was roughly 33 percent of the national population in 1931, 1941, and 1951, the provincial population is based on a calculation of 33 percent of the estimated national population. This population figure is rough, but it should suffice. See Statistics Canada online data: http://www.statcan.gc.ca/pub/11-516-x/sectiona/4147436-eng.htm#1.
13 "50-Cent Increase Seen on 40 Ounces of Liquor," *Globe and Mail,* 13 September 1939.
14 "40 Per Cent Drop in Liquor Revenue," *Toronto Star,* 23 November 1939.
15 "Hepburn Sees Taxes Aid to Bootlegging," *Toronto Star,* 13 September 1939.
16 "Bootleggers Grow Busy, So Liquor Price Is Cut," *Globe and Mail,* 15 December 1939.
17 "Says Beer Vendors 'Allies of Hitler,'" *Toronto Star,* 29 October 1939.
18 "Wartime Prohibition," letter, *Globe and Mail,* 21 September 1939.
19 "Charges War Effort Weakened by Liquor," *Toronto Star,* 9 November 1939.
20 "Nation Needs Temperance," *Toronto Star,* 25 September 1939.
21 "Stop Liquor Trade in War Temperance, Workers Urge," *Toronto Star,* 2 October 1939.
22 Tutte to Hepburn, 6 November 1940, AO, RG 3-9-0-394 Premier Mitchell F. Hepburn Public Correspondence, "Resolutions–Liquor Control."
23 See G.M. Smith, Presbytery of Dundas Grenville United Church, to Hepburn, 30 October 1940; United Church Muskoka Presbytery, resolved 20 February 1941; and J.S. Veals to Hepburn, 27 February 1941, all in AO, RG 3-9-0-394 Premier Mitchell F. Hepburn Public Correspondence, "Resolutions – Liquor Control."
24 "Stop Liquor Trade in War Temperance, Workers Urge," *Toronto Star,* 2 October 1939.
25 "Sugar for Liquor, None for Canning," *Globe and Mail,* 7 October 1939.
26 "War Curbs on Liquor Ruled out by Hepburn," *Globe and Mail,* 29 November 1939. Irwin later argued that he had not asked soldiers to be banned from drinking (for which he was accused of discrimination against soldiers), but three reporters who had attended the meeting concurred with the premier's story; see "Hepburn Offers Irwin Apology If in Error over 'Dry' Debate," *Globe and Mail,* 7 December 1939; and "Irwin and Dry Deputation Say Hepburn Twisted the Issue," *Toronto Star,* 2 December 1939.
27 "Hepburn Sees Taxes Aid to Bootlegging," *Toronto Star,* 13 September 1939.
28 "Bootleggers Grow Busy, So Liquor Price Is Cut," *Globe and Mail,* 15 December 1939.
29 "Hotels Plan to Absorb Beer Gallonage Tax Rise," *Globe and Mail,* 21 September 1939.
30 Leslie Reid, Congregational Secretary of the United Church of Canada, Baltimore, Ontario, to Conant Resolution of January 31 1943, 18 March 1943, AO, RG 3-15 "Liquor Control #1 – Conant."
31 Ethel [?] A. Childs [Mrs. Herbert Childs] to Conant, 9 March 1943, AO, RG 3-15 "Liquor Control #1 – Conant."
32 Arthur Smith, Secretary, to Conant, 28 December 1942, AO, RG 3-15 "Liquor Control #2 – Conant."
33 McPhail Baptist Church, Telegram, to Conant, 23 December 1942, AO, RG 3-15 "Liquor Control #2 – Conant."
34 Jeffrey A. Keshen, *Saints, Sinners, and Soldiers: Canada's Second World War* (Vancouver: UBC Press, 2004), 71-72.
35 "Liquor Stores Jammed as Citizens 'Stock Up,'" *Globe and Mail,* 13 September 1939; "Tariff Boosts Taken in Good Part, No Rush of Hoarders Invades Shops," *Globe and Mail,* 14 September 1939.
36 See Keshen, *Saints, Sinners, and Soldiers,* 58-59.

37 In May 1943 the LCBO initiated a system of beer-ration coupons for all individuals twenty-one years and over. Individuals were permitted twenty-four pints of beer per month. See "Notice," ad, *Globe and Mail,* 17 May 1943.
38 Amounts for wine and spirits were reduced even more: by 20 percent and 30 percent, respectively. See "Liquor Sales to be Curtailed," *Globe and Mail,* 17 December 1942; and Sharon A. Jaeger, "From Control to Customer Service: Government Control of Liquor in Ontario, 1927-1972" (PhD diss., Department of History, University of Waterloo, 1999), 120-21.
39 Gaskin to Associated Services Company, 10 November 1943, AO, RG 36-8 Seacliffe Hotel (Leamington).
40 "Kingston Given Larger Beer Ration," *Globe and Mail,* 11 March 1943.
41 In 1944 the provincial Conservative government and the Dominion Liberals argued repeatedly about who was to blame for increased restrictions and quotas. This was a major source of newspaper copy in March and April of that year.
42 R.H.E. to Kieswetter, 3 February 1943, AO, RG 36-8 Grand Hotel (Bridgewater).
43 AHMCR, 25 January 1944, AO, RG 36-8 Capital Hotel (Ottawa).
44 Denaburg to Elmhirst, 14 April 1943, AO, RG 36-8 Danforth Hotel (Toronto).
45 Sanson to LCBO, 30 November 1943, AO, RG 36-8 Elliott Hotel (Niagara Falls).
46 MacDonald to Gaskin, 6 October 1943, AO, RG 36-8 Longlac Hotel (Longlac).
47 Kozak to LCBO, 18 November 1943, AO, RG 36-8 Klondike Hotel (Fort Erie).
48 John Rumig to LCBO, 22 September 1942, AO, RG 36-8 Imperial Hotel (New Hamburg).
49 Reaume to Elmhirst, 3 August 1943, AO, RG 36-8 Lakeshore Terrace (Kingsville).
50 AHMCR, 22 May 1942, AO, RG 36-8 Royal Hotel (Fort Erie).
51 AHMCR, 23 May 1942, AO, RG 36-8 Anglo-American Hotel (Niagara Falls).
52 Smith to Buchanan, 3 May 1941, AO, RG 36-8 Esquire Hotel (St. Catharines).
53 Ruth Roach Pierson, *They're Still Women after All: The Second World War and Canadian Womanhood* (Toronto: McClelland and Stewart, 1986).
54 AHMCR, 25 August 1943, and Bernhardt to LCBO, 16 September 1943, AO, RG 36-8 Drake Hotel (Windsor).
55 AHMCR, 6 October 1943, AO, RG 36-8 East End Hotel (East Windsor). See also Reaume, Memo, 28 January 1944, AO, RG 36-8 Grand Hotel (Windsor).
56 Reaume to Elmhirst, 19 June 1942, AO, RG 36-8 Europe Hotel (Windsor).
57 Simington to Elmhirst, 23 March 1943, AO, RG 36-8 Auto Stop Inn (Leamington).
58 Jennifer A. Stephen, *Pick One Intelligent Girl: Employability, Domesticity and the Gendering of Canada's Welfare State, 1939-1947* (Toronto: University of Toronto Press, 2006), 61-64.
59 Mrs. Henry Ritter to LCBO, [c. 4 October 1940], AO, RG 36-8 Dominion Hotel (St. Jacobs).
60 Mrs. Davidson to LCBO, 2 March 1943, AO, RG 36-8 Beardmore Hotel (Beardmore).
61 J. O'Shea to Smith, 23 February 1940, AO, RG 36-8 Avion Hotel (Toronto).
62 H.H. Shale to Board, 9 April 1940, AO, RG 36-8 Ulster Arms Hotel (Toronto).
63 Mair to Corcoran, 20 December 1940, and Mair to Corcoran, 31 December 1940, AO, RG 36-8 Ulster Arms Hotel (Toronto).
64 This story extended over several letters. See Payne to Mair, 25 October 1940, AO, RG 36-8 Canadian Legion No. 65 (Toronto).
65 Berges to Mair, 5 November 1940, AO, RG 36-8 Dominion Hotel (St. Jacobs).
66 Authority Holder's Conduct Report (AHCR), 31 October 1939, AO, RG 36-8 Alexandra Hotel (Toronto).
67 Mrs. Taylor to LCBO, [c. 9 October 1941], AO, RG 36-8 Empire Hotel (Niagara Falls).
68 Ottawa Police Department, Report, 3 September 1941, AO, RG 36-8 Grad's Hotel (Ottawa).
69 AHMCR, 7 February 1942, AO, RG 36-8 St. Louis Hotel (Fort William).
70 AHMCR, 7 September 1942, AO, RG 36-8 Association Athletique Montagnard (Ottawa).
71 AHMCR, 18 September 1942, AO, RG 36-8 Association Athletique Montagnard (Ottawa).
72 Kidd, Memo, to Board, 29 November 1941, AO, RG 36-8 Barclay Hotel (Toronto).
73 Elmhirst to St. Catharines Hotel Ltd., 11 December 1942, AO, RG 36-8 Leonard Hotel (St. Catharines).
74 Murray C. MacDonald, Memo, to Board, 3 July 1940, AO, RG 36-8 Kimberly Hotel (Port Arthur).
75 MacDonald to Smith, 11 July 1940, AO, RG 36-8 Lakeland Hotel (Port Arthur).

76 AHMCR, 7 February 1942, AO, RG 36-8 St. Louis Hotel (Fort William).
77 Kidd to Smith, 1 March 1940, AO, RG 36-8 Picadilly Hotel (Toronto).
78 Major Stuart C. Bates to LCBO, 19 July 1941, AO, RG 36-8 Imperial Hotel (Crystal Beach); AHMCR, 9 December 1941, AO, RG 36-8 Spadina Hotel (Toronto); F.G. Jerome, Command Assistant Provost Marshal for Air Officer Commanding, to Mair, 10 March 1942, AO, RG 36-8 Avonmore Hotel (Toronto).
79 Ralph S. Gallen to LCBO, 22 October 1941, AO, RG 36-8 Empire Hotel (Niagara Falls).
80 AHMCR, 29 September 1942, AO, RG 36-8 Lord Elgin Hotel (Ottawa).
81 Simington, Memo, 8 July 1942, AO, RG 36-8 Piccadilly Hotel (Toronto).
82 Ibid.
83 Steve Hewitt, "Preparing for the Next One: Canadian Internal Security and the Beginning of the Cold War, 1939-1951," in *Engaging the Enemy: Canada in the 1940s,* ed. Andrew Hiscock and Muriel Chamberlain, 98-111 (Llandybie, UK: University of Wales Canadian Studies Group, 2006); Michelle McBride, "From Indifference to Internment: An Examination of the RCMP Responses to Nazism and Fascism in Canada from 1934-1941" (MA thesis, Department of History, Memorial University, 1997).
84 Advertisement for Angelo's Restaurant, *Globe and Mail,* 21 June 1940.
85 Kidd to Smith, 3 July 1940, AO, RG 36-8 Old Angelo's Restaurant (Toronto).
86 Price Waterhouse and Company, Controllers for the Custodian of Enemy [Alien] Property, to Mair, 12 March 1941, AO, RG 36-8 Old Angelo's Hotel (Toronto).
87 Price Waterhouse and Company to Smith, 24 April 1941, AO, RG 36-8 Old Angelo's Restaurant (Toronto).
88 For confidentiality reasons, the specific hotel file cannot be identified.

Conclusion

1 "Note and Comment," *Toronto Star,* 16 February 1944.
2 "Control of Beverage Rooms," editorial, *Globe and Mail,* 28 March 1944.
3 Sharon A. Jaeger, "From Control to Customer Service: Government Control of Liquor in Ontario, 1927-1972" (PhD diss., Department of History, University of Waterloo, 1999), 129.
4 Steven Maynard, "Through a Hole in the Lavatory Wall: Homosexual Subcultures, Police Surveillance and the Dialectics of Discovery, Toronto, 1890-1930," *Journal of the History of Sexuality* 5 (1994): 207-42; David S. Churchill, "Mother Goose's Map: Tabloid Geographies and Gay Male Experience in 1950s Toronto," *Journal of Urban History* 30 (2004): 826-52. Using the names of the known gay hotels in Churchill's article, I reviewed my records of those same hotels and could find nothing to indicate homosexuality. This is not to say that there was no gay sociability taking place, just that it was not blatant in the records.
5 "Anti-prohibition Sentiment Is Declared at a New High," *Toronto Star,* 1 April 1944.

Appendix

1 Neil F. Morrison, *Garden Gateway to Canada: One Hundred Years of Windsor and Essex County, 1854-1954* (Toronto: Ryerson Press, 1954), 308-9, 317-23.
2 This has been discussed well by Karen Dubinsky, *The Second Greatest Disappointment: Honeymooning and Tourism at Niagara Falls* (Toronto: Between the Lines, 1999).
3 John English and Kenneth McLaughlin, *Kitchener: An Illustrated History* (1983; reprint, Waterloo, ON: Wilfrid Laurier University Press, 1996), 144.
4 See ibid., 158-61.
5 W. Robert Wightman and Nancy M. Wightman, *The Land Between: Northwestern Ontario Resource Development, 1800 to the 1990s* (Toronto: University of Toronto Press, 1997), esp. ch. 4.
6 Ibid., 245.

Bibliography

Aaron, Paul, and David Musto. "Temperance and Prohibition in America: A Historical Overview." In *Alcohol and Public Policy: Beyond the Shadow of Prohibition – Panel on Alternative Policies Affecting the Prevention of Alcohol Abuse and Alcoholism,* ed. M. Moore and D. Gerstein, 127-81. Washington, DC: National Academy Press, 1981.

Anderson, Benedict. *Imagined Communities: Reflections on the Origin and Spread of Nationalism.* Rev. ed. London: Verso, 1983.

Anderson, Kay. *Vancouver's Chinatown: Racial Discourse in Canada, 1875-1980.* Montreal and Kingston: McGill-Queen's University Press, 1995.

Arthur, T.S. *Ten Nights in a Bar-Room and What I Saw There.* London: Houlston and Stoneman / W. Tweedie, 1854.

Avery, Donald. *Dangerous Foreigners: European Immigrant Workers and Labour Radicalism in Canada, 1896-1932.* Toronto: McClelland and Stewart, 1979.

–. *Reluctant Host: Canada's Response to Immigrant Workers, 1896-1994.* Toronto: McClelland and Stewart, 1995.

Behling, Laura L. "'The Woman at the Wheel': Marketing Ideal Womanhood, 1915-1934." *Journal of American Culture* 20 (Fall 1997): 13-32.

Blocker, Jack S. Jr. *American Temperance Movements: Cycles of Reform.* Boston: Twayne, 1989.

–. *Give to the Winds the Fears: The Women's Temperance Crusade, 1873-1974.* Westport, CT: Greenwood, 1985.

–. *Retreat from Reform: The Prohibition Movement in the United States.* Westport, CT: Greenwood, 1976.

Blocker, Jack S. Jr., and Cheryl Krasnick Warsh, eds. *The Changing Face of Drink: Substance, Imagery and Behaviour.* Ottawa: Les Publications Histoire sociale-Social History, 1997.

Boddington, Steven Paul. "The Alberta Liquor Control Board, 1924-1935." MA thesis, Department of History, University of Alberta, 1990.

Burnham, John C. *Bad Habits: Drinking, Smoking, Taking Drugs, Gambling, Sexual Misbehaviour and Swearing in American History.* New York: New York University Press, 1993.

–. "New Perspectives on the Prohibition 'Experiment' of the 1920's." *Journal of Social History* 2 (1968): 51-68.

Bushman, Richard L., and Claudia L. Bushman. "The Early History of Cleanliness in America." *Journal of American History* 74 (1988): 1213-38.

Campbell, Robert. *Demon Rum or Easy Money? Government Control of Liquor in British Columbia from Prohibition to Privatization.* Ottawa: Carleton University Press, 1991.

–. "Liquor and Liberals: Patronage and Government Control in British Columbia, 1920-1928." *BC Studies* 77 (1988): 30-53.

–. "Making Sober Citizens: The Legacy of Indigenous Alcohol Regulation in Canada, 1777-1985." *Journal of Canadian Studies* 42 (Winter 2008): 105-26.

–. "Profit Was Just a Circumstance: The Evolution of Government Liquor Control in British Columbia, 1920-1988." In *Drink in Canada: Historical Essays,* ed. Cheryl Warsh, 172-92. Montreal and Kingston: McGill-Queen's University Press, 1993.

–. *Sit Down and Drink Your Beer: Regulating Vancouver's Beer Parlors, 1925-1954.* Toronto: University of Toronto Press, 2001.

Chen, Xiaobei. *Tending the Gardens of Citizenship: Child Saving in Toronto, 1880s-1920s.* Toronto: University of Toronto Press, 2005.

Churchill, David S. "Mother Goose's Map: Tabloid Geographies and Gay Male Experience in 1950s Toronto." *Journal of Urban History* 30 (2004): 826-52.

Clark, Norman H. *Deliver Us from Evil: An Interpretation of American Prohibition.* New York: W.W. Norton, 1976.

Comacchio, Cynthia. "Dancing to Perdition: Adolescence and Leisure in Interwar English Canada." *Journal of Canadian Studies* 32 (Fall 1997): 5-35.

–. *The Dominion of Youth: Adolescence and the Making of Modern Canada, 1920-1950.* Waterloo, ON: Wilfrid Laurier University Press, 2006.

Conor, Liz. *The Spectacular Modern Woman: Feminine Visibility in the 1920s.* Bloomington and Indianapolis: Indiana University Press, 2004.

Cook, Sharon Ann. *Through Sunshine and Shadow: The Woman's Christian Temperance Union, Evangelicalism, and Reform in Ontario, 1874-1930.* Montreal and Kingston: McGill-Queen's University Press, 1995.

Corrigan, Philip. "Viewpoint: Power/Difference: Some Elementary Forms of a Post-'sociological' Modernity: Further Remarks on Moral Regulation Celebrating the End of *the* 'Stratification Paradigm,' *the* 'Logic' of 'Society' and All That." *Sociological Review* 39 (May 1991): 309-34.

Corrigan, Philip, and Derek Sayer. *The Great Arch: English State Formation as Cultural Revolution.* London: Blackwell, 1985.

Dandeker, Christopher. "Patronage and Bureaucratic Control – The Case of the Naval Officer in English Society, 1780-1850." *British Journal of Sociology* 29 (1979): 300-20.

Dean, Mitchell. *Governmentality: Power and Rule in Modern Society.* London: Sage, 1999.

Delottinville, Peter. "Joe Beef of Montreal: Working-Class Culture and the Tavern, 1869-1889." *Labour/Le Travailleur* 8-9 (1981-82): 9-40.

Dominion Bureau of Statistics. *Employment, Payrolls and Average Weekly Earnings, 1939-1946, with Index Numbers of Employment, 1921-1938.* Ottawa: Dominion Bureau of Statistics, 1946.

Dubinsky, Karen. *The Second Greatest Disappointment: Honeymooning and Tourism at Niagara Falls.* Toronto: Between the Lines, 1999.

Duffin, Jacalyn. "In View of the Body of Job Broom: A Glimpse of the Medical Knowledge and Practice of John Rolph." *Canadian Bulletin of Medical History* 7 (1990): 9-30.

Duis, Perry R. *The Saloon: Public Drinking in Chicago and Boston, 1880-1920.* 1983. Reprint, Chicago and Urbana: University of Illinois Press, 1999.

Elden, S. *Mapping the Present: Heidegger, Foucault and the Project of a Spatial History.* London: Continuum, 2001.

English, John, and Kenneth McLaughlin. *Kitchener: An Illustrated History.* 1983. Reprint, Waterloo, ON: Wilfrid Laurier University Press, 1996.

Eyler, John M. "The Sick Poor and the State. Arthur Newsholme on Poverty, Disease and Responsibility." In *Framing Disease: Studies in Cultural History,* ed. Charles E. Rosenberg and Janet Golden, 275-95. New Brunswick, NJ: Rutgers University Press, 1992.

Filey, Mike. *I Remember Sunnyside: The Rise and Fall of a Magical Era.* Toronto: Dundurn, 1996.

Forestell, Nancy. "Bachelors, Boarding-Houses and Blind Pigs: Gender Construction in a Multi-ethnic Mining Camp, 1909-1920." In *A Nation of Immigrants: Women, Workers, and Communities in Canadian History, 1840s-1960s,* ed. Franca Iacovetta, Paula Draper, and Robert Ventresca, 251-90. Toronto: University of Toronto Press, 1998.

Foucault, Michel. *The Birth of Biopolitics: Lectures at the College de France, 1978-1979.* Trans. Graham Burchell. New York: Palgrave Macmillan, 2004.

–. *Discipline and Punish: The Birth of the Prison*. Trans. Alan Sheridan. New York: Vintage, 1979.

Genosko, Gary, and Scott Thompson. "Administrative Surveillance of Alcohol Consumption in Ontario, Canada: Pre-electronic Technologies of Control." *Surveillance and Society* 4 (2006): 1-28.

Gerth, Hans H., and C. Wright Mills, eds. *From Max Weber: Essays in Sociology*. London: Routledge, 1970.

Gidney, Catherine. "'The Dredger's Daughter': Courtship and Marriage in the Baptist Community of Welland, Ontario, 1934-1944." *Labour/Le Travail* 54 (2004): 121-50.

Gordon, Alan. "Patronage, Etiquette and the Science of Connection: Edmond Bristol and Political Management, 1911-21." *Canadian Historical Review* 80 (March 1999): 1-31.

Gutzke, David. *Pubs and Progressives: Reinventing the Public House in England, 1896-1960*. DeKalb: Northern Illinois University Press, 2006.

Hallowell, Gerald A. *Prohibition in Ontario, 1919-1923*. Ottawa: Ontario Historical Society, 1972.

Heilman, Ann, and Margaret Beetham, eds. *New Woman Hybridities: Femininity, Feminism, and International Consumer Culture, 1880-1930*. New York: Routledge, 2004.

Heron, Craig. *Booze: A Distilled History*. Toronto: Between the Lines, 2004.

–. "The Boys and Their Booze: Masculinities and Public Drinking in Working-Class Hamilton, 1890-1946." *Canadian Historical Review* 86 (2005): 411-52.

Hewitt, Steve. "Preparing for the Next One: Canadian Internal Security and the Beginning of the Cold War, 1939-1951." In *Engaging the Enemy: Canada in the 1940s*, ed. Andrew Hiscock and Muriel Chamberlain, 98-111. Llandybie, UK: University of Wales Canadian Studies Group, 2006.

Hodgetts, J.E. *From Arm's Length to Hands-On: The Formative Years of Ontario's Public Service, 1867-1940*. Toronto: University of Toronto Press, 1995.

Hoerder, Dirk. *Creating Societies: Immigrant Lives in Canada*. Montreal and Kingston: McGill-Queen's University Press, 1999.

Horton, Mrs. K.C. "Men or Women for the Small Hotel." *Canadian Hotel Review and Restaurant* 8 (July 1930): 26, 48.

Hose, Reginald. *Prohibition or Control? Canada's Experience with the Liquor Problem, 1921-1927*. Toronto: Longmans, Green, 1928.

Hoy, Suellen. *Chasing Dirt: The American Pursuit of Cleanliness*. New York: Oxford University Press, 1996.

Huxley, Margo. "Geographies of Governmentality." In *Space, Knowledge and Power: Foucault and Geography*, ed. J. Crampton and Stuart Elden, 185-204. London: Ashgate, 2007.

–. "Spatial Rationalities: Order, Environment, Evolution and Government." *Social and Cultural Geography* 7 (2006): 771-87.

Iacovetta, Franca, Paula Draper, and Robert Ventresca, eds. *A Nation of Immigrants: Women, Workers, and Communities in Canadian History, 1840s-1960s*. Toronto: University of Toronto Press, 1998.

Iacovetta, Franca, Roberto Perin, and Angelo Principe, eds. *Enemies Within: Italian and Other Internees in Canada and Abroad*. Toronto: University of Toronto Press, 2000.

Jaeger, Sharon A. "From Control to Customer Service: Government Control of Liquor in Ontario, 1927-1972." PhD diss., Department of History, University of Waterloo, 1999.

Kealey, Gregory S., and Bryan Palmer. *Dreaming of What Might Be: The Knights of Labor in Ontario, 1880-1900*. New York: Cambridge University Press, 1982.

Kerr, K. Austin. *Organized for Reform: A New History of the Anti-Saloon League*. New Haven, CT: Yale University Press, 1985.

Keshen, Jeffrey A. *Saints, Sinners, and Soldiers: Canada's Second World War*. Vancouver: UBC Press, 2004.

Kirkby, Diane. *Barmaids: A History of Women's Work in Pubs*. Cambridge, UK: Cambridge University Press, 1997.

Kobler, John. *Ardent Spirits: The Rise and Fall of Prohibition*. Greenwich, CT: Fawcett Books, 1973.

Kukushkin, Vadim. *From Peasants to Labourers: Ukrainian and Belarusan Immigration from the Russian Empire to Canada*. Montreal and Kingston: McGill-Queen's University Press, 2007.

Kümin, Beat, and B. Ann Tlusty, eds. *The World of the Tavern: Public Houses in Early Modern Europe.* Aldershot, UK, and Burlington, VT: Ashgate, 2002.

Kyvig, David E. "Objection Sustained: Prohibition Repeal and the New Deal." In *Alcohol, Reform and Society: The Liquor Issue in Social Context,* ed. Jack S. Blocker Jr., 211-33. Westport, CT: Greenwood, 1979.

–. *Repealing National Prohibition.* 2nd ed. Kent, OH: Kent State University Press, 2000.

Langtry, James. "The History of Keno." Keno.cd. 18 January 2006. http://www.keno.cd/keno-history.html.

Leland, Joy. *Firewater Myths: North American Indian Drinking and Alcohol Addiction.* New Brunswick, NJ: Rutgers Center of Alcohol Studies, 1976.

"The Leonard Hotel." *Canadian Hotel Review and Restaurant* 7, 10 (October 1929): 15-18.

Little, Margaret Jane Hillyard. *"No Car, No Radio, No Liquor Permit": The Moral Regulation of Single Mothers in Ontario, 1920-1997.* Oxford, Toronto, and New York: Oxford University Press, 1998.

Luciuk, Lubomyr, and Stella Hryniuk. *Canada's Ukrainians: Negotiating an Identity.* Toronto: University of Toronto Press, 1991.

Malleck, Dan. "An Innovation from Across the Line: The American Drinker and Liquor Regulation in Two Ontario Border Communities, 1927-1944." *Journal of Canadian Studies/Revue d'études canadiennes* 41, 1 (Winter 2007): 151-71.

–. "Leisure, Liquor and Control: Negotiating Recreation in the Beverage Rooms of Post-Prohibition Ontario, 1927-1939." *Annals of Leisure Research* 11 (2008): 368-85.

–. "Priorities of Development in Four Local Woman's Christian Temperance Unions in Ontario, 1878-1895." In *The Changing Face of Drink: Substance, Imagery and Behaviour,* ed. Jack S. Blocker Jr. and Cheryl Krasnick Warsh, 189-208. Ottawa: Les Publications Histoire sociale-Social History, 1997.

–. "'Their Medley of Tongues and Eternal Jangle': Liquor Control and Ethnicity in Ontario, 1927-1944." In *The Real Dope: Social, Legal and Historical Perspectives on the Use and Regulation of Drugs in Canada,* ed. Ed Montigny, 123-47. Toronto: University of Toronto Press, 2011.

Mancall, Peter. *Deadly Medicine: Indians and Alcohol in Early America.* Ithaca, NY: Cornell University Press, 1995.

Markoff, John. "Governmental Bureaucratization: General Processes and an Anomalous Case." *Comparative Studies in Society and History* 17 (1975): 479-503.

Marquis, Greg. "'Brewers and Distillers Paradise': American Views of Canadian Alcohol Policies, 1919 to 1935." *Canadian Review of American Studies* 34 (2004): 135-66.

–. "'A Reluctant Concession to Modernity': Alcohol and Modernization in the Maritimes, 1945-1980." *Acadiensis* 32 (2003): 31-59.

Martynowych, Orest T. *Ukrainians in Canada: The Formative Period, 1891-1924.* Edmonton: Canadian Institute of Ukrainian Studies, 1991.

Maynard, Steven. "Through a Hole in the Lavatory Wall: Homosexual Subcultures, Police Surveillance and the Dialectics of Discovery, Toronto, 1890-1930." *Journal of the History of Sexuality* 5 (1994): 207-42.

McBee, Randy. "'He Likes Women More Than He Likes Drink and That Is Quite Unusual': Working-Class Social Clubs, Male Culture, and Heterosocial Relations in the United States, 1920s-1930s." *Gender and History* 11 (April 1999): 84-112.

McBride, Michelle. "From Indifference to Internment: An Examination of the RCMP Responses to Nazism and Fascism in Canada from 1934-1941." MA Thesis, Department of History, Memorial University, 1997.

McLaren, Angus. *Our Own Master Race: The Eugenic Crusade in Canada.* Toronto: McClelland and Stewart, 1990.

Miron, Jeffrey A., and Jeffrey Zwiebel. "Alcohol Consumption during Prohibition." *American Economic Review* 81 (1991): 242-47.

Moore, Stephen T. "Bootlegging and the Borderlands: Canadians, Americans, and the Prohibition-Era Northwest." PhD diss., Department of History, College of William and Mary, 2000.

–. "Defining the 'Undefended': Canadians, Americans, and the Multiple Meanings of Border during Prohibition." *American Review of Canadian Studies* 34 (2004): 3-36.

Morrison, Neil F. *Garden Gateway to Canada: One Hundred Years of Windsor and Essex County, 1854-1954*. Toronto: Ryerson Press, 1954.

Morton, Suzanne. *At Odds: Gambling and Canadians, 1919-1969*. Toronto: University of Toronto Press, 2003.

Nicholls, James. *The Politics of Alcohol: A History of the Drink Question in England*. Manchester, UK: University of Manchester Press, 2009.

Noel, Jan. *Canada Dry: Temperance Crusades before Confederation*. Toronto: University of Toronto Press, 1994.

Noel, S.J.R. *Patrons, Clients, Brokers: Ontario Society and Politics, 1791-1896*. Toronto: University of Toronto Press, 1990.

"The Old Mill and Spa History." The Old Mill and Spa online, http://www.oldmilltoronto.com/about/history.

Parr, Joy. *Gender of Breadwinners: Women, Men and Change in Two Industrial Towns, 1880-1950*. Toronto: University of Toronto Press, 1990.

Patrias, Carmela. *Patriots and Proletarians: The Politicization of Hungarian Immigrants in Canada, 1923-1939*. Montreal and Kingston: McGill-Queen's University Press, 1994.

. "Relief Strike: Immigrant Workers and the Great Depression in Crowland, Ontario." In *A Nation of Immigrants: Women, Workers, and Communities in Canadian History, 1840s-1960s*, ed. Franca Iacovetta, Paula Draper, and Robert Ventresca, 322-58. Toronto: University of Toronto Press, 1998.

Pennock, Pamela E., and K. Austin Kerr. "In the Shadow of Prohibition: Domestic American Alcohol Policy since 1933." *Business History* 47 (2005): 383-400.

Pickstone, John. "Dearth, Dirt and Fever Epidemics: Rewriting the History of British 'Public Health,' 1780-1850." In *Epidemics and Ideas: Essays on the Historical Perception of Pestilence*, ed. Terence Osborn Ranger and Paul Slack, 125-48. Cambridge, UK: Cambridge University Press, 1992.

Pierson, Ruth Roach. *They're Still Women after All: The Second World War and Canadian Womanhood*. Toronto: McClelland and Stewart, 1986.

Potter, Ryan. "Enforcing National Prohibition along the Detroit River." MA thesis, Department of History, University of Eastern Michigan, 2000.

Powers, Madelon. *Faces along the Bar: Lore and Order in the Workingmen's Saloon, 1870-1920*. Chicago: University of Chicago Press, 1998.

Purdy, Sean. "Building Homes, Building Citizens: Housing Reform and Nation Formation in Canada, 1900-20." *Canadian Historical Review* 79 (1998): 492-523.

Radforth, Ian. "Finnish Radicalism and Labour Activism in the Northern Ontario Woods." In *A Nation of Immigrants: Women, Workers, and Communities in Canadian History, 1840s-1960s*, ed. Franca Iacovetta, Paula Draper, and Robert Ventresca, 293-315. Toronto: University of Toronto Press, 1998.

Roberts, Barbara. *Whence They Came: Deportation from Canada, 1900-1935*. Toronto: University of Toronto Press, 1988.

–. "'A Work of Empire': Canadian Reformers and British Female Immigration." In *A Not Unreasonable Claim: Women and Reform in Canada, 1880s-1920s*, ed. Linda Kealey, 185-201. Toronto: Women's Press, 1979.

Roberts, Julia. *In Mixed Company: Taverns and Public Life in Upper Canada*. Vancouver: UBC Press, 2009.

Roizen, Ron. "How Does the Nation's 'Alcohol Problem' Change from Era to Era? Stalking the Social Logic of Problem-Definition Transformations since Repeal." In *Altering American Consciousness: The History of Alcohol and Drug Use in the United States*, ed. Sarah Tracy and Caroline Acker, 61-87. Boston: University of Massachusetts Press, 2004.

Rose, Kenneth D. *American Women and the Repeal of Prohibition*. New York: New York University Press, 1996.

Rosenzweig, Roy. *Eight Hours for What We Will: Workers and Leisure in an Industrial City, 1870-1920*. London: Cambridge University Press, 1983.

Rubin, Jay. "The Wet War: American Liquor Control, 1941-1945." In *Alcohol, Reform and Society: The Liquor Issue in Social Context*, ed. Jack S. Blocker Jr., 234-58. Westport, CT: Greenwood, 1979.

Sangster, Joan. *Dreams of Equality: Women on the Canadian Left, 1920-1950.* Toronto: McClelland and Stewart, 1989.

Saywell, John T. *"Just Call Me Mitch": The Life of Mitchell F. Hepburn.* Toronto: University of Toronto Press, 1991.

Schrad, Mark Lawrence. "Constitutional Blemishes: American Alcohol Prohibition and Repeal as Policy Punctuation." *Policy Studies Journal* 35 (2007): 437-63.

Simpson, Jeffrey. *The Spoils of Power: The Politics of Patronage.* Toronto: Collins, 1988.

Smith, Virginia. *Clean: A History of Personal Hygiene and Purity.* Oxford: Oxford University Press, 2007.

Solande B. *Becoming Modern: Young Women and the Reconstruction of Womanhood in the 1920s.* Princeton, NJ: Princeton University Press, 2000.

Sprecher, Hanna. "'Let Them Drink and Forget Our Poverty': Orthodox Rabbis React to Prohibition." *American Jewish Archives* 43 (1991): 135-79.

Srigley, Katrina. "Clothing Stories: Consumption, Identity, and Desire in Depression-Era Toronto." *Journal of Women's History* 19 (2007): 82-104.

Stephen, Jennifer A. *Pick One Intelligent Girl: Employability, Domesticity and the Gendering of Canada's Welfare State, 1939-1947.* Toronto: University of Toronto Press, 2006.

Strange, Carolyn. *Toronto's Girl Problem: The Perils and Pleasures of the City, 1880-1930.* Toronto: University of Toronto Press, 1995.

Stretch, Dianne Kathryn. "From Prohibition to Government Control: The Liquor Question in Alberta, 1909-1929." MA thesis, Department of History, University of Alberta, 1979.

Thompson, Scott, and Gary Genosko. *Punched Drunk: Alcohol, Surveillance and the LCBO, 1927-1975.* Black Point, NS: Fernwood, 2009.

Tomes, Nancy. *The Gospel of Germs: Men, Women and the Microbe in American Life.* Boston: Harvard University Press, 1998.

Tyrrell, Ian. *Woman's World/Woman's Empire: The Woman's Christian Temperance Union in International Perspective, 1880-1930.* Chapel Hill: University of North Carolina Press, 1991.

Valverde, Mariana. *The Age of Light, Soap and Water: Moral Regulation in English Canada, 1885-1925.* Toronto: McClelland and Stewart, 1991.

–. *Diseases of the Will: Alcohol and the Dilemmas of Freedom.* Cambridge, UK: Cambridge University Press, 1998.

–. "'When the Mother of the Race is Free': Race, Reproduction and Sexuality in First-Wave Feminism." In *Gender Conflicts: New Essays in Women's History,* ed. Franca Iacovetta and Mariana Valverde, 3-26. Toronto: University of Toronto Press, 1992.

Warsh, Cheryl Krasnick. "Dominion Alliance for the Total Suppression of the Liquor Traffic." In *Alcohol and Temperance in Modern History: An International Encyclopedia,* ed. Jack S. Blocker Jr., David M. Fahey, and Ian R. Tyrrell, vol. 1, 197-98. Santa Barbara, CA: ABC-Clio, 2003.

–, ed. *Drink in Canada: Historical Essays.* Montreal and Kingston: McGill-Queen's University Press, 1993.

–. "Oh, Lord, Pour a Cordial in Her Wounded Heart: The Drinking Woman in Victorian and Edwardian Canada." In *Drink in Canada: Historical Essays,* ed. Cheryl Krasnick Warsh, 70-90. Montreal and Kingston: McGill-Queen's University Press, 1993.

Warsh, Cheryl Krasnick, and Dan Malleck, eds. *Consuming Modernity: Changing Gendered Behaviours and Consumerism, 1919-1945.* Vancouver: UBC Press, forthcoming (Spring 2013).

Wasserman, Suzanne. "Cafes, Clubs, Corners and Candy Stores: Youth Leisure-Culture in New York City's Lower East Side during the 1930s." *Journal of American Culture* 14 (1991): 43-48.

Weber, Max. "Bureaucracy." In *Economy and Society,* ed. Guenther Roth and Claus Wittich, 856-1005. Berkeley: University of California Press, 1978.

–. *Economy and Society: An Outline of Interpretive Sociology.* Ed. Guenther Roth and Claus Wittich, trans. Ephraim Fischo et al. New York: Bedminster Press, 1968.

–. "Politics as Vocation." In *From Max Weber: Essays in Sociology,* ed. Hans H. Gerth and C. Wright Mills, 77-128. London: Routledge, 1970.

–. "Science as Vocation." In *From Max Weber: Essays in Sociology,* ed. Hans H. Gerth and C. Wright Mills, 129-56. London: Routledge, 1970.

Wightman, W. Robert, and Nancy M. Wightman. *The Land Between: Northwestern Ontario Resource Development, 1800 to the 1990s*. Toronto: University of Toronto Press, 1997.

Wright, Clare. *Beyond the Ladies Lounge: Australia's Female Publicans*. Melbourne, Australia: Melbourne University Press, 2003.

Wright, Cynthia. "'Feminine Trifles of Vast Importance': Writing Gender into the History of Consumption." In *Gender Conflicts: New Essays in Women's History*, ed. Franca Iacovetta and Mariana Valverde, 229-60. Toronto: University of Toronto Press, 1992.

Index

Note: Abbreviations used in this index: LCA, meaning Liquor Control Act (LCA), and LCBO, meaning Liquor Control Board of Ontario (LCBO). The Niagara Region is divided into Lincoln County; Niagara Falls, Ontario; and Welland County, to conform to the historical divisions of the day. It should also be noted that "hotel" may refer to a licensed *or* an unlicensed hotel.

Printed and bound in Canada by Friesens

Set in Stone by Artegraphica Design Co. Ltd.

Copy editor: Robert Lewis

Proofreader: Grace Yaginuma

Indexer: Natalie Boon